Party Polarization in America

This book develops a general explanation for party polarization in America from both historical and contemporary perspectives. Prior polarization studies focused exclusively on the modern era, but this work traces party polarization from the constitutional convention of 1787 to the present. Using such a broad historical perspective shows that what was unusual in American history was the period of low polarization from the Great Depression through 1980, rather than the period of high polarization of the modern era. Polarization is the norm of the American system, not the exception, and is likely to persist in the future. More theoretically, party polarization in America has been due to class-based conflict and rent-seeking by the patrician and plebian classes in various historical eras, rather than conflict over cultural values. As in earlier historical eras, modern party polarization has largely been elite-driven, with party entrepreneurs cunningly and strategically using polarization to their advantage.

B. DAN WOOD is a professor in the department of political science at Texas A&M University. His other books include *Presidential Saber Rattling* (Cambridge University Press, 2012), *The Myth of Presidential Representation* (Cambridge University Press, 2009, and recipient of the 2010 Richard Neustadt Award), *The Politics of Economic Leadership* (2007), and *Bureaucratic Dynamics: The Role of Bureaucracy in a Democracy* (1994). He is a widely cited author of many articles in leading political science journals. Wood has also taught statistical methods at the Essex Summer School (Colchester, United Kingdom), the Inter-university Consortium for Political and Social Research (University of Michigan), and the European Consortium for Political Research (Vienna, Austria).

SOREN JORDAN is an assistant professor at Auburn University. His research focuses on lawmaking in Congress, especially how lawmaking strategies have evolved over time as a result of the polarization between the two political parties. His work has appeared in *Social Science Quarterly, Research & Politics*, and *The Forum*. He is also the author (with Kim Quaile Hill and Patricia A. Hurley) of *Representation in Congress: A Unified Theory* (Cambridge University Press, 2015). Prior to coming to Auburn in 2016, he was a postdoctoral research associate in the department of political science at Texas A&M University after earning his Ph.D. there in 2015.

Party Polarization in America

The War Over Two Social Contracts

B. DAN WOOD
Texas A&M University

with

SOREN JORDAN
Auburn University

CAMBRIDGE
UNIVERSITY PRESS

CAMBRIDGE
UNIVERSITY PRESS

University Printing House, Cambridge CB2 8BS, United Kingdom

One Liberty Plaza, 20th Floor, New York, NY 10006, USA

477 Williamstown Road, Port Melbourne, VIC 3207, Australia

314-321, 3rd Floor, Plot 3, Splendor Forum, Jasola District Centre, New Delhi - 110025, India

79 Anson Road, #06-04/06, Singapore 079906

Cambridge University Press is part of the University of Cambridge.

It furthers the University's mission by disseminating knowledge in the pursuit of education, learning and research at the highest international levels of excellence.

www.cambridge.org
Information on this title: www.cambridge.org/9781107195929
DOI: 10.1017/9781108164450

First published 2017

A catalogue record for this publication is available from the British Library

Library of Congress Cataloging in Publication data
NAMES: Wood, B. Dan, author. | Jordan, Soren, author.
TITLE: Party polarization in America : the war over two social contracts / B. Dan Wood, Soren Jordan.
DESCRIPTION: Cambridge, United Kingdom ; New York, NY : Cambridge University Press, 2017. | Includes bibliographical references and index.
IDENTIFIERS: LCCN 2017005648 | ISBN 9781107195929 (Hardback)
SUBJECTS: LCSH: Political parties–United States–History. | Polarization (Social sciences)–United States–History. | Political culture–United States–History. | Elite (Social sciences)–Political activity–United States–History. | BISAC: POLITICAL SCIENCE / Government / General.
CLASSIFICATION: LCC JK2265 .W66 2017 | DDC 324.273–dc23 LC record available at https://lccn.loc.gov/2017005648

ISBN 978-1-107-19592-9 Hardback
ISBN 978-1-316-64700-4 Paperback

At the constitutional convention of 1787, Governeur Morris of Pennsylvania expressed disdain for the "commoner" class, stating, "Give the votes to people who have no property, and they will sell them to the rich ... We should not confine our attention to the present moment. The time is not distant when this Country will abound with mechanics and manufacturers who will receive their bread from their employers. Will such men be the secure and faithful Guardians of liberty?" (Madison 1787, August 7) His answer was a definitive no.

This book is dedicated to the ordinary citizens of America,
past, present, and future.

Contents

Figures

Tables

Preface and Acknowledgments

This book develops a general explanation for party polarization in America from both historical and contemporary perspectives. It also evaluates whether modern polarization is good or bad for the health of American democracy.

Of course, polarization is nothing new in world or American history. In ancient Athens, factional conflict led to the world's first democracy. During the seventh century BCE, the Archons (lords) and Areopagus (a council chosen by powerful noble families) ruled Athens. The great mass of the people served noble families and had no say in government whatsoever. Fearful of the population, the Athenian nobility enlisted King Archon Draco in 621 BCE to codify a new set of laws. "Draco's laws were most notable for their harshness: there was only one penalty prescribed, death, for every crime from murder down to loitering" (Blackwell 2003). By the sixth century BCE, most Athenians had been enslaved to the rich. Selling oneself or family into servitude to pay debts was common; most people had lost their land and become tenant farmers for the wealthy. By 594 BCE, it was clear that class conflict might erupt into rebellion.

Residents of the Athenian city-state were hopelessly split into two factions: wealthy oligarchs and poor democrats. The wealthy wanted to maintain their positions in society. The poor wanted to level the political and economic playing fields. The Athenians chose a new King Archon, Solon, to revise their laws. Solon reshaped political power by granting citizenship to every free resident of Athens and the surrounding area. Athens under Solon had many elements that would later be a part of Athenian democracy – democratic juries, an Assembly, a Council, and selection of most officials by lottery rather than election. The Athenians believed that lotteries were far more egalitarian than elections, because elections always favored the wealthy (Hansen 1999, 84). Solon's laws did not establish Athenian democracy as such, but nevertheless became the template for its development over the next 200 years (Blackwell 2003).

Why is this story worth recounting? Not much has changed over the roughly 2,600 years since the birth of Athenian democracy. World history is replete with struggles between the wealthy and the masses. American history is no exception. The American Constitution was framed in a setting where wealthy property holders were pitted against those who would take their property through popular democracy. The struggle between the American commercial class and those who supported it with wage slavery continued from the early American Republic through the nineteenth century and up to the Great Depression. The same struggle continues today, as the wealthy seek tax advantages, free markets, and a regulatory regime that favors the acquisition and retention of even greater wealth. In contrast, the masses seek to retain advantages gained as a result of New Deal and Great Society reforms.

This book is partially about gaining a historical perspective on the nature and severity of modern party polarization. Citizens, pundits, politicians, and social scientists alike lament the extent of polarization and governmental dysfunction in the modern era. However, focusing on present conditions sidesteps the real reason for studying party polarization: it is an important research concept worthy itself of scientific investigation. History reveals much about party polarization in America. Therefore, this book develops a comparative historical perspective on polarization in earlier eras.

A primary theoretical purpose of this book is to develop a general explanation for why party polarization existed in earlier American historical eras, as well as in recent history. Basically, the book argues that party polarization has always been rooted in class-based economic conflict. Much as in ancient Greece or Rome, a patrician class secured advantage and sought to maintain its advantage. Later, a plebian class obtained advantages of its own, and sought to maintain that advantage. Thus, the struggle for class advantage has been a defining characteristic of American party polarization.

A secondary theoretical purpose of the book is to examine the implications of party polarization for democracy and representation. Some have argued that party elites drive polarization in the American system, rather than the electorate. If so, then that does not suggest effective democratic representation. Further, if elected officials are more polarized than those who elected them, then there may be a representation gap. On the other hand, if elected officials are polarized because the electorate is polarized, then American democracy may be healthy. This book provides an initial effort to determine whether party polarization is healthy for American democracy.

The research reported in this book started in the fall of 2010, with various conference papers delivered from 2011 through 2016. Fellow panelists at these conferences provided useful comments, and their work also informed this work. As with any project of this duration, thanks are owed to many. Jon Bond was very helpful in sharing insights on party polarization in Congress. George Edwards was a reliable sounding board for ideas regarding the presidency. As Director of the American Politics Program, with help from Jon Bond,

Paul Kellstedt, and Joseph Ura, Texas A&M provided financial support through a Strategic Development Grant funding two mini-conferences on polarization, one focusing on American political institutions and the other focusing on the electorate. Participants at the institutional polarization mini-conference included Sean Theriault, Jeff Stonecash, Hans Noel, Laurel Harbridge, Kim Hill, Paul Kellstedt, Jon Bond, and Soren Jordan. Participants at the mini-conference on electoral polarization included Marc Hetherington, Chris Ellis, Jan Leighley, Corwin Smidt, Christina Wolbrecht, Grant Ferguson, Antje Scweinnicke, Rick Lau, Paul Kellstedt, Kim Hill, and Francisco Pedraza. University funds also enabled visits by Keith Poole, Alan Abramowitz, Mike Crespin, Kim Fridkin, and Chris Wlezien. Thanks to all for providing excellent discussions and sharing ongoing research. Insightful suggestions also came from three anonymous reviewers, most of which were implemented in the final manuscript.

A debt of thanks is also owed to those providing research assistance for this project. In particular, Clayton Webb and Kelly Arndt provided invaluable data collection and research support. Clayton is now a faculty member at the University of Kansas, and also team teaches the time series course at the University of Michigan's ICPSR summer methods program. Kelly shows high promise and will soon join the academy.

Robert Dreesen of Cambridge University Press was very helpful in advising on how to pitch the manuscript. He encouraged writing in a style that would be inclusive of readers at all levels. Accordingly, the focus is on theoretical substance, with the most technical materials relegated to appendixes. Hopefully, the materials in this book are not so complex as to deter serious readers. If so, then Robert deserves credit. He was also a pleasure to work with as an editor, especially in securing expert reviewers and facilitating the review and acceptance process.

In the interest of future research, replication is encouraged, as well as further application of the data. Thus, all of the data on party polarization reported in the empirical parts of the book are available at http://people.tamu.edu/~b-wood/replication.html.

Theoretical Perspectives on Party Polarization in America

On February 28, 2012, Senator Olympia Snowe (R-Maine) announced her decision to retire after eighteen years in the U.S. Senate. Explaining her decision, she said,

I have spoken on the floor of the Senate for years about the dysfunction and political polarization in the institution. Simply put, the Senate is not living up to what the Founding Fathers envisioned ... During the Federal Convention of 1787, James Madison wrote in his *Notes of Debates* that "the use of the Senate is to consist in its proceedings with more coolness, with more system, and with more wisdom, than the popular branch." ... Yet more than 200 years later, the greatest deliberative body in history is not living up to its billing ... everyone simply votes with their party and those in charge employ every possible tactic to block the other side. But that is not what America is all about, and it's not what the Founders intended. (Madison 1787, June 7; Snowe 2012)

Senator Snowe was not alone in her frustration with the polarization and dysfunction of the U.S. Congress. In the 2010 and 2012 election cycles, twenty-five senators and sixty-five House members either retired or resigned (Chamberlain 2012), with another seven senators and forty-one House members retiring in 2014 (Ballotpedia 2016). Many of these incumbents expressed sentiment similar to Senator Snowe's. Referring to the poisonous nature of politics in Washington, Representative Steve Latourette (R-Ohio) stated, "I have reached the conclusion that the atmosphere today and the reality that exists in the House of Representatives no longer encourages the finding of common ground." LaTourette told reporters that to rise in party ranks, politicians must now hand over "your wallet and your voting card" to party extremes, and he was uninterested (Helderman 2012). Similarly, Senator Ben Nelson (D-Nebraska) observed, "Public office is a place for public service ... It's about promoting the common good, not the agenda of the radical right or the radical left. It's about fairness for all, not privileges for the few" (FoxNews. com 2011). And Representative Jim Cooper (D-Tennessee), one of the last remaining Blue Dog Democrats, noted, "We don't have a Congress anymore, we have a parliament ... We moderates are an endangered species, but we are also a necessary ingredient for any problem solving" (Steinhauer 2012).

This perceived environment of polarization and dysfunction also had profound impacts for the American presidency. John Dean, former Nixon White House Counsel, wrote shortly after the 2012 election, "Republican partisans (with whom I have spoken) are planning to continue their efforts to frustrate President Obama with ongoing obstructionism and increasingly shrill politics, which they understand will further polarize Americans ... Making government unworkable is totally consistent with their philosophical feelings towards government" (Dean 2012).

Exasperated over this Republican strategy, President Obama said in a 2012 interview with CBS News, "And, if you asked me what is the one thing that has frustrated me most over the last four years, it's not the hard work, it's not the enormity of the decisions, it's not the pace, it is that I haven't been able to change the atmosphere here in Washington to reflect the decency and common sense of ordinary people – Democrats, Republicans and Independents – who I think just want to see their leadership solve problems" (Rose 2012). Four years later the president echoed the same sentiment in another interview with CBS News when he said, "The one thing that gnaws on me is the degree of continued polarization. It's gotten worse over the last several years" (Cowan 2016).

Popular pundits have increasingly sounded alarms over the extreme polarization and dysfunction in Washington. CNN commentators David Gergen and Michael Zuckerman wrote, "As each of the parties has moved toward ideological purity, our politics have become ever more polarized, our governing ever more paralyzed. Extremists increasingly run the show" (Gergen and Zuckerman 2012). Darrell West, vice president and director of governance studies at the Brookings Institution, remarked, "It's worse now than it's been in years ... Our leaders are deeply polarized, and 'compromise' has become a dirty word ... They seem less interested in actually solving problems than in presenting some doctrinaire view that's not getting anything done" (cited in Cohen 2012). And Thomas Mann and Norman Ornstein (2012), co-directors of the Brookings/American Enterprise Institute Election Reform Project, observed "with more than 42 years each of experience immersed in the corridors of Washington at both ends of Pennsylvania Avenue, this dysfunction is worse than we have ever seen it, and it is not limited to Capitol Hill. The partisan and ideological polarization from which we now suffer comes at a time when critical problems cry out for resolution, making for a particularly toxic mix."

Observing these conditions, political scientists have been highly attentive to party polarization in both Washington and among the public. For example,

a web search of http://scholar.google.com on August 25, 2015, for the words
"political polarization" and "America" (but not "Latin") for the years
2009 through 2015 returned 5,410 records. By way of comparison, the same
search conducted for years 1971 through 1977 yielded only 195 records.
Obviously, there is relatively new and ongoing scholarly discourse about
this topic.

Some scholarly work has received more attention than others. For example,
McCarty et al. (2008) (*Polarized America: The Dance of Unequal Riches
and Ideology*) had been cited over 1,300 times as of August 25, 2015. These
scholars studied polarization in Congress. They claimed that congressional
polarization was at a peak, and "closely parallels measures of economic
inequality and of immigration for much of the twentieth century" (2008, 6).
Similarly, Fiorina et al. (2011) (*Culture War? The Myth of a Polarized
America*) had a roughly equal number of citations. These authors studied
polarization in the electorate. They claimed that it is a myth that the American
public is highly polarized. Rather, "a polarized political class makes the
citizenry appear polarized, but it is largely that – an appearance" (Fiorina
et al. 2011, 9).

This book enters into this scholarly discourse by evaluating the basis of
both mass and elite polarization in the United States from both a historical
and causal quantitative perspective. Chapters 2 through 6 are largely historical,
with some quantitative evidence interspersed within. Shifting rather starkly,
Chapters 7 and 8 are primarily quantitative and statistical, measuring modern
polarization among the mass public and political institutions for the purpose of
evaluating the implications for democracy and representation. Both research
styles offer distinctive insights into the nature of party polarization in America.

ACHIEVING HISTORICAL PERSPECTIVE: FORESTS AND TREES

As an initial motivation, this book is partially about gaining a historical
perspective on the nature and severity of modern party polarization. As noted
above, elected officials, popular pundits, and social scientists alike express great
alarm that polarization may be at an extreme. Because of deep philosophical
divisions between the political parties, and the nature of American political
institutions, leaders are seemingly incapable of resolving the important issues
facing the nation. These issues include who should pay for government, how
large government should be, how free should markets be, how to rein in a
massive and growing federal debt, resolving the impending crises in entitlement
spending, protecting American jobs, immigration reform, and gun violence, etc.

If one accepts at face value the widespread belief that the American system is
dysfunctional due to polarization, then there would appear to be a need to
reform the system. However, are elected officials, popular pundits, and some
social scientists missing the big picture? Are they so focused on the present that
they are missing the forest for the trees?

Is the current level of polarization really unusual when considered against the larger backdrop of American political history? Or has polarization actually been the historical norm? Relative to history, is modern polarization now at a zenith, as some have argued? Or have there been other periods when polarization was as high or even higher? Is the current level of dysfunction so unusual that the institutions created by the Founders should be reconsidered? Or is the current degree of polarization and dysfunction the norm for a political system that constitutes the oldest functioning democracy in the world?

One theme of this book is that the current alarmist view of polarization lacks historical perspective (see also Brady and Han 2006). Specifically, the historical analyses to follow suggest that if we are currently at a zenith of polarization, then it is probably not all that unusual when considered against the larger backdrop of American political history. Indeed, the historically low levels of polarization that existed from 1933 through the late 1970s were the unusual phenomenon when considered against this backdrop.

Party polarization viewed dynamically across American history has not been an unbounded trend, continuously moving toward the polar extremes. Rather, it has been a time series random walk. A random walk through time will sometimes increase and other times decrease. Systematic public opinion data on mass polarization are not available before the late 1940s. However, data on both mass and institutional polarization are of reasonably high quality for the period since the late 1940s. These are the data that most scholars use to reach their conclusions. However, these data represent only a short segment of a much longer time series process. If one uses data for only a short segment of a long random walk, as is typical for most analyses of polarization, then the data may appear to be trending. However, that appearance will be deceptive, because the trending short segment will always reverse at some point. Thus, the trend in polarization from the 1980s to present may only appear to have reached a critical zenith. That zenith will at some point reverse toward moderation, as it did in earlier eras.

Of course, the system may well be at a *localized* zenith of polarization and systemic dysfunction. However, one cannot make this judgment without understanding the larger backdrop of polarization through American history. One must make comparisons with earlier eras to make this determination. Accordingly, the next two chapters develop analyses of polarization from the Founding Era up to the Great Depression.

The Founding Era was one of especially high polarization, starting even before the drafting of the Constitution. Indeed, the original Constitution can best be understood as a document intended to protect one segment of a polarized system from the other segment. Even in the absence of political parties, the two poles of the founding system were class-based. During the Founding Era, the patrician class pitted itself against the plebian class in constructing the new American government.

A wealthy faction feared the "too democratic" tendencies of popularly elected state governments, and sought to limit these tendencies through federal power. Wealthy property owners feared that the masses might take their property through taxation or inflated paper money. They sought economic advantages through the new form of government, including constraints on popular democracy and a design enabling the accumulation of even greater wealth. One aspect of this effort was establishing a federal government intended more for obstruction than for action. Another was that the new federal government would be supreme in certain economic matters over threatening state governments.

THE PRIMARY THEORETICAL FOCUS: EXPLAINING PARTY POLARIZATION

Placing modern polarization in historical context is a worthy endeavor from the standpoint of focusing people and scholars on objective reality. However, the primary motivation for this work is theoretical. This study offers a *general explanation for why party polarization existed in earlier historical eras, as well as in recent history.*

In particular, this work answers the following questions. Why were political parties so polarized during the Founding Era over taxation, tariffs, a National Bank, subsidies for the commercial class, the Jay Treaty, and the war in Europe? Why was party polarization so high during the latter part of the nineteenth century up to 1932 over tariffs, taxation, the gold standard, economic and social regulation, and social welfare? Why was party polarization so low from the New Deal through the late 1970s over many of these same issues? Finally, why has party polarization been so high since the 1980s over taxation, regulation, social welfare, and various cultural issues?

Obviously missing from the preceding list of questions is any treatment of polarization associated with slavery and the slavery events of the nineteenth century. Slavery was clearly a polarizing issue, perhaps the most polarizing issue of all time, as were the events surrounding the Missouri Compromise, the Kansas-Nebraska Act, the Dred Scott decision, and the Civil War. However, *polarization over slavery was not about party polarization*, the subject of this book.

Pulitzer Prize–winning historian Arthur Schlesinger, Jr. (1945b; see also Nichols 1948; Wilentz 2005) showed that slavery did not cleanly divide the political parties during the first half of the nineteenth century. Both Democrats and Whigs, the two major political parties, were internally split on the issue, largely based on regional interests. These internal splits resulted in a party realignment in the 1850s when anti-slavery Democrats and Whigs combined to form the Republican Party. However, even after the formation of the Republican Party, the remaining Democratic Party was unable to establish an official party line on slavery.

In 1860, the Democratic Party held three national conventions (Wikipedia 2016a). The first was unsuccessful in nominating a consensus presidential candidate. At the second convention, the Democrats nominated Senator Stephen A. Douglas of Illinois, and adopted a platform that was noncommittal on slavery (National Democratic Platform – Douglas Faction 1860). However, many Southerners defected and held yet a third Democratic convention. They selected John C. Breckinridge as their nominee, and adopted a platform that was clearly pro-slavery (National Democratic Platform – Breckinridge Faction 1860). Both Douglas and Breckinridge claimed to be the official Democratic candidate. Later in 1864, President Lincoln selected Southern Democrat Andrew Johnson as his running mate on the National Union Party ticket, again reflecting the split within the Democratic Party.

Thus, polarization due to slavery was about regional economics and the great moral issue of the time: could human beings be considered property? Because polarization due to slavery was not about party polarization, polarization associated with slavery is left for others to consider and is omitted from analyses below.

The core theme running throughout this book is that *party polarization in American history has always been rooted in economic class conflict over who benefits from government, and at whose expense.* Class conflict has been encouraged during different historical eras by two different interpretations of the American social contract, the Founders' social contract and the New Deal social contract.

Laid out in the original Constitution, the Founders' social contract placed the patrician class at a significant economic advantage at an expense to the plebian class. The benefits obtained by the patrician class were substantial, including very low taxes, high tariffs, monetary certainty, cheap money, and freedom from federal regulation. Through the rules of the game laid down by the original Constitution, the patrician class remained so advantaged through 1932.

Political warfare occurred over these issues from the early American republic, through the nineteenth century, and up to the Great Depression. That warfare was largely about whether previously obtained advantages by the patrician class would be maintained. However, there was never a time during these eras when the patrician class did not have the ability to block change, through either Congress or the courts. Therefore, polarization from 1789 through 1932 was largely about maintenance of the Founders' social contract.

However, the collapse of the American economy between 1929 and 1932 yielded a new interpretation of the American social contract. Under the New Deal social contract, the plebian class began to receive significant benefits of their own through New Deal programs and altered constitutional interpretations. The New Deal social contract also removed significant benefits from the patrician class by instituting higher taxes on the wealthy, reduced tariffs, devalued credit instruments, increased regulation, and greater government intrusiveness. Then, starting in the 1960s, Great Society programs greatly expanded these benefits for the masses, again to the disadvantage of those who had previously been advantaged. Predictably, class conflict subsequently increased as a result of the shift in economic advantage for the American system.

After a long period of one-party dominance from 1933 through the late 1970s, a confluence of conditions enabled Old Guard Republicans to challenge the New Deal social contract. They sought to restore the Founders' social contract and its advantages for the patrician class. They also sought to remove advantages to beneficiaries of the New Deal social contract. Thus, political warfare since the 1980s has again been about contract maintenance, but now maintenance of policies associated with the New Deal social contract. As in earlier eras, the basis of modern polarization is about who benefits from government, and at whose expense.

The conflicts that have produced party polarization throughout American history *can also be framed theoretically in terms of rent-seeking or rent-maintenance.* Public choice economist Gordon Tullock (1967; 1993) originated the idea of rent-seeking, but Ann Krueger (1974) invented the label. People are said to seek rent from society when they try to obtain benefits for themselves without paying for them and at a cost to others (Henderson 2016). Rent-seekers do so through the political arena by getting a subsidy, a tariff, a tax break, a favorable constitutional or legal provision, or a regulation that gives them a special advantage.

Nobel Laureate economist Robert Shiller (2013) gives a clear example of rent-seeking as that of a feudal lord who erects a barrier across a river that flows through his land and then hires a collector to charge passing boats a fee to withdraw the barrier (i.e., charges rent for a section of the river for a short time). No additional production results from the barrier or the collector, but there is a cost to those who pass. The lord has made no improvements, but is simply finding a way to make money from something that was previously free.

Rent-seeking can be distinguished from investment in a particular economic class using the Pareto criterion (Lockwood 2008). The Pareto criterion states that if there are improvements to one person's welfare while no one is made worse off, then the world is a better place. Applying the Pareto criterion, if the rich get richer through a tax break, and no one is harmed in the process, then this outcome would be fine. However, if a particular economic group obtains advantage by a tax break causing others to pay higher taxes or lose benefits, then this would be rent-seeking. As expressed by another Nobel Laureate economist Angus Deaton, "[I]f no one gets hurt in some other dimension, better off is better. But if people use that money to undermine my well-being – my access to public education or better health care, or there's more military spending and, so, less for social programs – then I have to pay those taxes, live in that system" (Deaton 2013, 2014).

Rent-seeking virtually always produces economic inequality, which can become an irritant of class conflict. For example, yet another Nobel Laureate economist, Joseph Stiglitz (2012), argued that rent-seeking contributes significantly to income inequality in the United States. He notes that partisan efforts to secure government policies allowing the wealthy and powerful to increase their income, not as a reward for creating wealth, but by grabbing a larger share of the wealth produced without their effort, is a type of rent-seeking. Similarly, Piketty et al. (2011) analyzed international economies and changes in tax rates, and concluded that much of income inequality across nations results from rent-seeking by wealthy taxpayers.

Of course, rent-seeking is not exclusive to the patrician class. Other examples of rent-seeking include the poor lobbying for welfare benefits; small businesses lobbying for tax advantages; lawyers or doctors lobbying for regulations that restrict competition from unlicensed lawyers or doctors; labor seeking policies enabling easier formation of unions; the elderly lobbying for increased health care or Social Security benefits. The list is extensive.

The historical analyses in this book show that rent-seeking and the class basis of party polarization in America have remained consistent through time. Political parties that developed early in the American republic were based largely on class interests. Most of the Founders said that they detested the idea of political parties, arguing that they were more likely to comprise factions antithetical to representation in the common interest. Nevertheless, from the Founding Era, through the nineteenth century, Progressive Era, Great Depression, and up to the present there have always been two political parties separated largely along class lines.

One political party has consistently pursued the interests of economic elites, arguing that what was good for the commercial class was best for the nation. The name of that political party has changed through time (Federalists, Whigs, Republicans), but the motivations have remained the same. The other political party (Democratic-Republicans, Democrats) rejected this philosophy, arguing that what was good for the larger citizenry was best for the nation and business. Government has a positive obligation to protect the masses from the evils of a wealth-dominated system. Of course, this same philosophical divide has separated Democrats and Republicans since the 1980s.

Partisan behaviors through time have always been strategic and purposeful. The Constitution and the dominant partisan regime from 1789 through 1932 strategically engaged in rent-seeking and rent-maintaining behavior. As will be shown in the next chapter, the Constitution itself was a veiled exercise in rent-seeking by the patrician class (Beard 1913; McGuire and Ohsfeldt 1984). Subsequently, the Washington administration and Hamilton's three plans for the economic development of the nation involved rent-seeking and secured significant economic benefits to the patrician class that became very controversial.

The largely successful battles by the dominant Republican Party from the latter part of the nineteenth century through 1932 over tariffs, the gold standard, taxation, economic and social regulation, and social welfare were rent-maintaining efforts by the dominant partisan regime. Polarization during this era involved the opposition Democratic Party seeking to curtail those rents and obtaining economic advantages for their own partisans, many of whom were an underclass suffering the inequities of a wealth-dominated system.

Subsequently, the Great Depression realigned the partisan balance of the American system. The result was a purposeful effort by Democrats to change which citizens benefited from government, and at whose expense. The New Deal social contract provided many new rents to the plebian class, now at an expense to the patrician class. These rents were directed toward the poor, jobless, hungry, elderly, unhealthy, and underdeveloped, as well as those seeking union representation, experiencing injury or disability, suffering discrimination, etc. The New Deal social contract also curtailed many rents to the patrician class. Taxes on the upper class increased after 1933, tariffs decreased, the nation removed itself (temporarily and later permanently) from the gold standard, economic and social regulation expanded greatly, etc. Such changes were abrasive to an economic class that had received special treatment by government for almost a century and a half.

Starting in the early 1980s, Old Guard Republicans represented by Ronald Reagan deliberately and strategically sought to restore earlier rents to the patricians. Of course, Democrats sought to maintain rents for the plebian class, resulting in ever increasing polarization. Post-1980, Old Guard efforts involved cutting taxes for the wealthy, deregulation, curtailing social welfare, and generally making free markets, small government, and deregulation "holy" again. The Old Guard also cunningly attempted to bring new adherents into the Republican Party by connecting economic and cultural issues. Republicans partially succeeded in no small measure because of their efforts to expand the Republican base through the emotional appeal of cultural issues. At the core, however, party polarization since 1980 was about restoring rents for the privileged class and removing rents from the masses.

THE OTHER THEORETICAL FOCUS: DEMOCRACY AND REPRESENTATION

For a significant part of this book, attention is directed toward showing that the explanation for party polarization throughout American history has been class-based economic conflict and shifting economic advantage due to the transition between the Founders' and New Deal social contracts. However, party polarization is also theoretically interesting because of its potential implications for democracy and representation. From a theoretical standpoint, *polarization may (or may not) weaken American democracy and representation*. In the later chapters of this book, this matter will be the primary concern.

The dominant theory of party representation among political scientists and economists has always been the centrist theory, also called the median voter theory. The centrist theory argues that elite partisan actors strategically move toward the ideological center in order to maximize their chances for reelection and effectuate their policies. Under this theory, political parties do not stray too far from the median voter for fear of losing political support.

Downs (1957) first proposed the centrist theory using a simple graphical depiction showing that it was rational for political parties to move toward the political center. Davis and Hinich (1966) subsequently initiated the mathematical modeling literature from this perspective, which became manifest through numerous formal and empirical analyses (see, e.g., Aldrich 1983; Austin-Smith and Banks 1988; Davis et al. 1970; Enelow and Hinich 1981, 1982, 1984; Riker and Ordeshook 1973; Wittman 1983). Indeed, the notion that politicians move toward the median voter to maximize their political support is so embedded in scholarly thinking that it could be called an established paradigm of elite political behavior.

Consistent with centrist theory, a large body of empirical research has stressed the importance of mass political preferences to policy outputs from American political institutions (e.g., see Canes-Wrone 2006; Canes-Wrone and Shotts 2004; Canes-Wrone et al. 2001; Erikson et al. 2002; Page and Shapiro 1985, 1992; Stimson et al. 1995; Wlezien 1996). For example, Erikson et al. (2002; see also Stimson et al. 1995) claimed that mass preferences affect policy stances by all three major U.S. political institutions.

Others have argued that partisan elites cater to the median voter only when they need to. According to this perspective politicians are calculating actors who use their knowledge of public opinion to pursue their own objectives and evade responsiveness to mass political preferences. For example, Jacobs and Shapiro (2000, chapter 2) use case study evidence to argue that a sophisticated understanding of public opinion combined with a variety of factors enabled politicians to engage in "crafted talk" to manipulate, rather than respond to the public. Partisans often face a tradeoff between pursuing partisan policy goals and pleasing the public. Thus, Jacobs and Shapiro (2000, 42–44) assert that only intermittently prior to elections and when they require broad public support do politicians pursue a centrist strategy (see also Canes-Wrone and Shotts 2004; Kriner and Reeves 2015). At other times, their cost–benefit calculations are weighted toward pursuit of policy goals and appeasing fellow partisans.

Regardless of whether elite partisans always or only sporadically move toward the political center, political parties that seek advantage for a particular economic class, whether patrician or plebeian, hold implications for American democracy and political representation. Specifically, political parties advocating for a particular economic class suggests that a more appropriate theoretical model would be one in which elite political actors cater to the median partisan in the electorate.

Wood (2009, chapter 4) provides empirical evidence that presidents cater to the median partisan, rather the median voter. More generally, observing contemporary party politics it is easy to see that modern election campaigns have featured increasingly extreme candidates and that once party representatives are in office their policy positions are also extreme. These facts seem more consistent with the idea that party elites are ideological, catering to their fellow partisans, rather than to the median voter.

Catering to the median partisan can also be rational. Political parties might still win elections and effectuate their policies by hyper-mobilizing fellow partisans. Instead of appealing to generally disinterested and uninformed citizens residing near the center who may be difficult to mobilize, partisans appeal to those who already share their ideology and are excited to participate. Such hyper-mobilization through advocating more extreme policies may be effective if much of their partisan electorate is also extreme.

Polarized partisans advocating extreme positions may or may not be consistent with good democratic representation. Resolving this matter requires determining whether partisan electorates are as polarized and extreme as the partisan elites representing them. Consider an ideological continuum running from most liberal to most conservative. Assume that the distribution of citizen preferences is unimodal and symmetrical. This assumption was the basis of Downs's (1957) core argument for why political elites move to the political center. It is also implicit in the central limit theorem that commonly describes a statistical distribution. A unimodal distribution is also implicit in much political science theory and empirical research grounded in the median voter theorem. Because most voters are assumed to lie near the political center, it is assumed rational for political parties to cater to the middle.

However, suppose the true distribution of citizen preferences is actually bi-modal. Downs recognized this possibility when he stated, "If voters' preferences are distributed so that voters are massed bi-modally near the extremes, the parties will remain poles apart in ideology" (1957, 118). Clearly, modern party elites are widely separated. Liberalism and conservatism for the parties, candidates, and elected officials are concentrated toward the ends of the liberal-conservative continuum. Further, it seems readily apparent that polarized representatives do not always cater to the middle. Rather, they move toward the poles for ideological reasons or to cater to their most politically mobilized constituents. As a result, American institutions better represent the ends of the political spectrum.

Given the preceding arguments, a fundamental question concerns whether the electorate actually is ideologically polarized along partisan lines. Past scholarly work has been divided over this question. For example, Fiorina et al. (2011; see also Levendusky 2009b) argue that electoral polarization is a myth. The electorate only appears to be polarized because they are given only extreme choices by political elites. In contrast, Abramowitz (2010; see also Abramowitz and Saunders 2008) argues that the electorate is polarized, especially those who are most politically aware and active (see also review articles by Hetherington 2009; Layman et al. 2006; Levendusky 2013; Schaffner 2011).

Settling this debate, the analyses reported in Chapter 7 show definitively that partisan electorates have become increasingly polarized through time on specific economic and cultural issues, as well as more generally along liberal and conservative lines. Some specific economic issues dividing partisan electorates include attitudes about size of government, free markets, taxation, support for equal opportunity, and support for the environment. Some specific cultural issues dividing partisan electorates include abortion, homosexuality, gun control, immigration, and welfare. More generally, partisan electorates have also grown increasingly separated through time in their identification as ideologically liberal or conservative.

A related set of questions about polarization and democratic representation addressed in Chapter 8 concerns the question of who leads whom: partisan electorates or partisan elites? Is elite polarization related to mass polarization? If there is a relationship, is it primarily bottom-up, top-down, or interactive? Does mass polarization cause elite polarization, as one might expect in a bi-modal Downsian situation? Does elite polarization drive mass polarization, as one might expect if democratic representatives are effective leaders and menu manipulators for the mass public? Are mass and elite polarization connected through an interactive relationship, whereby the causal arrows run in both directions between partisan electorates and partisan elites?

Knowing that the masses became increasingly polarized through time, a related question in democratic theory addressed in Chapter 8 concerns how the level of mass polarization compares with the level of elite polarization. If partisan elites are more polarized than partisan electorates, then one can say that American democracy is characterized by a representation gap. That is, the true preferences of partisan electorates are not reflected through the extreme policy choices made for them by partisan elites. For a representation gap to exist, partisan masses and partisan elites must have different levels of polarization. Yet past research has produced no measures placing mass and elite polarizations into a common measurement space.

In contrast, this work develops quantitative measures placing mass and elite polarization into the same metric. Specifically, the measures gauge the degree to which mass and elite partisans are ideologically divergent, narrowly dispersed around their ideological means, and skewed toward their left-right poles. Using these measures for mass and elite partisans enables observing the actual extent to which a representation gap exists due to elite polarization. The analysis in Chapter 8 shows that a representation gap has existed throughout the modern era. That is, elite partisans have almost always been more polarized than their fellow partisans in the electorate. However, the representation gap declined starting in 2003, as partisans in the electorate became increasingly polarized to draw closer to those representing them.

More generally and from a historical perspective, this book asks whether American political institutions and the citizenry are more polarized now than in earlier eras. If so, then what is the basis and magnitude of that polarization difference? Is the basis for modern polarization distinctively different from that in earlier eras, or is it the same? Is the current representational system more or less democratic than existed in the past?

ROAD MAP

Chapters 2 through 6 place modern polarization into historical context. Specifically, Chapter 2 contains an historical analysis of the Founding Era, with a focus on the motivations of the Founders. Original documents are evaluated. Early political science and modern scholarship are referenced to ascertain the likely motivations of the Founders. The Constitution itself is analyzed with respect to who benefited from the Founders' social contract. Finally, the domestic and foreign policies of the Washington administration (1789–96) are examined with regard to who benefited from early American government. Then, evidence is presented showing that polarization in the Founding Era was as high or higher than exists in the current era.

Chapter 3 contains a historical analysis of the consequences of the Founders' social contract from the Reconstruction Era up to the Great Depression (1872–1929). The work basically shows that the economic game was "rigged" against the plebian class through the American tax system (which relied heavily on tariffs and excise taxes), the monetary system (which was based on the gold standard), and an absence of economic and social regulation. As a result, great economic inequality emerged, with a very wealthy class, a very poor class, and few in the middle until the 1920s. Further, unfettered markets produced a plethora of economic evils, including white slavery, child labor, low wages, long working hours, abhorrent working conditions, tainted food and drugs, monopolistic behaviors, price discrimination, unstable economic conditions, etc. Resentment exploded against the rich, sparking a few Progressive Era reforms. However, the Supreme Court, seeking to maintain the Founders' social contract, posed a major obstacle to securing a more equitable system and market regulation through 1932. As with the Founding Era, evidence is also presented that polarization was very high during the latter part of the nineteenth century and the early part of the twentieth century.

Chapter 4 contains a historical analysis of the evolution of the New Deal social contract from the Great Depression through World War II (1933–45). The economic shock of the Great Depression was so extreme that it produced the near death of the Founders' social contract. It became very unpopular to be a Republican or a person of wealth, and remained so until the 1980s. The New Deal social contract unified the nation against the abuses of the market system and brought about many programs favorable to the plebian class and the nation-at-large. The patrician class financed the New Deal reforms through a revised monetary system, greater market regulation, and by paying higher taxes. World War II solidified national unity and produced a set of economic conditions favorable to expanding the New Deal social contract from the 1940s through the late 1970s. This period of American history was one of low polarization and partisan consensus that government should promote the general welfare of the nation, and not just benefit the commercial class. This chapter also argues that what is unusual in American history is not the modern extremes of party polarization, but the lack of party polarization from 1933 until the late 1970s.

Chapter 5 contains a historical and empirical analysis of the expansion of the New Deal social contract (1945–80). It covers the rationale for expansion, rooted in extreme economic inequality, discrimination, racial conflict, and a plethora of remaining economic and social problems. Modest expansion occurred during the Truman and Eisenhower administrations, but a conservative coalition of Southern Democrats and Republicans blocked major change. However, the Kennedy assassination and Lyndon Johnson's subsequent commitment to domestic reform sparked a plethora of programs targeting benefits toward the nation-at-large. Again, these benefits came at a cost to the patrician class. Significant expansion of the New Deal social contract also occurred during the Nixon administration, which cast itself as Modern Republican. However, Nixon's misbehavior set the stage for a takeover of the Republican Party by Old Guard Republicans. With the exception of the Era of Good Feelings (1815–25), party polarization was at its lowest in American history during the 1970s.

Chapter 6, the last historical chapter, traces the evolution of polarization from the late 1970s to the present. It outlines the conditions leading to the election of Ronald Reagan in 1980. These conditions included the Watergate scandal, Old Guard disgruntlement with Modern Republicans, the emergence of an intellectual paradigm rooted in free market economics, mobilization of the Christian Right, and renewed activism by wealthy entrepreneurs who established right-wing advocacy foundations and think-tanks. Reagan and those behind him attempted to revive the Founders' social contract. Accordingly, this chapter details the attacks during the Reagan administration on the progressive tax system, regulatory regime, and social programs intended to benefit the nation-at-large. Then, attention turns to party polarization during the subsequent presidencies of George H. W. Bush, Bill Clinton, George W. Bush, and Barack Obama. Polarization escalated continually during this period due to partisan conflict over which social contract is legitimate.

Shifting starkly in research style, Chapters 7 and 8 are quantitative and causal. Chapter 7 concentrates on whether the mass public really is polarized, and, if so, why. The previous chapter showed that Old Guard Republicans cunningly formulated a plan to connect their traditional economic values with cultural values. The first half of the chapter shows that after the 1980s Republicans and Democrats diverged ideologically on specific economic issues, including preferences for size of government, free markets, taxation, equality of opportunity, and the environment. They also diverged ideologically on specific cultural issues, including attitudes on abortion, homosexuality, guns, illegal aliens, and welfare. Further, the chapter shows that the partisan divergence on economic issues was strongly related to evangelical religious preferences. This result supports the idea that the Old Guard deliberately and cunningly connected economic and unrelated cultural issues in order to expand Republican support. The second half of Chapter 7 develops and reports a new measure of mass polarization using survey data. Polarization is precisely defined and illustrated graphically. A formal analysis of the potential theoretical mechanisms of mass polarization is given. Then, empirical measures are presented of polarization of the American electorate based on partisan divergence, dispersions, distributional skew, and the overlap between partisan distributions.

Chapter 8 concentrates on elite polarization and its relation to mass polarization. The first part of the chapter contains a text-mining analysis of party platforms from 1944 through 2012. The party platforms are a mechanism through which party elites control the menu of policy choices offered to their electorates. A cluster analysis is reported, showing that Republican platforms after 1980 were distinctively different from earlier Republican platforms, as well as Democratic platforms. The basis of this distinctiveness is revealed through a dimensional time series analysis. Republican platforms after 1980 focused more on economic and regulatory issues, with some increased attention to cultural issues. Hence, the menu of policy choices offered by Republican Party elites changed substantially after 1980.

The second part of the chapter develops measures of congressional and presidential polarization for the purpose of measuring and evaluating the nature of modern polarization and the implications for American democracy. Using these measures and the measure of electoral polarization developed in the preceding chapter, a causal time series analysis of possible relationships between mass and elite polarization is performed. Was the relationship, if it existed, elite-driven, electorate-driven, or interactive? Did mass polarization cause elite polarization, as one might expect in a well-functioning democratic system? Did elite polarization cause mass polarization, as one might expect if democratic representatives are effective leaders and menu manipulators? Were mass and elite polarization connected through an interactive relationship, whereby the causal arrows run in both directions between the masses and political elites? The general finding is that polarization is an elite-driven process, but with some evidence of mass to elite effects. Hence, polarization is interactive, with elites affecting the masses, and the masses affecting elites.

The last part of Chapter 8 uses the measures of electoral and elite polarization to evaluate the representation gap in America. The analysis shows that a representation gap has always existed in the modern era, with members of Congress and presidents being more extreme than those who elected them. However, the representation gap narrowed starting in 2003, as the electorate became increasingly polarized.

The final chapter places modern party polarization into historical context, noting that polarization has been the norm throughout American history. Generally, it argues that the Founders did not intend to create a system for resolving partisan conflict. Rather, they created a system intended to perpetuate conflict by institutionalizing rents for the patrician class. Empirical regularities are observed by comparing party polarization across eras. Unusually for a last chapter, a mathematical model is presented to describe how and why party polarization should be the norm of the American system. The model and empirical evidence suggest that party polarization should increase with the magnitude of class discontent and the efforts of party entrepreneurs to foment discontent in a competitive two-party system. Finally, advice is offered to future researchers concerning how party polarization should be studied as an important research concept.

2

Establishing the Founders' Social Contract from the Constitutional Convention through George Washington

On December 14, 1820, a frail eighty-five-year-old former President John Adams rose to address a convention of delegates meeting to revise the Massachusetts state constitution. The delegates were to decide whether to continue property ownership requirements for voting and holding office or move to equal representation for all white males. Noting that he was fearful of speaking because his voice and memory were failing, Adams passionately supported maintaining property requirements. He stated,

The Constitution declares, that all men are born free and equal. But how are they born free and equal? Has the child of a North American Indian, when born, the same right, which his father has, to his father's bow and arrows? No – no man pretends that all are born with equal property, but with equal rights to acquire property. The great object [of government] is to render property secure ... [If] it were left to mere numbers, those who have no property would vote us out of our houses. (*Daily Advertiser* 1820, 154)

Adams went on to argue that "universal suffrage" would lead the many to plunder the property of the few, similar to what had occurred during the French revolution.

Adams's disdain for popular democracy was reflective of an eighteenth-century Federalist philosophy that dominated the federal constitutional convention and early American government. However, the Federalist philosophy was out of favor by the time of Adams's speech. A push for greater democracy had emerged during the first term of the Washington administration. By the 1800 elections, Democratic-Republicans had gained control of both houses of Congress, as well as the presidency. Federalist opposition to the War of 1812 and the Hartford Convention resulted in the almost total demise of party loyalty. Accordingly, the Democratic-Republican movement saw most states abolish property requirements for both voting and holding office by 1820. And Massachusetts was about to do the same after the former president's speech.

THE CONSTITUTIONAL ORIGINS OF AMERICAN POLARIZATION

Two schools of political thought coexisted in the early American republic. One school advocated a government that protected the patrician class, which was viewed as wiser, less corruptible, and more capable of advancing the economic and political interests of the nation. The other school favored a government more sympathetic to the plebian class, which was deemed capable, trustworthy, and deserving of full consideration.

Those favoring the elitist view in the early American republic were called Federalists. Those more sympathetic to the common class were called anti-Federalists and later, when political parties formed, Democratic-Republicans. Continual from the early days of the republic, the struggle for dominance between these two schools of political thought has defined the history of party polarization in the United States.

The origins of the elitist view lay in early colonial governments and their British roots. For at least a decade before the federal constitutional convention, the colonies were writing their own suffrage laws and determining the qualifications of office holders. Their precedents were grounded in the British principle that only property owners should participate in representative government (Keyssar 2009, 4–7). Men who possessed property had a "unique stake in society – meaning that they were committed members of (or shareholders in) the community and that they had a personal interest in the policies of the state, especially taxation" (Keyssar 2009, 4–5). Further, "property owners alone possess sufficient independence to warrant having a voice in governance" (Keyssar 2009, 5). In other words, property owners were less likely to be corrupted by others or by the power of governing.

Federalists espousing the elitist view dominated the constitutional convention of 1787 and early American government. Past president of the American Political Science Association Charles A. Beard offered empirical evidence that the propertied class comprised a strong majority at the constitutional convention of 1787 in his *Economic Interpretation of the Constitution of the United States* (see especially Beard 1913, 189–216; more recently see McGuire 2003, 51–54). The delegates were chosen by state legislatures that had property requirements for holding office, thereby removing them from popular influence (Beard 1913, 64–72). Of the fifty-five delegates participating, nearly two-thirds were descended from old colonial families. Most were of British descent with demographics similar to the British ducal class. They were well educated and among the nation's most economically and politically advantaged. Sixty-two percent of the delegates were merchant-bankers and/or lawyers (mostly from New England and Middle Atlantic states), while another 12 percent were planter-farmers (mostly from Middle Atlantic and Southern states). Variations across regions reflected differences in sources of wealth, with those from New England reflecting the merchant-banker class and those from the South reflecting the plantation slave owner class (Brown 1976; McGuire and Ohsfeldt 1984). Not a single delegate to the convention represented the small farming or mechanic classes (Beard 1913, 149; see also McGuire 2003, 52–53).

Further, "The overwhelming majority of members, at least five-sixths, were immediately, directly, and personally interested in the outcome of their labors at Philadelphia, and were ... economic beneficiaries from the adoption of the Constitution" (Beard 1913, 149). Forty of the fifty-five delegates appeared in later records of the Treasury Department as holders of public debt; fourteen were land speculators; twenty-four were private creditors; eleven were involved in mercantile, manufacturing, or shipping enterprises; fifteen held slaves (Beard 1913, 150; more recently, see McGuire 2003, 54).

Under the Articles of Confederation, states were issuing paper money as legal tender for payment of debts. An earlier regime, in which gold and silver specie had been the only accepted currency, was supplanted under the Articles of Confederation by a regime that enabled debtors to pay creditors with paper money created under state-sanctioned inflation. "Large and important groups of economic interests were adversely affected by the system of government under the Articles of Confederation, namely those of public securities, shipping and manufacturing, money at interest; in short, capital as opposed to land." In response, "[T]he leaders in the movement set to work to secure by a circuitous route the assemblying of a Convention to 'revise' the Articles of Confederation with the hope of obtaining, outside of the existing legal framework, the adoption of a revolutionary programme" (Beard 1913, 63).

From the time of publication in 1913, Beard's *Economic Interpretation* was bitterly attacked by the popular press, with many deeming it unpatriotic and even Marxist in perspective. Nevertheless, Beard's interpretation of the founding became the dominant view of economic historians until the early 1950s (McGuire and Ohsfeldt 1986, 83).

Starting in the mid-1950s many historians began to challenge Beard's work, but with little systematic evidence. Kenyon (1955) argued that Beard had misinterpreted the motivations of the Founders. Commager (1958) questioned the logic of Beard's analysis. The most powerful critiques came from Robert Brown and Forest McDonald. Brown (1956) argued that early American society was not so undemocratic as portrayed by Beard. McDonald (1958, 349–57) descriptively examined the wealth, economic interests, and votes of those at the Philadelphia convention and at the state ratifying conventions. He concluded that economic interests were clearly important, but what motivated the Founders and those voting for ratification was too complex to be boiled down to pure economic self-interest. Debate over the motivations of the Founders continued until the mid-1980s, with no definitive conclusions (e.g., see Bensen 1961; Calhoun 1979; Diggins 1981; Hutson 1984; Jensen 1964; Main 1960, 1961; McCorkle 1984; McDonald 1965; Riker 1984; Rossiter 1966).

However, starting with McGuire and Ohsfeldt (1984, 1986), economic historians and public choice economists and political scientists definitively confirmed Beard's *Economic Interpretation*. The seminal analyses employed a theory of economic self-interest that took into account both the personal economic interests of the delegates to the convention and constituent economic interests. Using multivariate statistical methods and voting data from both the constitutional convention and state ratifying conventions, McGuire and Ohsfeldt (1984, 509) concluded, "[S]ignificant patterns related to economic interests are found in the voting, with the division of interests generally consistent with that outlined by Charles A. Beard seventy years ago." Extending this analysis, McGuire and Ohsfeldt (1986, 110) stated, "The voting patterns indicated by our statistical analysis generally support an economic interpretation of the Constitution because personal and constituent interests affected voting behavior on particular issues primarily when the interests could be significantly advanced by the outcome." McGuire (2003) later replicated and extended his work with Ohsfeldt, reaching the general conclusion that "Constitutions are the products of the interests of those who frame and adopt them" (2003, 8).

McGuire and Ohsfeld (1984, 1986) and MacGuire (2003) remain the definitive theoretical and empirical validation of Beard's *Economic Interpretation*. Flowing from their work, a consensus now exists among public choice economic historians that the personal economic interests of the Founders strongly affected outcomes at the constitutional convention (Whaples 1995). It should also be noted that while Beard is sometimes labeled a Marxist, scholars working from a public choice tradition are anything but Marxists. Rather, they often come from the rational choice perspective. Hence, the elitist view of the founding is grounded not in ideology but in theory and empirical evidence.

The theory and empirics associated with this economic view of the founding are also tied to similar work in constitutional economics (Voigt 1997), transaction cost economics (Macey 1988), principal-agent theory (McGuire and Ohsfeldt 1989), the theory of economic regulation (Stigler 1972), and the law and economics movement (Buchanan and Tullock 1961; Crain and Tollison 1979; Landes and Posner 1975; Posner 2007; Tollison 1988). These scholarly movements posit that economic self-interest is very important to the formation and behavior of all political institutions, constitutions, lawmaking, judicial behavior, and economic regulation. According to all of these perspectives, the Founders can be thought of as rent-seekers, trying to further their personal economic interests at a cost to the general population (Macey 1987, 1988).

Aside from these theory-driven quantitative analyses, a good case can also be made for the *Economic Interpretation* based on qualitative evidence. Twelve of the original states (Rhode Island boycotted) appointed seventy delegates, but only fifty-five attended. At the constitutional convention there was a notable absence of leading figures that would surely have favored greater representation for the masses. Samuel Adams, Richard Henry Lee, John Hancock, Patrick Henry, and others declined invitations believing the purpose of the convention was to trample Americans' rights. Other likely advocates of greater democracy were also missing. Thomas Jefferson was serving as ambassador to France; Thomas Paine had returned to Europe and was busy stirring up the French Revolution (McGuire 2003, 51; Rude 1964, 183).

However, a few dissenting voices were heard in the constitutional debates as reported in Madison's (1787) *Notes on the Debates in the Federal Convention*. For example, Benjamin Franklin said, "It is of great consequence that we should not depress the virtue and public spirit of our common people; of which they displayed a great deal during the war, and which contributed principally to the favorable issue of it" (Madison 1787, August 7). George Mason stated, "We ought to attend to the rights of every class of the people ... Every selfish motive therefore, every family attachment, ought to recommend such a system of policy as would provide no less carefully for the rights and happiness of the lowest than of the highest orders of Citizens" (Madison 1787, May 31).

Nevertheless, most delegates to the convention feared and loathed the concept of popular democracy. John Dickinson, one of the nation's wealthiest men, considered freeholders "as the best guardians of liberty; and the restriction of the right to them as a necessary defence against the dangerous influence of those multitudes without property and without principle with which our Country like all others, will in time abound" (Madison 1787, August 7). For Edmund Randolph the nation's worst problems were caused by "the turbulence and follies of democracy" (Madison 1787, May 31). Elbridge Gerry commented that democracy is "the worst of all political evils" (Madison 1787, September 17). Roger Sherman agreed, saying, "The people should have as little to do as may be about the Government" (Madison 1787, May 31). Governeur Morris also expressed disdain for the "commoner" class, commenting, "Give the votes to people who have no property and they will sell them to the rich ... The time is not distant when the country will abound with mechanics and [fabricators], who will receive their bread from their employers. Will such men be secure and faithful guardians of liberty?" (Madison 1787, August 7).

James Madison, a major architect of the Constitution, argued that "the freeholders of the country would be the safest repositories of republican liberty" (Madison 1787, August 7). Later in Federalist 10, Madison wrote, "Democracy is the most vile form of government ... democracies have ever been spectacles of turbulence and contention; have ever been found incompatible with personal security or the rights of property; and have in general been as short in their lives as they have been violent in their deaths" (1788b).

Alexander Hamilton was the most vehement in advocating the elitist paradigm. He stated, "All communities divide themselves into the few and the many. The first are the rich and well born, the other the mass of the people ... The people are turbulent and changing; they seldom judge or determine right. Give therefore to the first class a distinct, permanent share in the government" (Yates 1787, June 19).

Flowing from this Federalist perspective, the Constitution was a veiled attempt to squash democratic tendencies, provide security for the propertied class, and at the same time secure a document that could be ratified. The convention initially considered imposing specific property requirements for voting in federal elections, but decided that such requirements would make ratification difficult. As a result, the right to vote in federal elections was left to mirror existing requirements in the states by enfranchising only those who could vote in state elections for the most numerous branch of the state legislature (Madison 1787, June 21).

Of the original thirteen states, ten had property requirements for voting in state elections and seven had tax-paying requirements serving the same purpose (Keyssar 2009, tables A.2 and A.3). Twelve of the thirteen states imposed such high requirements that only white males with substantial wealth could vote. Pennsylvania was the most democratic, owing to the efforts of Thomas Paine and Benjamin Franklin, with all white tax-paying males eligible to hold public office. In contrast, Massachusetts required a member of the lower house to possess at least £100 in property (about $140,000 in today's currency), while those in the upper chamber needed at least £300 (about $420,000). In New Jersey a legislator had to show he was worth at least £1,000 (about $1.4 million). In South Carolina state senators needed estates worth at least £7,000 (about $9.8 million) (Aronson 1964, 35; Beard 1913, 64–72; McKinley 1905).

The final document from the constitutional convention established only one institution chosen by the people, the House of Representatives. Yet the House was counter-balanced by multiple institutions representing the propertied class. Members of the Senate were chosen by state legislatures, which were largely reflective of property holders. The president was chosen by an electoral college, which in turn was selected by state legislatures, most of which had no requirement that its members be reflective of a popular vote. The president appointed the judiciary, with the advice and consent of the Senate. Separation of powers, an appointed Senate representing property owners, an insulated Supreme Court, and a president wielding the veto erected major barrier to passing legislation disadvantageous to the propertied class.

Other specific provisions of the Constitution also solidified favor for the propertied class. Critical economic powers limited state power and were made exclusive to the national government. McGuire (2003, chapter 3) showed statistically that voting on these limitations was significantly affected by the personal economic interests of delegates. For example, the Contract Clause in Article 1, Section 10, read "No State shall ... coin Money; emit Bills of Credit; make any Thing but gold and silver Coin a Tender in Payment of Debts; pass any ... Law impairing the Obligation of Contracts ..." These limitations on states ended the popular practice of issuing paper money, thereby diluting debts and upholding the perpetual legitimacy of contracts. Prohibiting states from altering contracts and debt obligations advantaged creditors by guaranteeing payment, while taxpayers later had to pay the debt obligations. Making gold and silver the only currency for fulfilling contracts guaranteed creditors freedom from inflation, while the debtor class remained a perpetual victim of deflation. Thus, the original Constitution advantaged creditors, bankers, merchants, and holders of public securities to the disadvantage of debtors and taxpayers.

Article 6 stated, "All Debts contracted and Engagements entered into, before the Adoption of this Constitution, shall be as valid against the United States under this Constitution, as under the Confederation." This article made sure that creditors' notes would not be nullified by either states or the national government, and pertained especially to Revolutionary War debts. Many of the Founders held that war debt, and later benefited personally from this article (Beard 1913, 150; see also McGuire 2003, 54). They received certainty of monetary payment under the new Constitution for the debt that they had acquired, often through speculation rather than patriotic investment.

The Constitution granted Congress in Article 1, Section 8, plenary power to raise and support military forces, with the president having authority under Article 2, Section 2, to call these forces into action. Implicitly, the military was to be at the disposal of the president in executing national laws and guarding against renewed attempts by "desperate debtors" like Daniel Shays (Beard 1913, 171–75). Later, President Washington used this power to quell a popular uprising over taxes, the so-called Whiskey Rebellion (Elkins and McKitrick 1993, 461–85; Hogeland 2006; Slaughter 1986).

Further, the Constitution granted Congress in Article 1, Section 8, authority to lay and collect taxes, duties, imposts and excises, to pay the debts, and to borrow money on the credit of the United States. These powers clearly served the interests of the many delegates at the convention holding public debt, and who would benefit from protective and discriminatory tariffs favoring commercial interests. Through these powers, holders of public debt could be "paid in full, domestic peace maintained, advantages obtained in dealing with foreign nations, manufactures protected, and the development of territories go forward with full swing" (Beard 1913, 176).

Further, Article 1, Sections 2 and 9, prohibited direct taxation on any basis other than state population size. Under the new Constitution, people could not be taxed individually on the basis of their wealth or income. Prohibiting direct taxation of individuals gave rents to the propertied class, since the only other means for funding the government was through tariffs and excise taxes. These requirements implied that the patrician class would pay far less than the plebian class in taxes as a proportion of their wealth or income. The framers seemingly intended to place most of the national tax burden on the masses through tariffs and excise taxes (Beard 1913, 170–71, 176).

Thus, the social contract emerging from the constitutional convention reflected the economic class polarization of the early American republic. Class polarization existed between property holders and non-property holders, creditors and debtors, holders of public securities and taxpayers, wealthy and poor, etc. Given these obvious class biases, one might ask how the Constitution achieved ratification. Certainly, the phrase "We, the people of the United States"

(Wikipedia 2014b) does not adequately describe the ratification process. The Constitution was ratified by state conventions, with delegates elected by those qualified to vote in each state. In general, state legislatures imposed the same property requirements for voting as they applied for membership in the lower house of the state legislature. As a result, the Constitution was ratified by the vote of probably no more than one-sixth of the adult males in the United States (Beard 1913, 239–52, 325). As at the constitutional convention, economic self-interest was the primary factor affecting the votes of delegates to the state ratifying conventions (McGuire 2003, 159–61). The ratification process was not fully complete until May of 1790 when Rhode Island finally assented.

During the ratification process, partisan conflict had clearly emerged (McGuire 2003, 132–34). As expressed by Beard (1913, 292), "No one can pore for weeks over the letters, newspapers, and pamphlets of the years 1787–1789 without coming to the conclusion that there was deep-seated conflict between a popular party based on paper money and agrarian interests, and a conservative party centered in the towns and resting on financial, mercantile, and personal property interests, generally." Thus, even though there were no formal political parties, partisan polarization had already begun.

THE POLARIZING EFFECT OF THE WASHINGTON PRESIDENCY

George Washington was widely believed by delegates to the constitutional convention to be a unifying figure, as well as the embodiment of the Federalist values (Elkins and McKitrick 1993, 33–34). Accordingly, Washington was expected by the Founders to be the nation's first president. He was one of the wealthiest men in America. His plantation at Mount Vernon consisted of five separate farms on 8,000 acres of prime Virginia farmland. He was a slaveholder with over 300 of his own and 150 dower slaves owned by his wife Martha. She came from an even wealthier background, having inherited several plantations and much land from her first husband. More important, Washington understood the expectations of the Founders for the presidency (Elkins and McKitrick 1993, 34–46; Sharp 1993, 26–27) and presided over the constitutional convention; his prestige was highly instrumental in achieving ratification.

Washington lacked formal education, but was broadly perceived as a strong leader (Longmore 1999, 6–10; Moore 1927, xi–xv). As commanding general of the revolutionary forces, Washington was a war hero and exceedingly popular. Bolstering that popularity, he was viewed as wise and virtuous. Voluntarily returning to private life after the Revolution, he was compared during his day to the Roman general and hero Cincinnatus (519–430 BC), who had twice relinquished supreme power when it was no longer necessary (Hovde and Myer 2004). Washington was to most Americans an exemplar of leadership, courage, and sacrifice, and his election was a foregone conclusion.

The 1788 presidential election saw George Washington elected unanimously as president, with John Adams as vice president. Under the Federalist system only 38,818 citizens were qualified to vote. The 1790 Census counted a total U.S. population of 3.0 million, with a free population of 2.4 million and 600,000 slaves. Thus, initial voter participation under the new Constitution was about 1.3 percent of the population (Dubin 2002, 2–3; Rusk 2002, 171). After the 1788 election, the composition of the House of Representatives was 37 Federalist versus 28 anti-Federalist representatives (about a 60–40 majority) (Office of the Clerk U.S. House of Representatives 2012). The composition of the Senate chosen by state legislatures was even more skewed, with 18 Federalist versus 8 anti-Federalist senators (about a 70–30 majority) (United States Senate Office of the Clerk 2012).

Polarization in Domestic Affairs during the Washington Administration

President Washington was a unifying and popular leader who for many embodied the statesman ideal. However, his administration's actions in domestic affairs were quickly and visibly favorable to the patrician class. The Constitution had "rigged" the system to protect men of wealth and property from popular democracy. The Washington administration laid the groundwork for men of wealth and property to expand their wealth into the future.

In staffing the administration Washington chose mostly Federalists whose beliefs were similar to those framing the Constitution. Alexander Hamilton, a strong advocate of the British model (Madison 1787, June 18–19), was named Secretary of Treasury. Edmund Randolph, sponsor of the Virginia Plan for separated powers (Madison 1787, May 29), was named Attorney General. Of eleven cabinet appointments across his two administrations, Washington's only non-Federalist appointment was Secretary of State Thomas Jefferson.

Washington did not have the first-rate mind of many in his cabinet, but many argue that he had good judgment (Chernow 2004, 289–90). Understanding his own limitations, he relied heavily on his cabinet for guidance, and especially on Treasury Secretary Alexander Hamilton. Indeed, Hamilton was *the driving intellectual force* of the Washington presidency in both domestic and foreign affairs.

Hamilton's vision for the new nation more or less epitomized the Federalist philosophy. He and other appointees consistently pursued policies favoring the propertied class, and especially the merchant-bankers of the Northeast. Hamilton's grand vision was that of a great nation, expanding westward, with an economy rooted in commerce and banking. He favored a strong central government that would foster such development. The economic theory driving his policies was top-down, advocating an accumulation of wealth at the top that would employ the great mass of workers and citizens at the bottom. Trade internally and with other nations, especially with Great Britain, was an important ingredient for making his vision true. Accordingly, Hamilton supported a system that would promote commercial development, including tariffs and centralized credit and banking. He also wanted to protect and subsidize the men of property who would capitalize the new economy (Elkins and McKitrick 1993, 114–23).

The new government that would promote Hamilton's commercial utopia was initially funded by tariffs. The Tariff Act of 1789(1 Stat. 24), signed into law by President Washington on July 4 of that year, was the first substantive legislation passed by the first Congress. Section 1 read: "... it is necessary for the support of government, for the discharge of the debts of the United States, and the encouragement and protection of manufactures, that duties be laid on goods, wares, and merchandise imported."

House leader James Madison initially proposed the tariff bill. He sought to include provisions discriminatory toward Great Britain to induce more trade with France. Hamilton opposed Madison's discriminatory provisions, since he believed that the basis of American economic expansion would be trade with Great Britain (Elkins and McKitrick 1993, 113, 125; Miller 1960, 18–19). Most Federalists in Congress also opposed the discriminatory provisions for the same reason. The final legislation was not discriminatory toward the British, due to opposition from the administration and commercial class (Elkins and McKitrick 1993, 65–74).

The Tariff Act imposed duties that were costly to ordinary consumers, while protecting certain manufacturers. For example, an import tax was levied on rum and other distilled spirits, wine, ale, beer, cider, malt, sugar, molasses, salt, coffee, cocoa, tea, candles, cheese, soap, clothing, boots, shoes, buttons, gloves, hats, manufactured tobacco, snuff, fish, gunpowder, playing cards, etc. These items are consumed largely by the general public. A duty was also levied on imported tin, lead, pewter, brass, iron and brass wire, copper, wool, cotton, dyes, raw hides, furs, paint, cabinet wares, etc. These items are used primarily by domestic manufacturers. The Tariff Act was largely a consumption tax on the broad public, raising prices in an indirect and invisible way, while at the same time providing protection for manufacturers (Hill 1893).

Hamilton's subsequent plans for promoting American entrepreneurship were rooted in three reports to Congress issued during the first two years of the Washington administration. The first report on January 9, 1790, was called the *First Report on Public Credit* and proposed that the federal government assume all debts resulting from the American Revolution (referred to as the assumption plan below) (Hamilton 1790a, 15–25). The second report on December 13, 1790, was called the *Second Report on Public Credit* and proposed establishing a national banking system (referred to as the banking plan below) (Hamilton 1790b, 67–76). The third report on December 5, 1791, was called the *Report on Manufactures*, and recommended policies to protect and subsidize wealthy individuals who would expand American commerce (referred to as the tariff and subsidies plan below) (Hamilton 1791b, 971–1034). All three reports sparked significant controversy, and ultimately led to the formation of the first political parties.

Hamilton's assumption plan was for the federal government to assume all debts from the American Revolution, including those held by individual citizens and the states. The purpose of the assumption plan was to inject new capital into the American economy, specifically targeting those at the top of the economic system. Many wealthy individuals had invested heavily in the Revolution with the expectation that they would be repaid after independence. States had borrowed money from businesses and individuals, having exchanged promissory notes for supplies in support of the war effort. The Confederation had itself also borrowed substantial money from European powers. Yet under the Articles of Confederation there was little prospect that these debts would be repaid. Indeed, states and banks often paid war creditors in greatly devalued paper currency, making the debt essentially worthless (Markham 2002, chapter 2.1). As observed earlier, wealthy creditors were the biggest losers from this practice.

Hamilton believed that American commercial interests seeking to expand would never be able to do so until these war debts were paid. Paying the debts would generate new capital for wealthy entrepreneurs, as well as enable future borrowing. Hamilton's assumption plan was, therefore, an effort to inject new capital into a particular segment of the economic system. Underlying Hamilton's assumption plan was the belief that American economic development depended on the upper class (Chernow 2004, 297–301; Elkins and McKitrick 1993, 114–31). Under the assumption plan creditors were to be paid off by issuing U.S. government bonds yielding a guaranteed 4 percent interest.

Hamilton saw four primary benefits flowing from his plan. First, assumption would establish the full faith and credit of the nation, both at home and abroad. Second, assuming state war debts meant that the federal government would not be competing with states for certain revenues. Hamilton wanted to "preempt the best sources of revenue for the United States Treasury" (Chernow 2004, 299; Elkins and McKitrick 1993, 118–19). Third, centralizing war debts away from the states to the national government had the advantage of concentrating capital. Rather than leaving the debt dispersed, this approach was more likely to result in productive capital (Elkins and McKitrick 1993, 118). Finally, tying wealthy creditors who held the debt to the national government, rather than to state governments, increased their future commitment to the nation. Wealthy individuals were less likely to support state secession if they were to suffer great financial losses for such action. As expressed by Hamilton, a permanent and moderately sized public debt would form "the powerful cement of our Union" (Meyer 2007).

Initially, Hamilton's assumption plan was not well received. In April 1790, the House of Representatives voted it down. The opposition was led by House leader James Madison and Secretary of State Thomas Jefferson, who preferred a plan more beneficial to citizens and veterans of the American Revolution. After the American Revolution, veterans had been given promissory notes in lieu of back pay they were owed, and in reward for their service to the nation.

However, many of these veterans had grown uncertain that the notes would ever be honored. As a result, many sold them for a fraction of their face value to wealthy speculators. Madison saw Hamilton's plan as unfairly rewarding the wealthy, rather than the worthy individuals responsible for the success of the American Revolution. He proposed that "One of three things must be done; either pay both [the original holders and the assignees], reject wholly one or the other, or make a composition between them on some principle of equity" (Ellis 2002, 56). In other words, Madison's plan was to provide a modicum of justice for common Americans.

As a veteran himself, Hamilton certainly understood the justice in rewarding soldiers of the American Revolution. However, he staunchly opposed Madison's plan (Chernow 2004, 297–98). He argued that it would be a breach of contract to split payment between the original note holders and the assignees. Hamilton also argued that the principle contained in Madison's plan "was subversive of the public credit because it impaired the liquidity of public securities – their capacity, that is, guaranteed by security of transfer, to pass as money." Finally, and most revealing of Hamilton's mindset,

> He did not want holdings in the public debt widely dispersed. He wanted the resources which they represented concentrated as much as possible in the hands of a particular class of men, because he wanted those resources maximally available for productive economic uses ... For the capital created by a funded debt to become "an accession of real wealth," it must serve "as a New power in the operation of industry," and this would occur only if it went through the hands of men who would use it to build ships and factories, launch business ventures and augment commerce. (Elkins and McKitrick 1993, 117–18)

Jefferson and Madison also objected to Hamilton's plan because it discriminated against states that had already made substantial progress toward retiring their war debts. Jefferson and Madison's home state of Virginia had paid off a large part of its debt by 1789. In contrast, Massachusetts and South Carolina were still heavily burdened by their war debts (Elkins and McKitrick 1993, 119–20). It is probably no coincidence that many of the debt-ridden states were in the manufacturing regions of the Northeast, while most that had made progress in retiring their debts were in the South.

Despite the Federalist composition of Congress, the inequities in Hamilton's assumption plan were very divisive, evidenced by its initial failure to secure passage (Chernow 2004, 301–6). Opposition to the plan was rooted in both economic conflict (merchant-bankers versus planter-farmers) and sectionalism (the Federalist North versus the anti-Federalist South). However, a compromise with the encouragement of President Washington was reached between Hamilton, Madison, and Jefferson over dinner in June of 1790. Jefferson and Madison agreed to Hamilton's assumption plan on the condition that the nation's new capital be located in the Southern slave-holding states of Virginia and Maryland (Chernow 2004, 327–31). Virginia was also given financial compensation for its already retired war debts. The assumption plan finally passed Congress on July 26, 1790.

Later that year, Hamilton proposed his banking plan, which was an effort to establish a centralized credit system for commercial expansion (Chernow 2004, 344–55; Elkins and McKitrick 1993, 223–44). The plan was again especially beneficial to the merchant-banker class of the Northeast, and provided little or no benefit to the planter-farmers of the South. The proposal was to establish a First Bank of the United States through an initial sale of $10 million in stock. The U.S. government would purchase the first $2 million in shares, with the remaining $8 million available to the private investors. The government shares were to be funded by a loan from the bank, thereby increasing the federal debt on top of what was incurred with the assumption plan. In contrast, private investors were required to purchase their shares through a combination of specie (gold or silver) and acceptable notes. Through this plan, the First Bank of the United States would be capitalized at $10 million, "more than that of all existing American banks combined" (Elkins and McKitrick 1993, 226).

Hamilton drew inspiration for his banking plan from the Bank of England, established in 1694 to handle the finances and fund the overwhelming debt of Great Britain (Chernow 2004, 347). Indeed, Elkins and McKitrick (1993, 227) state that "in all likelihood he worked with a copy of the British statute at his elbow" (see also Hamilton 1904c, 332–33, 339, 439). However, there was a major difference between the Bank of England and the U.S. bank. The Bank of England was established solely to serve the government. In contrast, the First Bank of the United States was established to serve both the government and commercial interests.

The bank was to be the government's chief financial agent, issuing paper currency backed by gold or silver specie, holding government assets, collecting taxes, disbursing and transferring funds, and providing short-term credit in case of liquidity shortfalls. However, the most important function of the bank was carrying out commercial operations. It was to provide the mercantile community with a large base of credit for expanding their businesses (Elkins and McKitrick 1993, 226–27). Hamilton saw this concentration of capital through the national bank as essential to the future growth of the nation.

Hamilton's banking plan again sparked an uproar in Congress (Chernow 2004, 349–52). Maryland Representative Michael Stone declared, "This bank will swallow up the State banks; it will raise in this country a moneyed interest at the devotion of Government; it may bribe both States and individuals" (Gales 1834, February 7, 1791). Georgia Representative James Jackson stated that it "is calculated to benefit a small part of the United States, the mercantile interest only; the farmers, the yeomanry, will derive no advantage from it; as the bank bills will not circulate to the extremities of the Union" (Gales 1834, February 1, 1791). Of course, this was Hamilton's very purpose in establishing the bank. The bank would enrich its private stockholders and centralize economic power to Northeastern financial communities (Weisberger 2000, 63). As a result, it would give little benefit to planter-farmers in rural areas who were persistent borrowers.

While there was again an economic and sectional divide over Hamilton's bank proposal, a primary rationale of those opposing the bank was constitutional. Madison argued that it was not within the power of the Congress to establish a national bank. In House debates on February 2, 1791, he stated, "Reviewing the Constitution ... it was not possible to discover in it the power to incorporate a Bank" (Gales 1834). Madison went on to argue that none of the enumerated powers to Congress contained an explicit authorization to establish a bank. Therefore, under a strict construction view of the Constitution, doing so would be illegal.

Nevertheless, Hamilton quickly had sufficient votes to win passage of the bank plan (Chernow 2004, 350–51). The House voted 39 in favor and 20 opposed. Evaluating the votes, 33 of 39 yes votes came from representatives of Northern states, while 15 of 20 no votes came from representatives of Southern states (Weisberger 2000, 63–64). On the Senate side, the bill passed in the negative on third reading, with 6 yes votes and 16 no votes on a motion to reconsider the term of incorporation. Again, solid support for the bank came from senators representing Northern states, with all of the opposition to the bank coming from Southern senators (Gales 1834, January 21, 1791).

Madison recognized that there was little chance of stopping Hamilton's banking plan in Congress. Given this reality, he focused on persuading President Washington to veto the bank bill on constitutional grounds. Washington "held several free conversations" on the bank's constitutionality and listened attentively to Madison's arguments. The president even went so far as to ask Madison to pen a veto message in case he decided to veto the bill (Elkins and McKitrick 1993, 232). He also asked for the opinion of three officials within his administration, Attorney General Randolph, Secretary of State Jefferson, and Treasury Secretary Hamilton.

Randolph responded that he believed the bill was unconstitutional because, as Madison had argued, "there was no way of construing the incorporation of a bank from the Constitution's enumerated powers" (Elkins and McKitrick 1993, 232). Jefferson cited the Tenth Amendment, arguing, "The incorporation of a bank, and the powers assumed by this bill, have not, in my opinion, been delegated to the United States, by the Constitution" (Jefferson 1791).

Hamilton was the last to respond to Washington's request for advice, arguing that to employ such a strict construction of the Constitution was to deny the sovereignty of the national government. "[E]very power vested in a government is in its nature sovereign, and includes, by force of the term, a right to employ all the means requisite and fairly applicable to the attainment of the ends of such power, and which are not precluded by restrictions and exceptions specified in the Constitution, or not immoral, or not contrary to the essential ends of political society" (Hamilton 1791a). Under Hamilton's argument, sovereign governments have a right to do whatever enables the legitimate ends of government. Much to the chagrin of his anti-Federalist adversaries, Hamilton was likening the powers of the American national government to those of the British monarch.

President Washington received Hamilton's opinion on February 23, 1791, and signed the bank bill two days later. The president's alignment with Hamilton against Secretary of State Jefferson and House leader Madison opened a fissure that ultimately led to the first party system of the United States (e.g., see Chernow 2004, 349–55; Elkins and McKitrick 1993, 233–42). Madison and Jefferson quickly began to organize a political opposition to what they perceived as Hamilton's pernicious, aristocratic, pro-merchant-banker, pro-British, and unconstitutional plan for the nation.

As expressed by Elkins and McKitrick, they

spent much of the spring and summer of 1791 laying the basis for a systematic effort to obstruct Hamilton's program and to curtail his influence with Congress and the President ... [They] tested the political sentiments of various notables throughout the country, with an eye toward possible regional alliances ... [They] expended much anxious effort in ... [establishing a] newspaper there which might have a national circulation through which they could arouse public sentiment against the administration. (1993, 263–70).

The fruits of their efforts grew to maturity over the coming years. Between 1790 and 1808, the number of newspapers in the United States increased from 92 to 329. All but 56 identified with a political party. Jefferson and Madison provided encouragement, money, and a position in Jefferson's State Department for newspaper editor Philip Freneau to establish a Democratic-Republican newspaper, the *National Gazette*. The *National Gazette* became the leading critic of Federalist programs during its two-year existence. Equally important, their efforts led to the formation of many other partisan news outlets that continually aroused sentiment against the administration (Library of Congress 2013). Madison and Jefferson's anti-Federalist efforts paid off in the mid-term congressional elections the following year. Anti-Federalists took control of the House of Representatives (but not the Senate), and maintained their majority from 1793 through the remainder of the Washington administration.

The primary funding mechanism for the assumption and banking plans was the Tariff Act of 1789. However, tariff revenues were insufficient to fully fund the new public debt from the assumption and banking plans. Therefore, Hamilton also proposed a domestic excise tax on distilled spirits (Hamilton 1790a, 2067–70). Many poor workers were actually paid in whiskey, as it was a commonly bartered commodity. Distilled spirits were the preferred drink of the lower class, and especially workers in frontier regions and the South. Further, virtually all farmers raising grain possessed a still for converting some of their produce into whiskey for sale elsewhere. They objected strongly to paying a tax on their refined produce. The distilled spirit tax proved exceedingly unpopular with the masses, ultimately leading to the Whiskey Rebellion of 1794 (Hogeland 2006; Slaughter 1986).

The tax on distilled spirits also sparked sectional divisions. The moralistic culture of the Northeast saw the tax as a way of curbing the depravities associated with hard alcohol consumption, versus their own consumption of cider and beer. As stated in Hamilton's *First Report on Public Credit* (1790a, 2065), "The consumption of ardent spirits ... [is] very much on account of their cheapness, is carried to an extreme, which is truly to be regretted, as well in regard to the health and the morals as to the economy of the community." Hamilton presented a letter from the Philadelphia College of Physicians stating "domestic distilled spirits, the cheap drink of the laboring classes, had become a ravaging plague requiring immediate treatment" (Hogeland 2006, 63). Representative Samuel Livermore of New Hampshire commented that the distilled spirits excise is "an equal and just mode of taxation and, as such, will be agreeable to the people – they will consider it as drinking down the national debt" (Gales 1834, 1896).

In contrast, representatives from states with frontier regions and the South saw the tax as discriminatory. Senator William Maclay of Pennsylvania said the measure was "the most execrable system that ever was framed against the liberty of a people ... War and bloodshed are the most likely consequence of all this" (Maclay 1790, 386–87). Representative James Jackson of Georgia noted that it was "odious, unequal, unpopular, and oppressive, more particularly in the Southern states; ... as the citizens of those states have ... no breweries or orchards to furnish a substitute for spirituous liquors ... It will deprive the mass of [Southern] people of almost the only luxury they enjoy, that of distilled spirits" (Gales 1834, 1791).

Owing again to the Federalist majority in Congress, Hamilton's spirit tax easily passed. After a heated debate, the House of Representatives approved it on January 25, 1791, by a vote of 35–20. Of those representatives voting against the bill, all were from Southern states or districts in the frontier regions of Pennsylvania, New York, and Maryland. The bill passed the Senate on February 12, 1791, by a vote of 20–5, also along sectional lines. The excise tax on distilled spirits to pay for Hamilton's assumption and banking plans became law with President Washington's signature on March 3, 1791.

The final part of Hamilton's plan to promote the propertied class was contained in his subsidies and tariff plan. Hamilton's proposal was to establish a system of "pecuniary bounties" to encourage entrepreneurship. Specifically, he argued for bounties to be paid to potential investors, noting that subsidies are commonly used in other countries to encourage development. They are a direct method "to stimulate and uphold new enterprises, increasing the chances of profit and diminishing the risk of loss in first attempts" (Hamilton 1791b). Contrary to protective tariffs, subsidies do not produce greater scarcity, thereby increasing prices for the general population. However, Hamilton also proposed a system of additional tariffs to fund the bounties to be paid to the captains of commerce (Hamilton 1791b, 1009–16).

Hamilton recognized in his *Report on Manufactures* that bounties paid to wealthy entrepreneurs might be "less favored by the public than some other modes" (Hamilton 1791b, 1009). Further, as so often occurs in politics, the political environment had changed by the time Hamilton issued his subsidies and tariff plan to Congress in December of 1791. By this time, the efforts of Madison and Jefferson at organizing a political opposition were paying off. As a result, Hamilton's plan to subsidize the wealthy was viewed more critically.

Additionally, two attention-focusing events occurred soon after Hamilton issued his *Report on Manufactures*. President Washington received a dispatch on December 9, 1791, that Indians had massacred American militia and military under the command of General Arthur St. Clair in Ohio. Only 26 of the 920 officers and men in the engagement were unscathed, with 632 dead and 264 wounded. Virtually all of the 200 camp followers had been slaughtered (Eckert 1995). The House of Representatives began an investigation of the military debacle, as well as of the War Department. The investigation sidetracked congressional consideration of Hamilton's subsidy and tariff proposal (Elkins and McKitrick 1993, 270–72).

Another attention-focusing event was the financial panic of March and April 1792. This was the first of thirty-five such financial panics, recessions, and depressions through 1933. The cause of the 1792 financial panic, as with many later ones, was misbehavior by bankers and wealthy individuals (e.g., see Markham 2002, chapter 2.3). Wealthy speculators William Duer and Alexander Macomb attempted to drive up the prices of shares of public debt held by the newly established First Bank of the United States and the Bank of New York. At the same time, the Livingston family attempted to drive the prices down. The uncertainty produced by these competing speculators led to a run on banks and tightening of credit. These speculative activities produced a perception that the wealthy class could not be trusted. Making matters worse, Duer was an old friend and Treasury Department colleague of Hamilton (Chernow 2004, 292–94). While it was generally agreed that Treasury Secretary Hamilton performed admirably in combating the financial panic, there was nevertheless a pall of suspicion and soured taste by members of Congress for any measure that would continue favoring wealthy investors (Cowen et al. 2006; Elkins and McKitrick 1993, 272–76).

For these reasons, Hamilton's subsidies and tariff plan was dead on arrival in Congress and never considered as a complete package. As expressed by Elkins and McKitrick, "The rout of St. Clair's army by the Indians, and then the money panic of March 1792 – with their consequences and the emotions they produced – probably destroyed between them any likelihood there may have been of such a program's being undertaken, or even seriously considered ... The *Report on Manufactures* was not acted upon at all" (1993, 270–71). Similarly, Ferling observed that Hamilton's plan for manufacturing "which was at least a quarter century ahead of its time, died quickly in Congress without coming to a vote" (1992, 350).

However, these bleak assessments understate the success of Hamilton's subsidies and tariff plan. It is true that the bounty part of the plan received no serious consideration by Congress, except for an "allowance" made to American fisheries. However, virtually all of the added tariffs from the plan gained approval by Congress as a means of funding an army to regain control of the Western frontier from the Indians (Irwin 2003). Congress passed the tariff measure in March 1792, again with a sectional divide. Representatives of Northern states in the House voted 20–7 in favor of the bill, and those from the South voted 13 to 7 against it. According to Clarfield (1975), "Had circumstances been different, it is extremely doubtful that this tariff proposal would have stood much chance in Congress. By linking military appropriations to the impost, however, Hamilton managed to neutralize a good deal of the opposition" (Clarfield 1975, 459). Hamilton finessed congressional approval of tariffs favorable to the commercial class by advocating for national security, when in fact the enacted tariffs were lifted directly from his *Report on Manufactures*.

Polarization in Foreign Affairs during the Washington Administration

Hamilton's domestic vision for the nation was to promote economic development by expanding the American commercial class. However, his approach for doing this depended heavily on a steady supply of tariff revenues. The Tariff Act of 1789 was the primary revenue source for funding the credit and banking system upon which the American economic expansion depended. Tariffs had also expanded in 1792 as a measure to fund protecting the frontiers. Of course, these tariff revenues depended on maintaining trade with the rest of the world, and especially Great Britain.

The American commercial class depended heavily on the British commercial class for both imports and exports. Hamilton's vision also depended on westward expansion to the Mississippi, and beyond, to supply an abundance of natural resources for manufacturers, as well as land for settlers who would become future consumers and producers in his new commercial utopia. However, there were problems associated with these dependencies, rooted in complex foreign relations with the French, British, and the British allies in the West, the Indians.

The French Revolution began in 1789, the first year of the Washington presidency, and lasted for ten years. It threatened monarchies and aristocracies across Europe, both physically and philosophically. The French deposed their monarch and seized the estates of nobles benefiting from a tax system supporting their sumptuous and gluttonous lifestyles at the expense of the plebian class. The guillotine was applied liberally to silence anyone perceived as unfriendly to the French Revolution, and especially against the aristocracy. The French Revolution took an even more radical turn in April 1792, when the new French republic declared war on the Austrian Empire. In January

1793, the French executed their former monarch, and during this same month Spain and Portugal entered the war as part of the anti-French coalition. In February, the French declared war on Great Britain and the Dutch. The French revolutionary spirit directly challenged the divine right of sovereigns and the aristocracy, and those challenged responded accordingly. As a result, all of Europe was engulfed in a war that threatened American commercial interests and sharply polarized the nation (Sharp 1993, 69–91).

Anti-Federalists and most Southerners detested anything British. The British campaign through the South during the American Revolution had been especially brutal. Southern plantation owners had also chafed at their business experiences with the homeland prior to the Revolution (Chernow 2004, 313–14, 392–93; Elkins and McKitrick 1993, 83, 269). From an economic perspective, House Leader James Madison believed that as long as the nation was heavily dependent on British commerce, it could never be truly independent. British imports dominated the U.S. market, while American exports were severely restricted from Britain through a system of protective tariffs. With their dominant sea power, the British were also restricting American trade with the rest of Europe, even embargoing American shipping to the West Indies. In response, Madison revived his earlier calls for a discriminatory tariff system that would heavily penalize British trade with America (Elkins and McKitrick 1993, 381–88).

Ideologically, most ordinary Americans favored the French in their European war (Elkins and McKitrick 1993, 303–73; Sharp 1993, 69–74). After the French Revolution numerous private Jacobin societies arose in both North and South. The French Revolution was viewed popularly as an extension of the American Revolution to Europe. As Americans had done earlier, the French were casting off the chains of monarchy and aristocracy to establish a government of, by, and for the people. The French republic attempted to cultivate American support by sending Ambassador Edmund-Charles Genet to solicit money, provisions, and even an invasion force to attack Spanish Florida (Elkins and McKitrick 1993, 330–36; Ferling 1992, 337–38; McCullough 2001, 444–45; Sharp 1993, 69–91). American support for the French would, in fact, have been consistent with the Treaties of Alliance and Commerce of 1778 that were the primary basis for French support during the American Revolution.

In contrast, most Federalists preferred strong ties with Great Britain. Such ties were conducive to the commerce beneficial to the Northeast. Far more commerce occurred between America and Great Britain and its allies than between America and France (Elkins and McKitrick 1993, 70–72). Hamilton saw maintaining good relations with Britain as essential to the trade on which his new economic system depended. Funding the newly acquired federal debt and government was based largely on tariffs levied against foreign goods. Most of these goods were British. If trade with the British declined, then Hamilton's credit system and source of government revenues would likewise fail (Elkins and McKitrick 1993, 399).

More theoretically, Federalists saw the French Revolution as directly challenging the philosophical basis of the new American republic. They viewed the French Revolution as reflecting the same evils of popular democracy the Founders had sought to curtail when framing the new Constitution. Property was being indiscriminately confiscated by the French masses. The unicameral French assembly represented only popular interests and did not protect the propertied class. Most Federalists saw the new French government as nothing more than "mobocracy," destined to become yet another failed democracy piled onto the heap of failed democracies from times past. Vice President John Adams, representing the views of most Federalists, launched a philosophical attack on the French Revolution during 1790 and 1791 through a series of essays entitled "Discourses on Davila" published in the Federalist newspaper *Gazette of the United States*. In his rambling diatribe, Adams (1790) basically decried the radicalism and unbalanced democracy that was developing in France (Elkins and McKitrick 1993, 536; Ferling 1992, 340–41, 306–7, 364–65).

Because of these divisions between Federalists and anti-Federalists, when the French declared war on the British in February 1793 the Washington administration was in a precarious position. Favoring the British would have been politically unpopular and divisive. Favoring the French would have endangered essential trade relations with Great Britain. Thus, President Washington faced a difficult choice. On receiving word of the French declaration of war in April 1793, the president traveled quickly from Mount Vernon to Philadelphia to counsel with his cabinet. Arriving on April 17, the next day he sent his four cabinet officers a list of questions seeking advice on how to proceed. Interestingly, the president had already asked Treasury Secretary Alexander Hamilton to prepare the questions for the cabinet. This fact irritated Secretary of State Thomas Jefferson, who by right should have been the president's chief foreign policy advisor (Elkins and McKitrick 1993, 336–41).

A meeting occurred on April 19 in which cabinet members uniformly advised the president that the nation should steer a neutral course. Hamilton wanted a formal declaration of neutrality by the president. In contrast, Jefferson believed the nation should hold off a formal declaration, and simply behave in a neutral fashion. He also argued that it was not constitutionally within the president's power to declare neutrality (Elkins and McKitrick 1993, 336–41). Again siding with Hamilton, President Washington issued a Proclamation of Neutrality on April 22, 1793, without consulting Congress.

Of course, simply declaring neutrality did not prevent the warring parties from acting in ways hostile to American interests. In response, President Washington delivered a foreign policy address on December 5, 1793, focusing on American grievances. He noted in particular that the British had failed to carry out their obligations under the Peace Treaty of 1783 through their continued occupation of fortifications in the Northwestern territories. The British had also broadened their definition of what constituted wartime contraband.

The British Order in Council of June 8, 1793, declared it "lawful to stop and detain all vessels loaded wholly or in part with corn, flour, or meal, bound to any port in France, or any port occupied by the armies of France ..." (Elkins and McKitrick 1993, 377). Finally, Washington's message implied distress over the British system of restrictions on American maritime commerce requiring American goods to be transported on British ships. The implication of the president's message was that he considered Great Britain the greater threat to American interests after the outbreak of war in Europe.

Complicating the situation, President Washington received word in late March 1794 of a new set of British provocations. They had issued a new Order in Council on November 6, 1793, that ordered their navy to stop all American shipping through the West Indies whatever the destination. Over 250 American ships were subsequently seized, with the cargoes of around 150 confiscated. Many of the seized ships "were stripped of their sails and condemned, on the mere suspicion of intending to trade with the French. Sailors, all their possessions taken from them, were in considerable distress" (Elkins and McKitrick 1993, 391). Many American seamen were impressed into British service (Beschloss 2007, 2–3; Elkins and McKitrick 1993, 388–96; Sharp 1993, 114–15).

Most Americans viewed the British actions as an arrogant affront to national pride, and there was growing talk of renewed war. Congress immediately passed a thirty-day embargo on all British goods. However, President Washington recognized that the embargo was more harmful to American economic interests than it was to the British. Regarding war, the nation had no standing army or navy, and little ability to raise taxes and establish a military such as would be required to expunge British fortifications or defend American shipping. If a new war was to occur, the president wanted the nation to be ready (Beschloss 2007, 31; Sharp 1993, 121). More generally, war with Britain at this time would have been disastrous to the American commercial class and to government revenues, and very divisive to an increasingly polarized system (Elkins and McKitrick 1993, 424).

Given these circumstances, Washington deemed it better to negotiate a treaty with the British than to make war. Again, the president selected a strong Federalist to lead the negotiations. He chose John Jay of New York, who was the Chief Justice of the Supreme Court. Jay was descended from a family of wealthy merchants and government officials in New York City. While not a participant at the constitutional convention, he did author the second, third, fourth, fifth, and sixty-fourth *Federalist Papers*, all of which dealt with foreign policy. Jay was a strong advocate of centralized government and a leading opponent of slavery (Nuxoll 2012). Given his Federalist and abolitionist proclivities, it was virtually certain that his appointment and the resulting treaty would not be well received by anti-Federalist and Southern partisans.

Revealing of the president's mindset, Washington asked Treasury Secretary Alexander Hamilton, rather than Secretary of State Thomas Jefferson, to draft the instructions that Jay was to follow during negotiations with the British

(Elkins and McKitrick 1993, 396–403; Kafer 2004, 87). This unusual choice further alienated anti-Federalists. In drafting the instructions Hamilton primarily sought to defend his credit and banking system by assuring that tariff revenues from trade with Great Britain would not decline. However, his initiative was much bolder than mere defense of his domestic program. Hamilton wanted to stabilize and actually increase trade by removing British restrictions on American goods and open up the West Indies to American shipping (Elkins and McKitrick 1993, 399).

Additionally, Jay was to make "strenuous efforts" to gain compensation for British spoliations of American commerce and formulate rules preventing their reoccurrence. He was to insist that the British honor the Peace Treaty of 1783 by evacuating the Northwestern outposts. That treaty had also required indemnification for Southern slaves recruited and freed by the British. However, Hamilton saw this matter as less important. In his letter of instructions to Jay on May 6, 1794, he stated, "If you can effect solid arrangements with regard to the points unexecuted of the treaty of peace, the question of indemnification may be managed with less rigor, and may be still more laxly dealt with, if a truly beneficial treaty of commerce, embracing privileges in the West India Islands, can be established" (Hamilton 1904a). Of course, disregarding Southern interests on indemnification was certain to spark Southern opposition.

Hamilton listed several other matters as desirable. Jay was to seek the same "free ships, free goods" principle as was embodied in the 1778 Treaties of Amity and Commerce with France. He was to seek a provision allowing no assistance to the Indians (Hamilton 1904b). Jay was also to seek a commission to establish a boundary line with Canada. In return, America would guarantee American debts owed to British creditors. Disregarding anti-Federalist tariff preferences, Hamilton also directed Jay to give the British "most favored nation" trading status, assuring that American tariffs would be non-discriminatory and capped at a maximum of 10 percent.

Jay arrived in Britain for the negotiations in June 1794, and the treaty was finalized on November 19 (Elkins and McKitrick 1993, 406–10). Under the terms of the treaty, the United States and Britain mutually granted one another "most favored nation" trade status. No tariff discrimination was permitted toward one another's trade. The United States was also granted restricted commercial access to the West Indies. Britain relinquished control of their Northwestern outposts. Free navigation of the Mississippi River was guaranteed to both nations. The matter of American debts owed to British creditors was sent to arbitration by a commission of five representatives of both countries. Compensation for British spoliations of American commerce was sent to arbitration by a separate commission of identical design. The matter of the boundary between the United States and Canada was to be decided by yet another commission.

Hamilton got most of what he had wanted in stabilizing and improving commerce with Great Britain. However, there were some failures that became points of contention during the ratification process. Indemnity for American slaves freed by the British during the American Revolution was not granted, and per Hamilton's instructions, not pursued very vigorously (Elkins and McKitrick 1993, 411). The rights of neutral shipping embodied in the "free ships, free goods" principle was never a matter of serious negotiation (Elkins and McKitrick 1993, 410). The definition of what constituted contraband in British seizures of American goods was not settled. Thus, the British maintained their discretionary right to continue seizing American goods bound for France. The treaty also contained nothing about the impressment of American seamen (Elkins and McKitrick 1993, 411).

On March 7, 1795, the Jay Treaty arrived in Philadelphia (Elkins and McKitrick 1993, 417). On reading the Treaty, President Washington determined that it should be kept secret until after Senate ratification. On June 24 the Senate ratified the treaty along strict partisan lines by the precisely required two-thirds majority. Twenty Federalists voted for the treaty, and ten anti-Federalists voted against it. The anti-Federalists bitterly opposed the treaty for its alleged deference to the British, hostility to the French, and failure to achieve war reparations for Southern slave owners (Elkins and McKitrick 1993, 418–19).

Even before the treaty was made public, the partisan opposition had denounced it as traitorous, surrendering to the British monarchy and the American mercantile class. A series of fourteen essays decrying the treaty based on nothing but rumor appeared in the *Philadelphia Independent Gazetteer*. One article read, "there is not a nation upon the earth so truly and justly abhorred by *the People* of the United States as Great Britain; and if *their* temper and sensibility were consulted, no Treaty whatever would have been formed, especially at the expence of the *French Republic*" (Elkins and McKitrick 1993, 416).

When the text of the treaty was finally made public in early July after Senate ratification, mobs took to the streets. James Madison wrote that Virginians were almost unanimously opposed to the treaty in every "Town or county" with the exception of perhaps Alexandria. He also reported that in Boston, Portsmouth, New York, and Philadelphia, there had been unanimous "remonstrances" against the treaty. In Charleston, Boston, New York, and Philadelphia, copies of the treaty had been burned, along with effigies of John Jay (Combs 1970, 162). Graffiti appeared on walls in Boston reading "Damn John Jay! Damn everyone who won't damn John Jay!! Damn everyone that won't put lights in his windows and sit up all night damning John Jay!!!" One newspaper editor wrote, "John Jay, ah! the arch traitor – seize him, drown him, burn him, flay him alive" (McDougall 2008, 29). The British flag was dragged through the streets in Charleston. Rioters in Philadelphia broke the windows of British officials. At a town meeting in New York, Alexander Hamilton attempted to give a speech in support of ratification. However, he was "drowned out by hisses and catcalls, the mood of the audience being so ugly and the sentiment so hostile" that he was pelted by stones (Beschloss 2007, 1–17; Elkins and McKitrick 1993, 420–21; Sharp 1993, 119).

President Washington himself received numerous petitions warning that ratification of the treaty would mean the dissolution of the union. For example, citizens of Clarke County, Kentucky, told him that if he signed the treaty "western America is gone forever – lost to the union." Similar resolutions were passed in North Carolina. A Virginia newspaper declared that accepting the treaty would initiate a petition to the legislature that it secede from the union (Sharp 1993, 119). President Washington was also subject to personal attacks. In Virginia, Revolutionary War veterans toasted "A speedy Death to General Washington!" Newspapers published cartoons of the president being marched to a guillotine for favoring the British over the French. Several columnists alleged that Washington had been secretly bribed by the British (Beschloss 2007, 2). The president was also attacked for forming a closer union with "despotic" England, being hostile to France, and for having conducted his administration on principles incompatible with the spirit of republicanism and on precedents derived from the corrupt government of England (Sharp 1993, 126).

President Washington had his own reservations about the treaty. He considered the merits and demerits of signing for almost two months, but knew that he had to sign the treaty precisely because of the uproar it had caused. The nation was highly polarized between those supporting the British and those supporting the French, as well as between the mercantile class of the Northeast and the planter-farmer class of rural areas and the South. Under such conditions, the union could not survive a war. Further the nation's fledgling economy could not survive another war. Thus, he reluctantly signed the Jay Treaty on August 14, 1795.

Refusing to give up after the president's signing of the treaty, the anti-Federalists made a final attempt to block its implementation through the House of Representatives (Sharp 1993, 127–33). The Constitution gives the president the authority to negotiate treaties with the advice and consent of the Senate. However, the treaty required $90,000 to implement the three provisions requiring arbitration. The power of appropriations must originate in the House of Representatives, and both chambers must agree for passage. Due to Madison and Jefferson's earlier effort at organizing a political opposition, the anti-Federalists had gained control of the popularly elected House of Representatives starting in 1793, and controlled the House at this time by a margin of 59–47.

If the president and the Federalists were to prevail, then it was obviously necessary to persuade several anti-Federalist opponents to support funding the treaty. Recognizing this, Washington and the Federalists set about the task of changing public opinion. Washington remained the most highly respected leader in the nation, and his reputation was a powerful weapon in this effort. The Federalists organized petition campaigns in support of the treaty. They also used the anti-Federalist threats against the president to mobilize Washington's popular support. In a series of 38 essays published in newspapers across the nation under the pseudonym "Camillus," Alexander Hamilton and Rufus King vigorously defended the treaty (Elkins and McKitrick 1993, 432–36; Hamilton and King 1904). Contrary to what was claimed by the anti-Federalists, they argued, "the treaty made no improper concessions to Great Britain" (Sharp 1993, 121). They also framed the debate over the treaty as a choice between war and peace.

After a nine-month public relations campaign, public opinion had swung in the other direction toward support of the treaty. The appropriations measure passed the House of Representatives on April 30, 1796, by a vote of 51–48 (Elkins and McKitrick 1993, 441–49). The treaty was finally approved, but the nation would never be the same after the fight over the Jay Treaty. As observed by Elkins and McKitrick (1993, 415), "The outpouring of popular feeling over the Jay Treaty, as has long been understood, was more directly responsible than anything else for the full emergence of political parties in America."

Interestingly, the fight over the Jay Treaty was as much about class-based economic conflict as it was about love and hate toward the British and the French. Hamilton and the Federalists sought to defend and expand their tariff system, which supported British and American commercial interests. Madison, Jefferson, and the anti-Federalists sought to promote the mass egalitarian values of the French Revolution by restricting trade with the British in favor of the French. Thus, polarization over foreign policy during the Washington administration was also rooted in economic class conflict.

COMPARING EARLY AMERICAN POLARIZATION WITH MODERN POLARIZATION

How did polarization in the early American republic compare with polarization in the modern era? Quantitative historical measures of the degree of polarization among the population in early America do not exist. However, anecdotal evidence suggests that opposition to the Washington administration and its Federalist policies was quite strong. After the start of the French Revolution in 1789, support for the rights of the common man and democracy increased sharply in the United States through the formation of numerous private Jacobin societies. Starting in 1793, Democratic-Republican societies formed to promote democracy and fight the aristocratic tendencies of the new administration (Sharp 1993, 53–54, 69–70, 85–89). Members of these societies preached the equal rights of man and sought to restore what they considered the promise of democracy embodied in the American and French Revolutions.

Federalists were appalled at the formation of these democratic societies, viewing them as not sanctioned by the Constitution. Washington denounced the societies as "self-created," illegitimate, and dangerous extra-constitutional organizations. In the view of most Federalists, they were a threat to the government's authority, weakened the government's ability to govern, and threatened the stability of the new republic (Sharp 1993, 92–105).

Madison and Jefferson contributed greatly to increased mass polarization after 1791 as they began organizing a political opposition. Their opposition spurred the development of partisan newspapers and pamphleteers in every major American city. Of particular importance was Madison's publication of a series of eighteen essays in the anti-Federalist *National Gazette* that provided an intellectual basis for opposition to Hamilton's commercial utopia, an alternative view of American democracy, and a justification for emerging partisanship (Elkins and McKitrick 1993, 257–302). As a result, it became common for citizens to decry the aristocratic tendencies of the new administration. Madison and Jefferson also organized local factions for electoral competition with the Federalists. The result was that anti-Federalists gained control of the House of Representatives starting in 1793, and maintained their majority through the remainder of the Washington administration.

Regarding Congress, there are quantitative measures of the degree of polarization in the early American republic. Poole and Rosenthal (2012) gathered data on all roll call votes in the House of Representatives and Senate from 1789 to present. Using these data, they constructed measures of party unity and party cohesion by Congress for the two chambers over time. While not a precise measure of polarization (as will be presented in Chapters 7 and 8), unified and cohesive congressional factions are a good indicator of polarization as members cluster around their respective party positions. Figure 2.1 reports time series of their data from the 1st through 112th Congress. The shaded areas in the graphs mark periods of especially high party polarization. The lines and associated legends in panel A mark House and Senate party unity. The lines and associated legends in panels B and C mark the right party as the party representing the patrician class and the left party as representing the plebian class.

Focusing on the data in the first period of high polarization (first shaded area), the levels of polarization in Congress in the Founding Era can be compared with those of the modern era (third shaded area). One take on polarization is how frequently the majorities in the two parties lined up against one another in party unity votes. These data are in panel A of Figure 2.1. Considering the 3rd through 7th Congresses when political parties began to emerge, a majority of Federalists lined up against a majority of anti-Federalist/Democratic-Republicans in the House on average about 80 percent of the time. In the Senate a majority of Federalists lined up against a majority of anti-Federalist/Democratic-Republicans on average about 74 percent of the time. For the current era, the comparable figures for the 112th Congress were 75 percent for the House and 56 percent for the Senate. Thus, using this measure partisanship in Congress was stronger in the Founding Era than in the current era.

Another take on polarization is the rate at which party members vote with their party on roll call votes. This approach measures the relative cohesion of

(A) Party Unity Votes

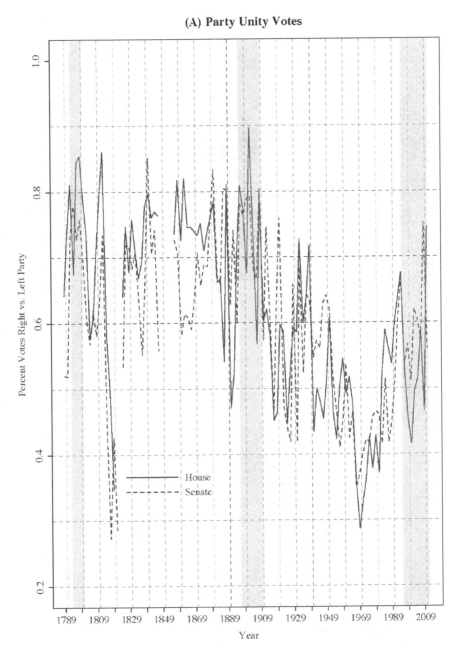

FIGURE 2.1 History of Party Unity (A) and Party Cohesion (B and C) in the U.S. House of Representatives and Senate

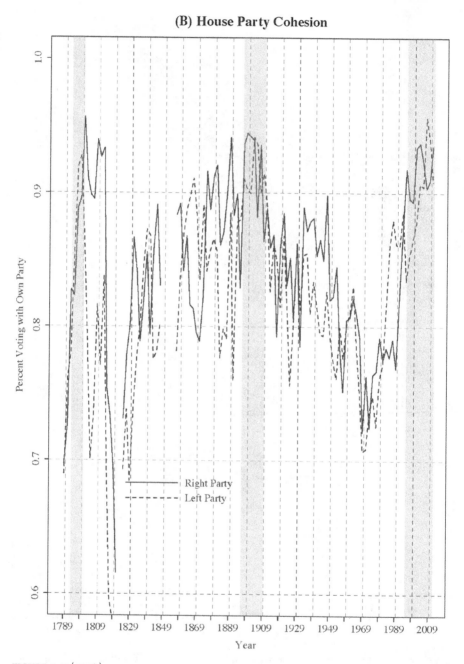

FIGURE 2.1 (*cont.*)

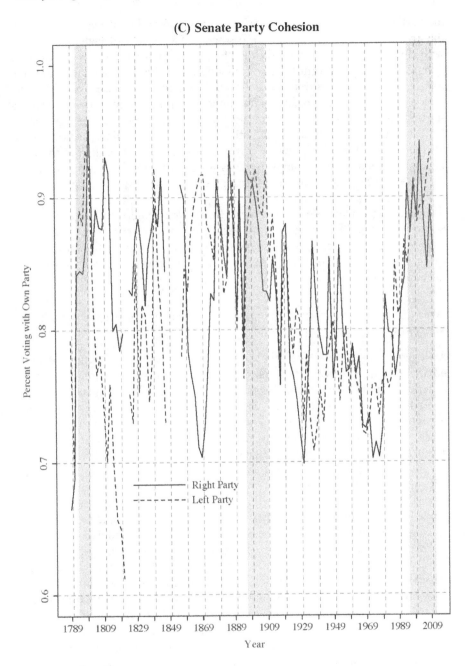

FIGURE 2.1 (cont.)

the parties in Congress. These data are in panels B and C of Figure 2.1. From the 3rd through 7th Congress, an average of 88 percent of Federalists voted with their party on roll call votes in the House of Representatives, reaching a maximum of 96 percent for the 7th Congress starting in 1801. The average for the anti-Federalists/Democratic-Republicans in the House over the same period was 89 percent, reaching a maximum of 93 percent for the 6th Congress starting in 1799. On the Senate side for the same period, an average of 87 percent of Federalists voted with their party, reaching a maximum of 96 percent for the 7th Congress starting in 1801. The average for the anti-Federalists/Democratic-Republicans was 90 percent, reaching a maximum of 94 percent for the 6th Congress starting in 1799. By way of comparison, the 112th Congress, which ended in 2012, found House Republicans voting with their party 93 percent of the time, with House Democrats at 91 percent. On the Senate side Republicans voted with their party 85 percent of the time, with Democrats at 93 percent. Thus, using this measure the level of polarization in Congress during the Founding Era was not much different from what exists in the current era.

IMPLICATIONS OF THE FOUNDING ERA FOR UNDERSTANDING POLARIZATION GENERALLY

An overarching purpose of this book is to understand the nature of party polarization in America. At the onset, it appears that polarization in the early American republic reveals much about American polarization generally.

Early American politics was characterized by conflict over who would benefit from government, and at whose expense. There is a scholarly consensus that the Founders' social contract, embodied in the original Constitution, was a veiled attempt by the patrician class to achieve economic advantage at the expense of the plebian class. The core principles of the Constitution made it difficult for the national government and states to confiscate income or wealth through taxation, currency inflation, or other means. The Constitution also limited taxation in such a way that income and wealth would not be taxed, placing the primary burden on the masses through tariffs and excise taxes.

Further, the activities of the Washington administration actually promoted the accumulation of wealth by the patrician class. This promotion occurred through debt assumption, a national credit system favoring economic elites, tariffs that protected commercial interests while raising the general price level for consumers, funding the government exclusively through imposts and excise taxes on the larger population, and a foreign policy that benefited the commercial class. Thus, at the core, early American polarization was a fight about economic advantage.

A fight over economic advantage has also been a common thread separating the two political parties though American history. This fight continued during the post–Civil War Reconstruction period through the industrialization era, the Progressive Era, and the New Deal. This same fight over economic advantage is at the core of polarization in the modern era. Conflict over taxing the rich, regulation, redistribution, trickle-down economics, and the degree to which the government should protect the population are essentially the same fights that occurred in the beginning. The two political parties that emerged during and after the Washington administration represented two distinctive viewpoints on who should benefit from government. Similarly, modern Republicans and Democrats continue to represent these viewpoints. Thus, the American party system has from the beginning involved a struggle between divergent views of the extent to which the patrician or plebian class should benefit from government.

An ancillary issue flowing from these fights over economic advantage has been the degree to which power should be centralized to the federal government versus reserved to the states. The two parties have also been divided over whether the Constitution should be interpreted strictly or flexibly. However, the two political parties have been opportunistic through time in their arguments for and against centralization, and for strict versus flexible interpretation. During the Washington administration Federalists (similar to modern-day Republicans) sought to centralize federal power relative to the states to protect and bolster the propertied class. The Constitution was viewed by Federalists as a flexible document that allowed the assumption of state debts, creation of a national bank, a proclamation of neutrality, and later the building of roads, canals, and infrastructure to enable commercial development. In contrast, the anti-Federalists believed in a strict interpretation limiting the powers of the national government.

However, as the federal government became more menacing to propertied interests through the latter part of the nineteenth century, the patrician party (i.e., Republicans) began to view centralization as a bad thing. Indeed, Republican-dominated courts of the late nineteenth and early twentieth centuries consistently used the Tenth Amendment and a strict interpretation of the Constitution to overturn efforts of the plebian party (i.e., Democrats) to intervene in markets. These same views on the virtues of centralization remain a matter that separates the two political parties today.

The next chapter turns to analysis of a second period of high polarization in American history. Specifically, it examines how partisan fights over economic advantage, centralization, constitutional interpretation, and market intervention manifested themselves in the polarized politics of national development from Reconstruction to the Great Depression.

3

The Consequences of the Founders' Social Contract from Reconstruction to the Great Depression

Nineteenth-century British historian and statesman Lord James Bryce wrote in *The American Commonwealth* of "certain dogmas or maxims which are [so] fundamental that ... one usually strikes upon them when sinking a shaft, so to speak, into an American mind" (1888, chapter 98). The maxims he observed were (1) Sovereign power resides in the people and is not conferred by divine right. (2) The rights of the individual, for example, the right to enjoy what one has earned free from excessive taxation or regulation, is "primordial and sacred." (3) When a governmental function can be done equally well by a central or local body, it should be done locally. (4) Government should be limited and kept in check by law. (5) The less government the better.

Lord Bryce also commented on what he saw as a contradiction between Americans' beliefs and their actions. He wrote, "The new democracies of America are as eager for state interference as the democracy of Britain ... [T]hough they conceive themselves to be devoted to *laissez faire* in principle, and to be in practice the most self-reliant of peoples, they have grown no less accustomed than the English to carry the action of the state into ever-widening fields" (Bryce 1888, chapter 98).

Contrary to popular belief, Republican governments of the nineteenth century were *not* advocates of laissez-faire, favoring free markets. Laissez-faire means "an economic environment in which transactions between private parties are free from tariffs, government subsidies, and enforced monopolies, with only enough government regulations sufficient to protect property rights against theft and aggression" (Wikipedia 2012). Virtually all of the departures from laissez-faire that Bryce wrote about involved Republican Party governments maintaining or giving new rents to the commercial class, and these rents generally came at a cost to the masses.

POST–CIVIL WAR REPUBLICAN DOMINANCE

From the Civil War to the Great Depression, the Republican Party dominated American politics. Of the fourteen presidents serving from 1861 through 1932, twelve were Republicans. The two Democrats winning the presidency during this period never received a popular vote majority. Republicans controlled the Senate for 62 of the 72 years, and the House for 50 of these years. A unified Congress with a Democrat president existed during only six of the 72 years. Thus, the Republican Party was the obvious dominant force in American politics from Reconstruction to the Great Depression.

The Birth of the Republican Party

The Republican Party was born in 1854 from abolitionist elements of the Northern Democratic and Whig parties (Foner 1995, 149–85; Mayer 1967, 23–47). The Whig Party had basically morphed from the Federalist Party in the early 1830s, and endorsed many of the same principles discussed in the previous chapter (Holt 2003, 2–3). Whigs favored rapid expansion of American wealth by developing a commerce-based system in which entrepreneurship and bank credit were widely available (Holt 2003, 64–70).

Following the War of 1812, future Whig Henry Clay proposed a national economic plan called the American System. The American System was very similar to Hamilton's economic plan, calling for high tariffs to protect American industry and generate revenues for the national government, preservation of the Bank of the United States, and a system of internal improvements, such as roads and canals, to promote commerce (Holt 2003, 2). Clay's American System was clearly not drawn from the bible of laissez-faire. His plan received strong support from bankers, merchants, businessmen, and entrepreneurs who sought benefit from government. The Tariff Act of 1816 implemented the tariff part of the American System. This law initiated high protective tariffs that remained in place through the Great Depression. Of course, such tariffs erected a barrier to trade that imposed costs on consumers through higher prices.

Democrats starting with Andrew Jackson opposed the American System as favoring the wealthy and as unconstitutional. Jacksonian Democrats advocated for the common man, especially yeoman farmers and laborers; opposed a government-granted banking monopoly; believed in a strict interpretation of the Constitution; and advocated a policy of laissez-faire economic expansion (Schlesinger 1945a, 306–21). The Jackson administration successfully terminated the Bank of the United States, and internal improvements were never fully funded until after the Civil War. Thus, party polarization over who should benefit from government continued through the Jacksonian Era and after the Civil War.

Whigs also espoused a broader social movement aimed at reforming American society. Their philosophy was rooted in moralistic evangelism and called for the abolition of slavery, free public education, schools to teach morality, and even support of prohibition to end the rampant liquor problem of early America (Holt 2003, 68–69; Howe 1984, 150–80). However, Northern and Southern Whigs differed on the issue of slavery (Holt 2003, 954–58).

This split resulted in the formation in 1854 of the Republican Party (Mayer 1967, 25–32). In 1856, Republicans contested the presidency by nominating John C. Fremont. Fremont made a strong showing in a four-candidate race, receiving 33.1 percent of the popular vote and 38.5 percent of the electoral vote. In 1860, Republican candidate Abraham Lincoln won the presidency in a four-candidate race, with 40 percent of the popular vote and 59 percent of the electoral vote.

The 1856 and 1860 Republican Party platforms stated the party's guiding principles. The 1856 platform read: "[W]e deny the authority of Congress ... to give legal existence to Slavery in any Territory of the United States ..." Both platforms called for a program of government-subsidized internal development directed at commercial expansion. The 1860 Republican platform called for a system of protective tariffs, stating that "while providing revenue for the support of the general government by duties upon imports, sound policy requires such an adjustment of these imports as to encourage the development of the industrial interests of the whole country" (Republican National Committee 1856, 1860).

Post–Civil War Republican Favor toward Business

The Northern victory in the Civil War resolved the issue of slavery once and for all. Because slavery was no longer an issue, subsequent politics was largely about the other Republican policies of protective tariffs, publicly subsidized internal development, and promotion of domestic commerce. However, federal regulation of business was not on the agenda of Republicans until the late nineteenth century, and then it was not pursued very vigorously. Business-friendly policies were easy to promote after the Civil War, because the Republican Party was the only viable party.

From Reconstruction through the Great Depression, Republicans continuously maintained protective tariffs. Excise taxes on tobacco and alcohol often supplemented tariff revenues. However, as noted in the previous chapter, both revenue sources were costly to consumers, who paid higher prices for both domestic and foreign goods.

Republicans also sought to subsidize business and industry indirectly through a government-funded program of internal development. Improvements such as roads, canals, and harbors were heavily financed by public money at a cost to taxpayers. More than 25 percent of the capital stock of railroads came from public money. These subsidies were especially important when private investment fell short. The federal government granted more than 100 million acres of public land to the railroads before 1880. Telegraph companies built their networks largely along railroad right of ways (Hughes 1991, 68–76).

A lack of economic regulation also facilitated the acquisition of great wealth by the commercial class through this era. The driving force for the accumulation of wealth was the hunger for profits. Free to carry on activities unregulated by government, the drive for profit became the central organizing force of the economic system. The search for profit produced ever-larger businesses, because large businesses almost always earn more money than small businesses. A natural result was that large businesses emerged that forced their competition out of business.

The American economy became increasingly concentrated between 1870 and 1900. By 1900 the number of textile mills dropped by a third; the number of manufacturers of agricultural tools fell by 60 percent; leather manufacturers by 75 percent. Two locomotive manufacturing companies remained in 1900, compared with 19 in 1860. In many industries single producers grew to monopolize their markets. For example, in steel manufacturing, United States Steel Corporation had more than half the market. Standard Oil monopolized between 80 and 90 percent of the nation's petroleum output. The American Tobacco Company controlled about 75 percent of tobacco output. Similar control of their industries also rested with the American Sugar Company, the American Smelting and Refining Company, United Shoe Machinery Company, and many more (Heilbroner and Milberg 2012, 80).

With an absence of competition, these companies were able to charge whatever consumers would bear for their products. As a result, great wealth was concentrated between 1870 and 1900 in the pockets of "robber barons" who ruthlessly and often illegally established empires in railroads, banking, steel, and oil (Heilbroner and Singer 1999, 151–72; Markham 2002, chapter 6.2).

The hunger for profit also caused businesses to employ what most would now consider immoral practices. Greater profits were often achieved by requiring very long working hours, paying subsistence wages, creating unsafe and unhealthy working conditions, using child labor, exploiting immigrants, minorities, and women, disregarding the environment, and marketing dangerous food and drugs (Heilbroner and Singer 1999, 216–41). Thus, unregulated markets resulted in serious harm to American workers, consumers, and the nation.

Protective tariffs, publicly supported transportation and communication systems, and a lack of economic regulation facilitated growth of American business that was nothing short of phenomenal. Total national wealth grew from $16 billion in 1860 to $88 billion in 1900, an increase of more than 550 percent over forty years. By 1900, America was richer than Great Britain, Germany, and France combined (Foner 2006, 581–84).

Commerce increasingly shifted from farms to cities. The urban population was a mere 10 percent of the total in 1870, but had grown to 42 percent by 1910 (Hughes 1991, 94). Farming's share of national income was 35 percent in the 1870s, but only 16 percent by 1912, a decline of 53 percent. In contrast, the nonfarm share of national income grew by about 730 percent over the same time frame (calculated from Hughes 1991, table 4.1). The transformation of America from a pastoral to a busy urban economy was stark.

This period also produced great economic inequality. At the close of the nineteenth century, men in manufacturing industries averaged about 75 percent higher pay than women. White men and women earned about twice what black men and women earned (Heilbroner and Singer 1999, 228). The number of low-paid child workers increased from around 850,000 in 1870 to 1.7 million in 1900, with about 9 percent of the industrial labor force comprised of children (Bercovitch 2003, 350). More broadly, in 1890 "the wealthiest 1 percent of families owned 51 percent of the nation's real and personal property; the 44 percent of families at the bottom of the economic ladder owned only 12 percent of all property" (Heilbroner and Singer 1999, 226).

The wealthiest Americans often justified their exalted status as a manifestation of social Darwinism. Many viewed it as only fair that the fittest ascend to the top of the economic ladder, while the unfit remained at the bottom. Of course, the unfit included the laborers, immigrants, blacks, women, and children who were the backbone of the American workforce. The wealthy often engaged in philanthropy, trying to mollify increasing opposition to their status. The wealthy also suggested that their increasing wealth was justified because it trickled down to workers through jobs, wages, and a better standard of living for all (Heilbroner and Singer 1999, 160–63). Thus, the entire system was alleged to benefit from the concentration of wealth at the top.

At the bottom, the percentage of Americans living in poverty grew very high. For the nation as a whole, it was estimated that poverty among wage earners was about 39 percent in 1900, before rising to 44 percent in 1909 (Hartley 1969, 135–37, 144, 153–63). Robert Hunter's study *Poverty* (1904) estimated that "half the population of New York City lived in absolute poverty – a number that seems neither an exaggeration nor unrepresentative of other large cities" (Katz and Stern 2001). A distinct urban underclass developed with seemingly little hope of advancement. Workers and immigrants were often housed in slums, receiving only subsistence wages, and enduring what were by all standards deplorable conditions. Asian and European immigrants were recruited as cheap labor to work on railroads and in the nation's factories and mills. Managers of these enterprises held the attitude that they should do their jobs without complaint, because they could easily be replaced by others willing to work under these conditions (Hartley 1969, 187–96).

Predictably, resentment exploded against the wealthy in the latter part of the nineteenth century. One manifestation of this resentment was increasing violence. Riots broke out in Oregon, Washington, and Wyoming during 1885 and 1886 against the use of cheap Chinese labor by industrial magnates (Center for the Study of the Pacific Northwest 2013). Violence also erupted in Pittsburgh in 1886 as Italian-Americans increasingly encroached into a working class

Irish-American neighborhood (Reporter 1886). The same year, riots occurred in Milwaukee and Chicago as workers protested long working hours, low pay, and poor working conditions (Foner 1986; Nesbitt 1985, 381–403).

Increasingly, workers organized against the industrialists. The labor movement and unions became a counterbalance to the concentrated power of business. Strikes often resulted in violence from both workers and management. By 1900, the specter of class warfare was a real possibility as the economic system produced ever greater economic disparities (Heilbroner and Singer 1999, 216–41; Mayer 1967, 251–52).

Republican Monetary Policy and Class-Based Economic Advantage

The Republican monetary system greatly exacerbated the class-based fight for economic advantage. Article 1, Section 10, of the Constitution forbade states from issuing "bills of credit" or making anything but gold and silver coin legal tender. The Coinage Act of 1792 established a bi-metallic monetary standard based on the prices of silver and gold and their ratio. However, there was no constitutional prohibition on the federal government issuing paper money or restricting the bi-metallic standard.

Nevertheless, the federal government did not issue paper money until 1862. Between 1789 and 1861, banks issued notes redeemable at face value for the equivalent in gold or silver. Debt contracts generally contained a "gold clause" requiring debtors to repay creditors in the equivalent amount of that metal. As stated by Jackson (1979, 98), "For many years lawyers had used with the regularity of a ritual a clause by which their contracts and mortgages, even farm and home mortgages, simply declared in substance that they were immune from the effect of any use Congress might find it necessary or expedient to make of its constitutional power to regulate the value of money."

The Civil War created a much stronger demand for money than could be financed through bonds or backed by existing gold or silver. In response, Congress passed the Legal Tender Act of 1862 authorizing the federal government to issue paper money, called greenbacks (Kleppner 1973, 1552). The greenbacks were legal tender, not backed by gold or silver, and creditors had to accept them at face value, regardless of the gold clauses in the original debt contracts (see Wikipedia 2016b). Greenbacks were a fiat currency and there was no promise of redemption by the government. Greenbacks introduced significant price inflation into the American economy. Before the Civil War an ounce of gold was valued at $20.67. By 1864, one greenback dollar was worth only about $1.85 in metallic specie (Friedman 1990).

With banks and creditors having the value of their debt obligations eroded by inflation, pressure emerged from the financial sector to remedy the situation. Thus, the federal government prepared to retire the greenback from circulation even before the Civil War had ended (Kleppner 1973, 1553). The accumulation of gold during this period initiated a long period of price deflation.

Nobel laureate economist Milton Friedman (1990; see also Friedman and Schwartz 1963, 89–128) discussed monetary policy history, with a special focus on the post–Civil War period, and especially the Coinage Act of 1873. He notes that historical precedent would have suggested a return to a bi-metallic standard such as existed from 1792 through the start of the Civil War. However, that is not what occurred. Republicans were the only viable political party after the Civil War. Their President, Ulysses S. Grant, and a business-friendly Republican Congress quietly passed the Coinage Act of 1873, which ended the free coinage of silver in the United States. The law created a de facto gold standard. Two years later Republicans in Congress used steamroller tactics to pass the Specie Resumption Act of 1875. This legislation authorized the accumulation of sufficient gold reserves to retire the greenback from circulation. The greenback was finally retired on January 1, 1879, and was no longer legal tender (Friedman 1990; Kleppner 1973, 1554).

Friedman (1990) reports that the period from 1875 through 1896 experienced deflation at a rate of about 1.7 percent per year. Deflation was considerably worse for the farm community, which saw deflation of about 3 percent per year. A $100 farm commodity in 1875 sold for only about $37 by 1896. These effects meant that farmers and other debtors had great difficulty paying their obligations. These were real economic hardships, putting the creditor class at an economic advantage, and the debtor class at a significant disadvantage. The Coinage Act of 1873 was decried by farmers and the laboring class as the "Crime of 1873" (Friedman 1990).

Figure 3.1 graphs the U.S. inflation rate from before the Civil War to 1932. Inflation is shown when the plot is above the zero line; deflation is shown when the plot is below the zero line. As shown, inflation was very high during the Civil War and World War I. Price deflation was prevalent from the end of the Civil War through 1900. Deflation was also prevalent after World War I and the period leading up to the Great Depression.

Price deflation helps creditors and people holding monetary instruments by making their money more valuable. After deflation, creditors' money buys more goods and services. Manufacturers pay less for raw inputs, and merchants reap higher profits by reselling cheaper commodities. In contrast, price deflation hurts debtors by making their money worth less, and more difficult to earn. After the deflation, debtors have more difficulty meeting their loan obligations. Commodity producers, such as farmers, have more difficulty selling their products at a good price. Thus, the price deflation between 1865 and 1900 created a zero-sum scenario. Bankers, manufacturers, businessmen, and the wealthy were made better off by deflation. Farmers, laborers, and those chronically in debt were made worse off. Thus, the Coinage Act of 1873 effectively created a rent paid to the creditor class by the debtor class during the period of deflation.

Deflation is also an important macroeconomic phenomenon. Price deflation encourages those with money to hoard it, rather than spend or invest it.

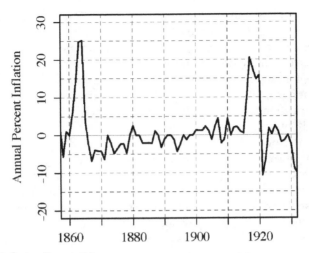

FIGURE 3.1 Inflation Rate, 1865–1932
Sources: Data from www.measuringworth.com/usgdp/ (Williamson 2014) and
wwwmeasuringworth.com/inflation/ (Officer and Williamson 2014).

The hoarding incentive occurs because the value of money increases with declining prices. Investors can simply wait until the price of what they want to buy declines to a lower value. The macroeconomic consequence of investors hoarding money is lower consumption and investment. Thus, deflation contributes directly to economic stagnation and depression.

Consistent with these facts, the Coinage Act of 1873 precipitated the Banking Panic of 1873, sparking what economists have called the Long Depression (Barga 2014; Bernstein 1956). The National Bureau of Economic Research (NBER) dates the Long Depression as lasting from October 1873 to March 1879. At 65 months, the Long Depression was the longest economic contraction in American history, eclipsing the Great Depression's 43 months of contraction (NBER 2014a; Wikipedia 2014g). Fels (1949) called the period from 1873 to 1897 the Long-Wave Depression, as depressed economic conditions were almost continuous from 1873 through the 1896 election.

Under these economic conditions, the creditor and debtor classes perpetually faced off during the latter part of the nineteenth century. The creditor class wanted a stable currency. A return to a metallic standard would provide security and protection for their wealth. However, the creditor class also feared that an influx of *both* silver and gold would inflate the currency, which would be harmful to their interests. Additionally, international considerations affected how returning to a bi-metallic standard might affect their money. Many merchants and bankers engaged in international transactions. Great Britain had at this point moved to a gold standard, as had many other countries around the world (Friedman 1990). Thus, the gold standard facilitated international commercial relations.

The debtor class sought to halt the post–Civil War price deflation through increased inflation. One approach to creating inflation was to issue more greenbacks, and to keep issuing them until the currency inflated. Farmers and labor preferred this option as most likely to enable receiving a fair price for their goods and services. Another option was a return to the pre–Civil War bi-metallic standard, allowing a large influx of silver potentially to inflate prices. Of course, price inflation, if it occurred, was beneficial to the debtor class, but was strongly opposed by the creditor class.

The softness of the Democratic Party in opposing the gold standard partially explains the emergence of two third parties between 1873 and 1892. In 1873, the Greenback Party formed around these issues. They fielded presidential candidates in the elections of 1876, 1880, and 1884, before finally merging into the Populist Party. The Greenback Party favored continued use of a fiat currency, believing that this policy would better support business and help farmers by raising prices and making debts easier to pay. The party changed its name in 1878 to the Greenback Labor Party, as it attempted to forge a farmer–labor alliance. In this effort, it added industrial and other reforms to its platform. In 1880, the Party also supported an income tax, an eight-hour workday, and allowing women the right to vote. The Greenback Party declined during the Cleveland administration, and died out completely during the second half of the 1880s, with its basic program reborn under the aegis of the People's Party, also known as the Populists (Kleppner 1973, 1549–66).

In 1892, the Silver Party formed advocating a return to the bi-metallic standard. Originating in Nevada, a major silver-producing state after the discovery of the Comstock Lode, this party drew support primarily from Western states where metals were produced and the farm population suffered from price deflation. The 1896 Silver Party Platform stated, "We are unalterably opposed to the single gold standard and demand the immediate restoration to the constitutional standard of gold and silver by the restoration by this Government, independent of any foreign power, of the unrestricted coinage of gold and silver as the standard money at the ratio of 16 to 1 and upon terms of exact equality as they existed prior to 1873 …" (Edwards 2014). The Party aligned itself with the Populists, and later the Democrats, and even co-nominated their presidential candidate William Jennings Bryan in 1896. The Silver Party was mostly absorbed into the Democratic Party by 1902.

THE MAJOR POLITICAL PARTIES DEFINE THEIR CLASS BIASES

After the Civil War in 1884, Democrats finally elected their first president, Grover Cleveland. Cleveland did not win a popular vote majority (49 percent), but did win the electoral vote (55 percent). He entered office with a House majority of 182 Democrats versus 140 Republicans. However, the Senate, still chosen by state legislatures, remained solidly in Republican hands, with 34 Democrats versus 41 Republicans.

Cleveland was a Bourbon Democrat. As such, he opposed free silver, inflation, and subsidies to business, farmers, or veterans. He was pro-business and supported the gold standard, but opposed protective tariffs. He was also a social reform advocate who drew support in 1884 from the like-minded Republican Mugwumps (McFarland 1975, 11–56). Cleveland voiced passionate disdain for the conditions he was observing in the American economy. Following is a lengthy quote from his 1888 State of the Union message.

[W]e find the wealth and luxury of our cities mingled with poverty and wretchedness and unremunerative toil ... We discover that the fortunes realized by our manufacturers are no longer solely the reward of sturdy industry and enlightened foresight, but that they result from the discriminating favor of the Government and are largely built upon undue exactions from the masses of our people. The gulf between employers and the employed is constantly widening, and classes are rapidly forming, one comprising the very rich and powerful, while in another are found the toiling poor ... As we view the achievements of aggregated capital, we discover the existence of trusts, combinations, and monopolies, while the citizen is struggling far in the rear or is trampled to death beneath an iron heel ... Under the same laws by which these results are produced the Government permits many millions more to be added to the cost of the living of our people and to be taken from our consumers, which unreasonably swell the profits of a small but powerful minority ... Our workingmen, enfranchised from all delusions and no longer frightened by the cry that their wages are endangered by a just revision of our tariff laws, ... demand through such revision steadier employment, cheaper means of living in their homes, freedom for themselves and their children from the doom of perpetual servitude, and an open door to their advancement beyond the limits of a laboring class ... Communism is a hateful thing and a menace to peace and organized government; but the communism of combined wealth and capital, the outgrowth of overweening cupidity and selfishness, which insidiously undermines the justice and integrity of free institutions, is not less dangerous than the communism of oppressed poverty and toil, which, exasperated by injustice and discontent, attacks with wild disorder ... He mocks the people who proposes that the Government shall protect the rich and that they in turn will care for the laboring poor. (Cleveland 1888)

The Cleveland presidency marked the start of extended partisan warfare over the U.S. system of tariffs and taxes, business regulation, the excesses of markets, and later the monetary system. Many industrialists reacted to the Cleveland presidency by becoming more involved in Republican politics. New Republican leaders emerged who built political machines for controlling the economic policy of government. Their guiding assumption was that the prosperity of business was equivalent to the prosperity of the nation. Unabashedly, Republican leaders sought to identify the party with the business class (Mayer 1967, 215).

In contrast, the Democratic Party increasingly identified more with those who sought to reform the system. They saw protective tariffs and unregulated markets as abusive of the working class and resulting in immoral outcomes such as perpetual poverty, monopolization, price fixing, child labor, white slavery, tainted food and drugs, and a host of other problems. Thus, polarization over government policies through this era was along class lines, just as it had been during the early American republic.

Partisan Fights over Reforming Tariffs and Taxes

As President Cleveland's speech indicated, the American tax system placed government as an advocate for the rich and powerful, producing unequal outcomes. The primary sources of government revenues before 1913 were tariffs and excise taxes. Tariffs were an indirect subsidy for the commercial class, while at the same time increasing prices for consumers. Excise taxes imposed a direct burden on consumers of the taxed goods. Thus, those seeking tax reform sought to shift the system from redistributing wealth from the masses to the commercial class toward a system that resulted in greater equity.

In demonstrating polarization over tax reform between 1885 and 1932, it is instructive to observe how the two political parties differed on this issue by looking at planks in the respective party platforms for each presidential election year. Table 3.1 reports excerpts from the party platforms stating their positions on tariffs. Reading these segments for each party in each year, one gains a clear sense that the two parties were continuously divided over the issue of tariffs. Republicans continuously favored maintaining protective tariffs all the way through the Great Depression. They consistently argued that high tariffs were needed to protect domestic business, jobs, and wages. Their argument relied on a top-down economic theory holding that as long as the upper class prospered, so also would the underclass prosper.

In contrast, Democrats were continuously opposed to protective tariffs as providing an excessive benefit to the upper class at the expense of the underclass and farmers. They viewed government protection of the propertied class as divisive, making the rich richer and the poor poorer. Democrats favored tariffs only insofar as they were needed to fund the government. Thus, the fight over tariff policy from 1885 through 1932 was basically a fight over redistribution of wealth.

The fight over tariffs shown in the party platforms can also be observed in actual public policy changes through this period. Figure 3.2 contains a time series graph of average U.S. tariff rates from 1860 through 2000. The graph shows tariffs increased sharply during the Civil War, as the Union needed vast new revenues to fund the war effort. With Southern Democrats gone, the Republican-controlled Congress greatly increased average tariff rates from about 20 percent in 1861 to about 47 percent by 1865. From this point through ratification of the Sixteenth Amendment in 1913, the average tariff rate continuously remained between 38 and 52 percent.

After the 1884 election, President Cleveland sought tariff and regulatory reform (Mayer 1967, 207–20; Nevins 1932, 280–82). However, Republican control of the Senate prevented reducing tariffs during his first term (Graff 2002, 88–89; Reitano 1994, 46–62). The subsequent presidential elections

TABLE 3.1 *Democrat and Republican Party Platforms on Tariffs, 1884–1932*

Year	Republican Platform	Democrat Platform
1884	The Republican party pledges itself to correct the inequalities of the tariff ... by such methods as will relieve the taxpayer without injuring the laborer or the great productive interests of the country.	[T]he Democratic party is pledged to revise the tariff in a spirit of fairness to all interests.
1888	We are uncompromisingly in favor of the American system of protection; we protest against its destruction as proposed by the President and his party.	The Democratic party indorses the views expressed by President Cleveland in his last annual message to Congress as the correct interpretation of that platform upon the question of Tariff reduction ....
1892	We denounce the efforts of the Democratic majority of the House of Representatives to destroy our tariff laws ...	We denounce Republican protection as a fraud, a robbery of the great majority of the American people for the benefit of the few.
1896	We demand such an equitable tariff on foreign imports which come into competition with the American products as will not only furnish adequate revenue for the necessary expenses of the Government, but will protect American labor from degradation and the wage level of other lands.	We denounce as disturbing to business the Republican threat to restore the McKinley law, which ... enacted under the false plea of protection to home industry, proved a prolific breeder of trusts and monopolies, enriched the few at the expense of the many, restricted trade and deprived the producers of ... their natural markets.
1900	The Republican party ... promised to restore prosperity by means of two legislative measures – a protective tariff and a law making gold the standard of value.	We condemn the Dingley tariff law as a trust breeding measure, skillfully devised to give the few favors which they do not deserve, and to place upon the many burdens which they should not bear.
1904	We replaced a Democratic tariff law based on free trade principles ... by a consistent protective tariff, and industry, freed from oppression and stimulated by the encouragement of wise laws, has expanded to a degree never before known...	We denounce protectionism as a robbery of the many to enrich the few, and we favor a tariff limited to the needs of the Government economically, effectively and constitutionally administered ...
1908	In all tariff legislation the true principle of protection is best maintained by the imposition of	We denounce ... as no less than a crime against the millions of working men and women, from

(*continued*)

TABLE 3.1 *(continued)*

Year	Republican Platform	Democrat Platform
	such duties as will equal the difference between the cost of production at home and abroad, together with a reasonable profit to American industries.	whose earnings the great proportion of these colossal sums must be extorted through excessive tariff exactions and other indirect methods.
1912	We reaffirm our belief in a protective tariff.	The high Republican tariff is the principal cause of the unequal distribution of wealth; it is a system of taxation which makes the rich richer and the poor poorer; under its operations the American farmer and laboring man are the chief sufferers; it raises the cost of the necessaries of life to them, but does not protect their product or wages.
1916	The Republican party stands now, as always, in the fullest sense for the policy of tariff protection to American industries and American labor and does not regard an anti-dumping provision as an adequate substitute.	We have effected an adjustment of the tariff, adequate for revenue under peace conditions, and fair to the consumer and to the producer. We have adjusted the burdens of taxation so that swollen incomes bear their equitable share.
1920	[T]he Republican party reaffirms its belief in the protective principles and pledges itself to a revision of the tariff as soon as conditions shall make it necessary for the preservation of the home market for American labor, agriculture and industry.	We reaffirm the traditional policy of the Democratic Party in favor of a tariff for revenue only and confirm the policy of basing tariff revisions upon the intelligent research of a non-partisan commission, rather than upon the demands of selfish interests, temporarily held in abeyance.
1924	We reaffirm our belief in the protective tariff to extend needed protection to our productive industries. We believe in protection as a national policy, with due and equal regard to all sections and to all classes.	We denounce the Republican tariff laws which are written, in great part, in aid of monopolies and thus prevent that reasonable exchange of commodities which would enable foreign countries to buy our surplus agricultural and manufactured products with resultant profit to the toilers and producers of America.
1928	We reaffirm our belief in the protective tariff as a fundamental	The Democratic Party has always stood against special privilege and

Year	Republican Platform	Democrat Platform
	and essential principle of the economic life of this nation. While certain provisions of the present law require revision in the light of changes in the world competitive situation since its enactment, the record of the United States since 1922 clearly shows that the fundamental protective principle of the law has been fully justified.	for common equality under the law. It is a fundamental principle of the party that such tariffs as are levied must not discriminate against any industry, class or section.
1932	The Republican Party has always been the staunch supporter of the American system of a protective tariff. It believes that the home market, built up under that policy, the greatest and richest market in the world, belongs first to American agriculture, industry and labor.	We advocate a competitive tariff for revenue with a fact-finding tariff commission free from executive interference, reciprocal tariff agreements with other nations, and an international economic conference designed to restore international trade and facilitate exchange.

Note: Extracted from party platforms as reported by the American Presidency Project, John Wooley and Gerhardt Peters, University of California, Santa Barbara. Available at www.presidency.ucsb .edu/sou.php#axzz2AzAAU3lb (accessed November 1, 2012).

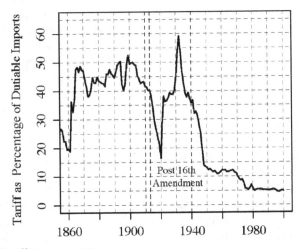

FIGURE 3.2 Tariff Percent, 1860–2000
Source: Data from *Historical Statistics of the United States*, table Ee424–430.

of 1888 and 1892 continued the debate over tariffs. Cleveland lost the presidential election of 1888 to Benjamin Harrison. Harrison worked with a Republican Congress to pass an even higher tariff dubbed the McKinley Tariff of 1890 (named for its author, Ohio Representative and future president William McKinley) (Taussig 1892, 291). The McKinley tariff was also highly discriminatory across different industries, with Republicans' industrialist supporters receiving the highest degree of protection as a reward for campaign contributions (Mayer 1967, 225).

Aided by the rise of a Populist third party, Grover Cleveland won the presidential election of 1892 (Mayer 1967, 231–38). That election also resulted in the first unified Democratic Congress since 1857, with a House majority of 220–156 and a Senate majority of 44–38. However, Cleveland's second term began with an economic disaster. The Panic of 1893 initiated a severe economic downturn that lasted for the remainder of his presidency. The mid-term congressional elections brought a Republican landslide. Before that happened, however, President Cleveland secured passage of the Wilson–Gorman Tariff Act of 1894, which somewhat reduced tariff rates (Mayer 1967, 241–42). However, the reduced rate was still near 40 percent. This legislation also enacted a 2 percent income tax to help redistribute the tax burden (Jeffers 2000, 285–87; Nevins 1932, 564–66). However, the income tax part of the Wilson–Gorman legislation was subsequently struck down by the Supreme Court in 1895 as an unconstitutional direct tax (*Pollack v. Farmers' Loan and Trust Co.*, 157 U.S. 428).

Republican William McKinley won the presidential election of 1896, and the Republican Congress quickly instituted the highly protective Dingley Tariff Act of 1897 (Gould 1980, 40–41). As a result, the tariff rate moved higher than it had been since before the Civil War at 52 percent. In the 1900 presidential election, Republican vice presidential candidate Theodore Roosevelt campaigned vigorously for the reelection of President McKinley on the promise of continuing high tariffs and the gold standard. After McKinley was assassinated in 1901, President Roosevelt assured mainstream Republicans that he would continue McKinley's policies (Mayer 1967, 275–79).

However, Roosevelt's Progressive Republican successor, William Howard Taft, aligned with Progressive Republicans and Democrats in Congress to pass the Payne-Aldrich Tariff Act of 1909 (Mayer 1967, 305–12; Thayer 2000, xxi). As shown in Figure 3.1, this legislation gradually reduced average tariff rates back to around 40 percent by 1912.

Coinciding with the Democratic presidency of Woodrow Wilson, tariff rates declined very substantially between 1914 and 1920. President Wilson enjoyed the support of a Democratic Congress during his first four years. As a result, the Underwood Tariff Act of 1913 was enacted. The Underwood Act also reimposed a federal income tax, which was finally enabled by ratification of the Sixteenth Amendment in 1913. Subsequently, the share of federal revenue coming from income taxes increased from 11 percent in 1914 to 69 percent in 1920 (Smiley and Keehn 1995, 285). Thus, the Wilson administration succeeded in shifting the tax burden upward through a reduction in tariffs and implementation of a progressive income tax.

However, Republicans regained control of the presidency and Congress in 1920, and remained in control through 1932. Predictably, tariff rates rose sharply again after 1921 to near levels existing before the Wilson administration. President Harding signed the Emergency Tariff Act of 1921 and the Fordney–McCumber Tariff Act of 1922, which renewed protection for American businesses. Then, shortly after the start of the Great Depression, President Hoover and a Republican Congress enacted the Smoot–Hawley Tariff Act of 1930. The Smoot–Hawley tariff raised the tariff rate to near the highest in American history at 59 percent (the tariff was slightly higher in 1830 at 62 percent). Many economists argue that the Smoot–Hawley tariff greatly exacerbated the Great Depression. It raised import restrictions, provoked protectionist retaliation by foreign governments, and damaged the spirit of peace, cooperation, and goodwill in combating the Great Depression (e.g., see the commentary in Econ Journal Watch 2007).

Following the Great Depression and World War II, as shown by Figure 3.1, tariffs declined sharply as Democrats entered a long period of government control. The tariff issue was replaced by partisan conflict over progressive taxation, and who should carry the heaviest tax burden. Republicans continuously favored lower taxes on the wealthy and corporations. In contrast, Democrats continuously favored higher taxes on the wealthy to promote greater equity and economic justice. More generally, the fight over tariffs and taxes was a battle over who benefits from government, and at whose expense.

Partisan Fights over Reforming Markets

The Republican approach to regulating markets was also strongly pro-business and anti-farmer, worker, and consumer. However, as observed by economic historian Jonathan R. T. Hughes, this was not a period dominated by free markets. He states, "It is odd indeed that the period roughly dated between 1870 and 1914 should have been viewed as the triumph of American capitalism, when it marked, in fact, the political beginning of nearly ubiquitous federal control. The extensive free-market capitalism of 1870 [was by 1914] an exotic species, as extinct as the dodo" (1991, 97–98).

Business regulation was an already established facet of the American economy by the 1880s. In closing his essay on the irony of Americans' professed belief in laissez-faire, Lord Bryce (1888, chapter 98) gave a lengthy list of state laws restricting business behavior. His list included state laws for antidiscrimination, women's rights, worker health and safety, minimum pay and hours of work, restrictions on child labor, pure food and drugs, occupational licensing, gambling and lotteries, agricultural subsidies, tobacco and alcohol regulation, regulation of monopolies and trusts, banking, railroad rates and practices, and the establishment of boards for trade dispute arbitration. However, Bryce's list did not include any *federal* regulation.

In this regard, a business-friendly U.S. Supreme Court initially bolstered state authority and limited federal involvement. It did so through restrictive interpretations of the Commerce Clause, the federal taxing authority, and the Tenth Amendment. Table 3.2 reports the major Supreme Court cases affecting federal involvement in the economy from 1877 through 1932. As shown, state regulation of interstate commerce was initially legitimized by the Supreme Court's 1877 decision *Munn v. Illinois* (94 U.S. 113). This decision validated state regulation of commerce occurring within their borders. States also used this authority to regulate a variety of interstate enterprises, including railroads, trusts, monopolies, and the plethora of other activities listed by Bryce.

Farmers dominated state legislatures until the twentieth century, and felt particularly aggrieved by the abuses that were occurring in the American economy (Hughes 1991, 98). As a result, dissatisfaction by farmers was largely responsible for the growth of state regulation. The Granger laws, passed by numerous state legislatures starting in the 1870s, were intended to rein in corporate power, and especially that of the railroad monopoly (Kanazawa and Noll 1994, 13–54). For example, four states passed legislation in 1873 and 1874 to prohibit the railroad monopoly from engaging in rate discrimination (Kanazawa and Noll 1994, 21). Rate discrimination made it more difficult for farmers to get their products to market.

With vigorous state regulation of businesses emerging, the Supreme Court did an about-face, severely restricting the ability of individual states to regulate interstate commerce in its 1886 decision *Wabash v. Illinois* (118 U.S. 557). An Illinois law prohibiting railroad rate discrimination was struck down, and more generally all of the Granger laws that affected interstate commerce. After the *Wabash* decision, the only alternative for regulation of interstate commerce was the federal government.

Accordingly, the federal government became the focus of increased pressure to regulate interstate commerce. One view is that farmer dissatisfaction moved from the state to federal level to provide the thrust for federal regulation of railroads (e.g., see Hughes 1991, 92–117). This view would be consistent with the "public interest" theory of regulation (e.g., see Posner 1974). According to the public interest theory, regulation occurs to protect the public from harmful economic outcomes.

A competing view is that the railroads themselves sought federal regulation as a way to shield themselves from vigorous and disparate state regulation, stabilize their rates and profits, and basically enable the apparatus of a business-friendly federal government (Kolko 1965). This view would be consistent with the so-called capture theory of regulation (e.g., see Posner 1974; Stigler 1972). The argument of capture theory is that the regulated are rent-seekers of economic advantage, such as protection from zealous state and local regulation, diverse state regulatory regimes, or the erection of barriers to market entry for competitors.

For whatever reason, after the *Wabash* decision the federal government became increasingly involved in regulating interstate commerce. Table 3.3

TABLE 3.2 *Major Supreme Court Cases on Government Reform of Markets,*
1877–1932

Year	Case	Summary
1877	*Munn v. Illinois*, 94 U.S. 113	Allowed states to regulate certain interstate businesses within their borders, including railroads.
1886	*Wabash v. Illinois*, 118 U.S. 557	Restricted Munn. Only Congress has the power to regulate interstate commerce and the interstate railroad business.
1895	*United States v. E. C. Knight Co.*, 156 U.S. 1	President Cleveland sued to block anti-competitive merger by American Sugar Refining Company. The Court held that manufacturing is a local activity not subject to congressional regulation of interstate commerce, thus limiting the government's power to control monopolies.
1895	*In re Debs*, 158 U.S. 564	President Cleveland ended railroad Pullman strike using Sherman Act. Court upheld his action, restricting the right to strike of railroad workers.
1895	*Pollack v. Farmers' Union and Trust Co.*, 157 U.S. 428	Struck down Congress's authority to impose an income tax as a violation of the Constitution's prohibition of direct taxation.
1898	*Smyth v. Ames*, 171 U.S. 361	Restricted the rate setting power of the Interstate Commerce Commission (ICC), stating that regulated industries have the right to a "fair return."
1904	*Northern Securities Co. v. United States*, 193 U.S. 197	Upheld the Commerce Clause right of the federal government to break up monopolies and trusts.
1906	*Lochner v. New York*, 198 U.S. 45	Invalidated federal and state statutes that sought to regulate working conditions, including hours of work.
1913	*Hoke v. United States*, 227 U.S. 308	Upheld the White Slave Traffic Act of 1910. The federal government has no right to regulate prostitution, but does have a right to regulate interstate travel for purposes of prostitution.
1918	*Hammer v. Dagenhart*, 247 U.S. 251	Invalidated the 1916 Keating–Owen Child Labor Act regarding products that may never enter interstate commerce.
1922	*Bailey v. Drexel Furniture Co.*, 259 U.S. 20	Invalidated the 1919 Child Labor Tax Law as an improper attempt by Congress to penalize employers using child labor.
1923	*Adkins v. Children's Hospital*, 261 U.S. 525	Invalidated federal minimum wage legislation for women in the District of Columbia as an unconstitutional infringement of liberty of contract.

traces the path of federal laws reforming markets from 1887 through 1932. Comparing the regulatory laws enacted in Table 3.3 with the judicial decisions in Table 3.2 yields a story of intra- and inter-institutional warfare over who benefited from governmental intervention and nonintervention in markets.

The very first federal regulatory enactment was the Interstate Commerce Act of 1887. This legislation occurred when there was a Democratic president, a Democratic House, and a Republican Senate. However, the legislation passed with broad bipartisan support in both the House (219 yea, 41 nay) and Senate (43 yea, 15 nay). The legislation created the Interstate Commerce Commission (ICC), the first independent regulatory agency. It required the Commission to establish "reasonable and just" shipping rates. It also prohibited long haul/ short haul rate discrimination. However, the new agency was basically power-less to enforce these mandates, probably by design if one subscribes to the capture theory of regulation. As shown in Table 3.2, in 1898 the business-friendly Supreme Court severely restricted the power of the ICC in *Smyth v. Ames* (171 U.S. 361), ruling that railroads have a right to a "fair return."

Responding to popular outcry over monopolistic business practices, a Republican president and Congress enacted the Sherman Antitrust Act of 1890. However, the enactment was so watered down in the Republican Senate that it did little more than reaffirm "the old common-law prohibition against illegal combinations in restraint of trade" (Mayer 1967, 227). The legislation was near unanimously approved in both houses of Congress, with only a single dissenting vote in the Senate. The legislation stated in Section 1, "Every contract, combination in the form of trust or otherwise, or conspiracy, in restraint of trade or commerce among the several States, or with foreign nations, is declared to be illegal." The Sherman Act provided the initial basis for regulation of monopolies and trusts. However, it is doubtful that it was actually intended to benefit consumers (Gould 2003, 107; Mayer 1967, 227).

The Sherman Act was largely ineffective over the next decade. Democratic President Grover Cleveland applied it in 1893 to halt an anti-competitive merger by the American Sugar Refining Company. However, as shown in Table 3.2, the president's action was quickly nullified in 1895 by the business-friendly Supreme Court's decision in *United States v. E. C. Knight Company* (156 U.S. 1). This decision also severely restricted application of the Sherman Act by future presidents (Heilbroner and Singer 1999, 208–10). Interestingly, President Cleveland also used the Sherman Act in 1894 to halt the railroad Pullman strike instigated by Eugene V. Debs, president of the American Railway Union, and subsequent Socialist Party candidate for president. This time the president's action was upheld by the Supreme Court's 1895 decision *In re Debs* (158 U.S. 564), which restricted the right to strike of railroad workers as placing a constraint on interstate commerce. Seemingly, the business-friendly Supreme Court was more prone to allow using the Sherman Act against organized labor than against those for whom the legislation was actually intended.

TABLE 3.3 *Major Federal Laws Instituting Market Reforms, 1887–1932*

Year	Party Control*	Law	Summary
1887	DP, DH, RS	Interstate Commerce Act	Created the Interstate Commerce Commission (ICC) to regulate railroad monopolies by requiring "reasonable and just" rates.
1890	RP, RH, RS	Sherman Antitrust Act	Prevent arrangements designed, or which tend, to advance the cost of goods to the consumer. Regulated monopolies and trusts.
1906	RP, RH, RS	Hepburn Act	Empowered the ICC to set maximum railroad rates and extended its jurisdiction to other transportation.
1906	RP, RH, RS	Pure Food and Drug Act	Regulation of meat products and the drug industry with respect to drug labeling and prohibition of poisonous patent medicines.
1906	RP, RH, RS	Meat Inspection Act	Regulation of adulterated or misbranded meat and meat products; ensure that meat and meat products used sanitary conditions.
1909	RP, RH, RS	Income Tax Amendment	President Taft's proposal for a constitutional amendment instituting a federal income tax passed unanimously in the Senate and in the House by a vote of 318–14. Finally ratified by the states in 1913 to become the Sixteenth Amendment.
1910	RP, RH, RS	White Slave Traffic Act	Prohibited the sale of women in interstate commerce for purposes of prostitution.
1910	RP, RH, RS	Mann–Elkins Act	Strengthened ICC authority over railroad rates and extended ICC jurisdiction to telephone, telegraph, and cable services.
1912	RP, RH, RS	Federal Radio Act	Required all radio stations in the United States to be licensed by the federal government.
1913	DP, DH, DS	Federal Reserve Act	Created the Federal Reserve System to ensure the elasticity of American currency, issue bank notes, and regulate banks.
1914	DP, DH, DS	Federal Trade Commission Act	Created the Federal Trade Commission (FTC) to regulate unfair and anti-competitive business practices, such as coercive monopoly.
1914	DP, DH, DS	Clayton Antitrust Act	Prohibited specific anti-competitive business practices, including price discrimination, exclusive dealings and tying, anti-

(*continued*)

TABLE 3.3 *(continued)*

Year	Party Control*	Law	Summary
			competitive mergers or acquisitions, and interlocking directorates.
1916	DP, DH, DS	Federal Farm Loan Act	Law increasing credit to rural and family farmers. Created an agricultural banking system, which made farmers more competitive and free from big banks.
1916	DP, DH, DS	Keating–Owen Child Labor Act	Prohibited the sale in interstate commerce of goods produced by factories employing children under fourteen, mines employing children younger than sixteen, and facilities where children under sixteen worked at night or more than eight hours daily.
1916	DP, DH, DS	Adamson Act	Established the eight-hour workday, with additional pay for overtime for interstate railroad workers. Predecessor to the Fair Labor Standards Act.
1916	DP, DH, DS	Army Appropriations Act	Empowered government during time of war to take possession or assume control of transportation systems. Used to nationalize the railroads during World War I.
1916	DP, DH, DS	Shipping Act	Established the Shipping Board and various nationally owned corporations including the Emergency Fleet Corporation, the U.S. Grain Corporation, the U.S. Housing Corporation, and the War Finance Corporation.
1917	DP, RH, DS	Revenue Act	Increased the top rate on the new progressive income tax from 7 percent to 67 percent, later rising to 77 percent, basically assuring that the wealthy would pay the bulk of costs for World War I.
1917	DP, RH, DS	Lever Food and Fuel Act	Wartime price controls over food and fuel. Licensed distributors, coordinated purchases, oversaw exports, acted against hoarding and profiteering, encouraged farmers to grow more crops. Government temporarily nationalizes to coal industry to insure production. Prohibits manufacture of alcohol.
1917	DP, RH, DS	Prohibition Amendment	Senate initiates the process of amending the Constitution to prohibit the sale, purchase, and transportation of alcohol. Bipartisan measure, with the Senate voting 65 to 20 in

Year	Party Control*	Law	Summary
			favor and the House voting 282 to 128 in favor. States finally ratified the Eighteenth Amendment in 1919.
1919	DP, RH, DS	Child Labor Tax Act	Imposed an excise tax of 10 percent on the net profits of any company that employed children as defined in the Keating–Owen Child Labor Act.
1919	DP, RH, RS	Volstead Act	Prohibition legislation to execute the Eighteenth Amendment. Forbid making, selling, and transporting alcohol, including beer, wine, and distilled spirits. The Republican House and Senate overrode President Wilson's veto.
1920	DP, RH, RS	Transportation Act	Railroads previously nationalized were turned back to private control, but with much regulation. Shifted vital aspects of managerial control to the ICC.
1925	RP, RH, RS	Air Mail Act	Provided for private contractors to carry the U.S. mail by air. Regulated routes and promoted development of air transportation.
1926	RP, RH, RS	Air Commerce Act	Predecessor to the Civil Aeronautics Board. Charged the Secretary of Commerce with promoting and developing air commerce, issuing air traffic rules, and general regulation of air commerce.
1926	RP, RH, RS	Federal Radio Act	Predecessor to the Federal Communications Commission. Created to regulate radio use "as the public interest, convenience, and necessity" requires.
1926	RP, RH, RS	Railway Labor Act	Predecessor to the National Labor Relations Board. Substituted bargaining, arbitration, and mediation for strikes to resolve railway labor disputes.

* DP, RP: Democrat and Republican presidencies, respectively; DH, RH: Democrat and Republican House of Representatives; DS, RS: Democrat and Republican Senate.

Class Warfare Intensifies with the Progressive Movement

In response to Republican policies on protective tariffs, movement to the gold standard, and unregulated markets, a Populist Movement emerged in 1891 comprised of farmers and other working people. Their goal was to achieve government action against low agricultural prices, low wages, high tariffs, banks, railroads, merchants, and corporate power generally (Hughes 1991, 98–101). In 1892, Populists organized into a third political party dubbed the People's Party. At their 1892 Omaha Convention they declared that the nation faced "moral, political, and material ruin." The government was corrupt, and this corruption even extended to "the ermine of the bench." Business was evil, labor was impoverished, and wealth was concentrated "in the hands of capitalists."

The People's Party platform called for the abolition of national banks, a progressive income tax, direct election of senators, a one-term limit for presidents, civil service reform, an eight-hour workday, restrictions on immigration, abolition of the Pinkertons (who had intervened violently in the Homestead strike), a boycott of certain goods produced by opponents of organized labor, nationalization of all railroads, telegraphs, and telephones, and a return to bi-metallism. They also demanded that lands given to the railroads and no longer needed be "reclaimed by the government and held for actual settlers only" (People's Party 1892).

The People's Party declined when the Democratic Party took up their cause in their 1896 platform. A highly polarizing period, the 1896 election has been called a realigning election, because it marked a shift in the cleavages in American politics (Burnham 1970; Mayer 1967, 255–56). The previous president, Grover Cleveland, was a Bourbon Democrat who supported the gold standard, alienating many agrarian Democrats. He had used the Sherman Act to end the Pullman strike, alienating organized labor. He had also attempted to reform tariffs and signed legislation creating the ICC.

In contrast, Progressive Democratic candidate William Jennings Bryan unified the reform movement in 1896, becoming the presidential nominee of the Democrats, the People's Party, and the Free Silver Party. In seeking the nomination, he decried the gold standard in his famous Cross of Gold Speech, stating, "[A]sk us why we say more on the money question than we say on the tariff question, I reply that, if protection has slain its thousands, the Gold Standard has slain its tens of thousands" (Bryan 1896). Bryan drew support from poor farmers, laborers, immigrants, and those advocating bi-metallism.

Republican nominee William McKinley drew support from the financial sector, railroads, businessmen, professionals, skilled factory workers, prosperous farmers, industrialists, and those advocating a gold standard (Mayer 1967, 244–45). As noted earlier, the nation had fallen into a deep economic depression during the second Cleveland administration. Republicans blamed Cleveland and his low tariff, anti-business policies for the poor economic conditions.

With these stark contrasts, the 1896 election was pivotal in sinking the fortunes of the Democrats and renewing the Republican hold on government. Voter turnout in the 1896 election was very high by modern standards at almost 80 percent (Peters and Wooley 2013). McKinley narrowly won the election with 51 percent of the popular vote, carrying 23 states versus Bryan's 22 states. His victory may have been due to the poor economy, or because his party employed a new means of financing presidential elections. Setting the precedent for modern campaign finance, Republicans relied heavily on donations from financiers and industrialists (Horner 2010, 193–201). As a result, McKinley outspent Bryan in the 1896 election by a factor of ten to one (Thayer 1974, 37–65).

When the economy recovered sharply at the start of the McKinley administration, it seemed an affirmation that the Republican pro-business policies were good for the nation. As noted earlier, McKinley quickly secured the Dingley Tariff of 1897 to protect manufacturers from foreign competition. He also obtained passage of the Gold Standard Act of 1900, finally moving the United States from the de facto gold standard of 1873 to the de jure gold standard that lasted until 1933. Both measures were highly polarizing, with Republicans in Congress overwhelmingly supportive and Democrats overwhelmingly opposed.

The McKinley administration coincided with a period of rapid economic growth. After this, the Republican Party gained the name Grand Old Party, and became a symbol of prosperity until the Great Depression (Mayer 1967, 255–56). Only one Democratic president, Woodrow Wilson, was elected during this period, and Democrats controlled Congress for only 4 of the next 36 years.

However, the 1896 election also marked the beginning of a rift in the Republican Party, with a conservative wing (called the "stand patters") continuing to advocate business interests, and a Progressive wing more sympathetic toward reform. The Progressive Movement was broad based, drawing support not only from farmers and workers, but also from the middle class, professionals, intellectuals, and some business people. By 1900, the Progressive Movement had become strong, and the Republican Party recognized the need to attract Progressive voters.

Against the wishes of President McKinley and the "stand patters," the Republican Party bosses selected Progressive New York governor Theodore Roosevelt to be his running mate in 1900. Roosevelt campaigned on the promise of continuing President McKinley's pro-tariff, pro-business policies, and support for the gold standard. Drawing Progressive support, the ticket won reelection in 1900 by a landslide (Mayer 1967, 268–71; Rutland 1996, 126–30).

As fate would have it, President McKinley was assassinated in September 1901, and, much to the consternation of the "stand patters" (Mayer 1967, 272), the Progressive Theodore Roosevelt became president. The subsequent Progressive Era extended to 1920, and was a period of increased governmental activism. The movement cut across party lines. Prominent Republican Progressives included Presidents Theodore Roosevelt and William Howard Taft, Senator Robert M. La Follette of Wisconsin, and Chief Justice of the Supreme Court Charles Evans Hughes. On the Democrat side, prominent Progressives included President Woodrow Wilson, and presidential candidates William Jennings Bryan (1896, 1900, 1908) and Al Smith (1928).

However, not all Progressives were created equal. Republican Progressives believed that economic concentration was an inevitable consequence of competition. Such concentration could be a good thing. However, when economic concentration led to bad behavior, then "bad" big businesses should be regulated. Thus, Republican Progressives focused on limiting evil market behaviors, while still supporting business interests.

In contrast, Democratic Progressives believed that all economic concentration was evil (Mayer 1967, 291–95; Neuman 1998). The goal of federal regulation should be to preserve competition. Unregulated businesses would always engage in immoral behaviors to make profits, and virtually always acted against the interests of consumers and workers. Therefore, Democratic Progressives saw the problem as emanating from the inherent greed of the commercial class.

Theodore Roosevelt aligned himself with the Republican Progressives, but because he was a Republican also needed to mollify the "stand patters." Nevertheless, as shown in Table 3.3, during his administration landmark legislation was passed to expand the authority of the ICC, regulate food and drug safety, and provide sanitary conditions in the meat packing industry. As chief executive, Roosevelt also halted the Anthracite Coal Industry Strike of 1902 by the United Mine Workers. As a result of federal intervention, workers received more pay and worked fewer hours. However, the federal government did not ultimately recognize the United Mine Workers as a bargaining agent. Roosevelt also acted to set aside public lands to prevent their unrestricted use by business interests.

Known popularly as the "trust buster," President Roosevelt acted in 1902 to break up what he considered a "bad" trust, the Northern Securities Company of J. P. Morgan and Associates (Heilbroner and Singer 1999, 210 note; Jenson 2001, 162; Mayer 1967, 279–81). As shown by Table 3.2, the Supreme Court upheld Roosevelt's action in 1904 through its decision in *Northern Securities Company v. United States* (193 U.S. 197). This decision modified the earlier *E. C. Knight* decision, upholding the power of the federal government to regulate trusts and monopolies through the Commerce Clause. Roosevelt also initiated action against the Standard Oil Company, the Swift & Company beef trust, the American Tobacco Company, and many more. All total, Theodore Roosevelt dissolved forty-four trusts during his two-term presidency.

The Supreme Court consisted largely of "stand patters." However, it allowed federal regulation of antitrust under Roosevelt, because it was within the purview of Congress to regulate interstate commerce, and monopolies and trusts clearly operated in an interstate context. However, the Court was less inclined to permit regulation along other economic dimensions. Table 3.2 shows that the Court in its 1906 decision *Lochner v. New York* (198 U.S. 45) struck down efforts by state and federal governments to regulate working conditions and hours of work. Thus, while a Progressive movement was ongoing, it faced an institutional roadblock from a Supreme Court appointed by earlier Republicans.

Although Theodore Roosevelt is known popularly as the "trust buster," he was neither anti-trust nor anti-business. Big corporations made far larger donations to his 1904 reelection campaign than were made to Democrats (Mayer 1967, 287). Further, during his administration the number of trusts actually grew from 149 in 1900 to 10,020 in 1908 (Mayer 1967, 280). As expressed by Schlesinger (1957, 22), "Trust busting seemed to him madness – 'futile madness.'" According to Roosevelt, "It is preposterous to abandon all that has been wrought in the application of the cooperative idea in business and return to the era of cut-throat competition. But acceptance of bigness could not be allowed to mean surrender to bigness: this was the test of democratic government" (Schlesinger 1957, 22). Thus, Roosevelt believed that "bad" trusts were deserving of destruction; he also believed that trusts could be "good" if they benefited the public (Mayer 1967, 290).

Roosevelt's hand-picked Republican successor, William Howard Taft, was less discriminating about eliminating trusts (Jenson 2001, 162; Mayer 1967, 300–305). President Taft's Justice Department went after more than twice as many trusts as Roosevelt. However, Taft was not the zealous conservationist Roosevelt had been. He opened public lands to business exploitation. These policies angered the former president, likely resulting in his running as a third-party candidate in 1912 (Mayer 1967, 316–18; Rutland 1996, 147–49).

As shown by Table 3.3, Taft also proposed and Congress passed legislation to amend the Constitution to authorize the federal income tax. The White Slave Traffic Act of 1910 prohibited the sale of women in interstate commerce for immoral purposes. As shown in Table 3.2, the Supreme Court upheld this law in *Hoke v. United States* (227 U.S. 308, 1913), stating that the federal government has no power to regulate prostitution per se, but does have a right to regulate interstate travel for the purpose of prostitution. The Mann–Elkins Act of 1910 further strengthened ICC authority over railroad rates and extended its jurisdiction to telephone, telegraph, and cable services. Finally, the Federal Radio Act of 1912 required federal licensing of all radio stations in the United States.

The election of 1912 greatly accelerated Progressive reform of markets when Democrats gained control of the presidency and both houses of Congress. The break between Taft and Roosevelt had produced a three-party race enabling the election of Woodrow Wilson. As a result, President Wilson was a minority president, receiving only 41.8 percent of the popular vote. However, he entered office with strong legislative majorities in both chambers. The new House comprised 291 Democrats, 127 Republicans, and 17 Progressives; the Senate split was 51 Democrats, 44 Republicans, and 1 Progressive. With such legislative majorities, Wilson acted definitively in positioning government as defender of common Americans, regulator of markets, and restrictor of big business (Mayer 1967, 336–37).

During the election campaign Wilson described his agenda as the New Freedom. Wilson's program consisted of action in four areas: (1) banking reform, (2) farm credit reform, (3) reform of big business, and (4) tariff and tax reform (manifest through the Underwood Tariff Act discussed above).

As shown in Table 3.3, banking reform came through the enactment of the Federal Reserve Act of 1913. The Federal Reserve Act established a central banking system, along with regional federal banks to provide relief from financial panics, unemployment, and business depression. Creating the central bank ended the "money trust" (Democratic National Committee 1912) by removing control of banking from Wall Street and eliminating the practice of depositing federal funds into private banks in exchange for political favors. The Federal Reserve Banks were empowered to issue notes, thereby increasing the elasticity of currency due to seasonal fluctuations and the business cycle.

As shown in Table 3.3, farm credit reform came through the Federal Farm Loan Act of 1916. This law increased the flow of credit to farmers and farm families. In doing so, it created a Federal Farm Loan Board, twelve regional farm loan banks, and many farm loan associations, which were cooperatives through which farmers could loan other farmers money. Thus, it created a credit system that freed farmers from dependence on wealthy bankers, who often charged predatory interest rates.

As shown in Table 3.3, reform of big business came through the Federal Trade Commission and the Clayton Acts, both passed in 1914. The Federal Trade Commission Act created the Federal Trade Commission (FTC) to regulate unfair and anti-competitive business practices, such as coercive monopoly. The legislation gave teeth to the much weaker Sherman Act by institutionalizing the process whereby trusts, monopolies, and other anticompetitive behaviors would be regulated. The legislation also exempted unions from the antitrust laws and limited the executive's power to seek injunctions to break strikes and prevent peaceful demonstrations. In addition, the Clayton Act extended the jurisdiction of the FTC by prohibiting specific anti-competitive business practices, including price fixing, price discrimination, exclusive dealings and tying, anti-competitive mergers or acquisitions, and interlocking directorates. Thus, the Wilson administration set in place tools for much more vigorous regulation of business.

A plethora of other Progressive reforms occurred during the Wilson administration. Organized labor had been a proponent of regulating child labor at the state level since the 1880s, but was largely unsuccessful in the South. The fortunes of the child labor movement changed when Wilson became president. As shown in Table 3.3, the Keating–Owen Child Labor Act of 1916 prohibited the sale in interstate commerce of goods produced by children in certain industries and under certain conditions. However, as shown in Table 3.2, the business-friendly Supreme Court struck down this law in 1918 in its decision *Hammer v. Dagenhart* (247 U.S. 251) as it pertained to products never entering interstate commerce. In response, Congress passed and President Wilson signed the Child Labor Tax Act of 1919, this time relying on the taxing power of the federal government for authority to regulate. In turn, the Supreme Court again struck down the law in its 1922 decision *Bailey v. Drexel Furniture Co.* (259 U.S. 20). The Court called the law a penalty, rather than a tax, again denying the constitutional authority of Congress to regulate child labor (Whittaker 2005).

Progressive Economic Activism during World War I

World War I broke out in Europe in 1914, but Americans were popularly opposed to U.S. involvement. Thus, the Wilson administration declared American neutrality (Wilson 1914). Nevertheless, the president wanted to be prepared for war. When nearly 500,000 railroad workers threatened a nationwide strike in August 1916 over work hours and pay, President Wilson saw this as a problem for the nation's preparedness. Accordingly, he presented emergency legislation to Congress to halt the strike by meeting the workers' demands. As shown in Table 3.3, the result was the Adamson Act of 1916, granting railroad workers an eight-hour workday, without reducing their pay, and overtime for extra hours. The Adamson Act was the predecessor to the Fair Labor Standards Act of 1938 establishing the eight-hour workday and overtime pay for all Americans.

As shown by Table 3.3, additional elements of President Wilson's wartime preparedness were the Army Appropriations Act of 1916 and the Shipping Act of 1916 (Higgs 2005). The Army Appropriations Act authorized the president during a time of war to take possession of transportation systems. The Shipping Act of 1916 established the Shipping Board (later the Federal Maritime Commission) and various nationally owned corporations including the Emergency Fleet Corporation, the U.S. Grain Corporation, the U.S. Housing Corporation, and the War Finance Corporation.

President Wilson narrowly won reelection in 1916 using the slogan "He kept us out of war!" In doing so, he received only 49.2 percent of the popular vote. The president's party retained a small majority in the Senate (now popularly elected after the Seventeenth Amendment), but lost control of the House of Representatives. President Wilson had attempted during his first term to mediate a settlement among the warring parties in Europe. However, Germany initiated unrestricted submarine warfare in January 1917, soon after his reelection, sinking seven American merchant vessels. As a result, Congress declared war in April 1917.

Funding the war required vast new federal revenues. In response, the Revenue Act of 1917 was passed, which significantly increased taxes on the wealthy and corporations. Income tax rates on the top 1 percent of Americans rose to 77 percent by 1918 (Tax Foundation 2013). Tax rates on corporate income rose from 1 percent in 1909 to 12 percent by 1918 (Internal Revenue Service 2013). Further, the legislation instituted an excess profits tax, with graduated rates from 20 to 60 percent on the profits of all businesses in excess of prewar earnings but not less than 8 percent of invested capital. Wilson's war funding effort intended to alleviate some of the tax burden from the middle and lower classes and shift it to the upper class. As expressed by Bank et al. (2008, 61–65), the focus was on "soaking the rich."

The Army Appropriations Act and Shipping Act gave President Wilson almost unlimited control over the U.S. economy (Hughes 1991, 126–35). Accordingly, he used the Army Appropriations Act to nationalize the railroads. He used the Shipping Act to confiscate over 400 ships under construction in shipyards, and took control of all existing steel ships, basically nationalizing the merchant fleet. In addition, Congress passed the Lever Food and Fuel Price Act of 1917, which imposed price controls on food and fuel. The legislation also licensed distributors, coordinated purchases, oversaw exports, acted against hoarding and profiteering, and encouraged farmers to grow more crops. Under the Lever Act, the government also took control of the coal industry. The legislation was also the predecessor to prohibition, forbidding the use of food and grain products to manufacture alcoholic beverages.

The more socialistic aspects of Wilson's emergency wartime regime expired after the war ended in November 1918. By presidential authority, price controls were removed, confiscated property was returned, and the nationalized coal industry was restored to private control. However, the Transportation Act of 1920 authorized continued federal control of the railroad industry. It remained heavily regulated and consolidated, and vital aspects of managerial discretion were shifted to the ICC. From this point forward, the ICC set minimum shipping rates, oversaw railroad finances, and authorized acquisitions and mergers. Thus, what was earlier a railroad monopoly problem was legislated away through national control.

THE "RETURN TO NORMALCY"

President Wilson's New Freedom, the new tax regime, and wartime economic controls sparked an intensely hostile postwar reaction. Business was subject to much greater regulation, including corporate size, business practices, what products could be produced, how much could be produced, what prices could be charged, how long people would work, who could be employed, and a plethora of other centralized government restrictions. Prior to the Wilson administration, the wealthy and corporations paid little to support a government that supported them through high tariffs and low taxes. During the Wilson administration the wealthy and corporations lost their protective tariffs and paid higher taxes than in all of American history. Government even restricted the amount of profit that could be gained through an excess profits tax. Predictably, conservatives saw the administration's actions as an attack on the American way of life, economic freedom, localized control, and the future prosperity of the nation.

The Rout of Progressivism in the 1920s

The presidential election of 1920 revolved around these issues, as well as President Wilson's idealistic internationalism associated with his proposed League of Nations (Bagby 1962, 13). President Wilson suffered a stroke in 1919, but nevertheless sought the Democratic nomination for a third time in 1920. However, Democrats nominated Ohio Governor James M. Cox for president and Assistant Secretary of the Navy Franklin D. Roosevelt for vice president. Cox and Roosevelt campaigned for a continuation of Wilson's Progressive policies (Bagby 1962, 146–50).

Republicans nominated Ohio Senator Warren G. Harding for president and Massachusetts Governor Calvin Coolidge for vice president. Harding's main campaign slogan was that America needed a "return to normalcy" (Bagby 1962, 158). Harding's "normalcy" implied a government that was again pro-business, pro-tariff, anti-tax, and anti-regulation. Harding advocated "more business in government and less government in business" and no more "pulling and hauling" of business by "weird economic and social theories." The government, he said, should be a partner of business, not its antagonist (Bagby 1962, 149). Thus, the campaign was largely a referendum on progressivism.

Arrayed against the Democrats were "men of boundless wealth who knew how to get what they wanted from a reactionary administration" (Bagby 1962, 130). The Republicans spent roughly four times as much as the Democrats on the 1920 campaign. The economic environment had also turned against the Democrats. World War I brought sharply rising incomes and a postwar boom. However, incomes and profits were eroded by high inflation. About the time of the party conventions, the postwar boom suddenly ended, with businesses sharply cutting production and laying off workers. Unemployment rose to nearly four million, and by the time of the election there was widespread economic distress.

Wilson administration officials suspected that big business was trying to injure the Democrats and affect the upcoming election. More broadly, Democrats believed that the sudden drop in business activity was a political conspiracy, perpetrated by Republican financiers and industrialists (Bagby 1962, 156–57). For whatever reason, the Republican ideology of supporting business to promote American prosperity came back into vogue.

Republicans won the 1920 elections with the largest landslide to that point since voting became widespread in America. Harding received 60.3 percent of the popular vote and carried 37 of 48 states. He won two-thirds of all U.S. counties. Harding received 404 electoral votes out of 531, losing only in the solidly Democratic South. Harding captured Tennessee, breaking the "solid South" for the first time since Reconstruction. The Republicans also carried the House of Representatives by 303 to 131 seats, giving them the largest majority in the history of the party. They also retained control of the Senate, gaining 10 seats to achieve a majority of 22 (Bagby 1962, 159–60).

The election of 1920 marked a resounding defeat for Progressives. After the landslide, the Democratic Party became impotent in national politics for the next decade. A rift emerged within the Democratic Party, largely rooted in agrarian versus pro-business elements. Divisions also included attitudes toward prohibition, religious fundamentalism, ethnic xenophobia, and the Ku Klux Klan (Schlesinger 1957, 98–100). The party organization fell into disrepair, deeply in debt, and did not even have a national headquarters in 1924 and 1928. From 1924 through 1932, the pro-business wing of the Democratic Party was the dominant faction. Democratic Wall Street financiers John J. Raskob and Bernard Baruch provided much needed financial support and policy leadership that was largely pro–Wall Street (Schlesinger 1957, 273–74).

However, progressivism did not die during the 1920s. A minority faction continued pushing Progressive ideas, and even developed a party manifesto of liberal principles (Schlesinger 1957, 93–94). Prominent among the remaining Progressives was Franklin D. Roosevelt, who circulated a letter to the delegates of the 1924 Democratic Convention stating that the Republican Party stood "for the control of the social and economic structure of the country by a small minority of hand-picked associates"; but the Democratic Party was "the party of progress and liberal thought" (cited in Schlesinger 1957, 103). In 1925, Roosevelt wrote that the Democratic Party must make itself "by definite policy the Party of constructive progress, before we can attract a larger following ... in the minds of the average voter the Democratic party has today no definite constructive aims." Portending the future, Roosevelt reviewed Claude Bowers's *Jefferson and Hamilton* for the New York *World* later that year, writing, "Hamiltons we have today ... is a Jefferson on the horizon?" (cited in Schlesinger 1957, 103–4)

Nevertheless, the economically prosperous 1920s made it appear that the Republican philosophy of business prosperity supporting the underclass was working. Times were good for those in urban areas, but not for the agrarian South and West. The weakened Democratic coalition consisted of morally conservative, native-born Southern White Protestants, along with disadvantaged Northern ethnics. The burning issues of the day were economic policy, immigration, and Prohibition. Democrats were persistently divided on these issues.

As a result, Democrats were the minority party in both Houses of Congress until 1933. Regarding the presidency, in 1924 they nominated Wall Street lawyer John Davis, who was just as conservative as Republican nominee Calvin Coolidge (Schlesinger 1957, 59–60). In 1928, Democrats nominated Progressive New York Governor Al Smith to run against Republican nominee Herbert Hoover. Smith was the first Roman Catholic presidential candidate in American history, and campaigned against Prohibition. Predictably, he did not fare well in the deeply Protestant and agrarian South (e.g., see Schlesinger 1957, 125–29, 273).

In contrast, Republicans did have a coherent agenda through the 1920s. They sought reduced taxes and regulation, and to reinstitute the earlier system of protective tariffs. Three Republican presidents, Harding, Coolidge, and Hoover, presided over efforts at returning to nineteenth-century policies. Coolidge was especially pro-business, and even religious about it. He said, "The chief business of the American people is business ... The man who builds a factory builds a temple ... The man who works there worships there." As much as Coolidge worshipped business, he detested government. He said, "If the Federal Government should go out of existence, the common run of people would not detect the difference in the affairs of their daily life ... The law that builds up the people is the law that builds up industry." And the chief way by which the federal government could serve business was to diminish itself through austerity and diminishing influence over the economy (Schlesinger 1957, 57).

Harding, Coolidge, and Hoover were pro-business, but the real intellectual force behind all three presidencies was Treasury Secretary Andrew Mellon, who served from 1921 through 1932 (Schlesinger 1957, 61–70). Mellon was a financier and industrialist before entering government service, and the third wealthiest American of his generation (Cannadine 2006, 349). On Mellon's advice, Congress passed "supply-side" tax cuts through the Revenue Acts of 1921, 1924, and 1926. As a result, the top marginal tax rate fell from 73 percent in 1919 to 24 percent in 1929 (de Rugy 2003). The rationale for Mellon's revised tax system was two-fold. He wanted to drastically reduce the size of the federal government to produce budget surpluses. He also wanted to free up capital for investment in the American economy (Mellon 1924).

Mellon also sought to reinstitute the system of protective tariffs that sheltered American businesses from foreign competition prior to the Wilson administration. As noted earlier, the Emergency Tariff Act of 1921 and the Fordney–McCumber Tariff Act of 1922 restored protection for American businesses to near what had existed prior to the Wilson administration. Then, the Smoot–Hawley Tariff Act of 1930 raised tariffs on imported goods to near the highest in American history.

Finally, Mellon wanted to ease business regulation. By 1925 pro-business Republicans constituted a majority of the FTC (Schlesinger 1957, 65). In effect, the FTC was "captured" by those it was intended to regulate (Davis 1962). A similar process occurred at the ICC. By 1926 Presidents Harding and Coolidge had appointed Republicans to a majority at the ICC. "[T]he ICC was transformed from an activist regulatory body committed to reducing competition and improving the efficiency of transportation services nationally and regionally to a timid federal agency pledged to a policy of noninterference with private, competitive, profit-oriented corporate decisions" (Revell 2000, 178).

Beyond these administrative changes, there was also a dearth of new legislative activity aimed at reforming markets. However, there were new enactments giving rents to businesses through regulation. As shown in Table 3.3, new regulatory enactments in the 1920s encouraged the development of the radio, air travel, and transportation industries. These enactments did so by erecting barriers to new entrants through licensing, as well as guaranteed returns for a select few businesses through government price fixing. Further, the adminis-trations of Harding, Coolidge, and Hoover opposed the rights of unions and support for farmers. Bolstering these Republican positions, the Supreme Court during this era stood "doggedly against social reform legislation" (Hughes 1991, 141).

Boom and Bust

The Republican policies of the 1920s are often put forward as an exemplar of how deregulation and low taxes on the wealthy can stimulate robust economic growth (Laffer 2013; Mundell 1971; Smiley and Keehn 1995; Wanniski 1978). Indeed, there was robust economic growth during the decade leading up to the Great Depression. Between 1922 and 1929 national income rose from $63.1 billion to $87.8 billion, a total increase of about 40 percent, and an average annual increase of 5.6 percent. Industrial production almost doubled between 1921 and 1929. Inflation and unemployment were tame , with an average annual price increase of 1 percent and unemployment averaging only 3.7 percent (Heilbroner and Singer 1999, 256). Between 1921 and 1929 annual real personal income increased from $660 to $857, an increase of about 30 percent.

Most urban Americans enjoyed the economic boom of the 1920s. It marked the beginning of a consumer revolution. New inventions, mass marketing, and factories yielded products like underarm deodorant, Coca-Cola, automobiles, telephones, radios, refrigerators, washing machines, phonographs, and a pleth-ora of consumer goods. Rapid electrification of cities meant that many Ameri-can households could use these products. However, one of the most wondrous inventions of the age was consumer credit. Before 1920, the average worker could not borrow money. By 1929, "buy now, pay later" had become a way of life (Sobel 2009). Consumer credit vastly increased corporate profits, while also allowing ordinary Americans to participate in the economic boom.

Accompanying the robust economic expansion of the 1920s was an increase in the stock market. The market value of shares listed on the New York Stock Exchange soared from $4 billion in 1923 to $87 billion on October 1, 1929, a 21-fold increase in about seven years. The value of the Dow Jones Industrial Average increased from a low of 63.9 on August 24, 1921 to a high of 381.2 on September 23, 1929, a 6-fold increase over about eight years. One reason stock values increased so phenomenally was that profits of most corporations were rising rapidly. Bolstered by protective tariffs, low taxes, weak regulation, and consumer credit, corporate profits in 1929 were triple those in 1920.

However, rising corporate profits did not justify the exaggerated stock price increases of the 1920s (Heilbroner and Singer 1999, 264–65). Stock prices were also increasing because profit-hungry banks and brokerage firms moved into the lucrative, but very risky business of making loans for purchases of unsecured stocks and bonds. Unregulated banks and brokerages encouraged people to buy these assets by lending vast sums to potential buyers. Ordinary people could buy stocks and bonds on margin, sometimes putting up only a tenth of the actual value (Hovde and Myer 2009). Margin buying lowered the risk for individuals and shifted those risks onto bank and brokerage depositors and shareholders. As a result, participation in the stock market became irresistible to many. Stock ownership increased from roughly 15 percent of American families in 1900 to about 28 percent by 1929 (Heilbroner and Singer 1999, 264–65).

Many Americans joined the euphoric "get rich quick" mentality brought on by the fortunes being made in the stock market. People listened to the advice of trusted men of wealth, who were not so trustworthy (Heilbroner and Singer 1999, 264–65). For example, Charles Mitchell, President of the National City Bank (later Citibank) popularized the idea of selling stocks and bonds directly to small investors. Mitchell and a group of bankers, brokers, and speculators grew even wealthier by forming pools to manipulate the stock market. These men included Wall Street financiers William Durant (General Motors founder), Jesse Livermore, and Michael Meehan, among others.

Under this scheme, wealthy investors would pool their money in a secret agreement to buy a stock, sell it to an unsuspecting public, and then inflate its price. Historian Robert Sobel (2009) observed that virtually all of the financial journals were "on the take," including the *Wall Street Journal*, the *New York Times*, the *Herald-Tribune*, and others. The pool would literally bribe journalists for successful press. Reading the favorable press, small investors would join the stampede for profit. When the price was high enough, the pool would then sell the stock, leaving small investors taking the losses. This shady, but legal, practice occurred throughout the 1920s (Hovde and Myer 2009).

Of course, this speculative boom had to end at some point. To be sure, the wealthy bankers and speculators who had created the boom did not want the frenzy to end. Market manipulation was highly profitable to an elite class of Americans, and a basis for boundless profits. Thus, when the stock market tumbled horrifically at the open on Thursday, October 24, 1929, Thomas Lamont of J. P. Morgan and Associates, joined by Charles Mitchell of National City Bank (Citibank), J. Albert Wiggin of Chase Bank, the directors of Bankers Trust, and several others attempted to prevent the crash by pooling their money to support the market (Lamont 2009; Mitchell 2009; Schlesinger 1957, 158). However, their efforts were futile.

The market crash continued on Monday, October 28, with a drop of 13 percent in the Dow Jones Industrial Average. As expressed in the PBS documentary *The Crash of 1929*, "It was like trying to stop Niagara Falls. Everyone wanted to sell. AT&T down 50 percent. RCA, once $110 a share, couldn't find buyers at $26. Blue Ridge 100 plunged to $3 and still no buyers. On the floor, they had never seen anything like it" (Hovde and Myer 2009).

On Tuesday, October 29, financier William Durant, members of the Rockefeller family, and other financial giants again sought to instill public confidence in the market by buying large quantities of stocks (Burns 1999). However, their efforts failed, with the market declining that day by another 12 percent. Over the next two weeks the Dow Jones Industrial Average dropped by over 60 percent.

The Great Depression had begun.

COMPARING POLARIZATION IN THE INDUSTRIALIZATION ERA WITH OTHER ERAS

Party polarization increased starting in the 1880s, peaked between 1897 and 1910, remained high during the Wilson administration, but declined during the economically prosperous 1920s. As in the Founding Era, polarization involved a split largely along economic class lines. The elite class benefited greatly from government policies enabling a great accumulation of wealth. Some have called these policies laissez-faire capitalism. However, the preceding analyses show that capitalism through this period was anything but laissez-faire.

Government tipped the scales toward the patrician class through protective tariffs, government subsidies to wealthy entrepreneurs, biased monetary policy, unregulated banking practices, unregulated working conditions, an absence of consumer protection, failure to protect the environment, and a plethora of other policies enabling and promoting big business. The wealthy paid very little in federal taxes until 1914. After World War I up to the Great Depression, taxes remained low on upper class. The government's policy was basically one of what is now called trickle-down economics: promote the elite class and the rest of the nation will be better off.

The underclass paid dearly for these special favors from government. Protective tariffs were effectively rent paid by ordinary consumers through higher prices for both imported and domestic goods. The banking and monetary systems were rigged to favor the "haves" over the "have-nots." The agricultural sector (employing most Americans) was especially disadvantaged due to deflation, high interest rates, and unstable agricultural markets. Before the 1920s, most average Americans could not make installment purchases or obtain home mortgages. As a result the average citizen was relegated to perpetual letting, with many living in slum conditions and without the commodities essential to good living. Common citizens, including women, children, and laboring men, worked long hours under unsafe and unhealthy conditions. The mass public was frequently exposed to tainted food and drugs and abysmal environmental conditions. More generally, the federal government was largely funded by the underclass, but the benefits of government flowed to the upper class. Thus, it is no wonder that polarization emerged in the latter part of the nineteenth century and extended up to the 1920s.

Throughout this period, polarization existed at both the mass level and within political institutions. No large-scale public opinion data exist to back up this assertion about mass polarization. However, there are other indicators of mass polarization through this era. Emerging social reform movements were one manifestation of class polarization. Third political parties arose calling for radical social change. The most prominent of these were the People's Party in 1892 and the Socialist Party in 1897. Their calls for change were widespread and soon coopted by the major political parties. A Progressive movement emerged consisting largely of Democrats and some elements of the Republican Party. In 1896, the Democratic Party coopted the agenda of the Progressive movement. However, the polarization of this era was not exclusively a two-party phenomenon. Progressive reforms were driven by both political parties, as well as by "fringe" parties seeking greater social justice.

Increasing social unrest was another manifestation of mass polarization during this era. Starting in the 1870s, workers began to organize against the abuses of management. Perhaps the first to organize were the railroad workers who struck against the B&O Railroad for cutting their wages. Dubbed the Great Railroad Strike of 1877, this action was the predecessor of many others by railroad workers against the railroad magnates over the next several decades. Workers in other industries also organized against the corporate giants, including steel workers, miners, textile workers, longshoremen, manufacturing workers, shoemakers, grain shovelers, sugarcane harvesters, printers, newsboys, etc. The urge to organize became widespread in America, often involving strikes that were national in character.

Figure 3.3A depicts counts of major strikes in the United States through time and across presidencies from 1873 through 1932. The graph shows that strikes increased sharply with the first Cleveland administration. Following the Cleveland administration, strikes remained fairly high up to the Wilson administration. The three Progressive presidencies of Theodore Roosevelt, William Howard Taft, and Woodrow Wilson saw the highest number of strikes excepting the first Cleveland administration. Strikes declined somewhat during the 1920s, perhaps because the Republican-dominated government was less sympathetic and more prone to federal intervention.

Further, strikes and other public gatherings often resulted in civil disturbances. Figure 3.3B reports the frequency of civil disturbances in the United States through time and across presidencies from 1873 through 1932. Civil disturbances are defined as events such as riots or violence either by or against workers. One example of a civil disturbance is the Haymarket Massacre in Chicago on May 4, 1886. This disturbance involved a bombing and police shootings at a peaceful rally of workers seeking an eight-hour workday. Other examples of civil disturbances through this era include the Homestead Affair of 1892 at the Carnegie Steel Company, where Pinkerton agents and the state militia were called in against striking workers, and the Lattimer Massacre of 1897, in which nineteen unarmed immigrant coal miners were murdered, leading to the expansion of the United Mine Workers. Figure 3.3B shows that increased frequencies of civil unrest came during the first Cleveland and

A

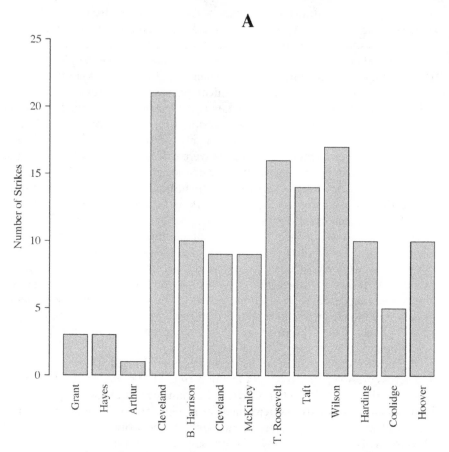

FIGURE 3.3 Strikes and Civil Unrest from the Post–Civil War Era to the Great Depression

Source: Calculated from http://en.wikipedia.org/wiki/List_of_strikes and http://en
.wikipedia.org/wiki/List_of_incidents_of_civil_unrest_in_the_United_States.

Theodore Roosevelt administrations and peaked sharply during the Wilson administration. Of course, the latter two presidencies are most associated with the promulgation of Progressive policies, perhaps as a response to these events. In either case, the incidence of civil disturbances suggests the high degree of mass polarization in the United States before the 1920s.

Regarding institutional polarization, there are quantitative measures of the degree of polarization through this era. As in the previous chapter, party unity and cohesion data on roll call votes in the House of Representatives and Senate compiled by Poole and Rosenthal (2012) are used for analysis. These data were reported in Figure 2.1. While not a precise measure of polarization, as will be developed in Chapters 7 and 8, unified and cohesive congressional factions are

B

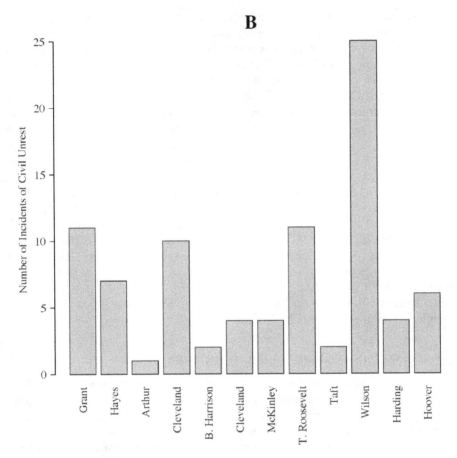

FIGURE 3.3 (*cont.*)

a reasonable indicator of polarization as members cluster around their respective party positions.

Using these data enables comparing the levels of polarization in Congress during the Progressive Era and the modern era. The focus is on the second shaded area of Figure 2.1, which consists of the seven Congresses from 1897 through 1910. Again, one take on polarization is how frequently the majorities in the two parties lined up against one another in what could be called party unity votes. Considering the 55th through 61st Congresses, a majority of Democrats lined up against a majority of Republicans in the House 74 percent of the time on average. In the Senate a majority of Democrats lined up against a majority of Republicans about 75 percent of the time. Party line voting was at a maximum for the House at 90 percent in 1903, and for the Senate at 81 percent in 1909. For the current era, the comparable figures for the 112th Congress are 75 percent for the House and 56 percent for the Senate.

Thus, party line voting was more frequent during the Progressive Era relative to the current era, especially for the Senate.

Another take on polarization is the rate at which party members vote with their party on roll call votes. This approach measures the relative cohesion of the parties in Congress. From the 55th through 61st Congress, an average of 93 percent of Democrats voted with their party on roll call votes in the House of Representatives, reaching a maximum of 94 percent for the 56th Congress starting in 1899. The average for the Republicans in the House over the same period was 91 percent, reaching a maximum of 92 percent for the 55th Congress starting in 1897. On the Senate side for the same period, an average of 89 percent of Democrats voted with their party, reaching a maximum of 92 percent for the 55th Congress starting in 1897. The average for the Republicans over this period was also 89 percent, reaching a maximum of 92 percent for the 58th Congress starting in 1903. Comparison of these percentages with the current era, the 112th Congress, which ended in 2012, finds House Republicans voting with their party 93 percent of the time, with House Democrats at 91 percent. On the Senate side Republicans voted with their party 85 percent of the time, with Democrats voting with their party 93 percent of the time. Thus, the level of polarization in Congress during the Progressive Era was not much different from what exists in the current era.

IMPLICATIONS FOR POLARIZATION GENERALLY

One purpose of this book is to develop a theoretical explanation for American party polarization encompassing earlier eras, as well as the modern era. Studying polarization in earlier eras provides a historical perspective on American polarization generally. The analyses in this chapter show that party polarization during the industrialization era was not much different from that of the Founding Era or the modern era.

Theoretically, the tariff and tax fights from the nineteenth century to the Great Depression can be viewed as battles over rent paid to the commercial class by consumers through higher prices or higher taxes. The movement to the gold standard from the bi-metallic standard of the Constitution maintained and increased the rent paid to creditors by debtors through increasing deflation. The absence of economic regulation can also be thought of as producing rents paid to the commercial class at an expense to those paying monopolistic prices, workers, immigrants, children, women, minorities, the environment, and all others suffering the externalities from non-regulation of business.

Again, a subsidiary issue flowing from these fights over economic advantage is the degree to which power should be centralized to the federal government versus reserved to the states. Table 3.2 showed that the Supreme Court was the ultimate decision-maker in this fight. Table 3.3 showed that Congress often passed legislation seeking more centralized control of interstate commerce, monopolies, worker rights, regulation of working conditions, child labor, etc.

However, the business-friendly Supreme Court repeatedly struck down these laws using a restrictive view of the Commerce Clause, the power to tax, and Tenth Amendment. Indeed, the "stand patter" Supreme Court restricted most federal involvement in the economy even into the heart of the Great Depression.

The next chapter turns to an analysis of how these partisan fights over economic advantage, centralization of government, and market intervention manifested themselves in the politics of the Great Depression, New Deal, and World War II.

4

Forging the New Deal Social Contract from the Great Depression through World War II

On October 22, 1928, presidential candidate Herbert Hoover delivered a campaign speech in New York's Madison Square Garden in which he lauded the prosperity of the previous seven and a half years of Republican administration. He said, "By adherence to the principles of decentralized self-government, ordered liberty, equal opportunity, and freedom to the individual ... [w]e are nearer today to the ideal of the abolition of poverty and fear from the lives of men and women than ever before in any land" (Hoover 1928, 168).

Hoover's philosophy of limited government, decentralization, and allowing individual initiative to decide economic outcomes appealed to most Americans in 1928. The nation was at a peak of prosperity. American families, at least those living in cities, were better off than ever before. As Hoover noted, people were better able to enjoy "the good life," rather than simply subsisting. Many urban families had an automobile, radio, refrigerator, homes, more food, and better clothing. Wages had increased, while the cost of living had decreased. Jobs were also seemingly more secure (Hoover 1928, 169–75).

Predictably, Herbert Hoover defeated Democratic candidate Al Smith in 1928 by the largest electoral vote margin (444–87) since 1864, as well as the second largest popular vote margin (58.2–40.8) since voting became widespread in the 1820s. Yet only one year after Hoover's speech, the nation entered a period of profound economic depression that would permanently alter American values and forever change the relationship between government, business, and citizens.

THE GREAT DEPRESSION AND NEAR DEATH OF THE FOUNDERS' SOCIAL CONTRACT

Between 1929 and 1932, an enormous economic shock altered people's faith in business leadership and Republican government. Americans' long-standing beliefs in the virtues of markets and limited government were shattered. By 1933, the nation had sunk into a fog of fear, and some argued was even on the verge of a revolution (see Schlesinger 1957, 166–76).

The Great Depression had a huge and lasting effect on the American psyche. The business-dominated economic system had failed catastrophically, as had Republican solutions. As a result, the depression and its aftermath tarnished the Republican brand in the near term, and for the next half-century or more.

Democrats became the dominant force in American politics from 1933 through the 1970s. Republicans lost the presidency in 1932, and did not regain it for twenty years. Once they did regain it, Republican presidents until 1980 labeled themselves Modern Republicans, espousing a philosophy more consistent with New Deal values than with older values. Between 1930 and 1936, Republicans lost large numbers of seats in Congress. By the 75th Congress (1937–38) there were only 89 remaining House Republicans (out of 435) and only 17 Senate Republicans (out of 96). Republicans regained a majority in Congress in 1947–48 and again in 1953–54. However, from this point forward Republicans did not control both houses of Congress until 1995. Republicans did not control both the presidency and Congress again until 2001, 72 years after the election of 1928.

The psychological effect of the Great Depression was akin to that from a foreign policy crisis or war. During a crisis or war, people unify and rally around a leader. Further, when the crisis is serious enough people ultimately accept most anything the leader wants to preserve the nation. Leaders responding to the Great Depression greatly expanded the role of the federal government in the economic and social spheres, effectively creating more broadly dispersed rents. Among the masses, belief in individualism, self-reliance, and faith in big business gave way to society-wide demands that government do more to help those suffering economic hardship and market injustice.

Starting in 1933, America unified around the programs of a New Deal that would dominate American politics, both philosophically and electorally, until the 1970s. An electoral realignment occurred, with many Republicans becoming Democrats, and the mobilization of many new Democratic voters (Burnham 1970, 6; Campbell et al. 1960, 153–56; Erikson and Tedin 1981; Sundquist 1983, 229–39). In response to the dominance of New Deal ideals, the Republican Party became more diverse, with many claiming to be Modern Republicans (i.e., moderates) or even liberal. Conservative Republicans were largely marginalized until the 1980s.

Nevertheless, from 1939 through the early 1960s the New Deal expanded only modestly, as a coalition of conservative Republicans and conservative Southern Democrats, called the Conservative Coalition, stymied significant change (Manley 1973; Patterson 1966). However, during the 1960s and '70s the New Deal philosophy returned with a vengeance as a plethora of transformative social and regulatory laws were enacted through the Great Society and its extensions. American values were forever altered and would never again return to the Federalist mindset that had prevailed from the constitutional convention to the start of the Great Depression.

The Economy of the Great Depression

Popular belief holds that the stock market crash of 1929 was the primary cause of the Great Depression (but for more nuanced views, see Bernanke 2000; Friedman and Schwartz 1963, 299–407; Heilbroner and Singer 1999, 273–86; McElvaine 1993, 25–50). The crash itself was a huge economic shock, wiping out vast amounts of personal and corporate wealth. Over the two days of October 28 and 29, 1929, commonly called "Black Monday" and "Black Tuesday," the New York Stock Exchange dropped by over $30 billion (Burns 1999), roughly ten times the annual federal budget for that year.

Between the crash and July 1, 1932, the stock market lost $74 billion (Vanderlip 1932). This was a fantastic sum at the time, given that the entire U.S. gross domestic product (GDP) in 1932 was only $59.4 billion (Bureau of Economic Analysis 2014b). In other words, the stock market loss was roughly 125 percent of the nation's entire national income. The loss amounted to $616 for every man, woman, and child in the United States (Vanderlip 1932). Average per capita personal income in 1932 was $402 (Bureau of Economic Analysis 2014e), so the loss per capita was roughly 150 percent of what all earners in the United States were making annually. Translating the stock market loss to the 2015 economy, the market decline would amount to a drop of $22.55 trillion in the present value of personal and corporate assets.

These numbers are staggering, and go a long way toward explaining why a depression followed the stock market crash. However, the bland numbers do not reveal the true human cost or the effect on the American psyche. As expressed by Frank Vanderlip (1932, 3–4), "The loss of $74,000,000,000 in the value of New York listed stocks is something more than a mere item of financial data. Implicated in it are ten million cruel heartaches. I am using 'million' as an adjective, and making an understatement. The laborious savings of an uncounted number of lifetimes have been swept away."

These circumstances saw a rise in the U.S. suicide rate from an average 12.1 per 1,000 population from 1920 to 1928 to 18.9 per 1,000 population during 1929 (Bureau of the Census 1970; but see Galbraith 2009). Further, the multiplier effects of the monetary losses on the larger economy were huge, resulting in countless bank failures, business closings, declines in business investment, mortgage foreclosures, unemployment, homelessness, and bread lines across the country.

The decline of the banking sector was a particular source of misery. As noted in the previous chapter, during the 1920s bankers entrusted with people's money engaged in very questionable lending practices. Unregulated banks and investment firms moved into the highly profitable but risky business of making loans on purchases of unsecured stocks and bonds. People bought stocks and bonds on margin, sometimes putting up only a tenth of the actual value (Hovde and Myer 2009). Margin buying lowered the risk for market participants, while shifting it onto depositors and shareholders.

This shift in risk fueled the stock market rise through the 1920s. However, following the stock market crash, the shift in risk also accelerated the crash. As the stock market dropped, banks and investment firms were losing their unsecured investments. Margin calls by financial institutions greatly accelerated the market decline, as investors were required to sell when the value of their stocks dropped below the institution's investment. Because of the rapidity of the crash, most stocks fell far below the institution's investment, leading to sales at huge losses. A vicious cycle occurred in which panicking financial institutions joined panicking investors to drive the decline in stock prices.

Nobel laureate Milton Friedman and coauthor Anna Schwartz observed that some 9,000 banks failed between 1929 and 1933, wiping out about one-third of the nation's money supply. Risky bank loans made before the stock market crash contributed to these failures. However, fear was also a factor. As word of the stock market crash spread, panicking depositors rushed to withdraw their money. "Runs" on banks were disastrous, requiring them to liquidate assets, further accelerating market declines, and losses in bank capital. Not having money on hand to pay depositors increased people's level of panic, accelerating the rate of bank failures. Thus, Friedman and Schwartz argued that the market crash itself did not cause the Great Depression. Rather it was the collapse of the banking system during successive waves of public panic from 1930 through 1933. The number of banks operating at the end of 1933 was only about half the number in 1929 (Friedman and Schwartz 1963, chapter 7).

As expressed by former Federal Reserve Chairman Ben Bernanke, "The two major components of the financial collapse were the loss of confidence in financial institutions, primarily commercial banks, and the widespread insolvency of debtors." In normal times, banks are an important source of economic security and expansion. However, following the stock market crash, bank credit dried up. Bank credit was scarce because there was less money to lend. Additionally, there was a general belief that debtors would be unable repay potential loans. Thus, bankers became far more risk averse after the crash (Bernanke 2000, 43–47).

A very important consequence of the bank failures was a drop in the amount of gold available to monetize the economy. As noted in the previous chapter, the United States was on a gold standard until 1933. All paper currency issued in the United States had to be backed by a fixed amount of gold. Paper currency was convertible on demand to gold. As people withdrew their money from banks and hoarded gold, the amount of gold available to back additional currency declined.

Exacerbating the scarcity of gold due to runs on banks, Great Britain left the gold standard in September 1931. Fearing the United States would do the same, foreign investors began converting their dollar assets into gold, further draining

the U.S. gold supply. Corresponding with these events, significant price deflation occurred between 1929 and 1933 (see Figure 3.1). Absent a sufficient
supply of gold, the Federal Reserve found it difficult to monetize the economy,
fund the increasing number of insolvent banks, and fund a government deficit
that could prime the pump for economic expansion (Eichengreen 1995, 1–28;
Elwell 2011; Engemann 2014).

On a more personal level, before the Emergency Banking Act of 1933, when
a bank failed, people lost all of their deposits. For obvious reasons, such losses
had huge economic and psychological effects. There was no federal deposit
guarantee, so putting money in a bank was a pure leap of faith. Because so
many banks failed, after the crash people viewed depositing their money in
banks as folly. It was preferable to bury money in the ground, rather than
deposit it in a bank (Schlesinger 1957, 474–75). As a result, there was little or
no possibility for banks to recapitalize under the existing system.

The failure of the banking system profoundly affected both individuals and
businesses. Potential homeowners relied on banks for mortgages, so home
building and new home ownership dropped precipitously. The number of
new home starts in 1928 was around 450,000. Fewer than 80,000 new homes
were under construction in 1932. New home construction declined every year
from 1929 through 1933, and did not recover to pre-depression levels until the
start of World War II (Wheelock 2008).

Loan delinquencies and mortgage foreclosures on existing homes soared due
to falling household incomes and property values. At the worst in 1933, banks
foreclosed on around 1,000 homes each day. In 1934 approximately half of all
urban houses in the United States were in default (Wheelock 2008). Homeowners lost their property when they could not pay their mortgages. As a result,
millions of Americans were forced out of the normal housing market, either
crowded in with relatives or left homeless.

Businesses also relied on banks for capital and expansion. Between November 1929 and January 1933, the number of business failures was 85,256
(NBER 2013b). The number of businesses operating in January 1929 was
234,000 fewer in January 1933 (NBER 2014b). Exacerbating business failures,
consumer demand dropped. Aggregate personal consumption expenditures fell
from $77.4 billion in 1929 to $45.9 billion in 1933, a drop of over 40 percent
(Bureau of Economic Analysis 2014d). Corresponding with this drop in consumer demand, business profits fell sharply. In 1929, net business profits were
at $6.15 billion. However, in 1932 they were negative at –$2.27 billion.
Businesses were not only unprofitable, but were bleeding cash. Business profits
did not come close to pre-depression levels until the start of World War II
(NBER 2013a).

When businesses face a decline in demand for their products, they typically
consolidate. From the preceding evidence it is clear that much of the consolidation involved complete closings. Businesses also did not invest during the
depression. Bank capital was not available for conducting business or for

expansion. Probably more important, businesses became risk averse and did not seek bank capital in the face of bleak consumer demand. As a result, U.S. gross private domestic investment declined from $17.2 billion in 1929 to only $1.8 billion in 1932, a drop of almost 90 percent. Again, business investment did not return to pre-depression levels until 1941 as the country mobilized for World War II (Bureau of Economic Analysis 2014c).

The upshot of the stock market crash, banking industry decline, and abysmal business conditions was misery for the masses. The civilian unemployment rate rose from 3.2 percent in 1929 to 24.9 percent in 1933. The Bureau of Labor Statistics later estimated that "12,830,000 persons were out of work in 1933, about one-fourth of a civilian labor force of over 51 million. March was the record month, with about fifteen and a half million unemployed" (Bernstein 2013). The civilian unemployment rate was above 20 percent from 1931 through 1934, fell to 14.3 percent by 1937, but a recession in 1937–38 increased it again to 19 percent to remain at high levels until the start of World War II (Bureau of Labor Statistics 2012).

Further, those who remained employed often went from full- to part-time work. The Hoover Administration recommended and many industries adopted work-sharing to preserve at least some income for workers. As expressed by Bernstein (2013), "[T]he United States Steel Corporation in 1929 had 224,980 full-time employees. The number shrank to 211,055 in 1930, to 53,619 in 1931, to 18,938 in 1932, and to zero on April 1, 1933. All who remained on the payroll on this last date were part-time workers, and they were only half as numerous as those working full-time in 1929." By the end of 1932, the average wage for iron and steel workers was 63 percent less than in 1929. This same process of moving from full- into part-time work and lower wages occurred across the entire economy (Schlesinger 1957, 249).

As people lost their jobs and/or earned less money, personal incomes dropped precipitously. Average annual personal income in 1929 was $700. However, by 1933 it was only $376. In other words, four years after the stock market crash people were earning only about half of what their income was before. Personal income remained low for the remainder of the 1930s, finally recovering to pre-depression levels at the start of World War II (Bureau of Economic Analysis 2014e).

Down on the Farm

Starting in 1931, migration from farms to cities slowed, and even reversed during 1932 and 1933, with the farm population actually increasing by 1.86 million over this period (Ferrie 2013; Olmstead and Rhode 2013a). In some ways, farmers were better off than those in urban areas. They could at least produce some of their own food. Most farm families had gardens, and canned vegetables and fruits. Dairy cows provided milk and cream; poultry supplied meat and eggs; farmers bought flour and sugar in bulk and baked their own bread. In some farm families the wife made clothing from flour and feed sacks. Thus, farmers were able to live with little money.

Nevertheless, farmers were also hurting. The depression started for farmers well before the 1929 market crash (Heilbroner and Singer 1999, 274–75; Schlesinger 1957, 105–10). World War I had seen farmers expand their production of crops and livestock to support the war effort and European demand. These increases were enabled not only by increasing the amount of land in production, but also because farming moved from "horse and plow" to "tractor and combine" (Cooper 2004, 15–16). Mechanization vastly increased farm productivity during the 1920s and made it harder for small farms to compete. Expanded production and oversupply after World War I produced agricultural price deflation during the 1920s, making it difficult for farmers to make money and pay their debts. By 1929, roughly four of every ten farmers had already lost their farms and moved into share-cropping or tenantry (Heilbroner and Singer 1999, 275).

With the depression, farmers' ability to pay off their debts deteriorated even further as agricultural prices dropped even more steeply. A bushel of wheat that sold in 1925 for $1.45 had declined by 1931 to $0.40; cotton fell from $0.34 cents to $0.16 per pound (Heilbroner and Singer 1999, 275). Farmers in the plains region of the United States also experienced extreme drought and "dust bowl" conditions, making it very difficult to produce a crop.

By 1935 farmers' mortgage debt as a percentage of their farm's value had increased to 50 percent. Between 1930 and 1935, about 880,000 farms were foreclosed, with 227,000 in 1933 alone (calculated from Alston 1983; Stam and Dixon 2014). During the same period, about one-third of all farms in the United States were lost to foreclosure (Cooper 2004, 28–29). At the beginning of 1933, 45 percent of all farms were delinquent in their mortgage payments (Bernanke 2000, 46). Roughly 40 percent of all remaining farmers in 1935 owed money to the bank (Olmstead and Rhode 2013b). Thus, many farmers defaulted to banks and sought work elsewhere to feed their families (Schlesinger 1957, 174–76).

Public Desperation and Anger

Public anger and blame for the deplorable economic conditions fell squarely on business leaders and the Republican administration (e.g., see Schlesinger 1957, 176). As tin, cardboard, and tarpaper shantytowns sprung up to house the homeless in virtually every city in America, the name "Hooverville" became a common epithet. Soup kitchens served stew known as "Hoover Stew." Newspapers became blankets for the poor and were known as "Hoover Blankets." Jackrabbits used as food were known as "Hoover Hogs." Cars with empty gas tanks pulled by mules were known as "Hoover Wagons." Cardboard used to line a shoe when the sole had worn through was called "Hoover Leather." An empty pocket turned inside out was called a "Hoover Flag." Clearly, it became very unpopular to be associated with Herbert Hoover and the Republican Party during the depression (Schlesinger 1957, 244–47).

People in the "Hoovervilles" lived day to day with little or no money or food, as well as ragged clothing. Of course, there was no public welfare system before the New Deal, and people in this plight often resorted to begging and local soup kitchens for their daily fare. Some food was distributed by private charities, and to a limited extent state and local governments. However, the situation was largely hopeless for many affected by the economic decline. People were literally going hungry.

Freedman (2005, 4) estimates that nearly 50 percent of children during the Great Depression did not have adequate food. In 1932, the New York City Health Department reported that 20.5 percent of the schoolchildren were undernourished. In 1933, a study in Boston found that about 18 percent of high school students were at least 10 percent underweight, and a study in Pennsylvania found that 23 percent had lost weight over the past six months. During the fall of 1933, Franklin Roosevelt's Labor Secretary Frances Perkins stated publicly that as many as one in five preschool and school children across the nation suffered from malnutrition, and many from rickets (Cohen 2003, 40–41; Freedman 2005, 15). In the mountain communities of Appalachia, entire families were living on dandelions, pokeweed, and blackberries for their basic diet. Some children were so hungry that they chewed on their own hands (Freedman 2005, 35).

Given American values of self-reliance and individualism, people were often ashamed of their low condition and angry at their inability to provide for their families (e.g., see Schlesinger 1957, 169–72). With economic devastation in both the cities and countryside, hopelessness and social unrest rose sharply from 1929 through 1932. Historian Arthur Schlesinger, Jr., vividly depicted depression-era conditions as follows.

The fog of despair hung over the land. One out of every four American workers lacked a job. Factories that had once darkened the skies with smoke stood ghostly and silent, like extinct volcanoes. Families slept in tarpaper shacks and tin-lined caves and scavenged like dogs for food in the city dump ... Thousands of vagabond children were roaming the land, wild boys of the road. Hunger marchers, pinched and bitter, were parading cold streets in New York and Chicago. On the countryside unrest had already flared into violence. Farmers stopped milk trucks along Iowa roads and poured the milk into the ditch. Mobs halted mortgage sales, ran the men from the banks and insurance companies out of town, intimidated courts and judges, demanded a moratorium on debts. When a sales company in Nebraska invaded a farm and seized two trucks, the farmers in the Newman Grove district organized a posse, called it the "Red Army," and took the trucks back. In West Virginia, mining families, turned out of their homes, lived in tents along the road on pinto beans and black coffee. (Schlesinger 1957, 3)

The Feeble Republican Response

Meanwhile, most business leaders and the Hoover administration clung to their long-held beliefs that local and individual initiative would soon restore economic prosperity. Hoover consistently viewed the role of the federal government as restricted to promoting voluntary cooperation between business, local authorities, and the masses. As always, Americans were to be self-reliant, the role of government was to be limited, and the free market economy would automatically mend itself (Schlesinger 1957, 161–64, 177–83).

However, it had become clear by 1932 that the depression would be a lasting phenomenon. Forced to act, the Hoover administration viewed the federal government as a means for helping businesses so that men of wealth could support the masses through employment and charitable endeavors. Underlying this perspective was the optimistic view that men of wealth were driven by benevolence. As expressed by Calvin Coolidge, "[Men of wealth] use their power to serve, not themselves and their own families, but the public"(Coolidge 1925).

The counterpoint to this perspective was the pessimistic view of many Republicans that the masses wanted a free ride. For example, President Hoover stated in 1931, "We have had one proposal after another which amounts to a **dole** from the Federal Treasury. The largest is that of **unemployment** insurance. . . . The net results of governmental **doles** are to lower wages toward the bare subsistence level and to endow the slacker" (Hoover 1931, emphasis in original). Of course, these views were deeply unpopular as suffering from the depression deepened.

As noted in the previous chapter, wealthy businessmen had initially attempted to prop up the stock market and prevent its crash. After their efforts failed, business leaders and politicians went into a period of denial and paralysis from 1929 through 1931 (Schlesinger 1957, 177–78). For example, Charles Schwab, chairman of Bethlehem Steel, professed roughly one month after the market crash, "Never before has American business been as firmly entrenched for prosperity as it is today." In the same month, John Edgerton, president of the National Association of Manufacturers, said, "I can observe little on the horizon today to give us undue or great concern." Automaker Henry Ford stated, "Things are better today than they were yesterday." George E. Roberts, president of National City Bank of New York (now Citibank), stated, "There are no great business failures, nor are there likely to be . . . Conditions are more favorable for permanent prosperity than they have been the past year." James Farrell, president of United States Steel, predicted in January 1931, "The peak of the depression passed thirty days ago" (Heilbroner and Singer 1999, 270; see also Schlesinger 1957, 162–63).

Mirroring these denials by wealthy businessmen, the Hoover administration also painted a rosy picture. In November after the crash, the president said, "[A]ny lack of confidence in the economic future of American enterprises is foolish" (Heilbroner and Singer 1999, 270). In early January 1930, Treasury Secretary Andrew Mellon stated, "I see nothing in the present situation that is either menacing or warrants pessimism" (Schlesinger 1957, 164). On March 3, 1930, Commerce Secretary Robert P. Lamont said, "As weather conditions moderate we are likely to find the country as a whole enjoying its wonted state of prosperity. Business will be back to normal in two months." Julius H. Barnes, who headed President Hoover's National Business Survey Conference, proclaimed, "American business is steadily coming back to a normal level of prosperity" (Schlesinger 1957, 165). In October 1930, President Hoover spoke to the American Bankers Convention, telling them, "During the past year you have carried the credit system of the nation safely through a most difficult crisis. In this success you have demonstrated not alone the soundness of the credit system, but also the capacity of the bankers in an emergency" (Hoover 1930). All the while, half the nation's banks were failing, credit was frozen, and businesses were dismissing hordes of workers and reducing their work hours and pay.

The Hoover administration did, however, support some measures to combat the depression. As business failures increased, the Republican president and Congress enacted the Smoot–Hawley Tariff of 1930 to protect American businesses from foreign competition. The legislation increased import tariffs to near their highest level in American history.

Many economists argue that this tariff was disastrous, greatly exacerbating the Great Depression (Econ Journal Watch 2007). It deprived foreign nations of a major source of revenue that would have enabled them to buy American goods. Further, the tariff provoked protectionist retaliation by foreign governments, hurting American businesses dependent on exports. By the fall of 1931 U.S. foreign trade was only 35 percent of what it had been when the tariff was enacted (Heilbroner and Singer 1999, 272). Nevertheless, the mindset of the Hoover administration was fixed on tariffs to promote American businesses.

Business leaders and the Hoover administration also clung to their long-standing belief that the federal government should balance its budget and steer clear of federal intervention (Schlesinger 1957, 172–74). Federal revenues had declined sharply as a result of four tax cuts enacted during the 1920s. As noted in the previous chapter, Republicans had enacted these tax cuts to reduce the size of the federal government. The decline in business activity and personal income due to the depression also significantly reduced federal revenues. President Hoover and the Republican Congress saw balancing the federal budget as key to solving the Great Depression. As a result, they enacted the Revenue Act of 1932, which instituted the largest peacetime tax increase to that point in American history. The law increased taxes on everyone, including the wealthy, with the top income bracket rising to 63 percent. The legislation also increased taxes on corporations (McElvaine 1993, 87). Of course, these moves were, as modern economic theory teaches, precisely the wrong approach to stimulating the economy.

As a result of these attitudes and failed policies, business leaders and the Hoover administration lost credibility. They also came across as lacking empathy for ordinary people. For example, the most visible and outspoken business leader in the nation, automaker Henry Ford, blamed the market crash and ensuing depression on people's laziness. He wrote in the *New York Times* that "[Americans] wanted something for nothing ... They didn't want to work. The crash was a good thing; it has made them start working and thinking again" (Ford 1930). Later he wrote, "The average man ... won't really do a day's work unless he is caught and cannot get out of it" (Ford 1931). John Edgerton stated, "Many of those who are most boisterous now in clamor for work have either struck on the jobs they had or don't want to work at all, and are utilizing the occasion to swell the communistic chorus" (Schlesinger 1957, 178–79).

Business leaders strongly opposed direct federal intervention in the economy. For example, Charles Schwab suggested that government remain passive while workers "just grin and keep on working" (Cohen 2009, 28). Henry Ford admonished: "Let the government stick to the strict function of governing ... let business alone" (Ford 1931). The president of the National Association of Manufacturers said, "Lifting the individual's economic responsibility by legislation is to promote the very habits of thriftlessness in his life which produce his dependency on such a process" (Schlesinger 1957, 178).

In compliance with advice from business leaders, the Hoover administration followed a "hands-off" economic policy up to 1932. The president frequently reiterated his belief that the economy would right itself if left alone, and argued that federal assistance to individuals would weaken the moral fiber of the American people, making them lazy and lacking in self-reliance. He also believed that federal intervention would stifle relief efforts by individuals, private charities, and local organizations. He frequently spoke against federal relief efforts and vetoed them when they passed Congress, asserting, "We cannot squander ourselves into prosperity" (Cohen 2009, 28–29; Hoover 1932).

Finally forced by Congress to intervene in 1932, Hoover did so reluctantly with concern about unbalancing the federal budget and violating his Republican principles (Miller Center 2013; Schlesinger 1957, 231–32). President Hoover asked Congress in January 1932 to establish the Reconstruction Finance Corporation (RFC). The RFC was again true to Republican beliefs about the proper role of business in relation to citizens. It was to funnel money to the wealthy and big business in the hope that it would trickle down to the masses.

Starting in July 1932, the RFC made roughly $1.2 billion available to the largest banks, insurance companies, railroads, and mortgage associations. This top-down pro-business approach assumed that those at the top of the economic structure would actually invest the money in the economy (McElvaine 1993, 89; Schlesinger 1957, 235–38). This did not occur. With an absence of consumer demand, there was little point in businesses taking out loans for expansion. As noted earlier, business investment continued its precipitous drop throughout 1932 and 1933, and the rate of bank and business failures showed no response to the availability of loans from the RFC.

In contrast, the administration was unwilling to help the neediest Americans. The federal government provided no money for direct relief to the homeless, hungry, or unemployed before 1933. Hoover vetoed bills in 1931 that would have set up a public works program, a stabilization board, and a system of employment agencies at the state level. He even declined to submit an appropriation for collecting unemployment statistics (Schlesinger 1957, 224–26). Hoover also vetoed a bill in July 1932 that would have expanded the function of the RFC to make loans for public works programs to relieve destitution through employment. Starting the same month, relief money was provided indirectly in the form of loans to the states. However, by December 1932 the government had allocated only about $30 million for this purpose (Schlesinger 1957, 240–41).

Hoover came across to Americans as callous and insensitive to their problems. For example, in 1930 he endorsed a $45 million appropriation to feed the livestock of farmers during a drought. At the same time, he rejected a $25 million appropriation for food for farmers and their families. He told reporters "No one is actually starving ... The hoboes, for example, are better fed than they have ever been. One hobo in New York got ten meals in one day." Later the president spoke of the many unemployed who eked out a living by selling apples on street corners. He said, "[M]any persons left their jobs for the more profitable one of selling apples" (Heilbroner and Singer 1999, 272; see also Schlesinger 1957, 170). As a result of such delusions, the president became increasingly isolated and unpopular (Schlesinger 1957, 243–47).

As the election approached, fear gripped the nation over the extent of suffering and the absence of an administration response to worsening economic conditions. The severity and duration of the economic decline had thoroughly debunked the Republican myth that free markets will automatically mend themselves. Faith in the business community and Republicans to lead the economy was shattered.

The Republican brand was badly tarnished. As expressed by George Sokolsky, "Confidence in the erst-while leadership of this country is gone. Mention the name of any of the great men of the postwar era, and there is only derision. No banker, no great industrialist, no college president commands the respect of the American people." Joseph P. Kennedy, himself a Wall Street investor, said, "The belief that those in control of the corporate life of America were motivated by honesty and ideals of honorable conduct was completely shattered." Columnist Walter Lippman wrote, "In the past five years, the industrial and financial leaders of America have fallen from one of the highest positions of influence and power that they have ever occupied in our history to one of the lowest" (cited in Schlesinger 1957, 459).

People even came to doubt the very foundations of American democracy, as their elected institutions seemed devoid of ideas for resolving the worst economic crisis in American history. In December 1932, President Hoover again proposed legislation for smaller government, a national sales tax, banking and bankruptcy, and a general mortgage discount system. However, a lack of party discipline in Congress made it exceedingly unlikely that anything would be done. Indeed, President Hoover himself said, "I don't want them [Congress] to do anything now," apparently hoping that the incoming administration would be crippled without a program (Schlesinger 1957, 456–57).

FRANKLIN D. ROOSEVELT AND ESTABLISHING THE NEW DEAL SOCIAL CONTRACT

Virtually any Democrat could have won against Herbert Hoover and the Republicans in 1932. However, the Democratic Party chose an inspirational leader promising a New Deal for the American people. The 1932 election was a landslide. Franklin Roosevelt defeated Herbert Hoover with 57.4 percent of the popular vote, carrying 42 of 48 states, producing an electoral vote margin of 472–59, or roughly 90 percent. A Democratic presidential candidate had not received a majority of the popular vote or won both the popular and electoral vote since 1852.

The congressional elections were equally lopsided. Democrats gained overwhelming control of Congress, picking up 90 seats in the House and nine in the Senate. The resulting Democratic majorities were 313 Democrats versus 117 Republicans in the House, and 59 Democrats versus 36 Republicans in the Senate. Roosevelt had veto-proof majorities in both the House and Senate, and did not need Republican support to implement change. However, most of his proposals also received support from the remaining Republicans (e.g., see Cushman 2012). Thus, the sweeping turnover in government produced a unified national response favoring the New Deal.

Roosevelt's Preparation for Governing

Franklin Roosevelt was intellectually prepared to lead the nation in a new direction. When he was five years old, his prominent father took him to meet President Grover Cleveland, who said he hoped "you may never be President of the United States" (Schlesinger 1957, 319–20). Roosevelt attended one of finest preparatory schools in America, Groton, and spent considerable time in Europe with a personal tutor. In the fall of 1900, he entered Harvard College. While at Harvard, his fifth cousin, Theodore Roosevelt, became president of the United States.

Franklin Roosevelt had a lifelong admiration for his Republican cousin (Schlesinger 1957, 330–31). Indeed, one could reasonably argue that his career paralleled that of Theodore. Like Theodore, Franklin was elected to the New York state legislature (1910), appointed Assistant Secretary of the Navy (1913), a vice presidential candidate (1920), and governor of New York (1928–32). Theodore had his Square Deal, while Franklin had his New Deal. However,

Franklin was a lifelong Progressive Democrat who campaigned for William Jennings Bryan in 1904 and Woodrow Wilson in 1912 and 1916, and was the leader of the Progressive wing of the Democratic Party through the "dark years" of progressivism in the 1920s.

In the spring of 1920, Franklin Roosevelt drafted part of the Democratic platform with a strongly Progressive tone. One of his proposals even called for government borrowing to finance public works during hard times, stating that "we believe such a policy to be the constructive preventive for acute depression" (Schlesinger 1957, 361). After the Republican landslide in 1920, he retired to practicing law, but remained occupied with Democratic Party politics over the next decade. In 1922, Roosevelt wrote of the necessity of keeping "the control of our government out of the hands of professional money-makers" and denounced Republicans as enacting laws "designed to make men very rich without regard to the rest of the nation" (Schlesinger 1957, 375).

Campaigning for New York governor in 1928, Roosevelt said, "[If] reduction of hours of women and children is Socialistic, we are all Socialists; and [if] public improvements for the hospitals of the State and the prisons of the State is Socialistic, we are all Socialists. And [if] bettering health ... [and] aid to the educational program of this State, if they are Socialistic, we are Socialists and we are proud of the name" (Schlesinger 1957, 384). As a Progressive, Franklin Roosevelt was outside the mainstream of Democratic politics through the 1920s. Nevertheless, he was an intellectual leader who believed that his time would come.

When the depression struck, Roosevelt was New York's governor. As governor of the most populous state, he experimented with programs that later became models for New Deal programs. For example, he developed programs to reduce the cost of electrical power through public ownership and development. He advocated conservation of public lands and planning as a way of improving the farm situation. He appointed Progressive social reformer Frances Perkins as Commissioner of the New York State Department of Labor. With her advice, they began planning a system of old age pensions for New York state. Once it became clear that the depression would have lasting effects, Roosevelt was also a pioneer in implementing public relief programs and unemployment insurance. Roosevelt was the first governor to call for state aid for public relief, and the New York Temporary Emergency Relief Administration was the first state public relief agency. He accomplished this Progressive agenda while facing a Republican legislature. Foreshadowing what was to become a major aspect of his presidential leadership, Roosevelt used radio addresses as governor to mobilize public support, essentially forcing the Republican legislature to accept his ideas (Schlesinger 1957, 389–95).

Another aspect of Roosevelt's preparation for the presidency was his so-called brain trust. In March 1932, Roosevelt was considering a run for the presidency and discussed with his long-time political advisor, Sam Rosenman, who he should consult for specific approaches to addressing the depression.

Rosenman responded that it should not be businessmen or politicians; they had had their chance and fallen on their faces. Rather, he said, "Why not go to the universities of the country?" (Schlesinger 1957, 398).

Subsequently, Roosevelt assembled a team of experts, the foremost of whom were political science professor Raymond Moley, economics professor Rexford G. Tugwell, and legal professor Adolph Berle, all from Columbia University. The "brain trust" advised Roosevelt on specific policy proposals throughout the 1932 campaign, and its members later became the main architects of the New Deal.

In winning the 1932 presidential election, Roosevelt and the Democrats pulled together a New Deal Coalition. The Coalition included the largely agricultural South where traditionalist Southern Democrats still resented the Republican Party for destroying slavery and the basis for Southern economies. It also included Populist farmers from other parts of the nation who felt disenfranchised by pro–Wall Street/pro-business Republican policies of earlier eras. Other groups in the New Deal Coalition were those loyal to urban political machines, including trade unionists, ethno-religious minorities (Catholics, Jews, African-Americans), anti-prohibitionists, as well as Progressive intellectuals from all parts of the country (Schlesinger 1957, 413–39). Of course, all of these groups were major beneficiaries of New Deal programs, and their leaders populated the offices of the incoming administration.

The First 100 Days

Inaugurated president on March 4, 1933, President Roosevelt delivered an inspirational address that was broadcast on radio to tens of millions of anxious Americans. Because fear and economic distress overwhelmed the nation, Americans were primed for a charismatic leader who would restore hope to their lives.

Roosevelt did not disappoint. The most memorable part of his inaugural address was the opening statement: "So, first of all, let me assert my firm belief that the only thing we have to fear is fear itself – nameless, unreasoning, unjustified terror which paralyzes needed efforts to convert retreat into advance" (Roosevelt 1933b). The speech struck a populist tone that attacked the class basis of the economic system, decried the "moneychangers," and laid out the broad outlines of the New Deal. He said,

[T]here must be an end to a conduct in banking and in business which too often has given to a sacred trust the likeness of callous and selfish wrongdoing ... This Nation asks for action, and action now ... Our greatest primary task is to put people to work ... It can be accomplished in part by direct recruiting by the Government itself, treating the task as we would treat the emergency of a war, but at the same time, through this employment, accomplishing greatly needed projects to stimulate and reorganize the use of our natural resources ... The task can be helped by definite efforts to raise the values of agricultural products and with this the power to purchase the output of our cities.

It can be helped by preventing realistically the tragedy of the growing loss through foreclosure of our small homes and our farms ... Finally, in our progress toward a resumption of work we require two safeguards against a return of the evils of the old order; there must be a strict supervision of all banking and credits and investments; there must be an end to speculation with other people's money, and there must be provision for an adequate but sound currency. (Roosevelt 1933b)

Roosevelt's inaugural address quickly changed the mood of the nation from one of despair to renewed hope. As expressed by humorist Will Rogers, "They know they got a man in there who is wise to Congress, wise to our so-called big men. The whole country is with him, just so he does something. If he burned down the capitol we would cheer and say 'well, we at least got a fire started anyhow.' We have had years of 'Don't rock the boat,' go and sink it if you want to, we just as well be swimming as like we are" (Rogers 1955, 167). Political columnist Walter Lippmann expressed the mood change in more highbrow language: "At the beginning of March the country was in such a state of confused desperation that it would have followed almost any leader anywhere he chose to go ... In one week, the nation, which had lost confidence in everything and everybody, has regained confidence in the government and in itself" (Schlesinger 1958, 13).

Roosevelt's inspirational words were quickly followed by actions. The next 100 days constituted the most productive period of legislative output in American history. Roosevelt's initial policies were directed toward reviving the collapsed economy. Not coincidentally, the initial policies also helped solidify support for the New Deal philosophy for generations to come. Table 4.1 provides a chronology of actions by the administration and Congress during the first 100 days.

Roosevelt's inauguration occurred in the midst of yet another banking panic. Thus, two days after the March 4 inauguration the president issued Proclamation #2039 declaring a national emergency and bank holiday. Over the next week banks were closed, thereby preventing further hoarding of money and coinage, as well as allowing a period of relative calm as new measures were adopted to restore people's confidence in the banking system. The proclamation also made it illegal to hoard gold or remove it from banks for export or speculation.

On March 9, the president called a special session of Congress. The first order of business was an emergency banking proposal, introduced that day and passed that same evening. The legislation passed the House by a voice vote and the Senate by a margin of 73–7, with 22 Republicans voting in favor and only 5 opposed. The Emergency Banking Act allowed only Federal Reserve–authorized banks to operate in the United States. It also committed the Federal Reserve to supplying unlimited currency to authorized banks, effectively creating de facto 100 percent deposit insurance. This guarantee assured bank depositors that their money was safe. The law also authorized the Treasury Secretary to order any individual or organization in the United States to deliver all privately held gold to the Treasury in return for legal tender.

TABLE 4.1 *Presidential Actions and Legislation Fighting the Depression during Franklin D. Roosevelt's First 100 Days*

1933	Action or Law	Summary
March 4	Inauguration	President Roosevelt delivers an inspirational inaugural address that was broadcast on radio to tens of millions of anxious Americans.
March 6	Bank holiday and prohibits gold speculation	Two days after his inauguration, the president proclaims a nationwide bank holiday as a first initiative in stabilizing the banking system. Additionally, the president's proclamation makes it illegal to remove gold from banks for hoarding, exporting, or speculative purposes.
March 9	Roosevelt calls special session of Congress	The president calls Congress into special session to enact measures to combat the Great Depression. The hundred-day session was the most productive legislative period in American history.
March 9	Emergency Banking Act	The Emergency Banking Act allowed only Federal Reserve authorized banks to operate in the United States. Along with a commitment from the Federal Reserve to supply unlimited currency to authorized banks, this legislation created de facto 100 percent deposit insurance. It also authorized the Treasury Secretary to order any individual or organization in the United States to deliver any gold that they possess to the Treasury in return for legal tender.
March 12	First Fireside Chat	American families gathered around their radios to hear the first of thirty evening radio addresses by the president from 1933 through 1944. The president assured Americans that banks are now safe.
March 13	Bank holiday lifted	Banks reopen with assurance that deposits are protected by the full faith and credit of the U.S. government. Within a few weeks the banking system is deemed stable.
March 21	Civilian Conservation Corps (CCC)	The president proposes the first work relief program. Passed by Congress on March 31, it was directed toward unemployed men (ages 18–25) from families on public relief.

1933	Action or Law	Summary
		The program involved low skilled work in national forests, parks, and other public facilities.
April 5	Gold made illegal for domestic commerce	The president issues E.O. 6102 requiring gold in various forms to be delivered to the government in exchange for notes. These actions increased the government's supply of gold, effectively allowing money supply expansion to stimulate the economy.
April 20	Gold standard ends	The president issues E.E. 6111 banning the export of gold to settle international accounts. This action effectively ends U.S. participation in the gold standard.
May 7	Second Fireside Chat	The president's second radio address to the American people lays out the details of the New Deal. The president also explains measures taken with respect to gold and reflation of the economy.
May 12	Federal Emergency Relief Act	Along with the CCC, the Federal Emergency Relief Administration (FERA) was the main relief agency prior to the Works Progress Administration (WPA) taking over its functions in 1935. The agency diminished household unemployment by creating unskilled jobs in local and state government. Under authority of this law, the president created the Civil Works Administration (CWA) on November 8 through E.O. 6420 to administer public works construction.
May 12	Emergency Farm Mortgage Act	The Emergency Farm Mortgage Act attempted to save the farms of those in arrears on their loans by extending repayment schedules and offering emergency financing. House: 383–11; Senate: 58–31.
May 12	Agricultural Adjustment Act	This legislation created the Agricultural Adjustment Administration (AAA) to supervise the largest New Deal farm programs. Also, farm subsidies were financed by a tax on processors of farm crops.
May 18	Tennessee Valley Authority (TVA)	This program was intended to alleviate poverty in the Tennessee Valley where the effects of the depression were especially acute. It did so by using experts to improve local farming techniques and rural electrification to improve living and working standards.

(continued)

TABLE 4.1 (*continued*)

1933	Action or Law	Summary
May 27	Federal Securities Act	Pursuant to the interstate commerce clause, this legislation required that all sales of securities in the United States be registered with the Federal Trade Commission (and after 1934 with the Securities and Exchange Commission). Registrants were required to create a registration statement, including a prospectus with full disclosure about the security. Registrants were made liable for false claims. The purpose was to ensure that investors had full information before purchasing a regulated security.
June 13	Home Owners' Loan Act	This legislation provided money for refinancing of home mortgages. Also, it established the Home Owners' Loan Corporation.
June 16	Farm Credit Act	Established the Farm Credit System (FCS), which oversaw a group of cooperative lending institutions in providing short-, intermediate-, and long-term loans for agriculture. President Roosevelt had earlier created by E.O. 6084 the Farm Credit Administration (FCA) that consolidated farm credit activities under one agency.
June 16	Banking Act of 1933	This legislation established the Federal Deposit Insurance Corporation (FDIC) to protect bank depositors from bank defaults. It also limited the activities of commercial banks by prohibiting combinations of commercial and investment banking, as well as "speculative" bank activities such as had occurred prior to the stock market crash. Also called the Glass–Steagall Act, this legislation remained a primary mechanism of bank regulation until the 1990s.
June 16	National Industrial Recovery Act (NIRA)	This legislation authorized the president to regulate industry to raise prices and stimulate the industrial recovery. It authorized industrial codes of fair competition to be administered by the executive branch, permitted regulation of working standards, guaranteed trade union rights, and controlled the price of petroleum products. The legislation also created the Public Works Administration (PWA), which was to provide employment by developing public infrastructure.

On March 12, President Roosevelt conducted his first Fireside Chat with the American people (Roosevelt 1933a). He used this first of thirty radio addresses to assure Americans that the banking system was now safe. The following day the president lifted the bank holiday, and authorized banks were opened for business. Citizens formed long lines to deposit their hoarded money. That same day the stock market registered its approval with its largest one-day percentage gain in American history. From this point forward, the banking system was stable.

Over the next three months, the president and new Democratic Congress acted decisively to bring relief to those Americans hit hardest by the depression. As discussed earlier, a hallmark of depression economics was deflation. As noted by Schlesinger (1958, 195), "On the day of Roosevelt's inauguration, the index of wholesale commodity prices was at 59.6 percent of its 1926 level, of farm commodities at 40.6 percent. The dead weight of debts contracted at higher price levels threatened to collapse the entire economy – unless prices could somehow be increased."

Further, as discussed in Chapter 3, price deflation produced an incentive to hoard money, and a disincentive for those with money to consume and invest. With prices in decline, the value of money was rising. As a result, holders of money could simply wait in predatory fashion for prices to drop sufficiently before resuming consumption and investment. For holders of money to return to normal patterns, an inflationary stimulus was required to make money less valuable when sitting idle.

The Roosevelt administration tackled these problems through a series of actions that removed the United States from the gold standard. Continued adherence to the gold standard meant that the money in circulation was restricted by the amount of gold held by Federal Reserve banks. As a result, the gold standard limited the ability of the central bank to increase the money supply, thereby increasing the general price level.

Historically, gold was widely understood to separate winners from losers in the American system. Indeed, paper money diluting the wealth of creditors had been one of the rationales of the Founders for framing the Constitution of 1787 (e.g., see Beard 1913, 32, 63). As discussed in Chapter 3, gold was also the basis for intense class conflict between 1873 and 1900, as a protracted period of price deflation occurred after the nation moved to a de facto gold standard.

Further, before 1933, a "gold clause" was a standard feature of most debt contracts. These clauses required repayment of debts in the dollar value of gold at the time of the contract. With the dollar value of gold fixed by the government at $20.67 per troy ounce, the "gold clauses" meant that farmers and small business owners selling their goods at depressed prices had great difficulty coping with their debts. Those who paid mortgages, owed debts, and lacked access to credit or currency were also losers. In contrast, gold was good for those who controlled currency, held gold, or issued loans. The wealthy commonly hoarded gold as a commodity oblivious to economic fluctuations.

They viewed gold as a means of protecting their wealth and were adamantly opposed to leaving the gold standard.

Taking a stand along class lines, Roosevelt took a series of actions that removed the nation from the gold standard. On March 6, the president issued a proclamation making it illegal to remove gold from banks for purposes of exportation or speculation. On March 9, the Emergency Banking Act authorized the Treasury Secretary to require holders of gold to exchange their gold for legal tender. A month later on April 5, the president issued E.O. 6102, requiring gold in various forms to be delivered to the Federal Reserve in exchange for notes, thereby removing it from commerce. The president's order, along with provisions of the Emergency Banking Act, criminalized the private possession of gold with certain exceptions. Finally, acting on the advice of his economic minions (Schlesinger 1958, 195–203), on April 19 the president announced in a press conference that the nation would no longer adhere to the gold standard. The next day the president issued E.O. 6111, which banned the export of gold to settle international accounts. Finally, in early June Congress supported the president's actions by approving a joint resolution "abrogating the 'gold clause' [in private and public contracts] and making legal tender [paper currency] acceptable in settlement of private debts and of government obligations" (Schlesinger 1958, 202).

Roosevelt's actions in removing the nation from the gold standard made clear his position relative to class divisions within American society. As expressed by Schlesinger (1958, 201), "the step involved the repudiation of obligations to pay in gold long written into the 'gold clause' of public and private contracts – an act which damaged all creditors who had hoped to make a killing out of the increase in the value of the dollar." Further, the influx of gold into the Federal Reserve freed it to expand the money supply very substantially. The money supply increased by 27 percent between December 1933 and December 1936. As a result, interest rates declined, prices increased, and industrial production grew by 56 percent. Former Chair of the President's Council of Economic Advisors Christina Romer showed statistically that the monetary expansion following Roosevelt's gold initiatives was responsible more than any other factor for stimulating the American economy between 1933 and 1937 (Romer 1992).

Simultaneous with these actions to level the playing field for debtors, the president pursued economic relief for those segments of the population most hurt by the depression. On March 21, the president proposed the first work relief program, the Civilian Conservation Corps (CCC). The CCC passed Congress ten days later by voice vote in both houses. The public works initiative employed young men (ages 18–25) from families on public relief. The program involved low skilled work in national forests, national parks, and other public facilities to improve conservation and infrastructure. By July 1933 there were 1,463 working camps with 250,000 youth enrollees, most sending money home to impoverished families (Ermentrout 1982, 15).

On May 12, Congress passed three measures to bring relief more broadly and to farmers. The Federal Emergency Relief Act created a Federal Emergency Relief Administration (FERA). The legislation passed the Senate by a voice vote, and the House by a vote of 331–42, with 74 of 117 Republicans voting in favor. This agency was the main relief agency before the Works Progress Administration (WPA) took over its functions in 1935. The agency attacked unemployment by creating unskilled jobs in local and state government. The FERA provided work for over 20 million people through construction projects, and production and distribution of consumer goods to those on public relief (Deeben 2012). Under authority of this legislation, the president created the Civil Works Administration (CWA) to administer public works construction through E.O. 6420. The CWA provided construction jobs to roughly four million workers to replenish buildings and bridges across the nation (Peters and Noah 2009).

The same day Congress passed the Emergency Farm Mortgage Act and the Agricultural Adjustment Act. The Emergency Farm Mortgage Act passed the House by a vote of 387–12, with 94 Republicans voting in favor, and the Senate by a voice vote. The Agricultural Adjustment Act passed the House by a vote of 315–98 with the support of 39 Republicans, and the Senate by a vote of 64–20, with 15 Republicans voting yes. The Emergency Farm Mortgage Act saved the farms of many behind on their loans by extending repayment schedules and offering emergency financing. The legislation enabled refinancing up to 40 percent of farm mortgages in the United States (Rose 2013). The Agricultural Adjustment Act created the Agricultural Adjustment Administration (AAA) to supervise the largest farm programs under the New Deal. The goal was to increase the flow of money to farmers so they could reach income "parity" with urban America. It did this by giving subsidies to farmers for restricting crop production, thereby raising crop prices and farm income. The subsidies were paid for by a tax on processors of farm crops, a method of financing later deemed unconstitutional by the Supreme Court.

On May 18, Congress passed legislation creating the Tennessee Valley Authority (TVA) by federal charter. The act passed the House by a vote of 306–92 with the support of 17 Republicans, and the Senate by a vote of 63–20, with 14 Republicans voting yes. The TVA was intended to alleviate poverty and backward conditions in the Tennessee Valley, where the effects of the depression were especially acute. The Tennessee Valley includes most of Tennessee, parts of Alabama, Mississippi, and Kentucky, and slices of Georgia, North Carolina, and Virginia. It functioned by using experts to improve local farming techniques, developing fertilizer manufacturing, flood control, and rural electrification to improve living and working standards (Schulman 2004, 183). In creating the TVA, Roosevelt and the Democratic Congress catered to core Southern supporters, as well as alleviated depression conditions in these states.

On May 27, Congress passed the Federal Securities Act pursuant to the Commerce Clause. Both houses passed the bill on a voice vote. This legislation regulated the sale of stocks and other securities, requiring that all sales of securities in the United States be registered with the Federal Trade Commission (and after 1934 with the Securities and Exchange Commission). Registrants were required to create a registration statement, including a prospectus with full disclosure about the security. Registrants were made liable for false claims. The purpose was to level the informational playing field between those issuing and those purchasing securities.

In April 1933, President Roosevelt asked Congress for legislation to protect homeowners from mortgage foreclosure. In response, Congress passed the Home Owners' Loan Act on June 13. The legislation passed the Senate by a voice vote, and the House by a vote of 383–4. This act provided for refinancing of home mortgages. The legislation also established the Home Owners' Loan Corporation (HOLC). By the mid-1930s this agency had refinanced almost 20 percent of all urban home loans in the United States (Schlesinger 1958, 297–98). Where earlier Roosevelt had secured legislation to protect farmers from creditors, the HOLC cast the net more broadly for all homeowners in danger of losing their homes. According to Schlesinger, "Probably no single measure consolidated so much middle-class support for the administration" (1958, 298) Again, the president was befriending himself to debtors.

Finally, on June 16, the last day of the special session, Congress enacted three laws punctuating the president's focus on ending the depression. The Farm Credit Act passed both houses of Congress on a voice vote. The legislation authorized the Farm Credit Administration (FCA) that had earlier been created by President Roosevelt's Executive Order 6084. The agency oversaw a group of cooperative lending institutions that subsequently provided short-, intermediate-, and long-term loans for agriculture, independent of private lenders. Henceforth, farmers were freed from reliance on bankers and financiers for securing credit.

The same day Congress passed the Banking Act of 1933 (also called the Glass–Steagall Act). The legislation passed the Senate by a voice vote and the House by a vote of 262–19. This legislation established the Federal Deposit Insurance Corporation (FDIC)) to protect bank depositors from bank defaults. It also limited the activities of commercial banks by prohibiting combinations of both consumer and investment banking, as well as "speculative" bank activities such as had occurred prior to the stock market crash. This legislation remained the primary mechanism of federal bank regulation until 1999 when parts of the legislation were repealed.

Finally, Congress passed the National Industrial Recovery Act (NIRA). This legislation passed the House by a vote of 325–76, with Republicans voting in favor by a margin of 54–50. The Senate vote for passage was 58–24, with 9 Republicans voting in favor. Initially supported by business leaders (Schlesinger 1958, 87–89), the NIRA was intended to regulate industrial activities and was an effort at national planning. As such, it was a clear move away from unfettered capitalism. Title I of the legislation authorized the president to regulate industry to raise prices and stimulate the industrial recovery. It also authorized the promulgation of industrial codes of fair competition. On the same day, Roosevelt created the National Recovery Administration (NRA) by E.O. 6173 to oversee these efforts (Schlesinger 1958, 87–176). The NIRA also authorized regulation of working standards, guaranteed trade union rights, and controlled the price of petroleum products. The legislation provided a legal mechanism through which workers could organize and pursue fair working conditions. Title II of the legislation created the Public Works Administration (PWA), which was to provide employment by developing public infrastructure such as dams, bridges, hospitals, and schools.

Roosevelt's first 100 days was a period of phenomenal presidential leadership, bipartisan congressional support, and national unity. The president sent fifteen messages to Congress, guided the enactment of fifteen major laws, delivered ten speeches, conducted two Fireside Chats, held press conferences and cabinet meetings twice a week, and made all major decisions in domestic and foreign policy (Schlesinger 1958, 21). As expressed by political scientist Raymond Moley, chief of Roosevelt's "brain trust," who led a bipartisan group in reforming the banking system, "We had forgotten to be Republicans or Democrats ... We were just a bunch of men trying to save the banking system" (Schlesinger 1958, 4–5). Given the veto-proof majority that President Roosevelt held in the Congress, there was little need for Republican support. However, virtually all of the legislation proposed by the president during the first 100 days passed Congress with strong, bipartisan support. More generally, Roosevelt's first 100 days helped consolidate a New Deal philosophy that would dominate American politics for the next forth-eight years.

Completing the New Deal Social Contract

The first 100 days of the Roosevelt administration was a start toward conquering the Great Depression. However, the president and his New Deal Coalition clearly had a more expansive goal in mind. They wanted to bring economic security for all time to those worried about their livelihoods, children, homes, farms, and old age (Schlesinger 1958, 297). By pursuing this more expansive goal, the administration sought to fundamentally alter the social contract between the American government and its people.

The Founders' interpretation of the social contract omitted any federal responsibility for public well-being. Federalist-style political parties from the Washington administration through the Great Depression also omitted this responsibility. It was not the actual wording of the Constitution that omitted this responsibility. After all, the preamble called for the federal government to "promote the general Welfare." Article 1 required Congress to "provide for the common defense and general Welfare of the United States" (Wikipedia 2014b). However, the Founders and subsequent political administrations only paid lip service to such concepts as "community welfare" and the "happiness of fellow citizens" (Wood 2009, 5–9).

The Founders' social contract sought to protect the patrician class and promote the expansion of their wealth. In return, the patrician class would provide for workers and the masses through employment and charity. This top-down Federalist mindset dominated American government from the constitutional convention, through the Hamiltonian initiatives of the Washington administration, through the industrial development era, and through the 1920s to the Great Depression. Excluding brief interludes, the federal government consistently supported the patrician class through protective tariffs (resulting in higher prices for the masses), excise taxes (paid by the masses), easy credit, no or low taxes on the wealthy, business subsidies, and freedom from federal regulation. However, the legitimacy of this top-down social contract was thoroughly debunked by the Great Depression and the moral and intellectual bankruptcy of the governing elite.

The Roosevelt administration and New Deal Coalition sought to replace the Founders' social contract with one in which the federal government became directly responsible for public well-being. In doing so, the president and New Deal Coalition vastly expanded the powers and role of the federal government. Previously, the Tenth Amendment had been interpreted as limiting federal authority to address matters not specifically enumerated by the Constitution or reserved to the states. The Supreme Court typically favored limited government, striking down a plethora of Progressive initiatives to regulate social conditions and redistribute wealth. However, the Roosevelt administration and New Deal Coalition interpreted the Constitution more flexibly as enabling the federal government to make all laws "necessary and proper" for the execution of all legitimate legislative and executive powers. Among these powers were regulation of interstate commerce and the taxing authority to provide for "the general welfare of the United States" (Wikipedia 2014b).

Using this more flexible interpretation, the Roosevelt administration pursued a variety of new initiatives securing rents for segments of the New Deal Coalition. Table 4.2 provides a chronology of initiatives occurring after the first 100 days. The first initiative involved business regulation and protection of worker rights. The last legislative action of the first 100 days was the NIRA. The NIRA sought to regulate industry to raise prices and stimulate the industrial recovery. As noted earlier, the legislation was implemented by the National Recovery Administration (NRA) and generated large numbers of regulations and industrial codes (Best 1991; Eisner 2000). Business leaders initially supported this part of the legislation (Schlesinger 1958, 87–102), but quickly reversed themselves once the implications became clear (Schlesinger 1958, 119–22).

Business leaders especially disliked elements of the NIRA enabling trade associations. Under the NIRA workers were guaranteed the right to organize and bargain collectively over wages, hours, and working conditions. The initial

TABLE 4.2 *Presidential Actions, Events, and New Deal Legislation through Franklin D. Roosevelt's Second Term*

Date	Activity	Summary
August 5, 1933	National Labor Board (NLB)	The NRA announces the creation of the National Labor Board (NLB) to enforce provisions of the NIRA pertaining to worker rights. The NLB authorizes workers to hold free elections to decide who would represent them in bargaining with management.
December 16, 1933	E.O. 6511	The president issues an executive order ratifying the NLB's past activities and giving authority to "settle by mediation, conciliation or arbitration all controversies between employers and employees which tend to impede the purpose of the National Industrial Recovery Act."
February 1, 1934	E.O. 6580	The president issues an executive order giving the NLB explicit power to authorize elections to determine majority status for worker representation. This order seemingly gave exclusive worker representation rights to the winning union, thereby limiting representation by company unions.
June 6, 1934	Securities Exchange Act	This legislation provided the basis for regulating financial markets and their participants in the United States. The Act also established the Securities and Exchange Commission (SEC), which is the agency primarily responsible for enforcement of U.S. federal securities laws.
June 28, 1934	National Housing Act	Congress passes the National Housing Act, creating the Federal Savings and Loan Insurance Corporation (FSLIC) and Federal Housing Administration (FHA). This legislation reduced risks for banks in making home loans, thereby lowering interest rates and making home loans more affordable for Americans.
June 29, 1934	E.O. 6763	President Roosevelt creates the National Labor Relations Board (NLRB). The NLRB replaced the earlier NLB in enforcing provisions of the NIRA pertaining to worker rights. The NLRB continues to this day as the primary guarantor of workers' rights to organize and achieve fair treatment.
April 8, 1935	Emergency Relief Appropriations Act	Congress passes the Emergency Relief Appropriations Act. On May 6, President Roosevelt issued E.O. 7034 creating the

(*continued*)

TABLE 4.2 *(continued)*

Date	Activity	Summary
		Works Progress Administration (WPA) to administer the law. The WPA was the largest New Deal relief agency, replacing both the CWA and PWA. It relieved unemployment in local communities by constructing public buildings, schools, roads, bridges, and parks.
May 11, 1935	E.O. 7037	President Roosevelt created the Rural Electrification Administration (REA) by E.O. 7037. The purpose was to bring electricity to rural areas. Congress later authorized the president's executive order through the Rural Electrification Act of 1936.
May 27, 1935	Supreme Court declares NIRA unconstitutional	The Supreme Court held in *Schechter Poultry Corp. v. United States* (295 U.S. 495) that the NIRA was unconstitutional. The Court argued that the Commerce Clause had been inappropriately applied. Also, the Court argued that the legislation delegated excessive authority to the executive branch.
July 5, 1935	National Labor Relations Act (Wagner Act)	Partially in response to the Supreme Court, Congress and the president passed the National Labor Relations Act, also called the Wagner Act, reestablishing the right of workers to collective bargaining that had been nullified by the *Schechter* decision.
August 14, 1935	Social Security Act	President Roosevelt's Secretary of Labor, Frances Perkins, drafted this legislation, which permanently changed the relationship of American citizens with their government. This sweeping social welfare legislation provided for old age assistance (i.e., Social Security retirement), unemployment insurance, Aid to Families with Dependent Children (AFDC), maternal and child welfare, public health services, and assistance for the blind.
January 6, 1936	Supreme Court declares AAA unconstitutional	The Supreme Court deemed the AAA unconstitutional in *United States v. Butler et al.* (297 U.S. 1). The legislation had imposed a tax on processors of farm products to pay for subsidies to farmers for reducing their production. The Court held that the tax was unconstitutional as part of a coercive contract. It also held that federal payments to farmers violated the Tenth Amendment.

Date	Activity	Summary
February 5, 1937	Roosevelt's "Court Packing" Plan	President Roosevelt proposes legislation allowing him to expand the membership of the Supreme Court to fifteen members, enabling him to overrule the conservative majority. On March 29, the Supreme Court published *West Coast Hotel Co. v. Parrish* (300 U.S. 379), upholding a Washington state minimum wage law. Associate Justice Owen Roberts had now switched to the wing of the bench more sympathetic to the New Deal.
April 12, 1937	Supreme Court upholds the Wagner Act	The Supreme Court held the Wagner Act as constitutional in *National Labor Relations Board v. Jones & Laughlin Steel Corporation* (301 U.S. 1). The decision is widely recognized as greatly expanding Congress's power under the Commerce Clause.
May 24, 1937	Supreme Court upholds the Social Security Act	The Supreme Court issued three opinions, all upholding provisions of the Social Security Act. *Helvering v. Davis* (301 U.S. 619) upheld the payroll tax used to fund Social Security. *Steward Machine Company v. Davis* (301 U.S. 548) and *Carmichael v. Southern Coal & Coke Co.* (301 U.S. 495) upheld unemployment compensation.
February 16, 1938	Agricultural Adjustment Act of 1938	Congress enacts legislation to reinstitute the AAA, replacing the tax on processors of agricultural products with general federal revenues. The legislation also established price supports for various crops, marketing quotas, and the Federal Crop Insurance Corporation (basically insurance for farmers during bad crop years).
June 25, 1938	Fair Labor Standards Act of 1938 (FLSA)	The FLSA introduced a maximum forty-hour work week, established a national minimum wage, guaranteed "time and a half" for overtime for certain jobs, and prohibited most "child labor."

reaction of businesses to these requirements was to create so-called company unions. Company unions actually prevented the development of true worker bargaining power. Management governed company unions, rather than workers. Recognizing this, the director of the NRA established the National

Labor Board (NLB) to mediate all labor issues arising under the NIRA. One of the first actions of the NLB was to rule that workers could choose which union would represent them, a company union or their own union. However, the NLB had no enforcement authority (Schlesinger 1958, 144–46).

Over the next two years, the president and Congress sought to increase worker rights through both executive orders and legislation. On December 16, 1933, Roosevelt issued Executive Order 6511 ratifying the NLB's past activities and giving it authority to "settle by mediation, conciliation or arbitration all controversies between employers and employees which tend to impede the purpose of the National Industrial Recovery Act." Regardless, many companies refused to comply with the president's executive order (Morris 2004, 32–34; Schlesinger 1958, 148–49).

In response, members of Congress led by Senator Robert Wagner (D-New York) asked the president to issue a new executive order strengthening the ability of the NLB to enforce compliance. On February 1, 1934, Roosevelt issued E.O. 6580 granting the NLB explicit power to decide union representation by majority rule. The president's order seemed to give the election winner exclusive rights of representation. However, this interpretation was widely disputed by business leaders, and noncompliance with the president's executive order continued to be widespread (Morris 2004, 34–36).

Because the NLB remained ineffective in protecting worker rights, members of Congress, again led by Senator Wagner, developed legislation to put "teeth" into the decisions of the labor board. Yet legislation requires time, and labor unrest over these and other issues was growing. As a result, Roosevelt submitted a resolution to Congress asking them to grant executive authority to set up labor boards empowered to conduct elections and enforce company compliance. Remarkably, the resolution passed Congress unanimously, with full support from both political parties. With congressional support in hand, the president issued E.O. 6763 on June 29, 1934. The order abolished the NLB and established a new National Labor Relations Board (NLRB). The president's order explicitly authorized the NLRB to conduct elections on behalf of workers and enforce the results (Schlesinger 1958, 149–51).

The president and New Deal Coalition also sought to increase government assistance for homeowners, local communities, and farm families. On June 28, 1934, Congress passed the National Housing Act. The legislation passed in the House by a vote of 176–19, and in the Senate by a vote of 71–12, with 21 Republicans voting in support. The legislation created the Federal Savings and Loan Insurance Corporation (FSLIC) and Federal Housing Administration (FHA). The FSLIC extended deposit insurance to those with deposits in savings and loan associations. The FHA made home ownership more affordable for Americans. It regulated interest rates and mortgage terms and provided government insurance against homeowner default. The FHA stimulated recovery in housing markets and has stood since 1934 as a mechanism through which government supports home ownership and protects citizens against potentially predatory lenders.

On April 8, 1935, Congress passed the Emergency Relief Appropriations Act to support local communities. The legislation passed the House by a vote of 341–38, with Republicans voting in favor by a margin of 62–31, and the Senate by a vote of 62–14, with 7 Republicans voting yes. Then, pursuant to this legislation President Roosevelt issued E.O. 7034 creating the Works Progress Administration (WPA) (Schlesinger 1960, 343–45). The WPA was the largest New Deal relief agency, replacing the earlier CWA and FERA. The WPA's initial appropriation of $4.9 billion was about 6.7 percent of the 1935 GDP (Dike-Wilhelm 2006). It supported local communities by relieving unemployment and improving community infrastructure through construction projects that had lasting impact. WPA projects included public buildings, schools, roads, bridges, and parks. Virtually every community in America benefited from the projects of this agency, many of which continue in use today (Jason Smith 2006).

Also flowing from the Emergency Relief Appropriations Act, President Roosevelt issued E.O. 7037 on May 11, 1935, creating the Rural Electrification Administration (REA). The REA developed electrical infrastructure for farmers (an indirect subsidy) to bring them to parity with urban dwellers. Of course, electricity is necessary for homes to have modern conveniences, as well as for making agricultural production more efficient. In 1935, only about 10 percent of rural dwellers had electricity, compared with about 90 percent of urban dwellers. The president's intention was to address this disparity (Schlesinger 1960, 379–84). Congress later authorized the president's executive order through the Rural Electrification Act of 1936. Again, this benefit to farm communities solidified Democratic support in the South and rural areas that lasted well into the 1970s.

Congress easily passed most New Deal legislation and accepted the president's executive orders without much question. However, business leaders were simultaneously working through the courts to challenge the greater role of government in regulating business and protecting citizens, workers, and the farm community. "[I]n 1935–36, federal judges issued some sixteen hundred injunctions preventing federal officials from implementing federal laws ... only 28 percent of the 266 federal judges were Democrats ... by the end of 1935 elaborate [district court] opinions were in circulation holding the TVA Act, the Holding Company Act, and the Labor Relations Act unconstitutional" (Schlesinger 1960, 447–49).

Then, on May 27, 1935, the Supreme Court handed down a landmark decision, *Schechter Poultry Corp. v. United States* (295 U.S. 495), holding that the entire NIRA was unconstitutional. The ruling pertained to the industrial codes, regulations, and all of the president's executive orders. The Court argued that the Commerce Clause had been interpreted too broadly. Also, the Court argued that the legislation delegated excessive authority to the executive branch (Schlesinger 1960, 281–83). Regarding worker rights and the ability of the government to regulate wages and hours, Supreme Court historian David

Currie wrote that the Court believed "to permit Congress to regulate the wages and hours in a tiny slaughterhouse because of remote effects on interstate commerce would leave nothing for the tenth amendment to reserve" (Currie 1990, 223). Hence, the Court declared the NIRA and everything flowing from it to be unconstitutional.

However, the Roosevelt administration and New Deal Coalition did not passively accept the judiciary's constrained view of national power. They acted quickly to pass new laws to replace those declared invalid, as well as expand the New Deal into additional areas. These additional areas included social security, public relief, banking regulation, public utilities, additional worker protections, and bills specific to particular economic sectors (Schlesinger 1960, 291–301).

Worker rights had long been on the congressional agenda due to labor unrest and the continuing efforts of Senator Robert Wagner. Accordingly, the Wagner labor bill was the obvious first choice of the administration for pushing back against the Supreme Court. Senator Wagner had been "opposed in his efforts by organized industry with a force and fervor and expenditure of funds perhaps unparalleled. It was vehemently opposed by almost all of the press" (Keyserling, 201–2). Nevertheless, Senator Wagner had succeeded in getting his labor bill passed in the Senate by a vote of 63–12, with 12 Republicans voting in favor. After the *Schechter* decision, the president indicated that he wanted the Wagner labor bill passed in some form by the House. The bill was rushed through the House in late June and passed by a voice vote. The president signed the bill on July 5, 1935 (Schlesinger 1960, 292). The National Labor Relations Act reinstituted the NLRB, and guaranteed worker rights to organize and bargain collectively for all industries engaged in interstate commerce.

The next item on the president's agenda was social insurance. On June 8, 1934, the president sent a message to Congress vigorously affirming his faith in social insurance. He stated that "among our objectives I place the security of the men, women, and children of the nation first" (Schlesinger 1958, 304). Soon afterward, he appointed a cabinet-level Committee on Economic Security headed by Secretary of Labor Frances Perkins. Before accepting her appointment, "she laid before the president an extensive agenda, including unemployment and old age insurance, minimum wages and maximum hours; and he told her to go ahead." Her "overriding objective, once emergency problems of hunger and want had been met, was to construct a permanent system of personal security through social insurance" (Schlesinger 1958, 300–301).

The Committee reported its work to the president on January 15, 1935. The president agreed with its omnibus recommendations, stating, "There is no reason why everybody in the United States should not be covered ... I see no reason why every child, from the day he is born, shouldn't be a member of the social security system ... Cradle to grave – from the cradle to the grave they ought to be in a social insurance system" (Schlesinger 1958, 308). Accordingly, the president sent a message to Congress on January 17 requesting social insurance legislation based on the Committee's recommendations (Schlesinger 1958, 308–9).

Congress passed the Social Security Act on August 14, 1935. There were strenuous objections from the business community, with many leaders arguing that the legislation would end the American way of life. It would allegedly destroy capitalism, end individual initiative and responsibility, discourage thrift, and create a socialist state modeled on the European system (Schlesinger 1958, 311–12). Nevertheless, Republicans in Congress overwhelmingly rejected the business community position. The Social Security Act passed in the House by a vote of 372–33, where Republicans supported the measure by a margin of 79–18. The Social Security Act passed in the Senate by a vote of 77–6, where Republicans voted in favor by a margin of 15–5. Hence, the legislation had strong bipartisan support.

The Social Security Act brought sweeping change to the scope of federal involvement in public welfare. It provided unemployment compensation jointly funded by states, private enterprise, and the federal government (Title III). Within two years, all states had passed unemployment compensation laws in compliance with the legislation. The legislation also gave states assistance in dealing with aged citizens (Title I), needy citizens through Aid to Families with Dependent Children (Title IV), Maternal and Child Welfare (Title V), public health services (Title VI), and the blind (Title X). Further, the Social Security Act created an old age, survivor, and disability retirement system that operated independent of annual tax revenues (Title II).

Payments to recipients were financed by current workers and employers, half as a payroll tax and half paid by the employer. The principle is that workers fund annuities during their working life to be paid out after retirement, survivorship, or disability. President Roosevelt personally insisted on this mode of financing. He said, "We put those payroll contributions there so as to give the contributors a legal, moral, and political right to collect their pensions ... With those taxes in there, no damn politician can scrap my social security program" (Schlesinger 1958, 308–9). Roosevelt was right.

At the same time Roosevelt was successfully extending the New Deal through legislative enactments, more judicial challenges were working their way through the Courts. On January 6, 1936, the Supreme Court issued another landmark decision, *United States v. Butler et al.* (297 U.S. 1), declaring the Agricultural Adjustment Act unconstitutional. The AAA had provided price supports and crop subsidies to farmers to lift the agricultural community from the depression. The constitutional justification of the AAA was Congress's taxing and spending power. Subsidies to farmers for restricting production were paid for by a tax imposed on processors of farm crops. However, the Court deemed this mode of financing as imposing an illegal coercive contractual obligation between grant recipients and processors. The Court also held that agriculture was fundamentally a local activity and beyond national authority. Therefore, Congress violated the Tenth Amendment through passage of the AAA (Schlesinger 1960, 472). The Court had earlier struck down the NIRA in the *Schechter* case based on excessive delegation of power to the executive and an overly broad interpretation of the Commerce Clause. With *Butler*, the Court relied on the Tenth Amendment and restricted the ability of Congress to use the taxing and spending power to expand federal authority.

The Court handed down the *Butler* decision at the start of the 1936 presidential election year. The Court also issued subsequent decisions that year hostile to the New Deal through *Carter v. Carter Coal Company* (298 U.S. 238) and *Morehead v. New York ex rel Tipaldo* (298 U.S. 587). These decisions, along with *Schechter*, became a major campaign issue in 1936, arousing great hostility toward the Court from farmers, labor, and citizens generally.

The Roosevelt administration, believing that the recently passed Wagner Act and Social Security Act would also soon fall, sought a way to remove the obstacle imposed by the Court. Initially, they considered a constitutional amendment restricting the Court's authority. However, they concluded that such an amendment was not politically feasible, given well-funded business opposition, and would still be subject to the interpretation of a hostile court majority. During the latter part of 1936, President Roosevelt asked the Attorney General to study the feasibility of expanding the size of the Court sufficiently to swing it in the liberal direction (Schlesinger 1960, 484–96). After the election, Roosevelt's "court packing" plan was submitted to Congress on February 5, 1937. The Supreme Court's interpretation of the scope of federal power changed abruptly soon afterward.

The 1936 Election Landslide

President Roosevelt was reelected in 1936 by a landslide, reflecting an overwhelming public endorsement of the New Deal. He received 61 percent of the popular vote, the second largest percentage in American history (only Lyndon Johnson received more in 1964). The president won 523 electoral votes, or 98.5 percent, losing only two states, Maine and Vermont. Relative to 1933, the House majority grew by another twenty seats, with the new House consisting of 333 Democrats versus only 89 Republicans. The Senate majority increased by a whopping sixteen seats, with the new Senate consisting of 75 Democrats versus only 17 Republicans.

With such a strong public endorsement of the New Deal, it could be that the Supreme Court bent to the popular will (Caldeira 1987). For whatever reason, the scope and magnitude of federal power increased without challenge from this point forward. On March 29, 1937, the Supreme Court published *West Coast Hotel Co. v. Parrish* (300 U.S. 379), upholding a Washington state minimum wage law. Associate Justice Owen Roberts had now switched to the wing of the bench sympathetic to the New Deal. On April 12, 1937, the Court upheld the constitutionality of the Wagner Act in its decision *National Labor Relations Board v. Jones & Laughlin Steel Corporation* (301 U.S. 1). This decision is widely recognized as greatly expanding Congress's power under the

Commerce Clause. Then, on May 24, 1937, the Court upheld the constitutionality of the Social Security Act through three separate decisions. The payroll tax to fund Social Security was upheld in *Helvering v. Davis* (301 U.S. 619). The unemployment compensation provisions were deemed valid through *Steward Machine Company v. Davis* (301 U.S. 548) and *Carmichael v. Southern Coal & Coke Co.* (301 U.S. 495).

On February 16, 1938, Congress and the president reinstituted federal support for farmers by reenacting the AAA. The Agricultural Adjustment Act of 1938 passed the House by a vote of 264–135, with the support of 14 Republicans and over the objection of 54 Democrats. It passed the Senate by a vote of 56–31, where 16 Democrats joined 12 Republicans in opposition. Bowing to the Court's earlier coercive contract doctrine and the potential illegitimacy of the tax on distributors of agricultural products, the new AAA paid for farm subsidies through general revenues. The legislation also established price subsidies for various crops, marketing quotas, and the Federal Crop Insurance Corporation (insurance for farmers during bad crop years).

Finally, on June 25, 1938, Congress and the president extended further protections to American workers through passage of the Fair Labor Standards Act. The legislation passed the House by a vote of 314–97, with Republicans voting in favor by a margin of 46–41. It passed in the Senate by a vote of 56–28, with 14 Republicans supporting the bill. This legislation established a maximum forty-hour work week and a national minimum wage, guaranteed "time and a half" for overtime for certain jobs, and prohibited most "child labor." Amended many times through the years, this legislation remains the primary mechanism through which hourly workers are guaranteed fair working conditions. With this legislation, the New Deal was complete.

The struggle for a new social contract between the national government and its people now stood on firm foundations, both popularly and legally. The landslide election of 1936 demonstrated overwhelming popular support. With the surrender of the Supreme Court, the new social contract was on a firm constitutional footing.

WORLD WAR II AND THE SOLIDIFICATION OF AMERICAN UNITY

Americans were unified in their response to the Great Depression. Due to strong presidential leadership, congressional support, and enactment of the New Deal, the American political system actually grew stronger during the crisis of the 1930s. However, other nations did not respond so benignly to the Great Depression. Some responded with ultra-nationalism, extreme ideology, political instability, repression, violence, and even war. Observing these developments, Americans were divided on how to respond to a changing international landscape.

In 1922, Fascist Party dictator Benito Mussolini came to power in Italy. Mussolini's response to the subsequent Great Depression was to launch nationalistic efforts to create a new Roman Empire extending across the entire Mediterranean region. Mussolini invaded Ethiopia in October 1935. In July 1936, Spanish Fascist General Francisco Franco led a failed coup d'etat sparking a three-year Spanish civil war. Fellow Fascist Mussolini quickly allied Italy with General Franco, providing arms and aircraft. Meanwhile, across the world Japanese nationalists were pursuing an Asian empire. Seeking land and natural resources, the Japanese invaded and occupied Chinese Manchuria in September 1931. They launched a full-scale invasion of China in July 1937, finally taking control of its Northern provinces (World War II Museum 2014b).

Political instability was also occurring in Germany. The onset of the Great Depression produced major gains for the Nazi Party in the German parliament in 1930, and they became the majority party in 1932. Nazi leader Adolph Hitler became German Chancellor in January 1933, and the effective dictator in March 1933 through the Enabling Act. The Nazi Party, under Hitler's leadership, sought to establish absolute German hegemony throughout Europe. In February 1938, Nazi Germany renounced its earlier alliance with China and entered into a new alliance with the more powerful Japan. In March 1938, Germany annexed Austria, provoking little response from European powers. A year later the Germans invaded Czechoslovakia and declared it a German protectorate, with other European powers again remaining passive. Finally, on September 1, 1939, Hitler invaded Poland. Two days later, Great Britain and France declared war on Germany, marking the start of World War II (World War II Museum 2014b).

These international conflicts raised tensions within the United States, which nevertheless sought to remain neutral. The Italians, Germans, and Japanese were clearly the aggressors in their respective wars. As a result, many Americans were predisposed to favor the British, French, and Chinese. The Roosevelt administration also favored these traditional allies (Office of the Historian 2014).

However, by the 1930s many believed that bankers and munitions traders with European business interests drove U.S. involvement in World War I. These beliefs fueled "isolationist" sentiment through the 1930s, arguing the United States should avoid future wars and avoid financial deals with countries at war. Isolationism was especially strong among Southerners and Republicans. Thus, Americans were divided over the American response to international events (Office of the Historian 2014).

Fueled by isolationist sentiment, Congress passed and the president reluctantly signed Neutrality Acts in 1935, 1936, 1937, and 1939. The Roosevelt administration lobbied Congress in 1935 to authorize sanctions on aggressor nations. However, Congress rejected the president's proposal, instead imposing a six-month embargo on trade in arms and war materials with all parties. In 1936 Congress extended the embargo for fourteen months, and strengthened it by forbidding loans or credits to belligerents on either side. In 1937, Congress passed a joint resolution forbidding arms trade with Spain, and made the earlier embargo permanent. However, Congress made a temporary concession to the president by allowing a "cash and carry" trade in non-arms materials, as long as they were paid for in cash and recipients arranged transport on non-U.S. carriers. In March 1939, after the German occupation of Czechoslovakia, the Roosevelt administration lobbied Congress to renew the "cash and carry" provisions of the Neutrality Act of 1937. However, the president's proposal was soundly defeated.

After Germany invaded Poland, and Britain and France declared war on Germany in September 1939, the president persisted. This time he prevailed over the isolationists. In November 1939, Congress repealed the Neutrality Acts of 1935 and 1937, and the arms embargo was lifted. However, the prohibition on loans remained, and American ships were forbidden to transport goods to belligerent ports (Office of the Historian 2014).

With the war going badly for American allies in Europe, U.S. neutrality finally ended on March 11, 1941, with passage of the Lend-Lease Act. This legislation authorized the Roosevelt administration to sell, loan, or give war materials to those countries the administration sought to support. As Lend-Lease began operating, German submarines repeatedly attacked American ships. In September 1941, the president announced that he had ordered the U.S. Navy to attack German or Italian war vessels for defensive purposes. After the Germans sunk the U.S. destroyer *Reuben James* on October 31, 1941, Congress repealed what remained of the Neutrality Acts.

Finally, on December 7, 1941, the Japanese launched a surprise attack the U.S. naval base at Pearl Harbor. Congress declared war on Japan the next day. Three days later Congress also declared war on Germany and Italy after they had first declared war on the United States (Office of the Historian 2014). Pearl Harbor shocked the nation. Before Pearl Harbor, America was a house divided over international affairs. After Pearl Harbor, the nation was strongly united in favor of war. Arguably, no other single event in American history unified the American people more than the Japanese attack on Pearl Harbor.

As expressed by Tom Brokaw (2001, 3), "Across America on that Sunday afternoon, the stunning news from the radio electrified the nation and changed the lives of all who heard it." After the attack, people were ardent in their support of the war effort. Patriotism increased sharply across all segments of American society. All partisan groups, economic classes, regions, age groups, races, and genders wanted to contribute.

President Roosevelt's leadership was very important in bolstering American unity. Two days after the attack he addressed the nation: "Powerful and resourceful gangsters have banded together to make war upon the whole human race. Their challenge has now been flung at the United States of America ... The Congress and the people of the United States have accepted that challenge ... We are now in this war. We are all in it - all the way. Every single man, woman and child is a partner in the most tremendous undertaking of our American history" (Roosevelt 1941).

Americans responded overwhelmingly to the president's radio address. After Pearl Harbor, legislation quickly passed Congress making men between the ages of eighteen and forty-five eligible for a military draft. However, there was little need for a draft, as men flocked to military recruitment centers to enlist. The number of active duty military personnel in 1940 was only 458,000. By 1945, about 16.35 million Americans had served in the military.

On the home front, families became less concerned with improving their living standards and more interested in contributing to the war effort. Taxes increased sharply to pay for the war, with little complaint. Encouraged by the government, people saved their money by purchasing war bonds (Kimble 2006). Businessmen and industrialists loyally converted production processes from consumer goods to war materials. As a result, consumer prices increased, and the government imposed rationing to distribute shortages equally across the population. Farm production rose sharply to feed the troops, as well as for exports to allies in Europe. The entire U.S. population was engulfed by a sense of shared national purpose.

The war effort finally ended the Great Depression. Indeed, the billions spent for rearmament and national defense did far more to revitalize the American economy than any of the New Deal programs. U.S. defense spending increased from $1.66 billion in 1940 to $83 billion in 1945. As a percentage of GDP, the United States went from spending 1.7 percent on national defense in 1940 to 37.5 percent in 1945 (White House 2013). GDP more than doubled during the war, from $102.9 billion in 1940 to $228.2 billion in 1945 (Bureau of Economic Analysis 2014a). Over the same time frame, the gross federal debt more than quintupled, increasing from $50.7 billion to $260.1 billion (Council of Economic Advisors 2014). Thus, the war effort brought a dramatic increase in defense spending, production, and an even more dramatic increase in government borrowing to finance the war.

Mobilization placed extraordinary demands on the labor force. With over 16 million men and women in uniform, labor was in short supply. As a result, employers welcomed many who had previously been excluded from high paying, skilled labor positions. At the end of the war there were almost 19 million more workers than there had been at the start (Brokaw 2001, 11). Unemployment virtually disappeared as a significant part of the population entered military service, and even more participated in the home-front mobilization. In 1940, the unemployment rate was 14.6 percent. By 1944 it had declined to only 1.2 percent (NBER 1957). Thus, the economy moved very quickly from one of deep lingering economic distress to one of considerably better than full employment.

The war effort also set the stage for important social and economic changes that followed the war. By 1945, about 35 percent of the workforce consisted of women (Brokaw 2001, 11). Over 19 million women worked outside the home, an increase of about five million over 1940 (Bureau of the Census 1976). That number never returned to prewar levels, dropping to about 17 million in 1946. In addition to women's labor force participation, a significant number also served in the armed forces. By 1945, more than 400,000 women were in uniform at home and overseas, serving as pilots, military trainers, nurses, pharmacists, clerks, cooks, mechanics, drivers, and administration. All but a few of these women were "mustered out" after the war. However, women's participation in the labor force and military service brought an expectation that females were no longer restricted to the home. (Women in Military Service Memorial Foundation 2014).

African-Americans also contributed greatly to the war effort. The home front mobilization saw African-Americans gain access to higher paying jobs from which they had always been excluded. As large numbers of African-Americans moved to the north and west to work in defense industries, discrimination persisted. Under pressure from civil rights leaders, in June 1941 President Roosevelt issued E.O. 8802 banning racial discrimination in defense industries. The order created a Committee on Fair Employment Practice to investigate and redress reported charges of discrimination. Subsequently, in May 1943 the president issued E.O. 9346, extending the coverage to include all federal contracts. These executive orders were the first federal actions in U.S. history to promote equal opportunity and prohibit racial discrimination.

African-Americans also entered the military in large numbers. In 1941, fewer than 4,000 African-Americans were serving. By 1945, over 1.2 million were in uniform at home, in Europe, and the Pacific. During the war, the segregation practices of the nation spilled over into the military. There were no integrated military units during World War II. Most African-Americans were in service roles, such as transport, supply, and combat support groups. However, a few all-black combat units served with distinction, including the Tuskegee Airmen, the 320th Anti-Aircraft Barrage Balloon Battalion, and the 761st Tank Battalion serving with General Patton (World War II Museum 2014a). After the war, President Truman abolished discrimination in the military and ended segregated military units by issuing E.O. 9981. Thus, World War II increased African-American expectations for greater equality and set the stage for the civil rights movement.

The war also affected more general changes in American society. It significantly reduced economic inequality. To pay for the war, the top marginal tax rate was increased to 94 percent, with the income level subject to the highest tax rate lowered from $5 million to $200,000. By 1944 most people who were employed were paying federal income taxes (compared with only 10 percent in 1940) (Perrett 1985, 300). During the war, the share of national income earned by the top 10 percent of the population dropped from about 45 percent on average between 1921 and 1940 to about 34 percent between 1941 and 1945. The change from 1940 to 1941 was very sharp, due to wage and price controls and changes in the tax code. The top 10 percent's share of national income did not rise from this level from the 1940s through the 1970s (Piketty and Saez 2003, table A3).

Further, during the war Americans saved money at an unprecedented rate. Saving was deemed patriotic, so people routinely put their money into war bonds to be paid back ten years after purchase (Kimble 2006, 23–24). In 1940, Americans saved about $16.8 billion, or about 5 percent of their annual disposable income. This amount increased sharply over the next five years. By 1944, Americans were saving about 25 percent of their annual disposable income. Between 1941 and 1945, Americans saved a total of $550 billion (NBER 1954a, 1954b). To provide some perspective, U.S. GDP in 1945 was $228.2 billion (Bureau of Economic Analysis 2014a), so "pent up" savings at the end of the war was more than twice national income. As Americans spent this money after the war, an economic expansion occurred, creating jobs and income for millions of citizens over the next several decades.

Legislation was also passed during World War II that became important for postwar American society. The Servicemen's Readjustment Act of 1944, also called the GI Bill, has been called the last of Roosevelt's New Deal enactments (Altschuler and Blumin 2009). The president, having observed the turmoil surrounding treatment of veterans after World War I and the Bonus March of 1932, proposed that Congress establish an economic support system for veterans after the war (Ortiz 2009). Widely endorsed by members of both political parties, the legislation provided several key benefits. Those benefits included a year of unemployment compensation, low interest business loans, low-cost home mortgages, and educational grants.

Less than 20 percent of the unemployment compensation funds were ever spent, as most veterans quickly found jobs or pursued an education after the war. The low-cost business loans allowed many veterans to start their own businesses, thereby expanding the commercial class. However, the most important elements of the GI Bill were the home loan mortgage and educational programs. The GI Loan program enabled millions of veterans to move out of rented apartments and into homes, with no down payment and low-interest mortgages. The GI Loan broadened American participation in the "good life" and reduced economic inequality. The GI educational benefit provided tuition and living expenses for veterans to attend high school, college, or vocational training programs. By the time the legislation expired in 1956, roughly 2.2 million veterans had used their educational benefits to pursue higher education. An additional 6.6 million had used it for other training (Bound and Turner 2002; Olsen 1973). Thus, World War II ushered in a new era in which class divisions were diminished.

CHARACTERIZING AMERICAN UNITY FROM THE GREAT DEPRESSION THROUGH WORLD WAR II

The Great Depression, New Deal, and World War II were an extraordinary period in American history. The cohesion that typified American society through this period stemmed initially from an economic shock. Subsequently, a sense of shared national experience enveloped the nation. A very large proportion of Americans suffered from the Great Depression. Not all were homeless, unemployed, hungry, in tattered clothes, or insecure. However, most Americans experienced significant adverse economic consequences. Those who went through the depression developed a common psychological bond that continued well into the modern era.

People came to expect much more from their government and the political system. The social contract flowing from the New Deal was starkly different from that of the Founders. Where the Founders saw the government's role as limited, the new social contract saw the government's role as expansive, doing whatever was appropriate to promote the common good. The landslide elections of 1932 and 1936 showed Americans' overwhelming support for the new social contract. New Deal enactments from 1933 through 1938 were simply the policy responses to people's changed expectations about government. Government became a regulator of business; a protector and promoter of savers, investors, workers, homeowners, rural residents, and farmers; and a guarantor of economic security for all Americans from cradle to grave.

World War II provided cement that solidified American unity. Just as the depression had been a rally event sparking the New Deal, so also was Pearl Harbor a rally event that gave the Roosevelt administration license to do what was required to win the war. The president spoke directly to Americans in highly personal terms about shared sacrifice and the magnitude of required effort. He invoked congressional support for a wartime mobilization that was unprecedented in world history. Americans responded overwhelmingly according to their abilities and characteristics.

About 16.35 million citizens served in the military between 1941 and 1945, of which 15.95 million were male. Roughly 73 percent of the nation's young male workforce served in the military (calculated from Bureau of the Census 2014b). American war casualties between 1941 and 1945 were 407,316 dead and 671,846 wounded, for a total of 1,079,162. Thus, many American families shared the anxiety and pain of having a family member potentially in harm's way, with some paying the ultimate price.

Those Americans remaining at home experienced shared sacrifice in other ways. Wage and price controls were implemented to conserve resources. Tax policy changed to pay for the war. Savings rates through war bonds increased sharply to fund the war. Increased taxes and savings meant that Americans had less money for consumption. As a result, Americans during World War II learned to live on less. Further, with so much of the American labor force entering the military, new segments of the population contributed by working in industries supporting the war. Thus, the shared sacrifices of World War II produced a common experience further unifying American society.

In this chapter we have continued to develop the historical background for understanding the causes and consequences of polarization in the modern era. Pundits and scholars of modern polarization commonly frame their work in terms of explaining why polarization is now so high. However, the background developed in the preceding historical chapters suggests that the level of modern polarization is not all that unusual. Our earlier analyses showed that modern polarization was as high in the Founding Era and from Reconstruction to 1920. Thus, polarization is a historical norm.

However, this chapter has shown that polarization virtually disappeared after 1933. Thus, what is unusual historically is the degree of nonpolarization that existed from the Great Depression through the 1970s. Perhaps scholars should be focusing on why Americans were not polarized from the Great Depression through the 1970s, rather than on why they are so polarized now.

The remainder of this book turns to an analysis of polarization in the modern era. The historical interpretation continues in the next two chapters. However, the availability of modern data from a variety of sources enhances that interpretation. Subsequent chapters will develop more systematic measures of mass and institutional polarization, enabling evaluation of the extent to which modern polarization exists, and its causes.

5

The New Deal Social Contract through the 1970s

On October 27, 1964, an up-and-coming fifty-four-year-old actor and politician named Ronald Reagan delivered a nationally televised speech supporting ultra-conservative Republican presidential candidate Barry Goldwater. He said:

In this vote-harvesting time, they use terms like the "Great Society," or as we were told a few days ago by the President, we must accept a greater government activity in the affairs of the people ... It must be replaced by the incentives of the welfare state ... [T]his was the very thing the Founding Fathers sought to minimize ... Welfare spending [is now] 10 times greater than in the dark depths of the depression ... [F]ederal employees number two and a half million ... These proliferating bureaus with their thousands of regulations have cost us many of our constitutional safeguards ... We need true tax reform that will at least make a start toward restoring for our children the American Dream that wealth is denied to no one ... (Reagan 1964)

Reagan's speech was considered radical at the time, as was the ultra-conservative philosophy of his Old Guard mentor, Barry Goldwater.

The 1964 election was a strong repudiation of their ideologies. Lyndon Johnson won by the largest popular vote landslide since voting became widespread in America in the 1820s (61.1 percent), and his electoral vote margin was the largest since Franklin Roosevelt in 1936 (90 percent). President Johnson entered office with the largest congressional majorities since the 1930s. The president's electoral mandate and veto-proof majorities spurred the most extensive social reform program since the New Deal. Thus, the nineteenth-century Republican principles of limited government, low taxes on the wealthy, non-interference in markets, and no redistribution remained near dead.

However, two years after the speech Ronald Reagan became governor of California. His message of low taxes and small government resonated in California. In 1968, Reagan entered the Republican presidential primaries as the Old Guard favorite. However, he did poorly against Richard Nixon in most states. In the aftermath of Watergate, Reagan again launched a presidential campaign in 1976. Running against Republican establishment candidate Gerald Ford, he again failed to win the nomination. Reagan was still viewed by most as too radical for the party and nation.

Nevertheless, just four years later Ronald Reagan was elected the fortieth president of the United States. To understand this rapid change in American attitudes, the period between World War II and the Watergate scandal must be examined. It was a period of continuing consensus and low party polarization.

CONSOLIDATING THE NEW DEAL FROM WORLD WAR II THROUGH EISENHOWER

From 1939 to the early 1960s only modest movement occurred in expanding the New Deal. Republicans made sizable gains in the 1938 mid-term elections, probably due to worsening economic conditions in 1937–38. Subsequently, an alliance of conservative Republicans and Southern Democrats, called the Conservative Coalition, blocked liberal legislation until the 1960s (Brady 2010; Manley 1973; Patterson 1966). Further limiting expansion of the New Deal were the World War II budgetary demands for funding the military and mobilization effort.

Modest Expansion under President Truman

On April 12, 1945, before the war's end, President Roosevelt died and was succeeded by his vice president, Harry S. Truman. On September 6, 1945, Truman delivered a special message presenting a twenty-one-point proposal attempting to set the postwar political and economic agenda (Truman 1945). The president proposed increasing the minimum wage, expanding the Social Security system, a federal housing program, new public works programs, federal funds for education, a national health insurance program, extension of the Fair Employment Practices Committee, expanding unemployment insurance, and legislation guaranteeing "full employment" for all Americans.

Most of Truman's proposals were dead on arrival in Congress, as the Conservative Coalition remained a potent force. One very important success did occur during Truman's first term. He secured passage of the Employment Act of 1946, placing responsibility for the nation's economy squarely on the president and national government. Truman relied on Keynesian principles in seeking "full employment" for all Americans. However, the final legislation fell short of a guarantee of "full employment" as the president had wanted. Opponents led by Old Guard Republican Senator Robert A. Taft argued that recessions and depressions are a natural product of a free market economy and that compensatory spending should rarely be used (Santoni 1986). Thus, the final bill was a compromise, removing all Keynesian markers (Rosenof 1997).

The law merely encouraged the federal government to "promote maximum employment, production, and purchasing power" (P.L. 79–304). It required the president to submit an Annual Economic Report to Congress. The law mandated a congressional Joint Committee on the Economic Report (later the Joint Economic Committee) to consider presidential recommendations. The legislation also established the Council of Economic Advisers within the White House to advise the president in formulating economic policy. As a result of this legislation (and the 1978 Humphrey–Hawkins Act), the post–World War II economy was no longer the big business capitalism that prevailed from 1789 through 1932 but became a centrally managed market economy.

In the 1946 mid-term elections, Republicans gained control of both houses of Congress for the first time since 1932. The election was largely a referendum on Truman's handling of a wave of postwar labor strikes and price controls (Leuchtenburg 2006). Over the next two years President Truman played defense with respect to the New Deal agenda. He cast 250 vetoes mostly on tax and labor policy, of which twelve were overridden (Senate 2014b). Truman's most significant veto concerned labor policy. Republicans in Congress passed the Taft–Hartley Act of 1947, amending the Wagner Act by limiting the activities and powers of labor unions. Truman vetoed the legislation, providing a litany of reasons the bill was unfair to workers (Truman 1947b). In response, the Republican Congress overrode the president's veto.

The president's veto of the Taft–Hartley bill solidified the president's labor support (Davis 2000, 90). Truman also vetoed two Republican tax cut bills that he believed favored the wealthy (Truman 1947a, 1948). He also rejected a Republican move to increase tariffs on imported wool (Truman 1947c). These positions, combined with a promise to repeal the Taft–Hartley Act, positioned the president as the main defender of the New Deal in the upcoming 1948 presidential election.

In the spring of 1948, Truman's approval ratings dropped as low as 36 percent, and he was not expected to win reelection (Gallup 2014; Hechler and Elsey 2006). Adding to this perception, the vigor with which he advocated civil rights reform split the Democratic Party. A faction led by South Carolina Senator Strom Thurmond walked out of the Democratic National Convention and formed a third political party dubbed the Dixiecrats (McCullough 1992, 525–722). The Dixiecrats carried four Southern states in the 1948 election. However, Truman shrewdly turned the 1948 presidential election into a referendum on the New Deal (Milkis and Nelson 1999, 279). To great surprise, Truman won the 1948 election with Democrats retaking both houses of Congress.

After the election, the president interpreted his victory as a mandate to pursue his program, the Fair Deal. Truman laid out his Fair Deal in the January 5, 1949, State of the Union address (Truman 1949). The proposed measures included federal aid to education, abolition of poll taxes, an anti-lynching law, a permanent Fair Employment Practices Committee, a farm aid program, increased public housing, an immigration bill, new TVA-style public works projects, establishing a Department of Welfare, repeal of the Taft–Hartley Act, an increase in the minimum wage from 40 to 75 cents an hour, national health insurance, expanded Social Security coverage, a large tax cut for low-income earners, and a $4 billion tax increase to finance these programs.

However, the Conservative Coalition remained a potent force limiting the president's ability to enact many of these proposals. Three of the president's Fair Deal proposals became law, but none of those that Neustadt (1954) claimed were the most important. On July 15, 1949, the president signed the Housing Act, which provided financing for urban renewal projects in American cities, increased funding for FHA mortgage insurance, authorized the FHA to extend financing to rural homeowners, and provided money for public housing. This enactment planted a seed that would later grow into a much larger federal role in housing (CQ Almanac Online 1950b). On October 26, 1949, Truman signed minimum wage legislation; the legislation also expanded worker safety protections to young people in industry under the Fair Labor Standards Act of 1938 (CQ Almanac Online 1950a). Finally, on August 28, 1950, the president signed the Social Security Act Amendments, which expanded the coverage of the Social Security system by about ten million recipients (CQ Almanac Online 1951).

President Truman was also determined to do something about racial segregation (Milkis and Nelson 1999, 281). Unable to move his civil rights agenda in Congress, the president turned to executive orders. On July 26, 1948, Truman issued E.O. 9980 creating a Fair Employment Board within the Civil Service Commission to eliminate racial bias in federal hiring. On the same day, he issued E.O. 9981 requiring equal treatment for members of the military. Finally, on December 3, 1951, Truman issued E.O. 10308 creating the Committee on Government Contract Compliance (CGCC, now called the Office of Federal Contract Compliance) within the Department of Labor. The CGCC was to assure compliance by federal contractors with the nondiscrimination provisions of Roosevelt's earlier E.O. 8802 and E.O. 9346. All three executive orders were important milestones to a much more expansive civil rights agenda in the 1960s.

By February 1952, President Truman's public approval had sunk to 22 percent, the lowest of any post–World War II president. He grew increasingly unpopular because of the grinding Korean War, price controls, and allegations of corruption at the Internal Revenue Service (Miller Center 2014). Thus, the prospects for a Democratic victory in the 1952 elections seemed dim.

More Modest Expansion under President Eisenhower

During 1951, President Truman attempted to persuade General Dwight D. Eisenhower to run for president as a Democrat. Many other Democrats assured him that he could win. Eisenhower was initially reluctant to run for president for either party (Mason 2014, 142–45). However, after Old Guard Republican Senator Robert A. Taft announced his presidential candidacy in October 1951, a "draft Eisenhower" movement developed among Republicans. They wanted to persuade Eisenhower to run as a moderate counterbalance to the conservative wing. With some difficulty, Eisenhower won the Republican nomination, and ran as a moderate in 1952 (Miller Center 2014). Eisenhower chose Richard M. Nixon as his vice presidential running mate.

During the campaign, Eisenhower criticized Truman's Fair Deal, but he did not share the extreme views of Old Guard conservative Republicans. Rather, Eisenhower was a moderate who supported many aspects of the New Deal. He sought to preserve individual freedom and the market economy, while providing needed assistance to the unemployed, poor, and elderly. He intended to lead the country "down the middle of the road between the unfettered power of concentrated wealth ... and the unbridled power of statism and partisan interests" (Mason 2014, 143).

A very popular war hero, Eisenhower easily won, carrying 39 states and 55.2 percent of the popular vote. Presidential coattails even brought a small Republican majority to Congress, with the new Senate consisting of 48 Republicans and 46 Democrats, and the new House consisting of 221 Republicans and 213 Democrats. The Republican majority was small and lasted for only one Congress, making major policy change unlikely. The president was also personally opposed to major changes in New Deal programs, and even supported limited expansion (Ambrose 1984, 545–46).

Eisenhower supported an alternative to the New Deal, later dubbed Modern Republicanism (Mason 2014, chapter 5). Modern Republicanism advocated protections for Americans, but was wary of centralizing solutions (Mason 2014, 156). During the unified Republican 83rd Congress of 1953–54, Republicans demonstrated a commitment to the New Deal legacy by enacting legislation expanding Social Security through payment increases, extension to new occupational groups, and a new class of entitlement – the disabled. Other legislation emerging from the 83rd Congress included an omnibus housing bill, extended unemployment coverage, and a more traditional Republican concern, tax reform (Mason 2014, 156–57). However, the tax reforms cut both ways, with reduced taxation of dividend income and acceleration of depreciation write-offs for business, but increased deductions for medical and child care expenses and reduced taxation of retirement income (CQ Almanac Online 1954).

Eisenhower also revived Truman's earlier proposals for Departments of Health and Welfare. On April 11, 1953, he issued Reorganization Plan No. 1 creating the Department of Health, Education, and Welfare (HEW). The president nominated and the Republican Senate confirmed its first Secretary, Texas Democrat Oveta Culp Hobby, director of the Women's Auxiliary Air Corps during the Roosevelt administration. HEW was made responsible for administering existing New Deal programs associated with its namesake.

However, the Republican 83rd Congress did not enact all of the president's proposals. Eisenhower's request that eighteen-year-olds receive the right to vote was denied. Congress also denied Eisenhower's proposal for voluntary, nationally subsidized health insurance. Finally, the Republican Congress stymied the president's proposal revising of the Taft–Hartley Act to make it deserving of the respect of both labor and management (CQ Almanac Online 1954).

Perhaps the most important evidence of Eisenhower's support of New Deal initiatives is the progress made on the American highway system. President Roosevelt had earlier proposed building a federal highway system. However, World War II interrupted these ambitions due to the expense of such a massive public works project. The Federal Aid Highway Act of 1938 directed the chief of the Bureau of Public Roads to study the feasibility of the project (Weingroff 1996). Marginal progress was made on highways through the Federal-Aid Highway Acts of 1944, 1948, 1950, and 1952.

Eisenhower extended these initiatives, proposing expansion of the federal highway system in his 1954 State of the Union address (Eisenhower 1954). The response by the Republican 83rd Congress was a federal expenditure of about $1.9 billion in fiscal 1956 and 1957. However, Eisenhower wanted more. In his 1955 and 1956 State of the Union messages, the president renewed his call for more highway funding (Eisenhower 1955, 1956). Eisenhower biographer Stephen Ambrose wrote, "Of all his domestic programs, Eisenhower's favorite by far was the Interstate System" (Ambrose 1984, 547). As stated later by the president, "More than any single action by the government since the end of the war, this one would change the face of America ... Its impact on the American economy – the jobs it would produce in manufacturing and construction, the rural areas it would open up – was beyond calculation" (Eisenhower 1963, 548–49).

Eisenhower had a good working relationship with Democratic House Speaker Sam Rayburn and Democratic Senate Majority Leader Lyndon Johnson (Collier 1994). Thus, following Eisenhower's lead the Democratic 84th Congress developed and passed the National Interstate and Defense Highways Act of 1956. With an original authorization of $25 billion for the construction of 41,000 miles of the Interstate Highway System over a ten-year period, it was the largest public works project in American history (Weingroff 1996). Eisenhower was, of course, right. The development of the Interstate Highway System changed the face of America, enabling economic expansion, citizen mobility, and work for literally millions of Americans to the present.

Eisenhower's proposals, successful and unsuccessful, demonstrated that the president and many Republicans in Congress were not enemies of the New Deal. Rather, they implicitly endorsed it in recognition of its popularity. Perhaps as a result, President Eisenhower enjoyed higher popularity than any president of the modern era (excluding the abbreviated presidency of John F. Kennedy). His approval ratings averaged 65 percent over his entire term, and fell below 50 percent only twice (Gallup 2014). Eisenhower was reelected in 1956 by a significant margin, with 57.4 percent of the popular vote and carrying 41 states. Nevertheless, congressional elections in 1954, 1956, 1958, and 1960 returned large Democratic majorities to the House and Senate. Those Republicans elected to the House through this period were also more moderate than existing members – an overall shift away from the Republican right (Mason 2014, 154).

Eisenhower's legacy on civil rights was mixed. He appointed five justices to the Supreme Court. All were more liberal than those being replaced (Bailey 2012; Martin et al. 2004; see especially the graphs at Wikipedia 2014d). His first appointment was Chief Justice Earl Warren in September 1953. Warren led the Court through 1969, presiding over a plethora of landmark decisions, including *Brown v. Board of Education* (1954, 347 U.S. 483), desegregating the public schools; *Engel v. Vitale* (1962, 370 U.S. 421), restricting school prayer; *Baker vs Carr* (1962, 369 U.S. 186) and *Reynolds v. Sims* (1964, 377 U.S. 533), securing fairer democratic representation; *Gideon v. Wainwright* (1963, 372 U.S. 335) and *Miranda v. Arizona* (1966, 384 U.S. 436), securing rights for the accused; and *Griswold v. Connecticut* (1965, 381 U.S. 479), securing a constitutional right to privacy, which later became the basis for the Supreme Court's abortion decision in *Roe v. Wade* (1973, 410 U.S. 113).

Some have argued that Chief Justice Warren was more liberal than Eisenhower had wanted, even suggesting that Eisenhower later thought the appointment was a mistake (Ambrose 1984, 189–90). However, the evidence is clear that Eisenhower intended to appoint a more liberal chief justice. As governor of California, Warren had been a progressive Republican who initiated New Deal–style public works projects, built up the state's higher education system, and raised taxes to fund a massive California highway program (Douglass 2000). The president even said that he wanted an experienced jurist who could appeal to liberals in the party, noting privately that Warren "represents the kind of political, economic, and social thinking that I believe we need on the Supreme Court" (Ambrose 1990, 337; Eisenhower 1996, doc. 460).

In addition to Warren, Eisenhower appointed associate justices John Harlan (November 9, 1954), William Brennan (October 15, 1956), Charles Whittaker (March 22, 1957), and Potter Stewart (October 14, 1958). Harlan was the most conservative of the Eisenhower appointees, who nevertheless supported the *Brown* decision and many other Warren Court decisions (Dorsen 2006). Brennan was a liberal Democrat who supported virtually all decisions of the Warren Court (Stern 2010). In between these extremes were Justices Whittaker and Stewart (Ball 2006, 126; Stern 2010, 357). Whittaker was confirmed in the Democratic Senate by unanimous voice vote. However, Stewart was strongly opposed by Southern Democrats, representing all ballots cast against him in the Senate confirmation vote (Poole 2014).

While it is clear that Eisenhower intended to shift the Court in a liberal direction, he did not publicly support civil rights reform. Ambrose wrote

"Although Eisenhower personally wished the Court had upheld *Plessy v. Ferguson*, and said so on a number of occasions (but only in private), he was impressed by the 9 to 0 vote and he certainly was going to meet his responsibility and enforce the law ... What hurt was not Eisenhower's private disapproval of *Brown*, but his refusal to give it a public endorsement ... Even as violence flared across the South, as the implementation of desegregation began, Eisenhower refused to ever say that he thought segregation was morally wrong." (Ambrose 1984, 190–91; see also Ambrose 1990, 368, 542–43).

In September 1957, Eisenhower was forced to act on civil rights after the Court ordered the desegregation of public schools in Little Rock, Arkansas, and Governor Orville Faubus resisted the order by mobilizing the National Guard to prevent black children from entering Central High School. Eisenhower sent the 101st Airborne Division to Little Rock to enforce the Court's order (Ambrose 1990, 447–48). The images of armed troops escorting nine young African-Americans into Central High School highlighted the desegregation issue to the entire nation. As expressed by Packard (2003, 257), it was "a real-life passion play instantaneously being broadcast into millions of homes via the shiny new medium of television."

Later that year, Congress passed and the president signed the Civil Rights Act of 1957 providing federal protection for voting rights, especially in Southern states where literacy tests, poll taxes, and other obstacles had prevented blacks from voting for almost a century. Finally, Eisenhower signed the Civil Rights Act of 1960, providing small advances over the 1957 legislation by expanding the authority of federal judges to protect voting rights and requiring local authorities to maintain comprehensive voting records for review. Still, these measures were only token actions that failed to address the larger problem of segregated public facilities and schools.

THE IMPACT OF THE NEW DEAL AND WORLD WAR II ON POSTWAR AMERICA

The New Deal, World War II, and its modest expansion through 1960 brought dramatic changes in American society. The market economy became more stable after 1933, relative to any earlier period of American history. A burgeoning middle class emerged as a result of New Deal and subsequent programs, reducing America's class bias. Many people became more optimistic about achieving "the good life," as incomes increased and they were able to purchase homes, automobiles, televisions, and a better education for themselves and their children. Almost everyone was better off as a result of the New Deal reforms, even the patrician class.

While most were better off, not everyone was well off. Poverty and inequality remained very high by 1960, especially among the nonwhite population, female heads of household, the elderly, in the South, and within inner cities. There was also an urban-rural dimension to poverty (Bernstein 1991, 17–20).

Greater Macroeconomic Stability

Evidence that the American macro economy became more stable after the New Deal and its extensions is straightforward. Figure 5.1 reports annual U.S. economic growth, measured as percent change in GDP, from 1790 through 2012. Figure 5.2 reports the annual inflation/deflation rate, measured as the percent change in consumer prices, over the same time frame. A solid vertical line at 1933 marks the break point for the New Deal reforms. The shaded areas are periods of economic recession.

Figure 5.1 shows that before 1933 annual economic growth was negative far more often and for longer periods than after 1933. The economy experienced thirty-five financial panics, recessions, and depressions from 1790 through 1932. Excepting the years 1794 and 1795, all periods of exceptional economic growth before 1933 were due to wars. All periods of extraordinary economic decline were due to bursting speculative bubbles, financial panics, government policies favoring the wealthy (e.g., movement to the gold standard in 1873), or the aftermath of wars (Moore and Zarnowitz 1986; Zarnowitz 1996, 220–30). After 1933, economic declines were far less volatile and intense. As discussed in Chapter 4, economic growth was phenomenal during World War II. Figure 5.1 shows that economic growth became increasingly steady after the war. Only nine recessions occurred between 1945 and 2012, most relatively mild. The one exception was the 2008 financial crisis, which, like many before 1933, was due to banker and financier misbehavior.

Figure 5.2 shows greater macroeconomic stability after 1933 reflected through inflation/deflation. Again excepting the years 1794 and 1795, all periods of very high inflation before 1933 were due to wars. Between 1790 and 1933, deflation was common. Since 1933, the economy has rarely seen deflation. As explained in Chapters 3 and 4, deflation benefits the creditor class and harms debtors and commodity producers such as farmers. Indeed, deflation and adherence to the gold standard after 1873 was a major source of class conflict from the nineteenth century to the Great Depression. Favoring the debtor class, Roosevelt removed the nation from the Gold Standard in 1933 (later restoring it in 1935). The post–World War II era has been one of steadily rising prices, creating an incentive to invest, rather than to save and hoard.

Note also in Figures 5.1 and 5.2 the differential duration of recessions before and after 1933. The NBER measures recessions and expansions monthly back to 1854 (NBER 2014a). From 1854 to 1919 the average recession lasted 22 months, and the average expansion lasted 27 months. From 1919 to 1945, the average recession lasted about 18 months, and the average expansion lasted 35 months. Of course, the Great Depression was much longer, with an official dating of 43 months. From 1945 to 2012, the NBER reports the average recession lasted just 11 months, and the average expansion lasted 58 months.

Why are these changes important? Recessions create monetary winners and losers by shifting assets across economic classes. Those with greater wealth

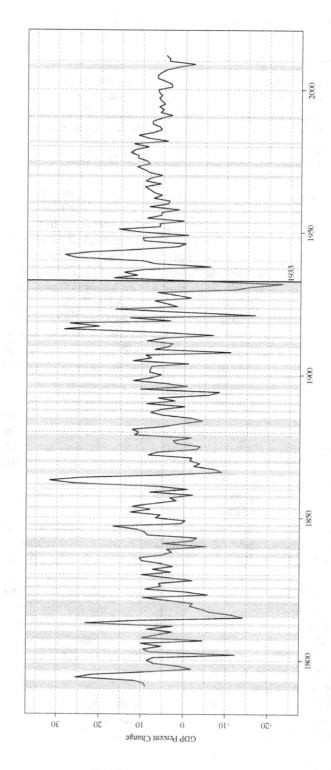

FIGURE 5.1 U.S. Economic Growth, 1790–2012

Source: Data from www.measuringworth.com/usgdp/ (Williamson 2014). Shaded areas show economic recessions. Recession dates before 1854 are from Thorp (1926, 107–145) and after 1854 from NBER (2014a).

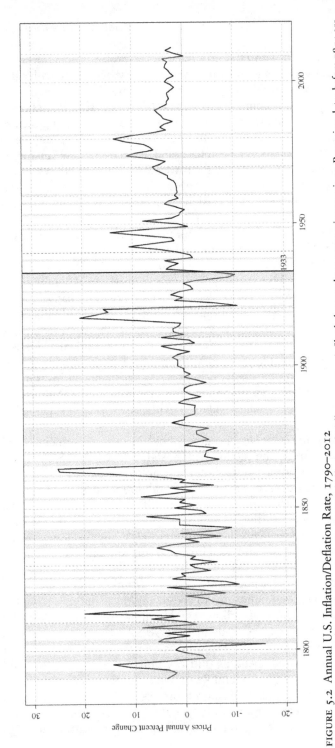

FIGURE 5.2 Annual U.S. Inflation/Deflation Rate, 1790–2012

Source: Data from www.measuringworth.com/inflation/ (Officer and Williamson 2014). Shaded areas show economic recessions. Recession dates before 1854 are from Thorp (1926) and after 1854 from NBER (2014a).

are better able to withstand economic downturns, and may even benefit from them. Those with less wealth are proportionately less able to withstand economic downturns, often resulting in bankruptcies, foreclosures, unemployment, and generally poor economic outcomes for the masses. Recessions and their associated deflation advantage wealthy individuals by making their assets more valuable, enabling them to buy commodities, labor, and properties at tremendous discounts. Bankruptcies and foreclosures are an opportunity for those at the top to multiply their wealth. Large enterprises also benefit by eliminating weaker competitors or absorbing them, thereby increasing their size. Thus, the overall result of recession or depression is a transfer of assets across economic classes.

Three factors explain the lower frequency and shorter duration of recessions after 1933. First, stabilization of the banking system made financial panics less likely, as depositors recognized their money was safe. Regulation of the financial sector through the Banking Act of 1933, the Federal Securities Act of 1933, and the Securities Exchange Act of 1934 made speculative misbehavior by bankers and financial institutions less likely. As described in Chapter 2, financial misbehavior and panics were occurring in the United States as early as 1792, when William Duer, Alexander Macomb, and the Livingston family attempted to manipulate shares in the public debt. As described in Chapters 3 and 4, speculation by the wealthy, banks, and financial institutions was also a major factor in the 1929 stock market crash and Great Depression. The New Deal reforms regulated speculation with other people's money, making it less likely.

Second, some New Deal programs implemented the principles of Keynesian economics to make the economy more stable. The Social Security Act of 1935 and postwar expansions established unemployment and social welfare benefits. Both programs operate as automatic stabilizers on the economy. When the economy is in decline, unemployment and welfare benefits increase, thereby pumping money into the economy. When the economy is robust, unemployment and welfare benefits decline, thereby reducing government expenditures. Thus, unemployment and welfare programs smooth out fluctuations in the business cycle.

Finally, the increasing centralization of macroeconomic policymaking since 1946 has been important to stabilizing the economy. Since the Employment Act of 1946, and subsequent Humphrey–Hawkins Act of 1978, the president, Congress, and Federal Reserve System have been responsible for the health of the economy. From Roosevelt through Obama, presidents and Congress have used spending and tax policy to address economic declines. Equally important, the Federal Reserve has become increasingly sophisticated in using monetary policy to smooth the ups and downs of the business cycle. Thus, the U.S. economy is no longer the business-friendly market economy that existed from 1789 through 1932, but is now a centrally managed market economy.

The Expanding Middle Class

Greater macroeconomic stability after the New Deal produced an environment in which more citizens could thrive, rather than scramble for the bare necessities of life. For this and other reasons, the postwar period experienced strong growth. U.S. GDP jumped from about $228 billion in 1946 to about $543 billion in 1960, an average growth rate of about 9.2 percent annually (Bureau of Economic Analysis 2014b). Annual personal incomes also rose sharply between 1946 and 1960 from about $1,292 per capita to about $2,338, a growth of about 5.4 percent annually (Bureau of Economic Analysis 2014e).

Economic stability, growth in the economy, and higher personal incomes had manifestations for the middle class. One manifestation was the strong demand for new homes, especially from returning GIs starting families after the war. As noted in Chapter 4, various government programs facilitated home ownership. The National Housing Act of 1934 enabled citizens to obtain risk-free FHA loans guaranteed by the federal government. The GI Bill provided easily affordable mortgages, loan guarantees, and incentives to returning veterans. The government promoted robust savings during the war through the War Bond program, resulting in pent-up capital. As a result, home ownership in the United States shot upward between 1940 and 1960. Decennial census data show that owner-occupied dwellings increased from about 44 percent in 1940 to about 62 percent in 1960 (Bureau of the Census 1940, 1960). Considering this change in terms of the number of new owner-occupied dwellings, it shifted from about 15.2 million in 1940 to about 33 million in 1960, almost doubling (Fetter 2014).

Another manifestation of the postwar economic boom was a more educated population. As noted in the previous chapter, the GI Bill provided returning war veterans with a significant education benefit. Millions took advantage. Families also wanted more for their children, and "baby boomers" were expected to pursue an education. In 1940 only about 38 percent of the U.S. population had a high school diploma; by 1960 that number had increased to around 65 percent. This trend continued to present, leveling off at between 85 and 90 percent (Bureau of the Census 2014a). In 1940 only 5.9 percent of Americans had a college education; by 1960 the number had more than doubled to around 13 percent. This trend continued to present, with about a third of the U.S. population over 25 currently having a college education (Bureau of the Census 2014a). The rising postwar educational attainment of Americans accelerated the rate of economic growth, expanded the middle class, and reduced economic inequality.

Another manifestation of growing middle-class affluence between 1945 and 1960 was an increase in the number of automobiles. The number of automobiles produced by American automakers quadrupled between 1946 and 1955 (Department of State 2014). Increased production provided literally millions of

American jobs, and a very powerful industrial sector. By 1960, 72 percent of households owned an automobile (Bernstein 1991, 21). The number of registered automobiles increased from about 31 million in 1945 to almost 74 million in 1960, a growth of almost 140 percent (Federal Highway Administration 2014).

The increase in automobile ownership had several side effects. It altered the lifestyle of most Americans from a local to a global character. Automobiles enabled moving about more freely, leading to a sense of affluence and freedom. The increase in automobile ownership also increased people's demand for better roads and highways. Accordingly, the Highway Act of 1956 resulted in the construction of more than 41,000 miles of federal roads linking all parts of the nation. People were no longer restricted to cities. The transportation revolution enabled people to live further from work and to migrate more readily to suburbs or across the country, producing a more broadly dispersed population. In response to middle-class demand, the housing industry shifted production from concentrated urban areas to suburban developments. As suburbs grew, businesses moved into the new areas and out of old areas. The number of shopping centers in the United States rose from eight at the end of World War II to 3,840 in 1960 (Department of State 2014).

Another manifestation of increased middle-class affluence between 1945 and 1960 was the spread of television. In 1950, fewer than 10 percent of American households had a television. By 1955, the number had increased to 64.5 percent; by 1960 it had increased to 87.1 percent; after 1960 the number of households with television finally saturated at around 98 percent (TV history. TV 2014). Television brought the nation and world into people's homes and became the most important medium for molding public attitudes.

"The power of television to sell opinion and products was not lost on American politicians, journalists, and business leaders" (Diggs-Brown 2011, 52). Broadcast news drew the world closer in vivid depiction. Further, television commercials became an effective and popular method for selling consumer goods. Television drove people's wants, resulting in an increase in what people thought they needed. The resulting consumer revolution produced a vast expansion in the range of products manufactured, sold, and purchased in the United States (Bernstein 1991, 21). Hence, television not only affected the middle class, but also spurred a broader commercial expansion.

The Groups Left Behind

While most were better off with the postwar economic expansion, a significant proportion of the American population lagged behind. In 1960, poverty and inequality were very high for the nonwhite population, female heads of household, the elderly, in the South, and within inner cities (Katz and Stern 2001). The 1940 census, conducted near the end of the depression, showed that about 42.5 percent of Americans lived in poverty. By 1960, that number had dropped to around 21 percent, or about one-fifth of the total population. Nevertheless, the total number of people in poverty was almost 40 million (DeNavas-Walt et al. 2013, table B-1). Obviously, the postwar economic boom did not bring economic security to all Americans.

Poverty was far greater among the nonwhite segment of the population. Figure 5.3 shows poverty rates in census years from 1940 through 1960 for white, black, and Latino Americans (Katz and Stern 2001). The poverty rate for whites dropped from 38.6 percent in 1940 to 16.5 percent in 1960. The Census Bureau's Current Population Reports (DeNavas-Walt et al. 2013, table B-1) shows that the total number of whites living in poverty in 1960 was about 28 million.

The poverty rates for blacks and Latinos in 1940 were an astounding 75.4 and 69.6 percent, respectively. By 1960, the poverty rates for these groups had declined to a still astounding 54.9 and 43.2 percent. The Census Bureau's Current Population Reports (DeNavas-Walt et al. 2013, table B-1) shows about ten million blacks and seventeen million Hispanics (overlapping with black) were in poverty. Thus, the percentage of African-Americans and Hispanics living in miserable conditions had declined by 1960, but was still much higher than for the white population. Predictably, high poverty among blacks and Hispanics instilled anger and resentment toward the dominant white society.

Poverty was even higher for female-headed households through this period. Without a male income earner, women and children were hugely disadvantaged. Figure 5.4 reports the poverty rates for white, black, and Latino female householders for decennial censuses from 1940 through 1960. The 1940 poverty rate for white female householders was 58.7 percent. This number had declined to 41.5 percent by 1960. Compared with the overall white poverty rate of 16.5 percent in 1960, this result implies a significant disadvantage for living in a home where there was not a white male income earner.

The situation was far worse for black and Latino female householders. The 1940 poverty rates for black and Hispanic female householders were a startling

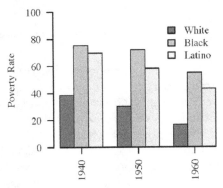

FIGURE 5.3 White, Black, and Latino Poverty
Source: Decennial censuses with pre-1960 data extrapolated by Katz and Stern (2001).

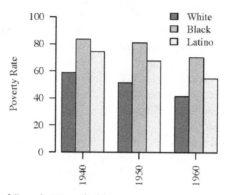

FIGURE 5.4 Poverty of Female Householders
Source: Decennial censuses with pre-1960 data extrapolated by Katz and Stern (2001).

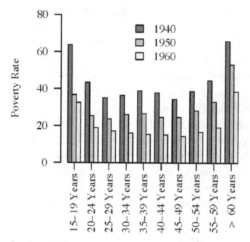

FIGURE 5.5 Poverty by Age Cohort
Source: Decennial censuses with pre-1960 data extrapolated by Katz and Stern (2001).

83.6 percent and 74.5 percent, respectively. By 1960, these numbers had dropped to a still startling 70.2 and 54.7 percent for the two groups. Compared with the overall poverty rates in 1960 for blacks and Latinos of 54.9 and 43.2 percent, this result again implies a significant disadvantage for living in a home where there was not a male income earner.

Another way of dissecting the poverty rate is to consider the data by age cohort for census data from 1940 through 1960. Figure 5.5 shows the poverty rates by age cohort for each census. Poverty was lowest for all three censuses in the prime earning years of 25 through 55 years old. Poverty was highest in the low earning years of 15 through 25 and in the lower earning years of 55 through death. Of course, the young end remedies itself with the progression of time as workers age to gain more education and skills. However, the highest age cohort is problematic from a public policy standpoint. After 55, workers become less desirable to employers and may be the target of age discrimination. Older workers also have greater health needs.

The geographic distribution of poverty is another important dimension. Figure 5.6A graphs the distribution of poverty by whether individuals lived in rural, central city, or suburban areas (Katz and Stern 2001). The graph shows that the 1940 poverty rate was highest in rural areas at almost 60 percent. By 1960, the rural poverty rate remained high at about 30 percent. Much of this decline in rural poverty was due to individuals moving from farms to cities and suburbs after World War II.

Figure 5.6A also shows that the 1940 poverty rate in central cities and suburbs was about equal at 30 percent. However, the poverty rate in central cities and suburbs had diverged by 1960. The central city poverty rate was 17.1 percent, while the suburban poverty rate was only 11.5 percent. This disparity probably reflects the flight of the middle class away from central cities to the suburbs, enabled by highways, automobiles, and business translocation. Increased segregation occurred as a result of middle-class flight away from central cities. That segregation was both racial and economic, as those who were unable economically to move remained in the cities. Businesses moved out of inner cities, giving the remaining residents fewer jobs and economic opportunities. Urban tax bases depreciated, due to the lower wealth and income of remaining residents. Reduced tax bases resulted in urban decay and decreased governmental services. Poverty became increasingly concentrated in inner cities, with many of the remaining residents nonwhite, living in slums, and angry (Bernstein 1991, 17–20).

Finally, Figure 5.6B graphs the geographic distribution of poverty in the United States by region from the 1940 through 1960 censuses (Stern 1991). The 1940 poverty rate was lowest for Northern whites at about 37 percent. By 1960, the Northern white poverty rate had declined to about 15.7 percent. The poverty rate for Southern whites in 1940 was 52.6 percent, but had only declined to 31.7 percent by 1960. Of course, this disparity suggests the depressed state of economic development in the South relative to the North.

The 1940 poverty rate for Northern blacks was 55.6 percent, while that for Southern blacks was an astounding 84.6 percent. By 1960, the poverty rate for Northern blacks had declined to 31.7 percent, while that for Southern blacks remained a shocking 62.4 percent. One can speculate that some of this differential was due to the lack of good jobs in the South, as with the disparity between Northern and Southern whites. However, another potential explanation is that Southern blacks were subject to racial discrimination, and systematically excluded from high skill, high paying jobs.

The evidence in this section concerning who was left behind in the post–World War II economic boom points the direction of New Deal expansions in the 1960s and 1970s. In 1960, poverty was widespread, and racial, ethnic, gender, and age discrimination were rampant in America. Anger was high

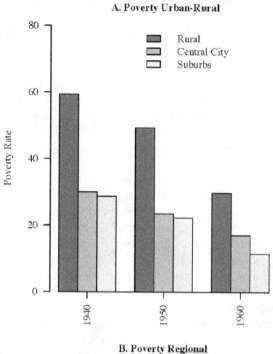

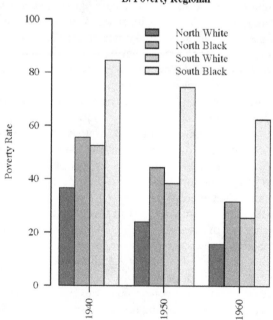

FIGURE 5.6 Geographic Distribution of Poverty
Source: Decennial censuses with pre-1960 data extrapolated by Katz and Stern (2001) and Stern (1991).

among those subject to these conditions. As a result, social unrest increased from the mid-1950s through the 1960s (e.g., see Wikipedia 2014f). Made increasingly sensitive to these conditions by television, many citizens came to view these conditions as unacceptable.

EXPANDING THE NEW DEAL FROM THE NEW FRONTIER THROUGH THE GREAT SOCIETY

The 1960s started with what seemed likely to be more of the same. The Democrats held a large majority in Congress with roughly 65 percent of both chambers. However, many of those Democrats were members of the Conservative Coalition. Given the composition of Congress, it was unlikely that the presidential election of 1960 could produce a mandate for addressing the serious problems of race, inequality, poverty, and social injustice in America.

The Inspirational Leadership of John F. Kennedy

The liberal wing of the Democratic Party heavily endorsed John F. Kennedy for the 1960 presidential nomination (Schlesinger 1965, 26–32). Kennedy was young and Roman Catholic, both of which worked against him in the early 1960s. Against the wishes of liberals, Kennedy chose Lyndon Baines Johnson, the Senate Majority Leader from Texas, to be his vice presidential running mate. Kennedy wanted to pursue a progressive agenda, but knew he needed to carry the South and would have to contend with Southern opposition in Congress (Schlesinger 1965, 45–50).

Republicans nominated Eisenhower's vice president Richard M. Nixon to carry their presidential banner. As the candidate of Modern Republicanism with experience, he represented a continuation of the restrained Republican policies of the 1940s and 1950s.

The election was a dead heat, with Kennedy receiving 49.7 percent of the popular vote and Nixon receiving 49.6 percent. The electoral vote outcome was controversial, because a shift of only 9,000 votes in Illinois and 23,000 votes in Texas would have swung the electoral vote to Nixon. Republicans claimed extensive voter fraud in both states. Nevertheless, the presidential election was certified in both states (Posner 2000).

The congressional elections were also indecisive. Unusually for a presidential election, Kennedy had no legislative coattails. Republicans actually gained two seats in the Senate and 22 seats in the House of Representatives. The Democratic majority in both chambers remained intact at 262–175 for the House and 64–36 for the Senate. However, the congressional election was not a mandate for change. The Conservative Coalition remained strong after the election. Thus, Kennedy would need help for any significant expansion of the New Deal.

Despite the absence of a mandate, Kennedy had asked Americans in his Los Angeles nomination acceptance speech to be pioneers for a New Frontier. He touted a "frontier [of] uncharted areas of science and space, unsolved problems of peace and war, unconquered problems of ignorance and prejudice, unanswered questions of poverty and surplus" (Kennedy 1960). He later called for the United States to put a man on the moon by 1970, address problems of poverty, end racial discrimination, protect the environment, conserve wilderness areas, and provide public funding for the arts.

At the presidential inauguration, the contrast between the outgoing and incoming presidents could not have been starker. Eisenhower was the oldest man to occupy the White House, and the last president born in the nineteenth century; at 43, Kennedy was the youngest man elected to the presidency. Eisenhower had grandchildren; Kennedy had a young wife, a three-year-old daughter, and an infant son. Eisenhower had been reluctant to take on divisive causes; Kennedy wanted to be a leader at the center of action.

In his inaugural address Kennedy stated that "the torch has been passed to a new generation of Americans – born in this century, tempered by war, disciplined by a hard and bitter peace, proud of our ancient heritage – and unwilling to witness or permit the slow undoing of those human rights to which this nation has always been committed ... And so, my fellow Americans: ask not what your country can do for you – ask what you can do for your country" (Kennedy 1961).

After the inauguration, Kennedy enjoyed enormous popular support. His first post-inaugural Gallup approval poll was 72 percent, a bump from the election outcome of over 20 percent. His public approval continued at this high level throughout his presidency, averaging 70.1 percent and never dropping below 56 percent. Kennedy was the most popular post–World War II president (Gallup 2014). Armed with this popularity and charisma, Kennedy sought to move the nation into a new era of space exploration, world peace, and social justice. He accomplished a start, but that start was ominously incomplete when his presidency abruptly ended.

After the election, Kennedy confronted the most conservative Congress since 1953–54. The balance of power had swung to the Conservative Coalition, which had blocked progressive legislation since the late 1930s (Sorensen 1965, 340). Nevertheless, Kennedy actively sought to shape the legislative agenda (Hall 1962). He proposed a variety of initiatives, including a volunteer Peace Corps to assist underdeveloped countries, a Medicare program, a program to combat intellectual disabilities, federal aid to education, raising the minimum wage and broadening its coverage, raising Social Security benefits, improved housing, creation of a department of urban affairs, and expanded power for the federal government to deal with recession (Kennedy 1961).

Kennedy's most significant legislative proposals were not adopted. He established the Peace Corps by executive order, even before seeking enabling legislation, with the result that it was in full operation by the time legislation passed six months later (Sorensen 1965, 347). Social Security benefits were increased, as was the minimum wage. The Housing Act of 1961 provided funding for new housing, housing for the elderly and low-income families, and urban renewal. Kennedy entered office in the midst of a recession. In response, the president proposed and Congress passed the Area Redevelopment Act (ARA) of 1961 and the Manpower Development and Training Act (MDTA) of 1962. The ARA provided training for unemployed workers in areas of serious unemployment, especially the Appalachian region. MDTA was a broader law that applied to the unemployed and underemployed generally. However, the 87th Congress denied Kennedy's proposals for federal aid to education, creating a department of urban affairs, mental retardation, and Medicare (CQ Almanac Online 1961, 1962).

Kennedy's Special Counsel Theodore Sorensen (1965, 342) wrote, "Of all his narrow losses, the most discouraging to Kennedy was the defeat of his 'Medicare' bill – the long-sought plan enabling American working men and women to contribute to their own old-age health insurance program under Social Security instead of forcing them, once their jobs and savings were gone, to fall back on public or private charity." Kennedy was also very disappointed about education. From the start and throughout his presidency, "[education was] the one domestic subject that mattered most to John Kennedy ... Throughout his campaign and throughout his presidency, he devoted more time and talks to this single topic than to any other domestic issue" (Sorensen 1965, 358). Yet he was unable to get any movement from Congress on aid to education.

The 1962 mid-term elections produced little change in Congress. The Democrats picked up three seats in the Senate but lost three seats in the House. Thus, the 88th Congress offered little advantage for Kennedy in pursuing a progressive agenda. Nevertheless, Kennedy persisted. He proposed and Congress passed the Equal Pay Act of 1963, which aimed to eliminate pay discrimination based on gender. In October 1963, Congress passed the Community Mental Health Centers Act and Mental Retardation Facilities Construction Act (CQ Almanac Online 1963).

At the start of 1963, the economy remained sluggish, and the president proposed a Keynesian tax cut to get things moving. The House of Representatives passed the tax bill on September 25, 1963. However, conservative West Virginia Democratic Senator Robert Byrd showed every intention of dragging out hearings before the Senate Finance Committee (Schlesinger 1965, 1005).

The president also intended to propose an anti-poverty program after his tax proposal was passed (Schlesinger 1965, 1011–12). In November 1963, President Kennedy remarked to his advisor Joseph Schlesinger Jr., "The time has come to organize a national assault on the causes of poverty, a comprehensive program across the board" that would be the centerpiece in his 1964 legislative recommendations (Schlesinger 1965, 1012).

President Kennedy's most significant proposal to the 88th Congress was for civil rights legislation. While he had been supportive from the start of the civil rights movement and had made specific promises to movement leaders,

Kennedy had been slow to move on the issue. However, the issue threatened to explode by the spring of 1963. As discussed in the previous section, the black community was experiencing vicious poverty, especially in the inner cities and South. Black inequality persisted in schools, jobs, voting, and public facilities. Federal action had to occur, or risk revolutionary violence and civil unrest (Shank 1980, 174–210).

The story of the civil rights movement and President Kennedy involves numerous details that cannot be delineated here (but see Schlesinger 1965, chapters 35, 36). However, most analyses focus on a single event as critical in spurring presidential action: the Birmingham campaign starting in early May 1963. Martin Luther King Jr. was jailed, and wrote his famous essay "Letter from Birmingham Jail" during this time. On being freed from jail on bail, King launched a Birmingham children's crusade. The movement recruited schoolchildren to continue the demonstrations after many participants were locked up or had left. With jails full, the Birmingham police, under the direction of Eugene "Bull" Connor, decided to keep people out of the downtown area using physical violence. The police turned fire hoses on the schoolchildren, used police dogs to deter their movement, and generally used brutality to curb peaceful demonstrations.

These events were televised nationally and significantly affected media attention and public opinion (Bass 2001, 3). *New York Times* stories on race relations jumped from 332 in the calendar quarter immediately before the Birmingham campaign to almost 1,000 during the quarter of the campaign (Wood and Huss 2008). The images produced by the news media were graphic, vividly showing the nature of the repressive regime that maintained segregation in the South. Before Birmingham only 4 percent of Americans viewed race relations as the most important problem facing the nation; by September 1963 that number had grown to 52 percent (Wood and Huss 2008).

The Birmingham campaign has been identified as the stimulus causing President Kennedy to finally propose civil rights legislation after two years of what some perceived as stalling (i.e., see Beschloss 2007, 261–66; Carson 1998, 120; Wood and Huss 2008). In a nationally televised speech on June 11, 1963, the president condemned the failure of the American system to live up to promises of equality extending from beginning of the republic. He said, "We preach freedom around the world, and we mean it, and we cherish our freedom here at home, but are we to say to the world, and much more importantly, to each other that this is a land of the free except for the Negroes...?" (Kennedy 1963a). Kennedy then proposed sweeping changes to desegregate public education and facilities in the United States. The legislation was delivered to Congress on June 19, 1963.

Martin Luther King Jr. and other civil rights leaders subsequently pressured the president for full support of the legislation. They orchestrated the March on Washington for Jobs and Freedom. On August 28, 1963, about 250,000 demonstrators gathered on the Washington Mall. Martin Luther King delivered his famous "I have a dream" speech at this event. Nielson reported that television viewership of the March on Washington was 46 percent higher than was typical during daylight hours (Adams 1963).

The president's proposed legislation was sent to the House of Representatives and referred to the House Judiciary Committee. After a series of hearings on the bill, the committee strengthened the act following the bombing of a church in Birmingham killing four little black girls. The Judiciary Committee reported legislation out on November 20, but it needed to clear the House Rules Committee to proceed to a floor vote. However, the Rules Committee chairman indicated his intention to keep the bill bottled up indefinitely (Bernstein 1991, 107–13).

On November 22, 1963, President Kennedy was assassinated. His agenda for civil rights was incomplete, as were those for eradicating poverty, revitalizing the American economy, and putting a man on the moon. However, his ideas became the subsequent basis for major expansions of the New Deal social contract.

Many have judged Kennedy's performance relative to Congress negatively (e.g., see Fairlie 1973, 1; Heath 1975, 163; McConnell 1967, 45; Miroff 1976, 272; Parmet 1983, 353; Shank 1980, 263). Others using quantitative data have rated his performance more positively (Bernstein 1991, 292–94; Edwards 1989, 18; Sundquist 1968, 481–89). Whichever analysis one accepts, Kennedy's influence on American politics grew in his death, and became even greater as the nation unified around its fallen leader and his agenda. As stated by Sorenson (1965, 757), "history will remember John Kennedy for what he started as well as for what he completed. The forces he released in this world will be felt for generations to come. The standards he set, the goals he outlined and the talented men he attracted to politics and public service will influence his country's course for at least a decade." Sorenson was undoubtedly correct in this assessment.

Lyndon Baines Johnson and the Great Society

Kennedy's death was a huge trauma to the nation and world. Most Americans who lived through these times know precisely where they were when news came of the Kennedy assassination. It was the first crisis in American history receiving round-the-clock electronic media coverage. Graphic scenes of the assassination were broadcast continuously on television. The flag-draped coffin and funeral procession burned an indelible image into the American psyche. People from around the world mourned the fallen president (Doherty 2014; Schlesinger 1965, 1027–31).

Only hours after the assassination, Vice President Lyndon Baines Johnson was sworn in as president aboard Air Force One as it departed Dallas for Washington with the fallen president's body. American broadcasters immediately referred to him as "President Johnson"(Doherty 2014). Johnson was deeply affected by the president's death, and determined to carry out the president's agenda. In this regard, he benefited enormously from a surge of national unity in the coming years.

President Johnson's approval ratings rose even higher than Kennedy's had been when he was assassinated. The first Gallup public approval poll after the assassination showed his initial approval at 78 percent, an increase of about 20 percent over the last poll for the deceased president (Gallup 2014). Johnson's average public approval between December 1963 and November 1964 was 74.2 percent, roughly 4 percent higher than Kennedy's average (Gallup 2014). Also revealing is the partisan breakdown of Johnson's approval over this period. In the first poll after the assassination, precisely 78 percent of Republicans approved of the new president. Republican approval of President Johnson's job performance remained above 50 percent until July of the election year (Gallup 2014).

Within this environment of high presidential popularity and sympathetic media coverage, Johnson used his momentum to quickly accomplish and expand Kennedy's agenda. Speaking with his speechwriter Richard Goodwin and top aide Bill Moyers, he said, "I never thought I'd have the power ... I wanted power to use it. And I'm going to use it ... We've got to use the Kennedy program as a springboard to take on the Congress, summon the states to new heights, create a Johnson program, different in tone, fighting and aggressive" (Goodwin 1995, 270).

Following through, in his January 8, 1964, State of the Union address the president outlined his agenda: "Let this session of Congress be known as the session which did more for civil rights than the last hundred sessions combined; ... enacted the most far-reaching tax cut of our time; ... declared all-out war on human poverty and unemployment in these United States; ... finally recognized the health needs of all our older citizens; ... reformed our tangled transportation and transit policies; ... and as the session which helped to build more homes, more schools, more libraries, and more hospitals than any single session of Congress in the history of our Republic ... Let us carry forward the plans and programs of John Fitzgerald Kennedy – not because of our sorrow or sympathy, but because they are right" (Johnson 1964a).

Later, speaking at the University of Michigan, Johnson first coined the phrase "The Great Society." He told the students, "[W]e have the opportunity to move not only toward the rich society and the powerful society, but upward to the Great Society. The Great Society rests on abundance and liberty for all. It demands an end to poverty and racial injustice, to which we are totally committed in our time" (Johnson 1964b).

Even before the 1964 presidential election, Johnson had accomplished a strong start toward the Great Society. Table 5.1 summarizes Johnson's legislative accomplishments from the time he assumed office through the end of his second term. The same 88th Congress that had denied most of what Kennedy wanted delivered major enactments for Johnson (Sundquist 1968, 481–89). On December 17, 1963, the president signed the Clean Air Act of 1963. The bill

TABLE 5.1 *Laws and Actions during the Lyndon B. Johnson Presidency as Part of the Great Society*

Date	Law or Action	Summary
December 17, 1963	Clean Air Act	The first federal legislation for air pollution control, establishing a program within the U.S. Public Health Service and authorizing research into monitoring and controlling air pollution. It has been amended and strengthened through the years, with the most significant change occurring in 1970.
January 23, 1964	24th Amendment	Proposed by Congress on August 27, 1962, and finally ratified on this date. It banned the poll tax, widely used in Southern states to restrict blacks from voting in federal elections.
February 6, 1964	Tax Reduction Act	Securing the proposed Kennedy tax cut, it reduced the top marginal rate from 91 to 70 percent and the corporate tax rate from 52 to 48 percent, and created a standard deduction for individuals. The legislation is widely credited with spurring significant economic growth for the remainder of the decade and beyond.
July 2, 1964	Civil Rights Act	Landmark legislation that outlawed discrimination based on race, color, religion, sex, or national origin. It also banned discrimination in voting requirements, racial segregation in schools, employment, and public accommodations. Also created the Equal Employment Opportunity Commission (EEOC) to enforce the employment provisions.
July 9, 1964	Urban Mass Transportation Act	Provided initial funding for large-scale urban public or private rail projects to cities and states in the form of matching funds. Reauthorizations through the years have given San Francisco the BART, Washington the Metro, Atlanta MARTA, and cities across America thousands of buses and modernized transit systems.
August 10, 1964	Tonkin Gulf Resolution	A response to the Gulf of Tonkin incident, this authorized the president to use the military without congressional authorization in the

(*continued*)

TABLE 5.1 *(continued)*

Date	Law or Action	Summary
		conflict in Southeast Asia. Widely regarded as the start of U.S. involvement in Vietnam.
August 20, 1964	Economic Opportunity Act	The centerpiece of Johnson's War on Poverty, this established an Office of Economic Opportunity (OEO) to administer a plethora of programs, including Job Corps, Neighborhood Youth Corps, Work Study Program, Project Headstart, Foster Grandparents, Legal Services to the Poor, Community Health Centers, Community Action Programs, Adult Basic Education, and Volunteers in Service to America. The OEO was discontinued during the Reagan administration, but its programs continue. Only the National Youth Corps has ceased operation today.
August 31, 1964	Food Stamp Act	Augmented the War on Poverty by addressing problems of malnutrition and hunger among the 22 percent of Americans then living below the poverty line. Also benefited farmers by enabling them to sell their surplus to the government. Currently, about 47 million persons, almost all living below the poverty line, receive food stamps.
September 3, 1964	Wilderness Act	Created the National Wilderness Preservation System, which preserves designated wilderness areas for future generations.
April 11, 1965	Elementary and Secondary Education Act	Provided financial assistance to local educational agencies for educating children from low-income families. Also provided funds for libraries, textbooks, instructional materials, teacher training, educational research, and to strengthen state departments of education. Reauthorized every five years since initiation.
July 27, 1965	Cigarette Labeling and Advertising Act	Required labeling of tobacco products as dangerous to health and placed regulation of cigarette advertising under the Federal Trade Commission. Also required the Department of Health, Education, and Welfare to study and report the effects of smoking on human health.
July 30, 1965	Social Security Act	Established the Medicare and Medicaid programs under the Social Security System. Medicare provides federal health insurance

Date	Law or Action	Summary
		for the elderly regardless of income or medical history. Medicaid provides health insurance for the poor. Also, the legislation significantly expanded benefits and changed rules to reduce poverty among the elderly.
August 6, 1965	Voting Rights Act	Enforced voting rights guaranteed by the Fourteenth and Fifteenth Amendments to the Constitution. Enabled a mass enfranchisement of racial minorities, especially in the South where they were often excluded from voting through requirements such as literacy tests, poll taxes, property-ownership requirements, and moral character tests.
August 10, 1965	Housing and Urban Development Act	Greatly expanded funding for federal housing, adding new programs to subsidize the elderly, disabled, poor, and veterans. Also provided matching grants to localities for water and sewer facilities, community centers in low-income areas, and urban beautification. A month later the president signed legislation to create the Department of Housing and Urban Development.
September 29, 1965	National Foundation on the Arts and the Humanities Act	Created and funded two new federal agencies, the National Endowment for the Arts and the National Endowment for the Humanities, promoting research, education, preservation, and public programs in the arts and humanities.
October 2, 1965	Water Quality Act	Required states to establish and enforce water quality controls for all interstate waters within their boundaries. Also authorized the federal government to set standards if state standards were too lax.
October 20, 1965	Solid Waste Disposal Act	Amended the Clean Air Act to require environmentally sound methods for disposal of household, municipal, commercial, and industrial waste.
October 20, 1965	Motor Vehicle Air Pollution Control Act	Amended the Clean Air Act to set the first federal vehicle emissions standards, requiring reductions in hydrocarbon, carbon monoxide, and crankcase emissions from new vehicles manufactured after 1968.

(continued)

TABLE 5.1 (*continued*)

Date	Law or Action	Summary
October 22, 1965	Highway Beautification Act	Ladybird Johnson led the effort for this legislation to beautify the nation's highways. It required control of outdoor advertising, including removal of certain billboards and removal or screening of certain junkyards, and encouraged scenic enhancement and roadside development.
November 8, 1965	Higher Education Act	Appropriated funds to support community service and continuing education; library assistance, training, and research; strengthening developing educational institutions; student assistance; teacher programs; and facilities construction. Reauthorized many times, it has become the core program providing financial assistance to the two-thirds of the nation's college students receiving aid.
September 9, 1966	National Traffic and Motor Vehicle Safety Act	Inspired by Ralph Nader's book *Unsafe at Any Speed*, this empowered the federal government to regulate the safety of motor vehicles and roadways. It also created a National Highway Traffic Safety Bureau, later renamed the National Highway Traffic Safety Administration.
October 11, 1966	Child Nutrition Act	A national School Lunch Program had existed since the New Deal and was expanded during the Truman administration. This act established a national School Breakfast Program to provide low-cost or free breakfasts to children in public and nonprofit schools, as well as child care facilities.
October 15, 1966	Department of Transportation Act	Created the Department of Transportation to administer transportation-related programs.
November 3, 1966	Child Protection Act	Granted authority to the Food and Drug Administration to ban hazardous products encountered by children.
November 3, 1966	Demonstration Cities and Metropolitan Development	Also called the Model Cities Program, this authorized experiments in more than 150 American cities to develop new anti-poverty programs and alternative forms of city government. Deemed by conservatives as the most unequivocal failure of the Great Society, the program was terminated in 1974.
November 7, 1967	Public Broadcasting Act	Created the Corporation for Public Broadcasting, which established the Public

Date	Law or Action	Summary
		Broadcasting Service and National Public Radio, networks of television and radio stations, respectively, for the public interest.
December 15, 1967	Age Discrimination in Employment Act	Outlawed employment discrimination against persons 40 years of age or older in hiring, promotion, wages, and termination. It also prohibited mandatory retirement ages for most tenured workers, including college professors. The legislation is enforced by the EEOC.
January 2, 1968	Bilingual Education Act	An amendment to the Elementary and Secondary Education Act, this act provides funds to local school districts to improve the education of students with limited English proficiency.
April 11, 1968	Fair Housing Act	Provides equal housing opportunities for all Americans regardless of race, creed, or national origin by making discrimination in housing a federal crime. Also, it split the depression-era Fannie Mae into two agencies, Fannie Mae and Ginnie Mae, to promote easier home ownership through affordable mortgage programs.
May 29, 1968	Truth in Lending Act	Required creditors to disclose credit terms to borrowers and standardized the manner in which costs associated with borrowing are calculated and disclosed. It continues today to protect consumers against shady credit practices.
July 21, 1968	Aircraft Noise Abatement Act	Required the Federal Aviation Administration to develop and enforce safe standards for aircraft noise control.
October 2, 1968	Wild and Scenic Rivers Act	Initiated protection for rivers designated wild and scenic. Currently there are 156 rivers under this designation managed by the Forest Service, the Park Service, and a few managed by the Bureau of Land Management and the Fish and Wildlife Service.
October 22, 1968	Gun Control Act	A response to the John F. Kennedy, Malcolm X, Martin Luther King Jr., and Robert F. Kennedy assassinations, this act broadly regulates the firearms industry and gun owners. It focuses on regulating interstate commerce in firearms by generally prohibiting interstate firearms transfers except among licensed manufacturers, dealers, and importers.

was inspired by Kennedy's Special Message to Congress on Improving the Nation's Health, delivered on February 7, 1963 (Bell 2013; Kennedy 1963b). The Clean Air Act was the first federal legislation for controlling air pollution in American history and became the basis for later enactments.

On February 6, 1964, President Johnson signed the Kennedy proposed Keynesian tax cut into law. The vote was a consensual 326–83 in the House and 74–19 in the Senate. Many who had earlier opposed the legislation switched their votes after Johnson promised not to ask for a larger budget (Gittinger and Fisher 2004b). The Tax Reduction Act of 1964 is widely credited with spurring economic growth for the remainder of the decade (Barlett 2014).

Johnson also advocated strongly for civil rights legislation. Largely due to his efforts, and those of his vice president, Hubert Humphrey, the Civil Rights Act of 1964 passed both chambers of Congress with bipartisan support. Johnson's proposal easily passed in the House on February 10 by a vote of 290–130. Democrats supported the bill, but there was a sharp regional split. Northern Democrats voted 141–4 in favor, while Southern Democrats voted 11–92 in opposition. Of the 177 Republicans voting, 138 voted for the bill and 34, including 12 Southern Republicans, voted against it (Carmines and Stimson 1981, 41–42).

The civil rights bill faced more serious opposition in the Senate. Under the usual procedure, the bill would have been referred to the Senate Judiciary Committee, chaired by arch-segregationist Senator James Eastland (D-Mississippi). However, this process would have doomed the legislation. Side-stepping the normal process, Senate Majority Leader Mike Mansfield brought the bill directly to the Senate floor on March 9 (Gittinger and Fisher 2004a, 2004b).

At this point, 18 of 22 Southern Democratic senators plus West Virginia Democrat Robert Byrd initiated a filibuster, the longest in Senate history. Debate occurred over 60 days, including 7 Saturdays (Senate 2014a; Whalen and Whalen 1985, 124–48). After a compromise proposed by Illinois Republican Senator Everett Dirksen to gain Western and Midwestern Republican support, a cloture vote successfully ended debate. The cloture vote passed 71–29, with 27 Republicans and 44 Democrats voting to end debate. Only 6 Republicans opposed cloture, including Arizona Senator Barry Goldwater; all Southern Democrats but Texas Senator Ralph Yarborough opposed cloture. Shortly afterward, the Senate passed the bill by a vote of 73–27, and it went to the conference committee. On July 2, 1964, President Johnson signed the Civil Rights Act of 1964 (CQ Almanac Online 1964; Gittinger and Fisher 2004b; Jeong et al. 2009; Loevy 1985).

A week later, President Johnson signed the Urban Mass Transportation Act of 1964, augmenting the Housing Act of 1961 and Highway Act of 1962. The legislation was a direct response to Kennedy's April 5, 1962, Special Message to Congress on Transportation (Kennedy 1962). The purpose of the law was to assist states and localities in developing comprehensive and coordinated transportation systems to better serve metropolitan areas (CQ Almanac Online 1964; Smerk 1965).

On August 20, 1964, Congress passed the Economic Opportunity Act, the centerpiece of Johnson's War on Poverty. The legislation passed on a bipartisan vote of 61–34 in the Senate and 226–185 in the House. Ten Republicans and 11 Southern Democrats voted for the bill in the Senate; 22 Republicans and 60 Southern Democrats voted for the bill in the House. Signing the legislation, President Johnson stated, "Today for the first time in all the history of the human race, a great nation is able to make and is willing to make a commitment to eradicate poverty ... We want to offer the forgotten fifth of our people opportunity and not doles" (CQ Almanac Online 1964; Johnson 1964c).

The Economic Opportunity Act established an Office of Economic Opportunity (OEO), headed by President Kennedy's brother-in-law Sargent Shriver, to supervise numerous anti-poverty programs. The most important were the Job Corps (a domestic analogue to the Peace Corps), a Neighborhood Youth Corps (training for young people in impoverished areas), a Work Study Program (grants and part-time employment for low-income college students), Project Headstart (giving low-income elementary school students an early start), Community Health Centers (neighborhood access to health care), Urban and Rural Community Action programs (against neighborhood poverty), Adult Basic Education (adult reading and writing skills), and Volunteers in Service to America (VISTA) (training volunteers to work with states and communities to combat poverty).

Augmenting the Economic Opportunity Act, Congress also passed the Food Stamp Act of 1964 on August 31 to address problems of malnutrition and hunger. The legislation authorized and made permanent a pilot program initiated by President Kennedy on his first day in office through E.O. 10914. The legislation addressed problems of poverty, while at the same time benefiting farmers who could sell their surplus for distribution to the needy. Rooted in congressional logrolling, the program was attached to a larger appropriation bill that raised price supports for cotton and wheat. The bill was strongly supported by rural representatives who sought to avoid the dismantling of farm subsidies. Thus, the program was rooted as much in farmer self-interest as in a humanitarian desire to help the urban poor (CQ Almanac Online 1964).

The preceding major components of President Johnson's Great Society were enacted before the 1964 election. The public approved overwhelmingly of these initiatives, and Johnson continued to ride a wave of high popularity in the aftermath of the Kennedy assassination and strong economy. Thus, it is likely that no candidate put forward by the Republicans in 1964 could have won.

Perhaps as a sacrificial lamb, Republicans nominated ultra-conservative Arizona Senator Barry M. Goldwater to carry their 1964 presidential banner (O'Brien 1964). Goldwater was from a state with only five electoral votes and was half-Jewish. He had "consistently taken positions nicely calculated to alienate all major voting blocs in the country – labor, the aged, the teachers, the Negroes, the subsidized farmers, all the beneficiaries of the welfare state, the liberal-minded independent voters, and finally, just to make doubly sure, the inhabitants of the entire East Coast" (Alsop 1964, 19).

Goldwater opposed *Brown v. Board of Education* (Goldwater 1960, chapter 4), voted against the Civil Rights Act, all anti-poverty legislation, Kennedy's proposed tax cut, and virtually anything sympathetic to the New Deal. Goldwater was on record as opposing the progressive income tax, favoring selling the TVA, and opposing all farm subsidies, Medicare, the United Nations, a nuclear test ban treaty, and perhaps most damning for the 1964 campaign, even suggesting using nuclear weapons in Southeast Asia (Alsop 1964; Mann 2011, chapter 2).

Cynically, Goldwater's campaign was also the first to adopt the Southern Strategy of seeking white Southern support by appealing to racism against African-Americans (Black and Black 2002, 28–29; Gould 2003, 361–65). Goldwater's strategy failed. As noted earlier, Lyndon Johnson was reelected to the presidency in 1964 by the largest popular vote percentage since 1820.

In terms of the electoral vote, Johnson carried 44 of 50 states, losing only five states in the Deep South and Arizona. More important from the standpoint of expanding the New Deal agenda, the election produced historic Democratic majorities in both the House and Senate. Many Republican congressmen who had endorsed Goldwater were defeated (Goldberg 1997, 232–37). The Democrats picked up 37 House seats and two Senate seats. Both chambers now contained veto-proof majorities of 68–32 in the Senate and 295–140 in the House, and those majorities were highly supportive of the Great Society.

There was a widespread perception of a mandate, and the president wasted no time in putting his mandate to work. Table 5.1 shows significant movement after the 1964 election in pursuing the Great Society. Concerning the War on Poverty, Congress passed the Elementary and Secondary Education Act (ESEA) increasing resources for educating low-income children, as well as education generally. Later, the Bilingual Education Act amended the ESEA to provide money for improving education among non-English-speaking children. The Higher Education Act of 1965 appropriated funds for several purposes, but became the modern vehicle for extending financial assistance to the two-thirds of the nation's college students receiving financial aid. The Child Nutrition Act aimed through the School Breakfast Program to ensure that no child started a school day hungry. The Housing and Urban Development Act addressed housing needs for the poor, elderly, disabled, and veterans, and later institutionalized the means for addressing the nation's housing and urban needs through the Department of Housing and Urban Development (HUD). Finally, Medicare and Medicaid addressed problems of health care among the elderly, as well as impoverished Americans generally (CQ Almanac Online 1965).

Regarding civil rights and equality, the Voting Rights Act of 1965 enfranchised a great mass of new voters, especially in the South, who had previously been excluded from voting (Carmines and Stimson 1981, 49). The Age

Discrimination in Employment Act of 1967 outlawed employment discrimination against older Americans and prohibited mandatory retirement ages for most tenured workers (CQ Almanac Online 1967). The Fair Housing Act of 1968 made it illegal to discriminate in housing on the basis of race, creed, or national origin, thereby increasing integration of the nation's neighborhoods. The legislation also made it easier for Americans to own homes, especially low-income families (CQ Almanac Online 1968).

Regarding environmental protection, the Motor Vehicle Air Pollution Control Act of 1965 amended the Clean Air Act of 1963 to create the first exhaust emissions standards in automobiles. The Solid Waste Disposal Act of 1965 amended the Clean Air Act to regulate dumping of hazardous materials. The Water Quality Act of 1965 became the instrument for securing the safety of the nation's drinking water, cleaning the waterways, and regulating water pollution generally (CQ Almanac Online 1965). And the Aircraft Noise Abatement Act of 1968 regulated noise levels of aircraft, thereby protecting the hearing of workers and those living around airports (CQ Almanac Online 1968).

Concerning new areas of social regulation, the Cigarette Labeling and Advertising Act authorized the Federal Trade Commission to require tobacco producers to place warning labels on their products, and commissioned studies of tobacco-use safety (CQ Almanac Online 1965). The National Traffic and Motor Vehicle Safety Act empowered the federal government to regulate the safety of automobiles and roadways. The Child Protection Act authorized the Food and Drug Administration to regulate the safety of products encountered by children (CQ Almanac Online 1966). The Truth in Lending Act authorized the Federal Reserve Board to regulate terms of credit so as to protect debtors from shady credit practices. Finally, the Gun Control Act of 1968 required firearms dealers and distributors to be licensed, and prohibited the transfer of firearms across state lines by anyone other than licensed dealers (CQ Almanac Online 1968).

Much subsequent Great Society legislation aimed at improving the lives of ordinary Americans. The Wilderness Act of 1964 protects designated wilderness areas for future generations (CQ Almanac Online 1964). The Wild and Scenic Rivers Act of 1968 protects a large number of the nation's rivers from commercial spoliation (CQ Almanac Online 1968). The National Foundation for the Arts and Humanities Act of 1965 created the National Endowment for the Arts and the National Endowment for the Humanities. The purpose of these endowments was to enrich the culture of Americans (CQ Almanac Online 1965). Similarly, the Public Broadcasting Act of 1967 created the Public Broadcasting Service (PBS) and National Public Radio (NPR) to enable millions of Americans to enjoy free and commercial-free television and radio (CQ Almanac Online 1967). Similarly, the Highway Beautification Act of 1965 was intended to make American driving experiences more pleasurable (CQ Almanac Online 1965).

Overall, President Johnson made 252 major legislative requests after his election. Of those requests, Congress approved 226. In 1965, 93 percent of Johnson's proposals were approved; over his entire second term his proposal success rate was 81 percent. By a significant percentage, Lyndon Johnson was the most successful president of the modern era (Edwards 1989, 18). These numbers suggest an extraordinary degree of consensus about the Great Society through the mid-1960s. Further, most of the enactments listed in Table 5.1 continue as programs today, in either original or revised form, and are even taken for granted as part of modern American life.

Ironically, however, the president's appeal and that of his agenda eroded through time. One indicator of this erosion is that the president became less popular. The first poll after the 1965 inauguration showed the president's job approval at 71 percent. Over the next four years his approval declined to a low of around 35 percent in August 1968 (Gallup 2014). Another indicator is the president's party's losses during the midterm congressional elections. In 1966, the Democrats lost four seats in the Senate and 47 seats in the House, leaving their majority smaller in the two respective chambers.

Two social undercurrents were responsible for Johnson's falling approval and the declining appeal of his agenda: the Vietnam War and the perception that race relations had actually gotten worse in the United States. Protests over the Vietnam War became increasingly frequent between 1965 and 1968 (Wikipedia 2014i). These protests sometimes led to violent clashes between police and largely youthful demonstrators. Drugs and civil disobedience permeated the anti-war movement, leading to a mainstream perception of disorder and lawlessness. Highly visible protests occurred at the August 1968 Democratic National Convention. At this nationally televised event, police used dogs, tear gas, and beatings to deter protesters outside the convention hall. The images produced the appearance of Democrats in disarray.

The Vietnam protests also raised the salience of the issue for most Americans. A Gallup poll conducted in July 1968 asked respondents, "What do you think is the most important problem facing this country today?" About 46 percent answered "Vietnam." Another 18 percent answered, "Racial strife – arson, looting, riots, etc.," followed by 13 percent mentioning "civil rights," with an additional 9 percent mentioning "crime." Only about 3 percent mentioned "poverty," with another 1 percent mentioning "slums, urban renewal" (Gallup 1968b). Clearly, the salient issues for the nation during the 1968 presidential election were Vietnam and race relations.

Concerning Vietnam, a widespread belief existed among Americans that President Johnson's foreign policy had failed. A Gallup poll conducted in February 1968 revealed that 58 percent disapproved of the president's handling of Vietnam, with only 32 percent approving. Democrats, Republicans, and Independents shared about equally in this disapproval. The same survey showed that 54 percent of respondents thought that "[t]he U.S. made a mistake sending troops to fight in Vietnam." Among those thinking Vietnam was a mistake, 57 percent were Republicans, 50 percent were Democrats, and 58 percent were Independents (Gallup 1968a; see also Hetherington and Weiler 2009, 27). Thus, while Vietnam was a costly issue for the president, it was not a polarizing issue.

Americans also believed that race relations had gotten worse, even in the presence of Great Society programs promoting equality and nondiscrimination and reducing poverty. This perception flowed from increased racial violence between 1964 and 1968 (Wikipedia 2014a). On July 16, 1964, about two weeks after passage of the Civil Rights Act, a race riot broke out in Harlem. It lasted six days, involved about 4,000 residents, vandalism, widespread looting, and large-scale destruction of property. Race riots also occurred that year in Rochester, NY; Philadelphia; and Jersey City, Paterson, and Elizabeth, NJ, as well as Chicago (Wikipedia 2014h). The next year on August 11, 1965, just days after Congress passed the Voting Rights Act, a race riot started in the South Central Los Angeles neighborhood of Watts. The Watts Riot also lasted six days, but was far more destructive, with about $40 million in property damage, 1,032 people injured, 34 dead, and 3,438 arrested (Martin Luther King Research and Education Institute 2014).

In 1966, a Black Power movement emerged in competition with Martin Luther King Jr.'s pacifist approach. The movement was militant and confrontational. That militancy and confrontation made black dissatisfaction seem far more threatening to whites. In sympathy with the movement, two black athletes at the 1968 Olympics issued the Black Power salute on national television while receiving their medals.

However, the assassination of Martin Luther King Jr. on April 4, 1968, caused a racial explosion. Racial violence erupted in over 125 cities across the country, including Baltimore, Washington, New York, Chicago, Kansas City, Louisville, and Pittsburgh (Wikipedia 2014e). Widespread violence among blacks during the 1968 election year produced a very negative view among white Americans. President Johnson's approval ratings were in continuous decline through this period, and many believed that the Great Society had failed.

In September 1968, a Gallup Poll found that 54 percent of Americans thought the Johnson administration was "pushing integration too fast" (Gallup 1968c). In April 1968, a National Opinion Research Center (NORC) survey found that 88 percent of white Americans disapproved of the actions taken by blacks "to get the things they want," 79 percent said that their actions had not helped, and 53 percent reported that they had grown less favorable toward racial integration. Further, the partisan reaction among whites was uniform, as 87 percent of Democrats, 89 percent of Republicans, and 84 percent of Independents disapproved. Further, this disapproval did not vary significantly across regions, with those living in the North, Midwest, and West about as disapproving as those living in the South (National Opinion Research Center 1968). Thus, the political parties were also not polarized over race relations at the time of the 1968 election.

PRELUDE TO PARTY POLARIZATION

From the 1968 election through Nixon's resignation on August 9, 1974, the American electorate and political parties entered a state of flux. Social and regulatory policies protecting the masses at the expense of the commercial class expanded greatly through this period. Party polarization was low and a strong consensus continued in favor of the New Deal social contract. However, the seeds of change in the electorate and political parties were also being sown. The 1968 election opened fault lines over the issues of race and the efficacy of the Great Society. Later in this period, the national upheaval over Watergate subsequently weakened the credibility of Republican moderates, enabling Old Guard Republicans to rise within the party.

The Chaotic 1968 Election

Democrats were in great disarray before the 1968 election. In 1965, precisely half of voting age Americans identified as Democrats. That number had dropped to 42 percent by the time of the 1968 election. However, the percentage identifying as Republican had barely budged from about 25 percent to 27 percent. Those identifying as Independents had increased from 24 to 28 percent (Times Mirror/Pew Research Center 2012).

The Vietnam Tet Offensive started in January 1968, producing a public perception that the war was unwinnable. Based on opposition to Vietnam, challenger candidates emerged during the Democratic primaries. Minnesota Senator Eugene McCarthy joined the race in November 1967 and drew significant support in the March 1968 New Hampshire primary. Four days later, Massachusetts Senator Robert F. "Bobby" Kennedy entered the race in opposition to the war and advocating social justice.

Then, on March 31, 1968, after receiving word that he was behind in polling for the Wisconsin primary, President Johnson abruptly announced that he would not seek another term. Four days later, Martin Luther King Jr. was assassinated, sparking race riots across the nation. On April 21, 1968, Johnson's Vice President Hubert Humphrey entered the campaign as the establishment candidate.

Humphrey did not compete in the primaries, relying instead on securing delegates from nonprimary states. In 1968, only fourteen states chose their convention delegates through primaries. Nevertheless, competition for the primary vote was fierce between Kennedy and McCarthy. Before the California primary, McCarthy had won in Wisconsin, Pennsylvania, Massachusetts, and Oregon, while Kennedy had won in Indiana and Nebraska. On June 4, 1968, Bobby Kennedy won the California primary. However, the nation was again shocked on California election eve when he was assassinated. Within this tumultuous environment, the 1968 Democratic National Convention in Chicago chose Hubert Humphrey as the Party's presidential candidate, with Maine Senator Edmund Muskie as his running mate.

Given Humphrey's prominent identification with civil rights, many Democrats broke from the party to support third-party candidate George Wallace. Wallace was an ardent segregationist who, as Governor of Alabama stated, "I draw the line in the dust and toss the gauntlet before the feet of tyranny, and I say *segregation now, segregation tomorrow, segregation forever*" (Wikipedia 2014c). Later, Wallace attempted to prevent racial integration of the University of Alabama by standing in the schoolhouse door to prevent the entry of black students. He also attempted to prevent four black children from enrolling in an elementary school in Huntsville, Alabama. Thus, Wallace stood as a racist alternative for those in the Democratic Party favoring segregation.

The Republican Party chose Richard Nixon as their 1968 presidential candidate. Nixon selected Maryland Governor Spiro T. Agnew as his running mate. As vice president under Eisenhower, Nixon had been the president's point man in pushing Modern Republicanism in Congress. Modern Republicanism advocated protections for Americans and an active role for the federal government, but was wary of centralizing solutions (Mason 2014, chapter 5). Nixon advocated a New Federalism to revise, but not repeal, Johnson's Great Society. He largely ignored Vietnam as a campaign issue, stating only that he would achieve "peace with honor." His most important campaign issue was "crime and disorder." A very astute politician, Nixon understood that civil and racial disorder in America were hot-button issues for activating white opposition to the war protests and race riots preceding the election (American Experience 1990a).

With Democrats in disarray, Richard M. Nixon won the presidency in 1968 by a small plurality. He garnered only 43.4 percent of the popular vote; Humphrey received 42.7 percent; Wallace polled 13.5 percent. Wallace carried five Southern states, also proving popular among blue-collar workers, the less-educated, and low-income white voters of the North and Midwest. Wallace took many votes that might otherwise have gone to Humphrey (Himmelstein 1989, chapter 3, note 25; Lipset and Raab 1973, 358–90). Despite the Republican victory in the presidential election, Democrats retained control of both congressional chambers. After the dust had settled, the Democratic majority still stood at 58–42 in the Senate and at 243–192 in the House.

Significant Expansion of the Great Society under Richard Nixon

As a Modern Republican, Nixon participated energetically in expanding the Great Society. However, he wanted to revise the Great Society through a New Federalism involving greater participation by states and localities.

Nixon was slow to formulate this agenda. During the first quarter of 1969, Nixon sent only two significant domestic policy requests to Congress, one calling for a reorganization of the Post Office, and the other calling for safety improvements in coal mines (Warshaw 1991, 339). During the second quarter, the president asked for an Omnibus Crime Control Act to enable prosecuting organized crime (Warshaw 1991, 339–41) and a tax reform proposal to "lighten the burden on those who pay too much, and increase the taxes of those who pay too little" (Nixon 1969c). Only two major enactments occurred during Nixon's first year: the Federal Coal Mine Health and Safety Act and the Tax Reform Act (Wikipedia 2015b).

However, on August 8, 1969, President Nixon made a nationally televised address to reveal his New Federalism vision. The president asked for a shift in responsibility for many New Deal and Great Society programs to states and localities (Nixon 1969a). He sought to replace the existing welfare system (AFDC and Food Stamps) with a Family Assistance Plan (FAP) that would provide a floor of recipient income that could be augmented by states. The principle was similar to a negative income tax (Nathan 2011, 6–7). Nixon proposed a job training program to be managed by state and local governments. He also proposed revamping the Office of Economic Opportunity to stress innovation and local input. Finally, Nixon advocated revenue sharing in which states and localities would receive block grants to combat problems of urban decay and poverty (Nixon 1969a).

Nixon's proposals were well received by the media and appealed to many who believed the Great Society had failed to alleviate poverty and inequality in America (Nathan 2011, 3). After the speech, the president reorganized the Office of Economic Opportunity to make its administration more efficient, expand its functions, and solicit greater local input (CQ Almanac Online 1969; but see Schlesinger 1973, 241–42). The State and Local Fiscal Assistance Act became law, providing $30.2 billion in revenue sharing funds to state and local governments (CQ Almanac Online 1973d). Congress also enacted the Comprehensive Employment and Training Act, a federally supported state and local program for training the poor and chronically unemployed (CQ Almanac Online 1974a). However, Nixon's FAP was soundly rejected, as it came under heavy criticism from groups across the ideological spectrum (CQ Almanac Online 1970b).

The New Deal agenda expanded more under Nixon after 1970 than under any modern president other than Johnson. In his 1970 State of the Union address, Nixon called for improvements in voting rights; equal employment opportunity; new opportunities for expanded ownership; improved health care, education, housing, transportation; and other critical areas that affected the well-being of millions of Americans. In his 1971 State of the Union address, Nixon even proposed a national health insurance program similar to the 2010 Affordable Care Act (Nixon 1971a; see also Nixon 1972b).

Regarding school desegregation, Nixon was the by far most active post-1960s president (but see Schlesinger 1973, 240–41). Instead of relying on forced busing and federal coercion, the administration implemented locally controlled school desegregation. "Starting in Mississippi and moving across the South, the Nixon administration set up biracial state committees to plan and implement school desegregation. The appeal to local control succeeded ... By the end of 1970, with little of the anticipated violence and little fanfare, the committees had made significant progress – only about 18% of black children in the South attended all-black schools" (American Experience 1990b).

Beyond desegregating public schools, Nixon promoted equal opportunity for minorities and women in business and the workplace. Weeks after the inauguration, he met with Labor Secretary George Schultz on the disposition of Johnson's E.O. 11246, establishing affirmative action in businesses receiving federal money. Out of this meeting came the Philadelphia Plan, which aimed at dismantling institutionalized racism in the construction industry (Anderson 2004, chapter 4; Hood 1993). Nixon established an Office of Minority Business Enterprise within the Department of Commerce to promote minority entrepreneurship. He also issued E.O. 11625 directing federal agencies to develop a national Minority Business Enterprise (MBE) contracting program.

Nixon supported women by endorsing the Equal Rights Amendment to the Constitution (Nixon 1972a). He increased appointments of women, and created a Presidential Task Force on Women's Rights. Nixon asked the Justice Department to bring sex discrimination lawsuits under the Civil Rights Act. He ordered the Labor Department to add affirmative action to guidelines for the Office of Federal Contract Compliance, modifying it in 1971 to include women (American Experience 1990b).

Finally, on March 5, 1972, President Nixon signed the Equal Employment Opportunity Act of 1972 (Nixon 1972c). This law gave teeth to the Equal Employment Opportunity Commission by enabling the agency to file lawsuits in federal courts on behalf of victims of illegal discrimination.

Federal regulation also expanded greatly during the Nixon administration, though sometimes grudgingly. On January 1, 1970, the president signed the National Environmental Policy Act (CQ Almanac Online 1970a). This law established the Council on Environmental Quality within the White House to assess and coordinate environmental policy. It required all projects – federal, state, and local – involving federal funds or a permit issued by a federal agency to submit an Environmental Impact Assessment.

Shortly thereafter, President Nixon sent twenty-three proposals to Congress dealing with environmental problems, including air pollution, water pollution, and municipal wastes (Nixon 1970b). After the president's proposals, the first Earth Day occurred on April 22, 1970. The event was organized under the bipartisan leadership of Democratic Wisconsin Senator Gaylord Nelson and Republican California Congressman Paul McCloskey. Over 20 million Americans participated in the first Earth Day (Lewis 1985).

Perhaps in response to Earth Day, on July 9, 1970, President Nixon created the Environmental Protection Agency (EPA) and the National Oceanic and Atmospheric Administration (NOAA) by Reorganization Plan Numbers 3 and 4 (Nixon 1970a). The EPA was created to coordinate and implement the nation's environmental laws. NOAA was to do the same regarding matters relating to the oceans and atmosphere.

Responding to the popular appeal of protecting the environment, Congress passed and President Nixon signed the Clean Air Act Amendments of 1970 (CQ Almanac Online 1971). The legislation passed the Senate unanimously and was opposed by only one House member. The president signed the law but later used a highly secretive review process at the White House Office of Management and Budget (OMB) to weaken state implementation plans in favor of industry (Jones 1975, 240–44).

President Nixon also supported water pollution control, but within limits. Congress passed the Clean Water Act of 1972 to control industrial, agricultural, and municipal water pollution. The bill coming out of the House and Senate allocated $24 billion for construction of municipal waste treatment plants, about $18 billion more than the president had requested. Because he thought this expenditure was excessive, the president vetoed the legislation (Nixon 1969d). One day later, Congress overrode the president's veto (CQ Almanac Online 1973a). However, President Nixon then directed EPA Administrator William Ruckelshaus to spend only $5 billion of the allocated funds (McThenia 1973, note 2). This impoundment of water quality funds incensed members of Congress during an election year.

Three other environmental laws enacted during 1972 extended government protection to coastal areas, oceans, and wildlife (the Coastal Zone Management Act, the Marine Protection, Research, and the Sanctuaries Act, and the Marine Mammal Protection Act) (CQ Almanac Online 1973b, 1973c, 1973e). Additional landmark legislation during Nixon's first term included the Occupational Safety and Health Act of 1970 and the Consumer Product Safety Act of 1972.

On August 6, 1969, President Nixon sent a proposal to Congress aimed at protecting worker health and safety (Nixon 1969b). The president's bill lacked mandatory protections for workers and would have created a new board to implement the law. In contrast, the bill advocated by some members of Congress was more stringent, requiring the law to be implemented by the Labor Department (Ashford 1976, 53–57). A more liberal Senate version of the bill prevailed (Department of Labor 2014). Nevertheless, President Nixon signed the legislation on December 29, 1970.

President Nixon also proposed consumer protection legislation (Nixon 1971b). As more stringent legislation was moving through Congress, Nixon sent a letter to the Chairman of the Senate Commerce Committee advocating his weaker approach (*Public Papers of the Presidents* 1971). The legislation that emerged was again stronger than the president had proposed, and even insulated the policy from presidential control by creating a commission (Lewis 2003, 30). Nevertheless, President Nixon again signed the legislation creating the Consumer Product Safety Commission.

The Premature End of the Nixon Presidency

President Nixon had many positives going into the 1972 election. Numerous popular programs were enacted during his first term that were quite friendly to common Americans. Inflation and unemployment were tame, at about 3.2 percent and 4.6 percent, respectively (Bureau of Labor Statistics 2014a, 2014b). The U.S. economy was very robust, with GDP growth of 11.6 percent in the third quarter of 1972 (Bureau of Economic Analysis 2014b). Internationally, Nixon had achieved notable foreign policy successes, including rapprochement with China and moving closer to ending the Vietnam War. Given these positives, Nixon's approval ratings averaged 62 percent between January and November of the election year (Gallup 2014).

It was highly probable that Nixon would be reelected. Nevertheless, the president pulled out all the stops to assure reelection. As Goldwater had done in 1964, Republicans followed a Southern strategy. The president's campaign strategist, Kevin Phillips, explained the rationale in a May 1970 *New York Times* article: "From now on, the Republicans are never going to get more than 10 to 20 percent of the Negro vote and they don't need any more than that ... but Republicans would be shortsighted if they weakened enforcement of the Voting Rights Act. The more Negroes who register as Democrats in the South, the sooner the Negrophobe Whites will quit the Democrats and become Republicans. That's where the votes are" (Boyd 1970, 106).

The Nixon administration also followed some illegal paths toward reelection. Starting in mid-1971, the White House compiled an "enemies list" and requested IRS audits of Democratic allies (Safire 2008, 215–16) The Nixon campaign also solicited illegal campaign contributions from at least eighteen American corporations later convicted of violating U.S. election laws (Frum 2000, 31). They also employed a "dirty tricks" unit during the primary season to discredit Nixon's Democratic challengers. FBI investigators later revealed a letter forged by the unit to discredit Senator Edmund Muskie, thereby diminishing his Northeastern support (Woodward and Bernstein 2005, chapter 7).

Most visibly later, the White House established an extra-legal Special Investigations Unit within the White House after Daniel Ellsberg leaked the Pentagon Papers to the *New York Times* (dubbed the Plumbers Unit). The Plumbers Unit burglarized the office of Ellsberg's psychiatrist to obtain information to discredit him. Extending this pattern of criminal actions, the Plumbers Unit burglarized the Democratic National Committee headquarters in Washington to uncover the Democrats' election game plan. All of this occurred with the knowledge and direction of the president (Weiner 1997).

Nixon won reelection in 1972 by the second largest margin since 1936, with 60.7 percent of the popular vote. He won all states except Massachusetts, receiving 520 electoral votes. Nixon was the first Republican presidential candidate in American history to win all Southern states. As forecast by the president's campaign advisor, Kevin Phillips, the 1972 election accentuated the trend of transforming the South from a Democratic to a Republican bastion.

However, the president's 1972 coattails were nonexistent to weak. Democrats picked up two seats in the Senate, but the Republicans added thirteen seats in the House. The Democratic majority in Congress after the election was 56–44 in the Senate and 242–192 in the House. Regardless of the presidential election landslide, Nixon had no mandate. He faced a Congress incensed over his demonization of Congress during the campaign. Congress became even more incensed as news came of the illegal campaign activities.

The Nixon presidency lasted for another twenty-one months after the landslide reelection. During that time Congress passed several landmark laws signed by the president. These included the Endangered Species Act, the Comprehensive Employment and Training Act, the Disaster Relief Act, and the Health Maintenance Organization Act. All were passed on a bipartisan basis to improve the lives of ordinary Americans.

However, far more time was spent during this period dealing with what was considered by both Democrats and Republicans to be an out-of-control presidency. Constraining the president's war-making power, the War Powers Resolution of 1973 was adopted over President Nixon's veto (CQ Almanac Online 1974b). Congress enacted the Congressional Budget and Impoundment Control Act of 1974 to permanently remove the president's power to impound duly appropriated funds. The legislation passed the House by a vote of 401–6 and the Senate unanimously. Easily overridden, President Nixon signed this legislation one month before his resignation (CQ Almanac Online 1975).

The most time-consuming and painful aspect of the president's remaining twenty-one months was the Watergate scandal. Two *Washington Post* reporters, Bob Woodward and Carl Bernstein, spearheaded the media investigation. Between June 17, 1972, and August 9, 1974, the *Post* published nineteen stories about the evolving Watergate scandal (*Washington Post* 2012b). The first story reported the burglary of the Democratic National Committee headquarters at the Watergate hotel in Washington in an attempt to "bug" their offices. Between June 19 and October 10, 1972, Nixon aides and officials, including former Attorney General and Nixon campaign manager John Mitchell, were linked to the burglary. On January 30, 1973, Nixon aides G. Gordon Liddy and James W. McCord were convicted of conspiracy, burglary, and wiretapping in the Watergate incident. On April 30, 1973, Nixon's top White House staffers, H. R. Haldeman and John Ehrlichman, and Attorney General Richard Kleindienst resigned over the scandal. On the same day, White House Counsel John Dean was fired.

At this point, Congress became involved (*Washington Post* 2012a). A special prosecutor, Archibald Cox, was appointed by the Justice Department to lead the congressional investigation. On May 18, 1973, a Special

Senate Watergate Committee began nationally televised hearings that captivated the nation over the next fourteen months. During the hearings former White House Counsel John Dean told the committee that he had discussed the Watergate burglary and attempted cover-up with President Nixon at least thirty-five times, implicating the president personally in criminal activities. On July 13, 1973, the White House appointments secretary revealed to the committee that Nixon had used a taping system to record all conversations and calls to his offices.

Ten days after this revelation, the Watergate Special Prosecutor requested that the White House turn over the tapes. Citing executive privilege, Nixon refused, and on October 20, 1973 he fired Archibald Cox and abolished the Office of the Special Prosecutor. In protest, the Attorney General, Elliot Richardson, and Assistant Attorney General, William Ruckelshaus, resigned. These events were dubbed "The Saturday Night Massacre" and resulted in increased calls in Congress for impeachment.

A federal district court quickly deemed the president's actions illegal (*Washington Post* 2012a). Following the court's decision, Nixon was compelled to allow his new Attorney General Robert Bork to appoint a new Special Prosecutor, Leon Jaworski. On November 20, 1973, the White House lawyers informed the district court that there was an eighteen-minute gap on one of the key requested tapes. On April 30, 1974, the White House released more than 1,200 pages of edited transcripts of the tapes. However, the Committee insisted that the tapes themselves had to be turned over.

On July 24, 1974, the Supreme Court in *U.S. v. Nixon* (418 U.S. 683) rejected the president's claim of executive privilege and required the president to turn over the tapes (*Washington Post* 2012a). Several days after the Court's decision, the House Judiciary Committee passed three articles of impeachment amid weak Republican opposition. On August 5, 1974, the tapes were provided to the Committee and provided the "smoking gun" showing that President Nixon was deeply involved in the cover-up, and had even ordered Haldeman to stop the FBI investigation just six days after the Watergate break-in.

Following this revelation, remaining presidential support in Congress evaporated. On August 7, 1974, three Republican members of Congress, led by Senator Barry Goldwater, visited Nixon in the White House telling him that there was little chance of avoiding impeachment. They reported that only twelve to fifteen senators would support the president if it came to a trial (Glass 2007).

On August 9, 1974, President Richard M. Nixon became the first president in American history to resign from office. During the twenty-one months after the landslide election, Richard Nixon had gone from a very popular president to a criminal likely to be forced from office. Both Republicans and Democrats were happy to see him go. In the last public opinion poll before Nixon's resignation, fully 66 percent of Americans reported that they were in favor of impeachment (Harris 1974b). In the last Gallup poll in August before his resignation, Nixon's approval was only 24 percent (Gallup 2014), the lowest of any president since Truman. In the end, Watergate and Nixon's resignation were very painful for the nation. However, they were neither partisan nor polarizing.

CHARACTERIZING CONSENSUS AND CONFLICT FROM WORLD WAR II TO THE 1970S

As during the Great Depression and World War II, the postwar period up to the 1970s was characterized by relative consensus in both the electorate and Congress in favor of the New Deal social contract.

Concerning consensus in the electorate, there was no large partisan divide over implementing the New Deal social contract, evidenced by the frequency of crossover voting in elections. Party identification heavily favored the Democrats in all presidential elections from 1948 through 1976. Yet Modern Republican presidents Eisenhower and Nixon were elected in 1952, 1956, 1968, and 1972. These results imply that party loyalty was incomplete and that split-ticket voting often occurred (Burden and Kimball 2002, 65–66). Those who identified with a particular party became increasingly likely to vote for presidential candidates opposite from their own party identification.

Concerning consensus in Congress, strong evidence is again contained in the annual percentage of party unity votes, as was reported in Figure 2.1A. During the heyday of the Great Society and its extension (the 89th through 93rd Congress), the average percentage of votes where a majority of one party lined up against a majority of the other party was only 36 percent in the House and 40 percent in the Senate. Comparing these numbers with the current era, the comparable percentages for the 112th Congress were 75 percent for the House and 56 percent for the Senate. Interestingly, the low point of party unity voting during the Great Society heyday was the 91st Congress, when Richard Nixon was president. Corroborating evidence is contained in Figure 2.1 panels B and C for party cohesion.

Thus, a bipartisan consensus existed from World War II into the 1970s in support of the New Deal social contract. Recognizing its popularity, there was little partisan conflict over *whether* to accept it. Americans were largely supportive of the new programs, and it would have been perilous for either party to oppose them. However, partisan conflict did exist over *how* to implement it. The Democratic version of the contract emphasized the centralized role of the federal government. The Republican version called for greater decentralization and participation by states and localities. Thus, the question of *whether* to implement the New Deal social contract was a matter of consensus before 1980. The question of *how* to implement it was a matter of partisan conflict. However, starting with the Reagan administration, the question of *whether* to implement the New Deal social contract at all became the primary basis of party polarization.

6

Polarization over the New Deal Social Contract from the 1970s to the Present

On May 17, 2012, Republican presidential candidate Mitt Romney spoke at a $50,000-per-plate dinner at the home of private equity magnate Marc Leder in Boca Raton, Florida. He told the wealthy donors:

There are 47 percent of the people who will vote for the president no matter what. All right, there are 47 percent who are with him, who are dependent upon government, who believe that they are victims, who believe that government has a responsibility to take care of them, who believe that they are entitled to health care, to food, to housing, to you name it. That that's an entitlement, and the government should give it to them ... Forty-seven percent of Americans pay no income tax ... And so my job is not to worry about those people – I'll never convince them that they should take personal responsibility and care for their lives. (MoJo News Team 2012)

Romney did not intend his remarks to be heard outside of his wealthy audience. However, a bartender surreptitiously recorded the event. Four months later, he gave the recording to the press. With media coverage escalating, Romney's remarks became well known to most Americans and were likely a basis for his 2012 election defeat.

Romney's remarks are important here because they illustrate the ongoing nature of the partisan divide in America. They show the class-based struggle over two distinct visions of the American social contract. As discussed previously, the Founders' social contract held that the chief purpose of government was to protect the property of the patrician class from the ravages of popular democracy (e.g., taxes, redistribution, regulation). Indeed, early American government not only protected the patrician class, but also promoted it through rents to creditors, tariffs, subsidies, and a tax system where the wealthy paid little. Before 1913, the mass public paid most federal taxes through high excises and duties. Thus, the free enterprise system of the Founders was not actually free. It cost the masses substantially to support a government promoting the propertied class.

In contrast, the New Deal social contract envisioned the nation as a community that promotes and protects all of its members, rich and poor, young and old, regardless of religion, gender, ethnicity, or race. Starting in 1933, the federal government leveled the distribution of rents through social programs, regulation, and various protections from market evils. The tax burden for supporting these initiatives shifted upward. Constraints on economic activity affected the patrician class more than the masses. Reversing the situation from earlier America, many Americans were no longer required to pay income taxes. Indeed, government subsidized the poor, the elderly, the middle class, and even the wealthy through various tax expenditures (Tax Policy Center 2014).

Romney's remarks suggested that he wanted a return to a (not so) free enterprise system that would again favor his wealthy patrons, who might in turn take care of the masses through employment and charity. As with many of the Founders (see Chapter 2), Romney's remarks showed a class-based disdain for common Americans and an intention to suppress their newfound benefits. More generally, Romney's remarks to his wealthy donors reflected his support for the Founders' social contract.

The basis of modern party polarization is the ongoing debate over the relative legitimacy of the two social contracts.

REBUILDING POPULAR SUPPORT FOR THE FOUNDERS' SOCIAL CONTRACT

The Great Depression and New Deal almost ended popular support for the Founders' social contract. Markets and the prevailing political regime had failed to provide for the general welfare. After 1929, most Americans held virtually all well-to-do and Republican leaders in very low esteem. Misery was abject and widespread during the depression and left an indelible imprint on the American psyche. The Republican brand was tarnished for almost fifty years. As a result, many Republicans became more like Democrats from 1933 through the mid-1970s. Modern Republicanism even extended the New Deal during the Eisenhower and Nixon administrations. A consensus existed among Democrats and most Republicans that the federal government was indeed responsible for all Americans.

However, a residual of Old Guard Republicans remained. The most visible standard bearer for the Old Guard was Arizona senator and presidential candidate Barry Goldwater. Failing to win the presidency in 1964, his mentee, Ronald Reagan, ran for president in 1968 and 1976. However, in an era when New Deal prescriptions remained popular, Americans considered him too extreme.

After two failed attempts, Reagan finally won the presidency in 1980, initiating the modern era of party polarization. Reagan's election initiated renewed support for the Founders' social contract. Reagan questioned the progressive income tax, regulatory programs, the legitimacy of social programs, bureaucratic inefficiency, and big government. Support for Reagan's more conservative perspective grew steadily starting in the 1980s to peak near the present.

The Aftermath of Watergate

To understand how such a sharp turnaround in American politics could occur, one must understand the period following Watergate. Nixon's resignation brought disgrace to Republicans, especially the moderate base from which he came. After 1974, Old Guard Republicans increasingly influenced the Republican Party. Their ascendance involved rebranding the party and its philosophy. Selling the rebranded Republican philosophy was made easier by poor economic conditions and adverse world events near the end of the 1970s. Selling the rebranded Republican philosophy also required an intellectual basis, money, and a public face. Accordingly, conservative intellectuals, wealthy donors, religious activists, Old Guard Republican politicians, and an actor-turned-politician named Ronald Reagan drove the transformation.

Nixon's resignation on August 9, 1974, brought the first nonelected president in U.S. history. His vice president, Spiro Agnew, had himself been forced to resign on October 10, 1973. Agnew had been charged with bribery while serving as Baltimore County Executive, governor of Maryland, and vice president. The federal prosecutor allowed Agnew to plead no contest to a single charge of failing to report $29,500 of income in 1967, under the condition that he resign. Nixon replaced Agnew by appointing House Republican Minority Leader Gerald R. Ford of Michigan (under the Twenty-fifth Amendment).

The Watergate scandal, along with the resignation of Nixon's vice president, made it even less popular to be a Republican. Figure 6.1 plots the annual party identification of Republicans, Democrats, and Independents from 1939 through 2012. The heavy dashed vertical line marks 1973, the year the scandal broke. The graph shows that Republican Party identification was already declining from 1939 to 1973. However, the percentage identifying as Republican dropped to the lowest level in Republican Party history afterward. After Nixon's resignation only 21 percent of Americans identified as Republicans. This low percentage of Americans identifying as Republicans continued through 1980.

As president, Ford did little to help the Republican image. After being sworn in, he nominated liberal Republican Nelson Rockefeller as his vice president. Conservatives were very unhappy with Ford's choice. However, the president believed that Rockefeller would broaden the appeal of Republicans in the upcoming 1976 elections. The Senate confirmation hearings proved embarrassing once again for Republicans. Descended from the Rockefeller family that accrued enormous fortunes through banking and oil in the late nineteenth and early twentieth century, he was exceedingly wealthy. The hearings uncovered large gifts to senior Nixon administration aides, and he had also secretly financed a defamatory biography of one of his political opponents. Rockefeller had also not paid all of his taxes. Nevertheless, the Democratic Senate confirmed him (*Time* 1975).

A much more unpopular action by President Ford, and one that probably cost him the 1976 election, was his quick pardon of Richard Nixon. On

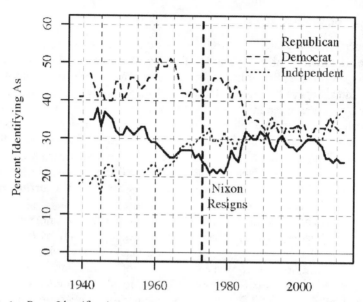

FIGURE 6.1 Party Identification, 1939–2012
Source: Pew Research Center, Trends in Party Identification from Gallup, 1939–1989, Times
Mirror/Pew Research Center, 1990–2012.

September 8, 1974, roughly one month after being sworn in as president, Ford
issued Proclamation 4311 granting "a full, free, and absolute pardon … for all
offenses against the United States which he … committed or may have committed or taken part in" (Ford 1974b).

Ford's pardon of Nixon was controversial, with many believing that a
"corrupt bargain" had been struck in exchange for the presidency (e.g., see
Woodward 1999, chapter 1). A Roper Center opinion poll in September
1974 showed that only 30 percent of Americans approved of Ford's
pardoning Nixon (Roper 1974). A Harris poll conducted the same month
showed that 60 percent of Americans believed that it was wrong to pardon
Nixon (Harris 1974a). Yet another poll asked, "Do you feel that President
Ford has or has not told the country the whole truth about the pardon of
former President Nixon?" Over 70 percent of respondents answered he "has
not" (*Time*/Yankelovich 1974). Thus, Ford's pardon of Nixon left a residual
of distrust.

Ford supported other policies disliked by conservatives. Neoconservatives
disliked his retention of Secretary of State Henry Kissinger, who had pursued
détente with the Soviet Union (Vaisse 2010, chapter 4). Others disliked Ford's
support for the Equal Rights Amendment for women (Ford 1975), higher taxes
on corporations and the wealthy (Ford 1974a), and several environmental
protection measures (Wikipedia 2015b). Ford later identified his position on
abortion as pro-choice (Larry King 2001).

Thus, conservatives did not back Ford's 1976 election attempt. Instead, they put forward their own candidate, Ronald Reagan. Moderate Maryland Republican Senator Charles Mathias considered entering the race as a moderate alternative to Ford and was critical of the conservative wing's Southern strategy. He also expressed concern about its apparent shift to the right. Referring to Reagan, he remarked that the party leadership was moving "in further isolation, in an extreme – almost fringe – position" (*Washington Post* 2010). The primary race between Ford and Reagan was close, and going into the Republican National Convention the outcome was too close to call.

The 1976 Republican Convention was the last convention not predetermined before the convention. Attempting to woo convention delegates, Ford narrowly won after dropping liberal Nelson Rockefeller and selecting Kansas Senator Bob Dole as his running mate. The 1976 Republican platform included several other concessions to conservatives. Responding to the Supreme Court's 1973 *Roe v. Wade* decision, the platform called for "a position on abortion that values human life." In another gesture toward the emerging Religious Right, it asserted that "[o]ur great American Republic was founded on the principle: One nation under God, with liberty and justice for all." Segments of the platform also mentioned excessive business regulation and high taxes and advocated decreased environmental protection (Republican National Committee 1976). The outlines for the rebranded Republican Party were beginning to take form at the time of the 1976 Republican Convention, but the platform remained fairly moderate.

The general election outcome was close, with Democrat Jimmy Carter winning the presidency with only 50.1 percent of the popular vote and 297 electoral votes. Ford won 48 percent of the popular vote and 240 electoral votes. As a Southerner, Carter carried all Southern states except Virginia, thereby nullifying the Republicans' Southern strategy. Carter ran as a conservative Democrat and a Washington outsider untainted by the Watergate scandal. In contrast, many were suspicious of President Ford's pardon of Nixon. More importantly, the failure of a moderate Republican to win the 1976 election further facilitated the ascendance of the Old Guard within the Republican Party.

A Conservative Intellectual Counter-Revolution

Rebranding the Republican Party and philosophy was further enabled by the emergence of a conservative academic program, originating from the Chicago School of Economics. Its philosophy was rooted in a reaction against Keynesian economics, New Deal liberalism, and the Great Society. Kaufman (2010, 133) characterized the Chicago School as having "an uncompromising belief in the usefulness and insight of neoclassical price theory, and a normative position that favors and promotes economic liberalism and free markets."

Even during the Great Depression, University of Chicago economists were the chief defenders of classical free market economics. The most influential early University of Chicago economists were Jacob Viner, Henry C. Simons, and Frank H. Knight. All three scholars advocated free market capitalism and were libertarians (Simons 1934, 40–77; University of Chicago Centennial Catalogues 2014). Knight was the Ph.D. advisor to three Nobel Laureates, Milton Friedman, George Stigler, and James M. Buchanan. Friedman was later the Ph.D. advisor to William Niskanen, a prominent official in the Reagan administration and later director of the libertarian Cato Institute.

The leader of the Chicago School movement was clearly Milton Friedman. Friedman spent decades campaigning on behalf of the macroeconomic approach known as monetarism. Monetarism aimed directly at Keynesian economics. Keynes had argued that under depression conditions, when businesses are psychologically disinclined to invest even with low interest rates, changes in the money supply can have little effect on the economy (Keynes 1936, chapters 13 and 15; Krugman 2007). In contrast, Friedman argued that the Federal Reserve ("Fed") should pursue a hands-off approach and not attempt to control the economy through either fiscal or monetary policy. According to monetarism, the money supply should grow at a slow steady pace, rather than attempting to prevent cyclical fluctuations (Friedman 1960).

Friedman and Schwartz's *A Monetary History of the United States* (1963) was seminal to the debate. They argued that the depth and duration of the Great Depression did not demonstrate a failure of the free market system (1963, 407–19). Rather, they claimed that the ineptness and bungling of government decision makers, notably the Fed, was responsible. According to Friedman, the 1929 market crash was a serious shock to the economic system, but the depth and duration of the Great Depression were wholly preventable. Adherence to poor monetary policies, and an absence of decisive action by the Fed to supply adequate bank reserves after the market crash and banking panics greatly exacerbated the Great Depression. Thus, according to Friedman, "money matters" even during times of depression.

Friedman was very effective in promoting monetarism through the 1970s. By 1979, the U.S. Federal Reserve and the Bank of England had adopted his monetarist approach. However, Friedman's *passive* monetarism was quickly abandoned in the early 1980s as the United States experienced the worst recession since the Great Depression. Nevertheless, Friedman convincingly established the notion that "money matters," resulting in *active* management of the money supply by the Federal Reserve to the present.

Beyond Friedman's contributions to popularizing monetary economics, he was also an ideologue opposed to *any* government intervention in the economy. He first became known as an advocate of free-market economics in 1945 when he published a book with Simon Kuznets proposing elimination of state licensing procedures for doctors (Friedman and Kuznets 1945). A year later, he published a pamphlet with George Stigler proposing elimination of post–World War II rent controls (Friedman and Stigler 1946). The pamphlet was published by the Foundation for Economic Education (FEE), an organization Rick

Perlstein later characterized as spreading "a libertarian gospel so uncompromising it bordered on anarchism" (Perlstein 2001, 113–14).

In ensuing decades, Friedman pushed free-market solutions to problems that most thought required government intervention, including illegal drugs, abolishing the Food and Drug Administration, privatizing public education and health care, pollution, and a negative income tax to address poverty (Krugman 2007). In 1980, Friedman pushed his libertarian philosophy in a book that became a ten-part television series broadcast on PBS, entitled *Free to Choose* (Friedman and Friedman 1980).

Free to Choose became a blueprint for many of Ronald Reagan's domestic policies (Ebenstein 2007, chapter 21). Friedman prepared several policy papers for Reagan even before the election. Starting in 1981, he was a member of Reagan's Economic Policy Advisory Board. He was socially connected with many officials in the Reagan administration, including Treasury Secretary Donald Regan and Labor Secretary George Schultz. Reagan often referred to Friedman in his regular radio addresses. Speaking before the National Conservative Political Action Committee (NCPAC), Reagan referred to Friedman as an intellectual leader "who shaped so much of our thoughts" (Ebenstein 2007, 206). Reagan presented Friedman with the Presidential Medal of Freedom in 1988. More generally, Friedman was probably the most important advocate of free-market economics of the twentieth century (Henderson 2008).

Several of Friedman's Chicago School colleagues also contributed to the intellectual rebranding of the Republican philosophy. George Stigler (1972) published "The Theory of Economic Regulation," which argued that government regulation usually results in rents to the regulated. Stigler also suggested that government regulation harms the public by reducing economic efficiency. Along with Milton Friedman and Austrian economists Friedrich Hayek and Ludwig von Mises, Stigler was a founding member of the libertarian Mont Pelerin Society, which advocates free markets (Novak 2012, 294).

Also of the Chicago School, James M. Buchanan co-founded with Gordon Tullock the subfield of political science and economics called "public choice" (Buchanan 2015). Public choice economics argues that the pursuit of rents by governmental actors generally leads to harmful results for the public (Tullock 1967, 1993). Among those harmful results are large public deficits and debt, as well as entitlements that place obligations on future generations that are difficult to honor (e.g., Social Security, Medicare). Buchanan blamed Keynesian ideas for excessive government spending during the 1960s and '70s, high taxes, large debts, big government, and excessive regulation (Buchanan 1977).

Finally, William A. Niskanen was another architect of Ronald Reagan's economic program and a member of his Council of Economic Advisors. His most prominent work was *Bureaucracy and Representative Government* (Niskanen 1971). Using mathematical modeling, this and later work (Niskanen 1975) purported to show that bureaucrats always seek to maximize their budgets. Because legislative oversight is weak or missing, bureaucracies have a distinct advantage over Congress, resulting in budgets that are consistently too large. Niskanen's work on bureaucracies and budgets was largely discredited by later work (see literature reviews in Blais and Dion 1991; Wood 2010). Nevertheless, his ideas were influential on Reagan's vigorous attack on bureaucracy and big government. On leaving the Reagan administration in 1985, Niskanen became the long-time chairman of the libertarian Cato Institute.

Big Money Paired with Conservative and Religious Activism

Another factor supporting the rebranded Republican Party was a cadre of wealthy conservative activists who supplied large amounts of money and support for Republican causes starting in the 1970s. A growing and synchronized group of foundations determinedly sought to make support for free markets the dominant force in American governance, political culture, and civic life (O'Connor 2010, 121–27).

A few free-market foundations had continued since the New Deal, including the FEE and the Earhart, W. H. Brady, Volker, and J. Howard Pew foundations. However, these were joined in the 1970s by the Coors, Koch family, Smith Richardson, Scaife, Bechtel, Lilly, DeVos, JM, Castle Rock, Bradley, and the Olin foundations. "In 1976, Nixon's former Treasury Secretary, Knight of Malta and Opus Dei supporter, William Simon, was appointed head of the Olin Foundation. Simon established 'clearinghouses' for corporate donations" through the Olin and other foundations (Clermont 2009, 40). Big money now supported Old Guard Republican causes.

Many of the activist donors were also religious zealots. As such, they sought to link the Keynesian revolution, the welfare state, and the "creeping socialism" of the New Deal and Great Society with immorality in America. The idea was to mobilize the evangelical community with an ideology teaching that regulation, social programs, and big government were somehow un-Christian and ungodly. Linking these concepts with traditional family values and hatred for abortion, pornography, and homosexuality made their task easier. This approach also played well with the Republican Southern strategy, because a concentration of evangelical white Christians in the South strongly resented the civil rights movement and social programs of the 1960s (Balmer 2007, 5–17).

In pursuing this approach, the conservative foundations created an infrastructure of think tanks, advocacy groups, and media outlets to break liberalism's strong hold on American civil society (O' Connor 2010, 133–34; Ricci 1994, 167–68). The most important of the think tanks were the Cato Institute, the American Enterprise Institute, and the Heritage Foundation. The Koch family, Olin, Scaiffe, Coors, and Bradley foundations funded the libertarian Cato Institute. Big donors to the pro-business American Enterprise Institute included the Smith-Richardson, Olin, Scaife, and Bradley foundations. However, the most influential recipient by far of conservative funding was the Heritage Foundation.

In 1973, Joseph Coors, Edwin Feulner, and Paul Weyrich started the Heritage Foundation. Coors provided the initial financing of $250,000.

Subsequently, John Mellon Scaife contributed $900,000, followed by substantial support from oil tycoon Edward Noble and the John M. Olin Foundation. The Heritage Foundation also received support from various corporate sponsors, including automobile manufacturers, coal, oil, chemical, and tobacco companies (Smith 1991, 200).

Beyond supporting free-market causes, the Heritage Foundation actively promoted evangelical values. Its founder, Paul Weyrich, often spoke to audiences of fundamentalist leaders about his policy positions and was highly influential in mobilizing the Religious Right (Hudson 2008, 70–72). In turn, Religious Right organizations regularly distributed voters' guides comparing Republican and Democratic candidates in and around evangelical churches before elections. These guides not only included references to moral issues, but also espoused the anti-government, anti-tax, free market positions of the conservative foundations (Black and Black 2002, 251–52).

Important conservative advocacy groups of the late 1970s were NCPAC (cofounded by closeted gay Christian conservative Terry Dolan), the Conservative Caucus (headed by evangelical Christian Howard Phillips), and the Committee for the Survival of a Free Congress (headed by the Heritage Foundation's Paul Weyrich) (see *Time* 1979). A Greek Catholic, Weyrich openly advocated uniting Protestant evangelicals and Catholics into a political bloc by emphasizing emotional "family issues" (Clermont 2009, 42). He was also the leader in defining what constituted "family issues" – including abortion, pornography, and homosexuality – to mobilize voters who were not necessarily conservative on other issues.

In 1977, Paul Weyrich and Robert Grant founded the first Religious Right advocacy group, Christian Voice. The impetus for its formation came from several California anti-gay and anti-pornography groups affiliated with the Unification Church led by the Reverend Sun Myung Moon. Evangelical minister Pat Robertson, who later founded the Christian Coalition, provided early financial support (Smith 2014, 99–100). Christian Voice operated directly out of the Heritage Foundation. However, a nasty fight erupted between the group and the Foundation leading to its eviction.

Soon afterward, Paul Weyrich cofounded the Moral Majority with the Reverend Jerry Falwell (Lernoux 1989; Rossi 2007, 109–10). The Moral Majority was an umbrella organization that included Baptists, Catholics, Mormons, and Orthodox Jews. In his television ministry, Falwell regularly connected free markets and limited government with morality and family values in America. His goal was "[t]o defend the free enterprise system, the family, Bible morality, and fundamental values" (Clermont 2009, 42).

The Moral Majority, the Christian Voice, the Religious Roundtable, and the National Christian Action Coalition all originated in the late 1970s with the goal of bringing morality back to America. They also sought to create a populist backlash against the progressive economic policies of the New Deal and Great Society by depicting them as somehow immoral and ungodly (Clermont

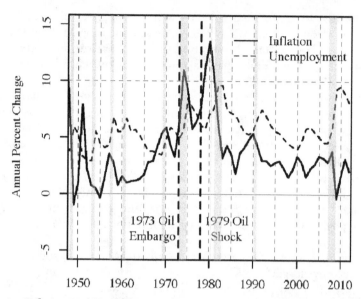

FIGURE 6.2 Inflation and Unemployment Rates
Sources: Inflation data are from www.measuringworth.com/inflation (Officer and Williamson 2014). Unemployment data are from Bureau of Labor Statistics series LNU04000000. Shaded areas show economic recessions. Recession dates are from NBER (2014a).

2009, chapter 4). During the 1980 election, the Religious Right formed a network of grassroots workers, funding for Ronald Reagan, and an important voting bloc.

Public Dissatisfaction with the Economy and the Iran Hostage Crisis

By 1980, Old Guard Republicans had a new intellectual basis, wealthy supporters, and a cadre of zealous workers committed to their cause. However, they had not yet persuaded a significant number of Americans that it was righteous to be a Republican. As shown earlier in Figure 6.1, the percentage of Americans identifying as Republicans in 1979 was only 21 percent, and had risen to only 23 percent by 1980. In contrast, the percentage of Democratic identifiers had increased to around 45 percent, while Independent identifiers remained stable. Thus, a confluence of conditions was needed for the Old Guard to be successful in the 1980 elections.

That set of conditions came from a poor economy and public dissatisfaction with how the Carter administration had handled economic and foreign policy issues. Figure 6.2 tracks the state of the economy with regard to inflation and unemployment from 1945 through 2012. The shaded areas mark economic recessions. Heavy dashed vertical lines mark the dates for two foreign policy events affecting the economy, the 1973 Arab oil embargo and the 1979 oil shock due to a cut off in Iranian production after the Iranian revolution.

The figure shows that starting in the late 1960s, and accelerating in the 1970s, inflation became a major problem. The inflation rate increased from less than 3 percent in 1967 to around 13.5 percent in 1980. The two foreign policy events strongly affected the rise in inflation. The 1973 oil embargo resulted in long lines at gas stations and widespread public anger. In response to the embargo, Nixon imposed gas rationing and price controls. Oil was a very important input to industrial processes, heating and cooling homes, and fueling automobiles. With the price of raw industrial inputs, energy, and fuel increasing, general price levels increased.

As shown by the shaded area of Figure 6.2, the inflation increase also coincided with an economic recession between 1973 and 1975. By 1978, inflation remained high, running at about 7.6 percent. However, the 1979 oil shock sparked an even more serious rise in inflation that lasted from 1979 through 1981. The inflation of 1979 was again followed by a recession during the 1980 election year.

While inflation was rising, people were losing their jobs. Figure 6.2 shows that unemployment rose steadily from a healthy 3.5 percent in 1969 to peak at around 7.1 percent during the 1980 election year. This phenomenon of simultaneous high inflation and unemployment has been called stagflation. According to prevailing economic theory at the time, inflation and unemployment were not supposed to increase together due to the operation of the Phillips (1958) curve. The Phillips curve predicted an inverse short-run relationship between inflation and unemployment (Chang 1997).

More important politically was the effect of stagflation on economic misery. Americans experienced widespread economic dissatisfaction due to higher prices and joblessness. President Carter received much blame for these conditions. A Gallup poll administered in September 1980 found that about 60 percent of Americans disapproved of "the way Carter is handling our domestic problems – that is, our problems here at home" (Gallup 1980a). Another Gallup poll administered in October 1980 reported that over 50 percent of Americans believed that the most important problem facing the nation was "inflation/high cost of living/high prices/economic situation/taxes" (Gallup 1980b).

President Carter's handling of the Iran hostage crisis also diminished presidential support in the 1980 elections. In 1979, the Iranian Revolution brought to power a religious regime under the Ayatollah Ruhollah Khomeini. Supporting Ayatollah, student revolutionaries captured and held hostage fifty-two U.S. citizens. President Carter engaged in patient negotiations with the Iranians to secure the release of the hostages. An abortive military attempt was also made to rescue the hostages. The Iranians held the American hostages for 444 days, during which time there was nonstop media coverage. The hostages were finally released the day Ronald Reagan was inaugurated.

The evidence shows that President Carter's failure to secure the hostages' release weighed heavily on the electorate. A NBC News/Associated Press poll in

October 1980 reported 55 percent of Americans disapproving of how President Carter had handled the hostage situation (NBC News/Associated Press 1980). A Cambridge Reports National Omnibus Survey the same month showed that around 77 percent of likely voters considered the hostage crisis very important to their votes (Cambridge Reports 1980).

RONALD REAGAN AND THE START OF MODERN POLARIZATION

Against this backdrop, Ronald Reagan won the presidency in 1980 espousing the most conservative views of any president since 1928. Of course, Reagan had failed voicing the same philosophy in 1964 in support of Barry Goldwater and when he ran for president in 1968 and 1976. What had changed in between were the Republican Party and the mood of the country. Old Guard Republicans now dominated and the mood of the country had soured toward the incumbent president.

However, support for Reagan's more conservative perspective was neither immediate nor substantial. Moreover, it was *not* the basis for his election. Americans were no more willing in 1980 to accept the pre–New Deal social contract than they had been in 1933. There was no public outcry to repeal Social Security, Medicare, unemployment benefits, the FDIC, the forty-hour workweek, the minimum wage, securities regulation, environmental protection, or the plethora of other social and regulatory programs enacted between 1933 and the 1970s. However, the economics and politics of the 1970s had produced doubts about the ability of Democrats to deliver the Great Society.

Reagan used those doubts over the next eight years to attack the foundations of the New Deal social contract, particularly as it pertained to the progressive tax system, the size of government, alleged bureaucratic bloat, regulation, and social programs. Early Reagan administration policy initiatives in each of these areas stealthily tipped the scales back toward the propertied class regarding who benefited from government.

The 1980 Elections

The 1980 elections did *not* reflect a massive upsurge of popular support for Reagan or the Republican Party. In the three-candidate presidential race, the vote percentages were 50.8 percent for Reagan, 41 percent for Carter, and 6.6 percent for John Anderson. The Republicans gained control of the Senate, 53–46, for the first time since 1954. Despite the gain, Republican Senate candidates actually lost the popular vote by over four million votes (Wikipedia 2015c). The Democrats lost 35 seats in the House, but still retained control by a majority of 243–192. However, many of the remaining Democratic House members were from the South and sympathetic to the conservative agenda.

Interestingly, polling data a few days before the election showed that Carter held a significant lead over Reagan. A poll conducted on October 26–27 put their respective percentages at 42 percent for Carter, 39 percent for Reagan, and 8 percent for Anderson (CBS News/*New York Times* 1980a). However, an exit poll of 15,201 actual voters conducted the day of the election reported that 25 percent of voters decided their vote in the last week (CBS News/*New York Times* 1980b). Most of the late deciders voted for Reagan, producing what at the time was considered a surprising outcome.

One factor hurting Carter was Democratic Party dissension, with a significant faction feeling that Carter was too conservative and had been an ineffective leader. An opposition liberal candidate, Massachusetts Senator Edward Kennedy, entered the race early in the primary season. Carter defeated Kennedy in 24 of 34 primaries and went into the convention with a sizable majority of the delegates. However, Kennedy refused to concede, even attempting to manipulate the rules of the convention to free Carter's delegates. A short-lived "Draft Edmund Muskie" movement occurred in June before the convention in case it became deadlocked (Robbins 2008).

The Democratic Party split materialized in the vote. According to the same election day exit poll (CBS News/*New York Times* 1980b), 26 percent of Democrats voted for Reagan, with another 6 percent voting for Anderson. Around 27 percent of liberals voted for Reagan, with another 11 percent voting for Anderson. Among Democrats, 24 percent of those favoring Kennedy voted for Reagan. Among union households, 44 percent defected to Reagan (Clymer 1980).

Another factor hurting Carter was the third-party candidate, Illinois House member John Anderson. A liberal Republican, Anderson ran as an Independent and did not win a single state. He represented a liberal alternative to both Carter and Reagan. As such, he drew voters away who would normally have voted Democratic. Anderson received most of his support in New England. His strongest showing was in Massachusetts, where he won 15 percent of the popular vote.

Reagan won all states of the Deep South except Carter's home state of Georgia, thereby revalidating the Republicans' Southern strategy. Reagan carried all states in the Northeast except Maryland and Rhode Island. In the rest of the country, Reagan won all states except Minnesota, Hawaii, and West Virginia. All total, Reagan won 44 states with 489 electoral votes. It was a lopsided electoral vote outcome.

The meaning of the election was a matter of debate for some time. One analyst examining the exit poll data (CBS News/*New York Times* 1980b) concluded that the results implied a profound displeasure with Carter, rather than an acceptance of Reagan and his more conservative agenda (Clymer 1980). The exit polls showed that 38 percent of voters leaving the voting booth gave their main reason for voting for Reagan as: "It's time for a change." Half of the 38 percent cited inflation as the most important campaign issue. The "It's time for a change" explanation was given more than twice as often as any other reason, and dwarfed the 11 percent who checked "He's a real conservative."

These percentages suggest a nonideological election, rather than a swing in popular sentiment toward the Republican Right.

Academics reached similar conclusions. Pomper (1981) evaluated the exit polls and other data and concluded that the 1980 election was a referendum on Carter and the Democrats being able to keep the country prosperous (see also Hibbs 1982; Lipset and Raab 1981; McWilliams 1981; Schneider 1981). Himmelstein and McRae (1984) showed that Reagan voters were not disproportionately social conservatives, more religiously oriented, or more alienated from government.

Thus, the 1980 election was fundamentally a referendum on Jimmy Carter. With high inflation, soaring gas prices, an election year recession, the Soviet invasion of Afghanistan, and sagging national confidence due to the protracted Iran hostage crisis, a majority of Americans voted to toss the president out. The Republican candidate, Ronald Reagan, was the beneficiary of this negative sentiment.

The Heritage Foundation and the Transition to Governing

While the 1980 election did not represent a fundamental shift in the ideology or loyalties of the American electorate, it did open an opportunity for a partial revival of the Founder's social contract. The Reagan administration hit the ground running toward this end. The major reason the Reagan team got off to such a fast start was the transition period work of the Heritage Foundation.

In the summer of 1980, the Heritage Foundation produced an 1100-page report entitled *Mandate for Leadership: Policy Management in a Conservative Administration* (Heatherly 1981). The report included thirty-two papers authored by Heritage Foundation–selected experts on how to shift policy in a conservative direction. Released to the Reagan transition team in November 1980 before it was published, it became the basis for many Reagan administration initiatives (Fuelner 1981).

The Heritage Foundation report called for reductions in the food stamp, school lunch, and other nutritional programs (Paarlberg 1981). It proposed curtailing the activities of the Office of Civil Rights in the Departments of Education and Health and Human Services (Docksai 1981; Winston 1981). The report called the Civil Rights Division of the Justice Department one of the "most radicalized divisions," recommending a curtailment of affirmative action programs and a repeal of President Johnson's Executive Order requiring government contractors to "take affirmative actions to ensure" nondiscriminatory treatment (Hammond 1981). It suggested abolishing the Department of Education or transferring many of its functions to the state and local levels. The report proposed having the Department of Commerce take the lead in reducing business regulation (Bradford 1981). The Heritage Foundation report recommended easing the burden on drug companies for bringing new drugs to market, and relaxing regulatory standards for food safety. It proposed large reductions in money and personnel for the Department of Housing and Urban Development, as well as relaxing regulatory standards in home construction, lead-based paint, and fair housing (Wall 1981). The report characterized the Labor Department as an advocate for organized labor and called for a less conflict-oriented approach to regulating worker safety and health (Hunter 1981). It called for the National Highway Traffic Safety Administration to exercise greater regulatory caution, and consider auto industry profitability (Swain 1981).

The Heritage Foundation report railed against excessive regulation and the costs for the U.S. economy. Twelve of the papers proposed abolishing or reining in specific independent regulatory agencies, including the Civil Aeronautics Board (CAB), Interstate Commerce Commission (ICC), Commodity Futures Trading Commission (CFTC), Consumer Product Safety Commission (CPSC), Federal Communications Commission (FCC), Federal Election Commission (FEC), Federal Maritime Commission (FMC), National Transportation Safety Board (NTSB), Securities and Exchange Commission (SEC), and Federal Trade Commission (FTC).

The FTC and Environmental Protection Agency (EPA) were particular targets of the report. The Heritage Foundation recommended divestiture of the FTC's anti-trust function and a narrowing of its rulemaking authority to preclude rules encompassing entire industries (Hinish 1981). A much longer paper was issued for the EPA, indicating its importance to curtailing business regulation (Hinish 1981).

Recognizing that it would be difficult to deregulate legislatively, the Heritage Foundation report called for the president to use an "administrative presidency" strategy (Nathan 1983; Waterman 1989). The appointment power was to be used to fill each agency's leadership with appointees sympathetic to the right-wing perspective. Finally, the new president was to choose targets of deregulation selectively. In particular, the recommendation was that the president focus on the EPA and its clean air standards, rather than on minor agencies.

The Treasury Department chapter contained the core recommendations for tax policy. It advocated the wholesale application of supply-side economics. The report called for a drastic overhaul of the tax system to move the tax code away from progressivity and toward a flat tax. Across the board personal income tax rate reductions (resulting in much more income for high-income groups) were recommended to increase the incentive for saving and investment. To increase savings and investment, the report advocated excluding some percentage of interest, savings, and dividends from taxation. Concerning businesses, the report called for accelerated depreciation allowances to increase investable income and bolster profitability. Corporate income taxes were to be reduced. The capital gains tax was also to be cut (Ture 1981).

According to the Heritage Foundation, the Reagan administration had implemented or initiated about 60 percent of the recommendations by the end of the first year. The Reagan administration offered high-level appointments to several dozen *Mandate* authors and placed more than 200 conservatives per year in government jobs. Many contributors to the report became officials of the Reagan administration, including FTC Chairman James C. Miller III, Interior Secretary James G. Watt, and Education Secretary William Bennett (Edwards 1997, 50–52). At the first meeting of Ronald Reagan's cabinet, the president gave each member a copy of the Heritage Foundation report. Never before in American history had a single foundation been so influential of an incoming presidential administration (Edwards 1997, 41–68).

Reagan and Taxes

The centerpiece of the Reagan strategy was reducing taxes. Between 1981 and 1988, the two largest tax cuts in American history were implemented through the Economic Recovery Tax Act (ERTA) of 1981, also known as Kemp–Roth, and the Tax Reform Act (TRA) of 1986 (Tempalski 2006). The ERTA lowered the top income tax rate from 70 to 50 percent over three years. The law accelerated the rate at which businesses could claim depreciation deductions and reduced the windfall profits tax on the energy industry. It reduced the taxes corporations paid by $150 billion over the next five years. It increased the estate tax exemption and lowered the tax by 15 percent. The ERTA reduced the capital gains tax from 28 to 20 percent (CQ Almanac Online 1981; Jacobson et al. 2006).

Another round of large tax cuts occurred in 1986. The TRA of 1986 consolidated income tax brackets from fourteen income levels down to two. The law drastically reduced the top rate from 50 to 28 percent starting in 1988, a huge boon to the wealthy. At the same time, the bottom rate increased from 11 to 15 percent, a penalty on low-income earners. The effect of this consolidation was to produce a system more closely resembling a flat tax. On signing the TRA, Reagan hailed the bill as the end of "the steeply progressive income tax" (CQ Almanac Online 1986).

The TRA also repealed the sales tax exemption for individual income tax deductions. It repealed the capital gains tax exclusion on home sales so that long-term capital gains became fully taxable starting in 1987. These changes heavily penalized the middle class, whose homes had appreciated rapidly during the inflationary period of the 1970s and '80s. The TRA also lowered the top corporate income tax rates from 40 percent to 34 percent (CQ Almanac Online 1986; Tempalski 2006).

The net effect of these changes was a tax system that became far less progressive and more favorable to the upper class. Figure 6.3 graphs the top marginal tax rates historically for individuals, estates, corporations, and investors (capital gains) from 1913 through 2012. The heavy dashed vertical lines mark the year of passage of the ERTA and TRA.

The figure shows that during World War I, as discussed in Chapter 3, taxes increased sharply for high-income individuals and corporations. Between 1921 and 1932, top rates dropped during three Republican administrations. With

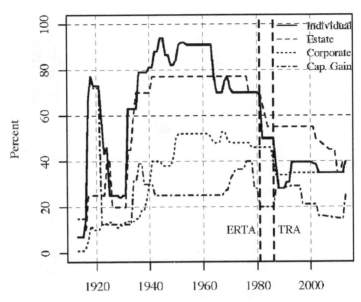

FIGURE 6.3 Top Marginal Tax Rates
Sources: IRS, Statistics of Income Division, historical tables 23 and 24, www.irs.gov/pub/irs-soi/ninetyestate.pdf; www.treasury.gov/resource-center/tax-policy/Documents/OTP-CG-Taxes-Paid-Pos-CG-1954-2009-6-2012.pdf.

the New Deal and World War II, taxes on high-income individuals, estates, corporations, and investors rose sharply again and remained high until 1981. From 1981 on, taxes on high-income groups were significantly lower. Indeed, the post-1986 individual tax rate paid by the highest income group was lower than at any time since the 1920s. Similarly, the capital gains tax was about equal to that in the 1920s. Corporate and estate taxes also dropped. Thus, the main beneficiaries of the Reagan era tax changes were those at the top.

Through time, tax policy became a major basis of polarization in the American system. Efforts to raise taxes on the wealthy were resisted with religious fervor by Republicans and tax ideologues such as Grover Norquist. At Reagan's request in 1985, Norquist formed the advocacy group Americans for Tax Reform. Norquist wielded considerable influence over Republican legislators by securing their pledge to oppose any and all tax increases. Indeed, his no new taxes pledge had been signed by 95 percent of Republican members of the 113th Congress (Americans for Tax Reform 2015).

These changes in the tax system coincide closely with increasing income inequality in the United States. This increasing inequality can be seen in Figure 6.4, which graphs the historical percentage of income received by the top 10 percent of all taxpayers. The data are from Piketty and Saez (2003), updated through 2012, and include income from all sources, including dividends, interest, and capital gains. The graph is broken down by income held for four percentiles from 90 to 99 percent, 99 to 99.9 percent, 99.9 to 99.99 percent,

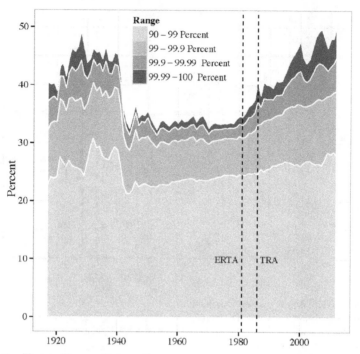

FIGURE 6.4 Top 10 Percent Income Shares, 1917–2012
Source: Calculated from Piketty and Saez (2003), table A3 updated to 2012 by the authors.

and 99.99 to 100 percent. Again, heavy vertical dashed lines show passage of the ERTA of 1981 and the TRA of 1986.

Figure 6.4 shows that income inequality dropped sharply in the 1930s and remained lower through 1980. The top 10 percent averaged about 35 percent of total income held between 1935 and 1980. However, after the ERTA of 1981 and the TRA of 1986, the top group's share of income increased steadily through 2012 to peak at around 50 percent. The inequality is progressively greatest for the highest income group. The largest gains between 1981 and 2012 were for the top 0.01 percent taxpayer group (the black region). The next largest gains came for the 99.99 group (dark gray). The next largest gains came from the 99–99.9 percent group (gray). The 90–99 percent group (light gray) experienced only a steady upward trend through time. Thus, there was a distinctly upper class bias to the American system after 1981.

This upper-class bias can also be seen by examining the increasing wealth share through time of the very richest people in America, shown in Figure 6.5. Saez and Zuckman (2016) compiled data on the total wealth held historically by percentile groups from 1917 through 2012. Figure 6.5 shows that wealth inequality was highest during the 1920s before the stock market crash and Great Depression. After this, wealth inequality declined steadily until around 1986. During this period, more and more Americans invested in home

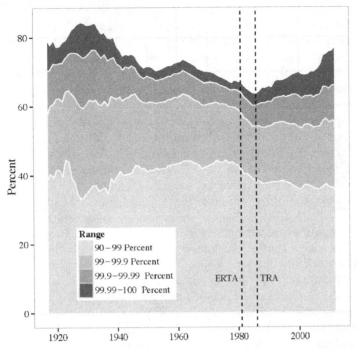

FIGURE 6.5 Top 10 Percent Wealth Shares, 1917–2012
Source: Calculated from Saez and Zuckman (2016).

ownership, the major source of wealth for most Americans. However, the TRA of 1986 eliminated the capital gains exclusion for individual home sales, a disincentive for middle-class Americans to invest in a home.

After 1986, the percentage of the nation's wealth held by the top 0.01 percent of the population (the black region) started to increase. The wealth held by the 99.99 percent (dark gray) group also increased. However, the wealth held by the 99–99.9 percent group (gray) dropped, as did that held by the 90–99 percent group (light gray). By 2012, more than three-fourths of the nation's wealth was concentrated in the top 10 percent of all taxpayers, with the top 1 percent holding 22 percent of the nation's wealth. Thus, Figure 6.5 shows that the rich got considerably richer between 1986 and 2012. Wealth became increasingly concentrated at the top of the economic system.

Reagan and Regulation

As recommended by the Heritage Foundation Report, the Reagan administration also waged a continuous assault on regulation. The first action occurred through E.O. 12291, issued barely one month after the president took office. This order substantially altered and suppressed the federal rulemaking process. It required each agency, before the issuance of major new rules, to perform a

Regulatory Impact Analysis of the costs and benefits of the rule to the extent allowed by law. The order defined a major rule as one having an impact of more than $100 million on the economy (*Federal Register* 1981)

E.O. 12291 was immediately controversial. Opponents asserted that it was an unconstitutional effort to override Congress and reduce environmental, health, and safety programs. They claimed that the order was little more than a veiled undemocratic effort to deregulate business and industry. Opponents also complained that the order "requires assigning dollar values to things that are essentially not quantifiable: human life and health, the beauty of a forest, the clarity of the air at the rim of the Grand Canyon" (Shabecoff 1981). The required cost–benefit analysis also involved normative judgments that were clearly manipulable by free-market friendly economists.

Regardless, the order was implemented and had a chilling effect on new regulations by federal regulatory agencies. In 1980 before the order, the number of new proposed rules published in the *Federal Register* was 5,347. After the president's order, the number dropped to 3,862, or by 27 percent, and continued declining through 1990. The total drop in new proposed rules between 1981 and 1990 was 2,177, or about 41 percent (see data at *Federal Register* 2014). Hence, the Reagan administration curtailed efforts by regulatory bureaucracies to implement legislatively enacted policies.

Reagan administration efforts to curtail regulation also extended to the implementation of existing regulatory programs. Wood and Waterman (1994) detailed the effects of Reagan administration appointees, budgets, and organizational authority on enforcement efforts by seven different federal regulatory agencies. They showed that, consistent with the Heritage Foundation recommendations, political appointments were by far the most important tool the administration used to suppress existing regulation.

At the EEOC, Reagan appointed Clarence Thomas chair of the Commission, and Michael Connolly as general counsel. Both opposed class-action lawsuits, setting goals, timetables, and hiring quotas in enforcing equal employment opportunity. Connolly even told the Commission soon after his confirmation by the new Republican Senate that he would no longer be pressing sexual harassment, age discrimination, equal pay, and class action lawsuits. This was in clear violation of the laws in these areas. A controversial figure, his tenure lasted only from November 1981 through September 1982. EEO litigations dropped during this period from about forty per month before his arrival to fewer than five per month at the time of his exit (Wood 1990; Wood and Waterman 1994, 38–42).

At the FTC, Reagan appointed James C. Miller III as chairman of the Commission. Miller had written the Heritage Foundation chapter on the FTC, and headed Reagan's Task Force on Regulatory Relief that produced E.O. 12291 (Harris and Milkis 1996). A Chicago School advocate, Miller's intentions were clear from the start in wanting to decrease the agency's consumer protection efforts and reducing industry regulation. Even before Miller's appointment, the Reagan administration had slashed the proposed FTC budget for 1982 by 23 percent. Confirmed in September 1981, enforcement activities after his appointment dropped by about 50 percent. The reduced vigor with which the FTC protected consumers and enforced industry regulations continued through 1988 (Wood and Waterman 1994, 43–48).

Reagan appointees also suppressed enforcement by the Nuclear Regulatory Commission, resulting in fewer safety citations by inspectors at nuclear power plants (Wood and Waterman 1994, 48–52). They curtailed the activities of the Anti-Trust Division of the Justice Department (Wood and Anderson 1993). Automobile safety enforcements were greatly diminished at the NHTSA (Wood and Waterman 1994, 58–62) and food and drug safety enforcements dropped at the FDA (Wood and Waterman 1994, 52–58). Reagan appointees also dramatically diminished safety enforcement by the Office of Surface Mining (Wood and Waterman 1994, 62–66).

However, the most visible and controversial Reagan administration efforts at deregulation were those at the EPA. The Heritage Foundation report and the Reagan administration viewed the EPA, and especially its clean air regulations, as a major threat to corporate and commercial interests. As such, a great effort was made to diminish EPA enforcement activities. Beginning in fiscal year 1982, large budget cuts occurred for virtually every program. In May 1981, an anti-environmental attorney, Ann Gorsuch (later Burford), was appointed to head the agency. After Burford's appointment massive personnel shifts occurred, with the most zealous officials transferred to remote locations. The number of full-time EPA employees dropped by 20 percent between 1981 and 1983. These changes sharply reduced enforcement activities at the Clean Air, Clean Water, Pesticides, and Hazardous Waste Divisions (Wood 1988; Wood and Waterman 1993; 1994, 66–71, 77–102, 117–26).

Reagan and Social Welfare

As recommended by the Heritage Foundation, Reagan entered office intent on shifting budget priorities away from social programs and toward national defense. This goal was accomplished through another important law, the Omnibus Budget Reconciliation Act (OBRA) of 1981.

In the 1970s, Reagan had been especially hostile toward women on welfare. He personally coined the term "welfare queen" during the 1976 election campaign to imply unwed African-American women were committing welfare fraud and having babies just to draw more and more benefits. Reagan's characterization of welfare recipients was blatantly false but struck a resonant chord with many who disliked African-Americans and welfare recipients and those seeking someone to blame for poor economic conditions. By 1981, the "welfare queen" hype had become a part of American popular culture (Douglas and Michaels 2005, 185–88).

As a result, OBRA passed easily and sharply cut spending for programs directed at the poor. Unemployment insurance was reduced by $17.4 billion (Midgley 1992). Spending on employment and training programs fell from about $28 billion to about $8 billion (in 1992 dollars) between 1979 and 1982.

OBRA authorized states to convert the Work Incentive (WIN) program into a block grant administered by state welfare agencies and to use workfare as a requirement for eligibility. While OBRA gave states flexibility to shape their AFDC programs, less money also became available. The major federal funding source for these programs, WIN, experienced annual budget cuts, with funding falling 70 percent between 1981 and 1987 (Caputo 2011, 31).

Toughening eligibility requirements and changing benefit calculations also drastically reduced AFDC participation. OBRA instituted maximum limits above which states could not make AFDC payments. In 1980, 42 states provided AFDC payments to a woman with two children with income at 75 percent of the poverty line; by 1984, only seven states provided this benefit. OBRA also eliminated the rule that enabled a welfare recipient to earn $30 a month before losing any benefits. Under OBRA, benefits were reduced by one dollar for every dollar earned above the income threshold (Moffitt and Wolf 1987). By the start of 1983, almost half a million recipients had been eliminated from the welfare rolls, or about 14 percent of all recipients (Danziger 1997, 23–31).

OBRA also reduced spending for the Food Stamp Program, the School Lunch Program, and social services. OBRA changed eligibility requirements for both Food Stamps and the School Lunch Program (Schuldes 2011, 342–73). The Congressional Budget Office estimated that the new OBRA eligibility standards would reduce participation in the Food Stamp Program by 20 percent and the School Lunch Program by 35 percent by 1983 (Hoagland 1984, 43–71). By 1983, the law had cut funding for "child nutrition programs by 28 percent, food stamp expenditures by 13.8 percent, and the Community Services Block Grant program by 37.1 percent" (Midgley 1992, 25) The inevitable consequence of all of these changes was increasing misery for poor Americans.

Figure 6.6 shows the number of Americans living in poverty from 1959 through 2012. The graph shows that poverty declined sharply from 1963 through 1979. It increased during the 1980 recession. However, by 1983, six million more people were living in poverty than in 1980. Part of this increase was due to the severe 1982 recession. However, the reduction of social welfare and unemployment benefits under OBRA enabled the continuing increase. By the start of the Clinton administration the number of people in poverty had risen to near the 1960 level. With the good economic times of the Clinton administration, poverty declined sharply again between 1993 and 2000. However, poverty resumed its upward climb after 2000, and grew to historic levels during the Great Recession. The implication is that the retreat from the family assistance programs of the 1960s and 1970s had a very negative long-term effect on the poor.

Reagan administration policies also affected another dimension of poverty, homelessness. OBRA reduced the eligibility rate for public housing from 80 percent to 50 percent of the local area's median income. Ceiling rents were eliminated, thereby making housing less affordable for many (Popkin 2000, 200). Federal funding for subsidized housing assistance fell from $26.6 billion in

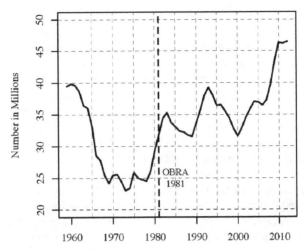

FIGURE 6.6 Americans Living in Poverty
Source: DeNavas-Walt, Proctor, and Smith (2013), table B-1.

1980 to $7.4 billion in 1989, a decline of almost 80 percent (Rubin et al. 1992). Coupled with changes in welfare programs, these changes in housing assistance led to a sharp increase in the number of homeless Americans. Homeless rates tripled between 1981 and 1989 (Burt 2010). By the late 1980s, the number of homeless in the cities of America had swollen to 600,000 on any given night – and 1.2 million over the course of a year (Dreier 2004).

Homelessness was made even worse by Reagan administration policies toward the mentally ill. Before Reagan assumed office, President Carter had signed the Mental Health Systems Act of 1980. However, the Reagan Office of Management and Budget (OMB) announced within one month that it would curtail the budget of the National Institute of Mental Health (NIMH), phase out training of clinicians, interrupt research, and eliminate services. Subsequently, OBRA repealed the Mental Health Systems Act and consolidated alcohol, drug abuse, and mental health programs into a block grant to be administered by the states. After this, the federal role in services to the mentally ill became one of providing technical assistance only (National Institute of Mental Health 2014). State mental health institutions lost federal support and lacked state funding. Without funding, state mental health institutions dumped their patients onto the streets, leading to a sharp increase in mental health–related homelessness in America.

Reagan, the Religious Right, and Cultural Issues

Before 1980, cultural issues had not been a major part of the Republican agenda. However, the Heritage Foundation pursued a deliberate strategy starting in

1979 of attempting to bring the Religious Right into the Republican Right by connecting economic issues with cultural issues. As noted, Paul Weyrich actually co-founded two evangelical organizations, Christian Voice and the Moral Majority. He also led efforts to indoctrinate evangelical pastors and their congregations about the godliness of free markets, small government, and deregulation. In return for their propagandizing, there was an implicit quid pro quo with the Religious Right of returning morality and family values to America.

Consistent with this strategy, Ronald Reagan did more than any other president to make evangelicals feel part of the Republican Party (Miller 2014). Reagan and the Republican Platform promised benefits that included a constitutional amendment on abortion, a restoration of prayer in the public schools, and the appointment of federal judges who would restore family values through the legal system (Republican National Committee 1980).

Many conservatives saw the Supreme Court as having conducted an assault on moral values during previous decades. *Engel v. Vitale* (1962) ruled that it was unconstitutional for a government agency like a school or government agents like public school employees to require students to recite prayers. *Stanley v. Georgia* (1969) supported a privacy right to pornography, ruling that people could view whatever they wished in the privacy of their homes. *Miller v. California* (1972) proscribed pornography by defining it, but also warned that states must tread carefully to avoid violating pornographers' First Amendment rights. Of course, the case that most incensed the Religious Right was *Roe v. Wade* (1973), which established a right to privacy under the Fourteenth Amendment due process clause extending to a woman's decision to have an abortion.

These Supreme Court decisions would be difficult to overturn legislatively, since they had been grounded in constitutional interpretation. Also, Republicans were at this time almost as divided as Democrats over these issues. Nevertheless, Reagan supported the constitutional amendment restricting abortion proposed by Utah Republican Senator Orin Hatch in September 1981, as well as the constitutional amendment cosponsored by Hatch and Senator Thomas Eagleton (D-Missouri) in January 1983 (NCHLA 2004). On May 17, 1982, Reagan also personally proposed a constitutional amendment to allow voluntary prayer in the public schools (Reagan 1982). All of these proposals failed to garner sufficient Senate support.

The Religious Right widely decried these legislative failures (ARL 1984). Many evangelicals blamed Reagan for not pushing their causes hard enough (Kyle 2011, 200). They were especially upset with his slow movement on abortion. Anti-abortion leaders met with him at the White House on January 22, 1982, and reported that he said he had not promised to give abortion a high priority or to use his political muscle to push an anti-abortion amendment. He was using his energy to focus on the economy and other issues deemed more pressing (Roberts 1982). Needless to say, evangelicals were unhappy over Reagan's lack of enthusiasm (Gary Smith 2006, 339–44).

Nevertheless, evangelicals did not abandon Reagan, working even harder for his 1984 reelection. The Religious Right had received far more consideration from the Reagan administration than had ever been given. Reagan appointed evangelicals to high-level administration positions, including Donald Hodel and James Watt as Secretaries of Interior, Elizabeth Dole as Secretary of Transportation, C. Everett Koop as Surgeon-General, and Bob Billings as Under-Secretary for Education (Gary Smith 2006, 239–40; Miller 2014). Reagan appointed William Bennett in 1981 to head the National Endowment for the Humanities, and he became Secretary of Education in 1985. Reagan had originally nominated Mel Bradford to this position, but due to Bradford's pro-Confederate views Bennett was appointed in his place (Gordon 2010). Evangelicals were also appointed to important positions in the Justice Department and Department of Health and Human Services. The White House even assigned several staff members to the Office of Public Liaison to work with key religious leaders and groups (Gary Smith 2006, 339–44).

Reagan especially wanted to connect with televangelists, giving them unprecedented access to the White House (Hadden 1993; Johnson 2003, chapter 16). The most prominent televangelists were Jerry Falwell (Liberty Channel), Pat Robertson (Christian Broadcasting Network), Jimmy Swaggart (Study in the Word), James Robison (Trinity Broadcasting Network), James Dobson (Focus on the Family), Oral Roberts (The Abundant Life), and Jim and Tammy Faye Baker (Praise the Lord Club). At the same time he largely snubbed the most established religious leaders in the nation (Gary Smith 2006, 239–40). Between 1978 and 1989, the number of Christian ministries broadcasting on television grew from 25 to 336 (Johnson 2003, 196–97). At their peak, they influenced as many as 25 million followers (Hadden 1993). Through the mid-1980s, the televangelists strongly aligned themselves with the Reagan administration and its policies, and were crucial to Reagan's 1984 reelection (Hadden 1993).

On judicial appointments, Reagan elevated one associate justice to Chief Justice (William Rehnquist, 1986), and appointed three new associate justices of the Supreme Court (Sandra Day O'Connor, 1981; Antonin Scalia, 1986; and Anthony Kennedy, 1987). The Religious Right wanted Reagan's judicial appointments to swing the Court back toward the moral America they wanted. However, as with Reagan's legislative initiatives, things did not work out that way.

In 1981, Reagan went against pro-life and fundamentalist groups that opposed the nomination of Sandra Day O'Connor to the Supreme Court. While she had been noncommittal on the abortion issue, it was suspected that she would not vote to overturn *Roe v. Wade* (Greenburg 2007, 141, 222–23). After the 1984 election, Reagan rewarded these groups with the elevation of William Rehnquist to Chief Justice and the appointment of Antonin Scalia. Rehnquist had been the most conservative associate justice on the Court from his initial appointment by Nixon in 1972. As a court clerk, he had written a memo arguing that *Plessy v. Ferguson* (1896), enabling "separate but equal" schools for blacks and whites, should not have been overturned. As an associate justice, he opposed the expansion of school desegregation and dissented from the majority on *Roe v. Wade*. As Chief Justice, Rehnquist remained the most conservative through the early 1990s. After the early 1990s, Scalia became even more conservative than Rehnquist. O'Connor and Kennedy were more moderate, often becoming important swing votes (Bailey 2012; Martin and Quinn 2002; updated in Wikipedia 2014d).

Scalia consistently voted to restrict abortion, usually joined by Rehnquist (e.g., see the landmark case *Planned Parenthood v. Casey*, 1992; but see *Webster v. Reproductive Health Services*, 1989). O'Connor and Kennedy generally voted to uphold Roe (*Planned Parenthood v. Casey*, 1992). Rehnquist and Scalia consistently defended state-sanctioned prayer in public schools, while O'Connor and Kennedy consistently deemed it unconstitutional (e.g., see *Lee v. Weisman*, 1991). On pornography, the same coalitions often emerged (e.g., see *Ashcroft v. Free Speech Coalition*, 1992). Scalia and Rehnquist regularly aligned on cases restricting gay rights, with O'Connor and Kennedy in opposition (e.g., see *Romer v. Evans* 1996). Thus, the Rehnquist court did little to alter established judicial doctrine on morality (e.g., see Merrill 2003).

With dim prospects for appeasing the Religious Right through legislative or judicial means, Ronald Reagan turned to symbolic politics. In early 1984, he published a ninety-five-page pamphlet entitled *Abortion and the Conscience of a Nation*, giving his reasons for opposing abortion (Reagan 1984). On July 12, 1984, NBC News broadcast a video of the president meeting at the White House with Reverends Jerry Falwell, Jimmy Swaggart, and other prominent televangelists. During 1983 and 1984, Reagan made three major speeches to religious groups (*Public Papers of the Presidents* 1983, 1984b, 1984c). Interestingly, a search of the *Public Papers* shows that Reagan made no other speeches to religious organizations after the 1984 election.

However, Reagan's silence on another issue, AIDS/HIV, is revealing of the increased importance of the Religious Right to Reagan and the Republican Party. The first AIDS deaths reported in the United States were those of five men in San Francisco in 1981. The disease spread exponentially across the United States population through 1993, at which point over 20,000 new cases quarterly were being reported. Between 1981 and 1987, over 50,000 AIDS deaths occurred as reported by the Centers for Disease Control and Prevention (CDC 2001).

This number is only somewhat less that the total number who died in the Vietnam War. Yet Ronald Reagan made no public mention of AIDS or HIV until September 17, 1986 (AIDS.gov 2014). On September 17, 1985, he even expressed the view at a news conference that children with AIDS should not be attending public schools (*Public Papers of the Presidents* 1984a), even after the Surgeon General had made clear that the disease could not be spread by casual contact.

Reagan's Secretary of Health and Human Services, Richard Schweiker, supported only meager research funding for AIDS/HIV (Rollins 1998). However, Surgeon General C. Everett Koop went against the administration by issuing a report on October 22, 1986, urging parents to initiate frank and open talks about AIDS emphasizing sex education and the use of condoms (AIDS. gov 2014). Reagan's Education Secretary, William Bennett, had attempted to prevent the report, fearing that it would alienate the Religious Right, which was virulently opposed to homosexuality (Rimmerman 1998, 399–400). Finally, on May 31, 1987, Reagan made his first public speech about AIDS in which he finally established a Presidential Commission on HIV (AIDS.gov 2014).

Throughout this period, evangelical preachers such as Jerry Falwell, Franklin Graham, Jimmy Swaggart, and Pat Robertson were saying that AIDS was a curse handed down from God on the homosexual community (McElvaine 2009, 35–39). Some have argued that Reagan's reluctance to speak publicly about AIDS was because the disease was strongly associated with homosexual behavior (Haider-Markel 1998; Rimmerman 1998; Rollins 1998). Whatever the reason for Reagan's silence on AIDS/HIV, it was clear that homosexuality and gay rights would become increasingly divisive in American society in coming years, just as did abortion, school prayer, and other cultural issues.

POLARIZATION AFTER RONALD REAGAN

Ronald Reagan was a highly polarizing president. However, most presidents since Ronald Reagan have also been highly polarizing. Examining partisan approval of the president's job performance through time reveals evidence of this polarization. Figure 6.7 tracks the absolute value of the difference in Democratic and Republican approval of the president from January 1953 through December 2012. The heavy dashed vertical lines mark the start of each presidency from Reagan through Obama.

Before Ronald Reagan the average difference in opposing partisans' approval of the president's job performance was about 35 percent. That difference shot up to 52 percent during the Reagan administration. His successor, George H. W. Bush, was far less polarizing until near the end of his term. Partisans were starkly divided over how Bush handled the economy during this period (e.g., see ABC News/*Washington Post* 1990). Polarization in presidential job approval ratings increased again during the Clinton presidency, and was at about the same level as during Reagan. The George W. Bush presidency saw similar polarization through September 11, 2001. However, polarization declined sharply after September 11. After Bush invaded Iraq, polarization increased to historic levels and remained high through the Obama administration.

Why did polarization continue and even increase after Reagan? Reagan followed the Heritage Foundation's strategy of restoring rents to the patrician class through low taxes, deregulation, and reduced social welfare, while linking

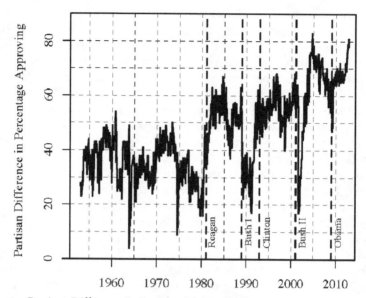

FIGURE 6.7 Partisan Difference in Presidential Approval
Source: www.gallup.com/poll/124922/presidential-apprpoval-center.aspx. The heavy vertical
dashed lines mark the starts of the Reagan, Bush I, Clinton, Bush II, and Obama administrations.
The shaded area marks the period from September 11, 2001, through the Iraq invasion.

these issues with highly emotional topics such as abortion, school prayer, and
homosexuality. Republicans since Reagan have also followed the Heritage
Foundation strategy.

Economic Polarization from 1989 through 2000

The dominant dimension separating the political parties since Reagan has been
economic. Specifically, conflict has escalated through time over who should pay
for and benefit from government. The debates over these issues have been
consistently grounded in a new problem created by Reagan's policies: deficits
and debt.

The Reagan tax cuts coupled with large increases in defense spending
roughly doubled the national debt between 1980 and 1989. By 1990, it
appeared that the national debt was increasing without bound. Calls emerged
from both political parties to find a solution. Of course, debt can be resolved
through increased taxes, reduced spending, or some combination of the two.
Thus, battles over taxes, spending, deficits, and debt have increasingly dominated American politics.

The annual federal budget battles have continually stoked the fires of polarization since 1989. Indeed, no other issue has unified Republicans more in the
post-Reagan era than their loathing for taxes, especially on the wealthy. Their
preferred approach to attacking budget deficits has been to hold the line

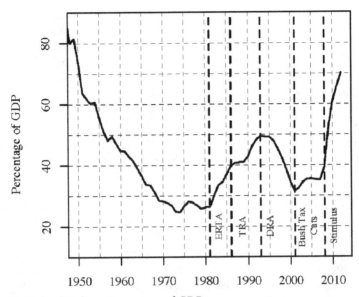

FIGURE 6.8 Federal Debt as Percentage of GDP
Source: Congressional Budget Office using end-of-calendar-year data on federal debt from the Department of the Treasury and the Board of Governors of the Federal Reserve System. Estimates of GDP come from the Bureau of the Census.

on taxes and cut spending, generally targeting New Deal and Great Society programs. In contrast, Democrats have perpetually favored lowering deficits and debt through reduced spending and increased taxes directed mainly toward the upper class.

The dynamics of taxing, spending, deficit, and debt politics become clear when observing data on the federal debt. Figure 6.8 plots the federal debt as a percentage of GDP from 1946 through 2012. When the percentage is decreasing, debt is being retired more rapidly than new debt is acquired. When the percentage is increasing, new debt is being acquired more rapidly than old debt is retired. Heavy vertical dashed lines mark the major budgetary events affecting change in the federal debt.

The graph shows that federal debt to GDP ratio declined steadily from the end of World War II through 1980. Starting with Reagan's ERTA of 1981 and continuing with the TRA of 1986, the federal debt began rising sharply. The increase continued through 1993 when a Democratic Congress and President Bill Clinton enacted the Deficit Reduction Act (DRA) of 1993. This law increased taxes somewhat on the upper class (see Figure 6.3). The budget was in surplus by 1997 and remained so through 2001. Then, President George W. Bush and a Republican Congress passed two large tax cuts in 2001 and 2003. The debt increased again after 2001 and continued a slow climb through 2007. Finally, the economic meltdown of 2007–8 was followed by huge amounts of stimulus spending, again sharply increasing the federal debt.

The polarized politics surrounding these dynamics started in 1990. Democrats, again controlling both the House and Senate, demanded higher taxes on the upper income group in exchange for spending cuts. In accepting the Republican presidential nomination, George H. W. Bush had made a very visible promise, stating, "Read my lips. No new taxes!" (Bush 1988). Nevertheless, Bush agreed to a budget compromise in which a new marginal tax rate was created for the highest income group. After the Reagan administration the tax rate on the highest income group was only 28 percent. After 1990, their rate increased by a mere 3 percent to 31 percent. Nevertheless, Bush's broken tax promise was politically costly.

Those most enraged by Bush's reversal were Old Guard Republicans, led by House Whip Newt Gingrich. Gingrich led over 100 House members in opposition to the budget compromise, resulting in a government shutdown from October 5 to 9, 1990. Bush's credibility with the Republican Right was destroyed, and he would receive only tepid support for the remainder of his term (Greene 2000, chapter 6). Bush's decision to compromise on taxes also served as an object lesson for future Republican politicians. Grover Norquist persistently pointed to Bush's broken tax promise in getting future Republicans to sign his tax pledge (Good 2012).

Bush's broken tax promise may also have cost him the 1992 election. An opposition candidate, right-wing ideologue Patrick Buchanan, emerged during the primary season with a candidacy based largely on the broken tax promise (Woodward 2005, chapter 10). After Bush received the Republican nomination, Buchanan stated, "We may have lost the nomination, my friends, but you and I won the battle for the heart and soul of the Republican Party" (cited in Woodward 2005, 146).

The 1992 election was a three-candidate race between Democrat Bill Clinton, Independent Ross Perot, and George H. W. Bush. Both Perot and Clinton also focused on Bush's broken tax pledge in their political advertising (Rosensteil 1992). An exit poll asking voters about the reasons for their presidential vote showed that 22 percent of voters based their decisions partially on "Bush breaking his no new taxes pledge" (VRS Election Day Exit Poll 1992).

Clinton won the 1992 election, garnering only 43 percent of the popular vote but with 370 electoral votes. Democrats retained both the House and Senate. Clinton ran on pledges to balance the budget, a tax cut for the middle class, universal health care, and the traditionally conservative policies of ending "welfare as we know it" and free trade. During a presidential debate on October 19, 1992, Clinton stated, "My [tax] plan says that we want to raise marginal [rates] on family incomes above $200,000 from 31 to 36 percent; ... that we want to use that money to provide over $100 billion in tax cuts for investment in new plant and equipment, for small business, for new technologies, and for middle class tax relief" (Clinton 1992).

However, a few days into his administration, Clinton met with Federal Reserve Chairman Alan Greenspan, who advised him that his highest priority should be the budget deficit. Based on this advice and that of economic advisor

Robert Rubin, Clinton had discarded the idea of a middle-class tax cut by the time of his first State of the Union address (Woodward 2001, chapter 7). Subsequently, Clinton delivered on his promised tax increase on high-income groups, but he reneged on the promise of middle-class tax relief.

Clinton signed the DRA on August 10, 1993. The marginal tax rate for joint filers earning more than $140,000 increased from 31 to 36 percent, and the rate for those earning more than $250,000 increased from 31 to 39.6 percent. The law left marginal tax rates intact for taxpayers below these limits, but other provisions increased taxes on low- and middle-income taxpayers. Itemized deductions were capped; the ceiling on the Medicare tax was removed; the taxable proportion of Social Security benefits was increased; and there was an increase in the gasoline tax (CQ Almanac Online 1993). Again, Clinton's broken tax cut promise was politically costly and a gift to Republicans.

The DRA had been highly polarizing in Congress. Every Republican member voted against the bill. The House passed the conference report by a vote of 218–216, with 175 Republicans and 41 Democrats voting against. The Senate passed the conference report by a vote of 51–50, with 44 Republicans and 6 Democrats voting against. Vice President Al Gore cast the deciding vote in the Senate (CQ Almanac Online 1993).

Clinton's tax increases were unpopular. One public opinion poll found 66 percent of Americans believing that the president's economic plan raised taxes too much and did not cut spending enough (ABC News/*Washington Post* 1993). Another poll found that 75 percent of respondents believed that the legislation would increase their taxes (NBC News/*Wall Street Journal* 1993).

In the run-up to the 1994 mid-term elections, Republicans emphasized Clinton's broken tax cut promise, painting him and the Democratic Congress as traditional tax and spend liberals. The result was a landslide victory for Republicans in the mid-term elections. Republicans gained 9 seats in the Senate and 54 seats in the House to become the majority party in both chambers for the first time since 1953.

Once again, the Heritage Foundation helped orchestrate the Republican victory. The Republican "Contract with America" was issued six weeks before the election. Many of the Contract's promises originated with the Heritage Foundation (Gayner 1995). The Contract, nominally coauthored by Newt Gingrich and Richard Armey, included proposals to cut taxes for families, small businesses, and seniors, a balanced budget amendment, welfare reform, term limits for legislators, social security reform, and tort reform. However, the Contract avoided controversial moral issues, such as abortion, school prayer, and homosexuality (Wikipedia 2015a).

Nonetheless, the Christian Right turned out heavily in the 1994 election. A national exit poll showed that 27 percent of all voters identified themselves as a born-again or evangelical Christian. Among evangelical Christians, 76 percent voted for Republican candidates. Economics also played a major role in the Republican landslide. Those with family incomes greater than $50,000 broke heavily for Republicans, suggesting that the tax increase and broken tax cut promise affected their decisions (Connelly 1994). All in all, the Republican landslide in the mid-term elections opened a wide cleavage within Congress and the electorate, and between Congress and the president.

Over the next three years, congressional Republicans and President Clinton engaged in trench warfare over taxing and spending policy. In 1995, the emboldened Republican Congress proposed sharp spending reductions that fell heavily on New Deal and Great Society programs. They initially proposed privatizing Medicare, converting it to a voucher system and encouraging seniors to move into a system of managed care (Chen 1995). Their 1995 budget would have cut federal Medicare spending by $270 billion. Stating their intentions, Speaker Newt Gingrich spoke to the Blue Cross/Blue Shield Association, saying, "Now we didn't get rid of it in Round 1 because we don't think that's politically smart and we don't think that's the right way to go through a transition. But we believe it's going to wither on the vine" (MacDonald 1995). The public reaction against the Republican plan to privatize Medicare was swift and strong, resulting in Republicans quickly abandoning their effort.

The 1995 Republican budget would also have included deep cuts in entitlements such as Medicaid, farm programs, food stamps, child nutrition and school lunches, and AFDC. It would have ended guaranteed welfare for poor children, cut funding for education, drastically reduced the Headstart program, eliminated Americorps, cut student loan programs, limited health care guarantees for the disabled, and reduced funding for the environment. The Republican plan would also have cut taxes by $245 billion, mostly for families earning $100,000 per year or more (CQ Almanac Online 1995; Rankin 1995).

From the start, Clinton said that he would veto such a budget. Faced with the veto threat, Republicans strategically delayed passing a FY1995 budget believing that the president would back down. The government was funded by a continuing resolution between October 1 and a November 13 deadline. Republicans and Democrats negotiated over the budget but failed to reach an agreement. After Republicans passed their budget along almost strict party lines (CQ Almanac Online 1995), the president vetoed the spending bill. The result was a government shutdown in which 800,000 federal workers were furloughed. The first shutdown lasted six days, ending when the President and Congress agreed to balance the budget in seven years, but stating no specifics.

Congress again passed a continuing budget resolution to fund the government that would expire on December 15. Again, no progress was made in breaking the stalemate by the deadline, so the government shut down a second time. On December 26, Republicans threatened to allow the federal government to default on its debt by not raising the debt ceiling. The president called this tactic "political blackmail" and again did not yield to Republican demands. The government shutdown finally ended after twenty-two days on January 6, 1996, after Clinton and Congress agreed to a seven-year balanced budget plan to be overseen by the Congressional Budget Office (Bancroft Library 2014; CNN Interactive 2014). Negotiations over the FY1995 budget continued well into 1996. During this period Republicans frequently attempted to use the federal debt ceiling as a bargaining chip. The last appropriations bill passed Congress on April 26, 1996.

In the end, Republicans received most of the blame for the government shutdowns of 1995–96. A January 6–7, 1996, public opinion poll found that 50 percent of respondents blamed Republicans, while only 27 percent found the president at fault (ABC News/*Washington Post* 1996). The shutdowns may also have affected the outcome of the 1996 presidential election. An election-day exit poll found that 21 percent of respondents reported that "standing up to the Republican Congress" affected their vote for president (*Los Angeles Times* Exit Poll 1996).

The 1996 presidential election was once again a three-party race between Bill Clinton, Kansas Republican Senator Bob Dole, and Independent Ross Perot. Clinton won, receiving 49.2 percent of the popular vote and 379 electoral votes. However, Clinton's congressional coattails were short to nonexistent. Democrats picked up only two seats in the House of Representatives and lost two seats in the Senate. Republicans retained control of both chambers for the first time since 1930. The Democratic president was still facing a Republican Congress, but one that was chastened and more subdued.

In 1997, Congress passed and the president signed two major pieces of legislation intended to balance the budget by 2002. The Balanced Budget Act of 1997 reduced spending by $127 billion between 1997 and 2002. Spending reductions were divided almost evenly between entitlement programs ($122 billion) and discretionary appropriations (about $140 billion). Medicare cuts – $115 billion over five years – comprised the largest reduction. These were accomplished by reducing payments to health care providers, such as hospitals, doctors, and nurse practitioners. The law increased spending on welfare and children's health care (CQ Almanac Online 1998a).

A companion tax bill moved through Congress at the same time. The Taxpayer Relief Act of 1997 cut taxes by $95 billion over five years. The two bills basically offset one another regarding the budget deficit. It should be emphasized that the law left intact the higher marginal tax rates established earlier by the Deficit Reduction Act of 1993. However, the law affected taxes in other ways benefiting both Democrats and Republicans. Republicans obtained the largest capital gains tax reduction since 1981, a drop from 28 percent to 20 percent. They also achieved a larger exemption for the estate tax and accelerated capital depreciation schedules for large businesses. Clinton and the Democrats won significant middle-class tax incentives for education, and a $500-per-child tax credit was made available to most working poor families, including some too poor to owe any income taxes (CQ Almanac Online 1998b). Thus, the Balanced Budget Act and Taxpayer Relief Act of 1997 marked significant compromises.

Economic Polarization after the 2000 Election

As noted earlier, the budget was in surplus between 1997 and 2001. A major issue of the 2000 presidential election campaign was this surplus. Democratic presidential candidate Al Gore proposed a modest tax cut, but wanted to use remaining surpluses to strengthen Social Security and put a lockbox on the Medicare trust fund (Gore 2000). In contrast, Republican presidential candidate George W. Bush proposed a much larger tax cut that especially benefited the wealthy (Bush 2000). Of course, the story of the 2000 election is well known. George W. Bush won, receiving a majority of the electoral vote, but decisively losing the popular vote. Republicans retained slim control of Congress.

Congress moved quickly to pass the Bush tax plan. The Economic Growth and Tax Relief Reconciliation Act of 2001 reduced the top marginal tax rate from 39.6 to 35 percent by 2006, a drop of 4.6 percent. Smaller tax cuts were extended to other taxpayers, with those in the 36, 31, and 28 percent brackets dropping by only 3 percent, and with the 15 percent bracket dropping back to 10 percent for very low-income earners. Major changes also occurred in the estate tax, with the top estate size subject to the tax increasing from $675,000 in 2001 to $3.5 million by 2009. The legislation passed the House with 211 Republicans voting yes and 153 Democrats voting no, and the Senate with 45 Republicans voting yes and 31 Democrats voting no. Enacted as an economic stimulus package, the 2001 law contained a sunset provision causing the tax cuts to expire and revert to the original rates on January 1, 2011.

Tax relief during the George W. Bush presidency continued with the Jobs and Growth Tax Relief Reconciliation Act of 2003. This law accelerated the rate at which 2001 reductions occurred and sharply reduced the capital gains tax on upper income groups. This time the bill passed along partisan lines, with 224 House Republicans voting yes and 198 Democrats voting no. In the Senate 48 Republicans voted yes, and 46 Democrats voted no. The 2003 law continued the sunset provisions of the 2001 law, creating the potential for a future fight over whether the Bush tax cuts would be allowed to expire.

In 2007, the economy started a nosedive into what would become the worst economic decline since the Great Depression. As with the Great Depression, the Great Recession started with misbehavior by bankers and asset management firms that had invested heavily in some very risky assets, mortgage-backed securities. These instruments became increasingly risky due to the high rate of mortgage defaults in 2007 and 2008. Investor panic ensued as housing prices declined, and it became apparent that many companies holding these securities were undercapitalized.

In March 2008, shares of Bear Sterns declined to near zero, and the Federal Reserve brokered its acquisition by J. P. Morgan Chase. In July, the fourth largest bank failure in U.S. history occurred, with the collapse of Indymac Bank. In early September, the federal government took over Fannie Mae and

Freddie Mac, which owned or guaranteed about half of the $12 trillion U.S. mortgage market. In mid-September, the largest bankruptcy in U.S. history occurred with the failure of Lehman Brothers. To prevent another large bankruptcy, the Federal Reserve injected $85 billion into American International Group to recapitalize a huge company, which was also heavily invested in mortgage-backed securities (Wood 2009, 184–85).

Against this backdrop, President Bush offered a plan to bail out the financial sector. He proposed that "the Federal Government reduce the risk posed by these troubled assets and supply urgently needed money so banks and other financial institutions can avoid collapse and resume lending ... the Federal Government would put up to $700 billion taxpayer dollars on the line to purchase troubled assets that are clogging the financial system" (*Weekly Compilation of Presidential Documents* 2008, 1252–53).

Remarkably, the president's proposal partially nationalized the U.S. financial sector by allowing the Treasury Department to buy shares of troubled institutions in exchange for government supervision. Of course, the post-Reagan Republican prescription was free markets with minimal government intervention. Thus, the president's proposal ran strongly against expectations for a Republican. To be sure, the plan was unpopular among the president's fellow partisans. On September 29 the House of Representatives rejected the "bailout" package by a vote of 228–205. The opposing votes included 133 Republicans, with only 65 members of the president's own party favoring the bill. The president's fellow partisans voted against it by more than two to one.

Much of the American public was also skeptical of the president's plan. During the week of September 19–22 before the speech, support for a bailout was at 57 percent, while for the same respondents during the week of September 27–29 after the speech it was only 45 percent (Pew Research Center 2008). Interestingly, support dropped significantly more among Republicans than it did among Democrats and Independents. Another poll showed that the president's approval rating declined after the speech to only 22 percent, with only 15 percent approving of the president's handling of the economy (CBS News 2008). Needless to say, the lack of public support and failed House vote were major political defeats for President Bush, who had tried to persuade the public through the televised address and also intensely lobbied wavering Republican legislators through personal phone calls (Calmes 2008).

The financial meltdown continued after President Bush's speech, with the collapse of Washington Mutual, the nation's largest savings and loan institution, and Wachovia, which was later acquired by Wells Fargo & Co. In the aftermath, many banks quit lending to one another. As had occurred during the Great Depression, credit effectively froze for businesses and consumers. Consumers and businesses became increasingly uncertain about the economy and were reluctant to make purchases or borrow money. The stock market also declined dramatically. On the day of the failed House vote, the Dow Jones Industrial Average dropped 778 points, or 7 percent of its total value.

Continuing to seek passage, on October 1 the Senate approved a sweetened version of the president's bailout package by a vote of 74–25, with 15 Republicans in opposition. Finally, on October 3 the revised bill passed the House of Representatives. Among Republicans, 91 House members voted for the final bill with 108 opposing. The president was still unable to muster a majority of his own party. Nevertheless, the president signed the financial bailout package on the same day it was passed. The Economic Stabilization Act of 2008 became law, providing an initial economic stimulus and initiating the large increase in the federal debt shown in Figure 6.8.

Against the backdrop of the worst economic downturn since the Great Depression, Republicans decisively lost control of the presidency and Congress in the 2008 elections. Barack Obama won over Republican John McCain, receiving 365 electoral votes and 52.9 percent of the popular vote. Democrats took control both houses of Congress for the first time since 1995. They had controlled the House since 2007, but extended their majority to 257–178. Democrats gained 8 seats in the Senate to hold a majority of 57–41.

The Democratic victory shocked many Republicans. They feared entering another period similar to the post-Depression era when they were vanquished for 50 years. However, the Republican reaction this time was not to move closer to the Democrats, as Modern Republicans had done from the 1950s through the 1970s. Rather, they did precisely the opposite. From the 2008 election through the end of the Obama presidency, the Republican Party became the party of "No!"

In early January 2009, party leaders adopted a deliberate strategy of keeping members united against virtually anything the president proposed (Draper 2012, prologue; Grunwald 2012a, chapter 7). Pete Sessions, the new Republican National Campaign Committee chair, asserted at a meeting of party leaders in Annapolis, Maryland, that the party's purpose was not to govern in this time of crisis, but "The purpose of the minority is to become the majority" (cited in Grunwald 2012a, 143). As expressed by Republican Senator George Voinovich, "If he was for it, we had to be against it" (cited in Grunwald 2012a, 19). Eric Cantor, the House Republican Whip, stated, "We're not here to cut deals and get crumbs and stay in the minority for another 40 years ... We're going to fight these guys. We're down, but things are going to change" (cited in Grunwald 2012a, 141–42).

Cantor believed that in order to produce that change, Republicans needed to be united and not lose the vote of a single member of their caucus. The Republican leadership also believed good public relations (PR), rather than governing, was required to move them back into the majority (Grunwald 2012a, 141). They wanted to paint Obama as a weak leader, unable to accomplish bipartisan change, and somehow responsible for the weak economy.

The Republican strategy materialized quickly as the Democratic president and Congress passed additional legislation to prevent the economy from falling into another Great Depression. On February 17, 2009, President Obama signed the American Recovery and Investment Act (ARIA). The legislation passed the House by a vote of 244–188, with 177 of 178 Republicans voting against. On the Senate side, the legislation passed by a vote of 61–37, with 37 of 40 voting Republicans against.

The ARIA was a Keynesian New Deal–style effort to save and create jobs. It provided temporary relief programs for those most affected and created public works programs. It included direct spending on infrastructure, education, health, and energy, federal tax incentives, and expansion of unemployment benefits and other social welfare provisions. The economic stimulus package was estimated to cost $787 billion, but was later revised to $831 billion (Congressional Budget Office 2012). Of course, the increased spending could not be paid for by the Bush era tax rates, so the inevitable result was ballooning federal deficits and increasing debt as shown in Figure 6.8.

Republican PR efforts painted the law as fiscally irresponsible, starkly increasing the federal debt, a manifestation of Democratic support for "big government," and disdainful of "free markets." Republicans were soon aided in their PR effort by passage of the Patient Protection and Affordable Care Act of 2010. The Affordable Care Act extended federal healthcare coverage to many millions of uninsured Americans, and was the first major expansion of the federal health care system since Medicare and Medicaid during the Great Society. The law passed both the House and the Senate without a single Republican vote. Lacking any semblance of bipartisanship, Republicans again painted Democrats as supportive of socialist solutions and "big government."

The Affordable Care Act was broadly unpopular among Republicans and Independents and became a major issue in the 2010 mid-term elections (ABC News/*Washington Post* 2010). Many would argue that the Affordable Care Act was responsible for the rise of the Tea Party movement and big Democratic losses in the 2010 mid-term elections. Democrats lost 64 House seats, making Republicans the majority party again by 242–193, just two years after the 2008 landslide election. Many incoming Tea Party Republicans were even more conservative than those already in the chamber. As noted in Chapter 1, the House also became more conservative through retirements and resignations of those frustrated with rabid partisanship in Congress. Democrats also lost 6 Senate seats, but retained the majority by 51–47. The Tea Party House Republicans, coupled with the continuing party of "No!" strategy, made it near impossible afterward for the Obama administration to enact new measures to stimulate the economy or to accomplish a meaningful policy agenda. Indeed, the 2010 election produced dangerous partisan showdowns through the 2012 elections.

Following the mid-term elections, Republican Senate minority leader Mitch McConnell reaffirmed the party of "No!" strategy in a speech to the Heritage Foundation on December 7, 2010: "Our top political priority over the next two years should be to deny President Obama a second term" (McConnell 2010).

House Republicans also engaged in a continuing politics of destruction through budgetary showdowns over allowing the Bush tax cuts to expire as scheduled on January 1, 2011.

The politics of resolving this issue finally came to a head as the cuts were set to expire in the lame duck session of Congress after the 2010 elections. At issue was whether the Bush tax cuts would be allowed to expire for all taxpayers or only for high-income taxpayers. President Obama wanted them to continue for low- and middle-income groups, but expire for those making over $250,000 annually. All 42 Republican senators were united in the position that, until the tax dispute was resolved, they would filibuster to prevent consideration of any other legislation, except bills to fund the government. Undoubtedly because the economy remained very weak, President Obama conceded to congressional Republicans to extend all Bush tax cuts for another two years with some additional provisions to stimulate economic growth. The Tax Relief, Unemployment Insurance Reauthorization, and Job Creation Act of 2010 passed the lame duck Congress on a bipartisan basis, with 81 senators and 277 House members voting yes.

Incoming Tea Party House Republicans were enraged by the compromise and also sought to prevent any future tax increases. Their tool for accomplishing these goals was to refuse to increase the federal debt ceiling. On April 4, 2011, Treasury Secretary Timothy Geithner informed Congress that the federal debt ceiling had been reached and that federal borrowing authority to fund the government would expire on August 2. Raising the federal debt ceiling had not been a partisan issue since Newt Gingrich during the Clinton era. However, this time House Republicans used the debt ceiling to coerce the administration into accepting deep spending cuts and promises of no future tax increases.

With the economy still weak, Republicans once again succeeded in coercing a presidential bargain, with passage of the Budget Control Act on August 2, 2011. The legislation established a process whereby the federal debt would be addressed through an automatic process of spending sequestration to occur at the end of 2012. The Bush tax cuts were also set to expire at the same time. The coincidence of these events soon acquired the label of "the fiscal cliff." Three days later, the Standard & Poors credit rating agency downgraded the long-term credit rating of the U.S. government for the first time in history, from AAA to AA+. In contrast with its previous assessments, the agency assumed that the government would go over the fiscal cliff due to dogged Republican resistance toward increased taxes.

With the approaching end of 2012, the ratings agency seemed correct in its assessment. Congressional Republicans were oblivious to the consequences of going over the fiscal cliff through the 2012 presidential election season. No action was taken as the deadline approached. However, their strategy of "No!" and making Obama a one-term president failed. President Obama won a second term over Republican Mitt Romney with 51.1 percent versus

47.2 percent of the popular vote and 332 versus 206 electoral votes. Republicans lost 8 seats in the House, but retained their majority. Democrats gained 2 seats in the Senate.

In the aftermath of the 2012 elections, Congress passed and the president signed the American Taxpayer Relief Act on January 3, 2013. The law restored the marginal tax rate of 39.6 percent on the highest income group, now set at $450,000 for joint returns. It also increased the tax on capital gains for this group, as well as increased the estate tax. However, the Bush tax cuts for low- and middle-income groups were made permanent and even reduced at the low end. The Senate passed the bill 89–8, with 49 Democrats and 40 Republicans in favor. The House passed the bill 257–167, with 172 Democrats and 85 Republicans and in favor and 16 Democrats and 151 Republicans opposed.

Polarization and legislative gridlock continued, with yet another government shutdown from October 1 to 16, 2013, as House Tea Party Republicans tried to defund the Patient Protection and Affordable Care Act. Republicans and the Tea Party got most of the blame, as 81 percent of Americans disapproved (*Washington Post* 2013). Regardless, the 2014 mid-term elections produced large gains for Republicans. Winning nine additional seats, they won control of the Senate for the first time since 2009. Republicans extended their majority in the House to the largest since 1928. Thus, polarization rooted in the war over two social contracts was guaranteed to continue for the foreseeable future.

CHARACTERIZING POLARIZATION FROM REAGAN THROUGH OBAMA

A confluence of factors enabled Ronald Reagan and the Old Guard to restore significant support for the Founders' social contract after 1980. Watergate and its aftermath enabled the rise of conservatives within the Republican Party. An intellectual movement, driven by Chicago School economic thought, relegitimized market capitalism. Big money donors successfully established a base of support for free markets, small government, and anti-social welfare values. They also connected their economic and cultural values by appealing to the Christian Right.

The evidence strongly suggests that Reagan was not elected in 1980 to implement an Old Guard agenda, but because he was not Jimmy Carter. Nevertheless, the Reagan team, with guidance from the Heritage Foundation, moved swiftly to attack New Deal and Great Society programs. By 1989, the tax system had become considerably less progressive, with huge tax benefits flowing to upper-income groups. The regulatory regime underwent substantial change as rulemaking was curtailed, and established regulatory agencies were suppressed through hostile political appointees and reduced budgets. Additionally, the social welfare system was starved for funding, and the poor felt the brunt of redirection of federal money toward national defense and the states.

It is important to understand from this chapter that polarization after 1980 did not "just happen." It resulted from the deliberate strategies of Old Guard Republicans. The same issues pushed by Ronald Reagan and the Heritage Foundation drove polarization through the 1990s, 2000s, and beyond. The acute basis of partisan conflict has been economic. However, Republican ideological support for low taxes, free markets, and less government has been strategically connected through time with culture politics.

More recent evidence of the deliberate basis of party polarization was the Republican reaction to the Great Recession and Democratic landslide in 2008. Fearing a return to 50 more years of wandering in the wilderness after the Great Recession, Republican Party leaders orchestrated a party of "No!" strategy. They used the strategy of not offering the incumbent president any support at all in dealing with the economic crisis. Instead, they adopted the PR strategy of trying to make the incumbent president look weak and Keynesian solutions appear ineffective.

Thus, the polarization of the American system after 1980 resulted from deliberate and calculating tactics intended to benefit the patrician class. Old Guard Republican elites hold an intense hatred for the New Deal social contract and desperately want to reverse it. As shown by Mitt Romney's remarks to his wealthy donors in Boca Raton, Florida, the class divide continues as the basis of party polarization of the American system.

7

Are Americans Ideologically Polarized?

Arguing against direct popular elections at the constitutional convention of 1787, Roger Sherman of Connecticut stated, "The people ... should have as little to do as may be about the government. They want information, and are constantly liable to be misled." Agreeing, Elbridge Gerry of Massachussetts stated, "The people do not want virtue, but are the dupes of pretended patriots ... [T]hey are daily misled into the most baneful measures and opinions, by the false reports circulated by designing men, and which no one on the spot can refute" (Madison 1787, May 31). Both men believed that wily leaders could easily sway ignorant citizens through emotional appeals.

The Old Guard and its benefactors cunningly and deliberately used emotional appeals to restore rents to the patrician class such as had existed under the Founders' social contract. They sought to make holy again low taxes on the wealthy, small government, and unregulated markets. In doing so, they tried to connect their economic agenda with culture politics. Accordingly, they consistently emphasized emotional matters such as abortion, homosexuality, school prayer, guns, and declining moral values in America, even though these issues were completely unrelated to their economic stances.

Did the Old Guard's efforts succeed in restoring significant support for the Founders' social contract, thereby producing a polarized mass public? Did these partisan efforts produce mass polarization over cultural issues? If so, were the economic and cultural dimensions connected, as would be suggested by the Old Guard strategy?

Past scholarship has reached opposing conclusions concerning whether the mass public is polarized. Fiorina (2011, 8) states, "Many of the activists do, in fact, hate each other and regard themselves as combatants in a war. But their hatreds and battles are not shared by the great mass of the American people." In contrast, Abramowitz (2010, x) argues that "there is no disconnect between the political elite and the American people. Polarization in Washington reflects polarization within the public, especially within the politically engaged segment of the public."

Also embedded in these scholarly debates is the question of whether polarization, if it exists, has been along a single dimension (economics) or multiple dimensions (economics plus cultural issues). Bartels states that "the hallucinatory appeal of 'cultural wedge issues like guns and abortion and the rest' continues to be 'far overshadowed by material concerns' " (2008, 86; see also Ansolabehere et al. 2006; Bartels 2006; Baker 2006). In contrast, Frank asserts that Republicans "systematically downplay the politics of economics. The movement's basic premise is that culture outweighs economics as a matter of public concern – that *Values Matter Most* ... citizens who would once have been reliable partisans of the New Deal [rally] to the standard of conservatism" (2004, 6; see also DiMaggio et al. 1996; Hunter 1991; Hunter and Wolf 2006; Layman and Carsey 2002; Mouw and Sobel 2001).

POLARIZATION OF THE AMERICAN ELECTORATE OVER SPECIFIC ISSUES

Was the Old Guard successful in making low taxes on the wealthy, small government, and unregulated markets holy again among a significant part of the mass public? To what extent did economic and/or cultural issues become the basis of polarization among the mass public? Is the mass public polarized, and if the mass public is polarized, is that polarization as visceral as that characterizing Washington?

This section addresses these questions using empirical time series data from the cumulative American National Election Studies (ANES 2015) and General Social Surveys (GSS 2015). Neither study has been administered annually or even biennially. Further, respondents are not asked all relevant questions in each administration of the surveys. However, sufficient data exist from both surveys to observe the patterns through time of issue polarization among the American electorate.

Mass Partisan Affect toward Liberals and Conservatives

There is virtually no scholarly debate over whether party elites in Washington are polarized. They are. Indeed, the acrimony between Republicans and Democrats in Congress and between presidents and opposing congressional partisans is so visceral that some observers suggest that Republicans literally hate liberals and Democrats literally hate conservatives. Is polarization among the mass public, if it exists, as visceral as that which seemingly characterizes Washington?

Leverage in answering this question is contained in the ANES feeling thermometer questions on Republican and Democratic affect toward liberals and conservatives. The feeling thermometer question reads: "We'd also like to get your feelings about some groups in American society. When I read the name of a group, we'd like you to rate it with what we call a feeling thermometer. Ratings between 50 degrees and 100 degrees mean that you feel favorably and warm toward the group; ratings between 0 and 50 degrees mean that you don't feel favorably towards the group and that you don't care too much for that group. If you don't feel particularly warm or cold toward a group you would rate them at 50 degrees" (ANES 2015, VCF0201).

The feeling thermometers toward liberals and conservatives are represented by two variables, ANES VCF0211 and VCF0212. Responses to these questions were separated out by respondents' partisanship. Figure 7.1A and B shows Republican and Democratic affect toward conservatives and liberals from 1968 through 2012. The graphs are on the same scale, so as to enable comparing the differences between partisans.

Focusing first on the Republican side, Figure 7.1A shows that Republicans among the mass public have always felt very positively toward conservatives and negatively toward liberals. However, their positive feelings for conservatives and negative feelings toward liberals have grown stronger through time. Republican sentiment toward liberals in 1968 was only slightly negative at 46.8 points and continued near this level through the mid-1970s. Falling only slightly below neutral, Republicans were thus somewhat indifferent toward liberals. Republican warmth toward conservatives was significantly more positive, hovering between 61 and 68 percent through the mid-1970s. After 1980 and Reagan's election Republicans grew significantly more negative toward liberals. However, between 1984 and 1990, Republicans were again almost neutral toward liberals. However, after 1990 Republican sentiment toward liberals dropped to below 40. By 2012, Republican sentiment toward liberals was only 28.5 points, suggesting intense dislike. At the same time, their warmth toward conservatives had increased to 70.7 percent. This is a difference of 41.9 percent. Figure 7.1A shows that Republican dislike for liberals grew increasingly intense after 2008, perhaps in acrimony regarding the election of President Obama or Keynesian measures addressing the Great Recession.

Comparing Figure 7.1B with Figure 7.1A, one observes a large difference between Republican and Democratic affect toward liberals and conservatives. Democrats registered dislike for conservatives in only two years, 1982 and 2012. They were either positive or indifferent toward conservatives in all other years. In 1968, there was virtually no difference in Democratic warmth toward liberals and conservatives. Democrats' liking for liberals and conservatives tracked quite closely until around 1988. After this, Democrats grew increasingly warm toward liberals and cold toward conservatives. However, the rate of change in these attitudes was slow. The largest gap between their warmth toward liberals and warmth toward conservatives before 2012 was only 11.8 percent, less than the 1968 gap for Republicans. This gap occurred in both 2000 and 2004. The year 2000 corresponds with the highly polarizing election between George W. Bush and Al Gore. The year 2004 was the election year

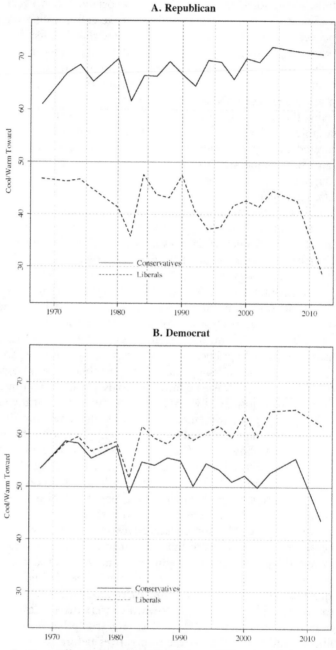

FIGURE 7.1 Partisan Affect toward Conservatives and Liberals, 1968–2012
Source: American National Election Study Cumulative File, 1948–2012, VCF0211, VCF0212.

following George W. Bush's tax cuts for the wealthy and the start of the Iraq war. In 2012, the gap widened, suggesting that Democrats too became more intense in their negative attitudes toward conservatives. However, the size of the 2012 gap was still relatively small compared with Republicans. The difference between Democrats' liking for conservatives and liberals was 18.1 percent, only slightly larger than the Republican gap in 1968. Thus, Figures 7.1A and B jointly suggest that Republicans have been far more visceral than Democrats in their feelings toward liberals and conservatives. These figures also suggest that mass polarization has been asymmetrical, driven largely by changing Republican attitudes.

Issue Polarization along the Economic Dimension

The New Deal social contract placed government in a more central position on economic matters. Government became the chief purveyor of economic equality, social justice, and regulating the market excesses that threatened ordinary Americans. Because Old Guard Republicans were largely vanquished from American politics between 1933 and the late 1970s, rents were more broadly dispersed among the mass public. The relation between the federal government and its citizens was dramatically transformed. However, the remaining Old Guard Republicans and their benefactors literally hated the broader dispersion of rents. Thus, the previous chapter showed that the Founders' social contract was partially resurrected starting with the Reagan administration, and economic issues increasingly became the basis of institutional polarization through time. Did that increasing institutional polarization extend to the mass public?

To reveal the nature of mass polarization along economic lines, five measures were chosen from the ANES and GSS. These measures capture partisan support for less government, free markets, lower taxes, economic equality, and environmental regulation. Of course, these were also issues emphasized by the 1980 Heritage Foundation report, the Reagan administration, as well as Republican partisan elites to the present.

Figure 7.2 plots the percentage of Republicans and Democrats from 1990 through 2012 saying they support smaller government. The precise question wording on each survey was: "I am going to ask you to choose which of two statements I read comes closer to your own opinion. You might agree to some extent with both, but we want to know which one is closer to your views. ONE, the less government the better; or TWO, there are more things that government should be doing" (ANES 2015, VCF9131).

Of course, the Republican Party has always favored small government. So, the gap between Republicans and Democrats in 1990 was a relatively large 26.1 percent. In 1990, 16.9 percent of Democrats and 43 percent of Republicans favored less government. However, the divergence between Republicans and Democrats had grown much larger by 2012 to 54.7 percent. In 2012, a full

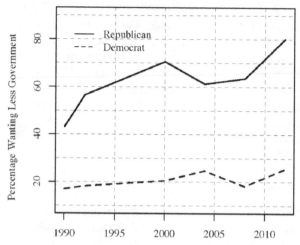

FIGURE 7.2 Partisanship and Size of Government
Source: American National Election Study Cumulative File, 1948–2012, VCF9131.

80 percent of Republicans said they support less government. In contrast, Democrats in 2012 were only somewhat more supportive of less government at 25.6 percent. The Republican percentage had increased by 37.4 percent over this time frame, while the Democrat percentage had increased by only 8.7 percent. Thus, the evidence is clear that Republicans became increasingly ideological through time on the "big government" issue, and diverged greatly from Democrats.

A similar pattern emerges when observing partisan support for free markets. Figure 7.3 plots the percentage of Republicans and Democrats who say they support free markets from 1990 through 2012. The question wording was the same as the preceding, except the two statements read: "ONE, we need a strong government to handle today's complex economic problems; or TWO, the free market can handle these problems without government being involved" (ANES 2015, VCF9132).

Interestingly, the gap between Republicans and Democrats in 1990 was relatively small at only 12.1 percent. Among Republican respondents, only 27.8 percent supported free markets versus 15.7 percent of Democrats. However, the gap had grown quite large by 2012. Among Republicans, 67.5 percent supported free markets versus only 14.1 percent of Democrats, a difference of 53.4 percent. Through time, Republican support for free markets increased by 39.7 percent, while Democratic support for free markets barely budged. Thus, the evidence again shows that Republicans grew increasingly ideological on the "free markets" issue and diverged greatly from Democrats.

Mass polarization over taxes can be observed using the GSS variable on partisans saying their taxes are too high. The variable used in the analysis was

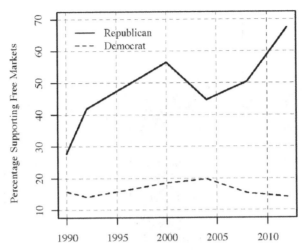

FIGURE 7.3 Partisanship and Free Markets
Source: American National Election Study Cumulative File, 1948–2012, VCF9132.

the GSS TAX variable, which asked respondents, "Do you consider the amount of federal income tax which you have to pay as too high, about right, or too low?" (GSS 2015, TAX). The variable was recoded into an indicator variable, with "too high" being the one category and "about right" and "too low" collapsed into the zero category. Initially, a probit analysis was used, controlling for respondents' family income (CONINC). However, the results did not differ appreciably from a simple graphical analysis of partisan attitudes on taxes. The GSS PARTYID variable separates partisanship by "strong" and "weak" for Republicans and Democrats.

Figure 7.4 reports the percentages for each category saying their taxes are too high for years from 1976 through 2012. A heavy dashed vertical line marks the year of passage of the Deficit Reduction Act of 1993, Clinton's highly polarizing measure that significantly increased the marginal tax rate on upper income groups. Of course, the discussion in the previous chapter suggests that this was a critical break point for institutional polarization over taxation. Did this event also affect mass polarization?

Figure 7.4 shows that before the Deficit Reduction Act of 1993 little difference existed between Republicans and Democrats on taxes. In 1982 after the Reagan tax cut, the percentage saying their taxes were too high declined steadily, with a small separation appearing between strong Republicans and strong Democrats. However, strong Republicans and weak Democrats actually tracked very closely in 1982. In other years before 1993, little separation existed between the four partisanship categories. However, after the 1993 Clinton tax increase, strong Republicans were much more likely than strong and weak Democrats to respond that their taxes were too high. By 1998, over 81 percent of strong Republicans

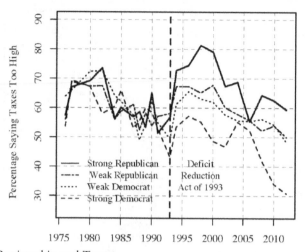

FIGURE 7.4 Partisanship and Taxes
Source: General Social Survey Cumulative File, 1972–2012. TAX recoded to binary TooHigh and NotTooHigh.

said their taxes were too high, while only 55 percent of strong Democrats responded this way. Weak Republicans also increasingly said that their taxes were too high, but the increase was smaller. The 1997 Clinton tax cut, and the 2001 and 2003 Bush tax cuts had no discernible impact. The implication is that the tax issue began resonating ideologically with Republicans starting around 1993, just as it had at the institutional level.

Issue polarization also emerged among the mass public on the question of whether government should ensure equal opportunity. The New Deal social contract produced greater governmental efforts toward this end. These efforts included a more progressive tax system, anti-poverty programs, and curtailing discrimination based on race, ethnicity, gender, and age. Yet the previous chapter showed that these initiatives were strongly opposed by Old Guard Republicans starting with Goldwater and continuing through Reagan to the present. Did the mass public also become polarized over governmental efforts toward ensuring a more equitable system?

In answering this question, the ANES variable on equal opportunity was chosen. The specific question wording was: "I am going to read several statements. After each one, I would like you to tell me whether you agree strongly, agree somewhat, neither agree nor disagree, disagree somewhat, or disagree strongly. Our society should do whatever is necessary to make sure that everyone has an equal opportunity to succeed" (ANES 2015, VCF9013).

Figure 7.5 plots the percentage strongly agreeing with societal efforts to ensure equal opportunity, broken down by partisanship, as reported by the ANES from 1984 through 2012. The smallest divergence between

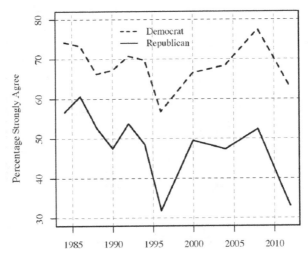

Democrat
Republican

FIGURE 7.5 Partisanship and Equal Opportunity
Source: American National Election Study Cumulative File, 1948–2012, VCF9013.

Republicans and Democrats occurred in 1986 when 60.6 percent of Republicans and 73.3 percent of Democrats were in strong agreement. The distance between Republicans and Democrats was only 12.6 percent near the end of the Reagan administration. However, by 2012 only 33.1 percent of Republicans believed strongly that society should ensure equal opportunity. The Democrat percentage remained high in 2012 at 62.9 percent. The divergence between Republicans and Democrats in 2012 had grown to 29.9 percent. The Democrat responses averaged 68.5 percent between 1984 and 2012 and remained relatively stable. In contrast, the Republican percentage trended downward through time. Between 1986 and 2012, the Republican percentage dropped by 27.6 percent. Thus, the evidence again suggests that the mass public became increasingly divided over societal efforts toward greater equality and that most of that division was driven by change in Republican attitudes.

A final economic issue concerns partisan attitudes toward the environment. The Heritage Foundation and Ronald Reagan sought deregulation generally, but the attack on the environment was especially vicious (e.g., see Wood 1988; Wood and Waterman 1993, 1994). Increasingly after Reagan, Republicans saw environmental protection as harmful to business and the economy. Therefore, Republican elites consistently sought to diminish environmental protection, while Democratic elites sought to maintain or increase it. Did partisan elite divisions over the environment extend to the mass public?

In answering this question, the ANES feeling thermometer toward environmentalists is chosen. The question wording is the same as reported above for partisan attitudes toward Conservatives and Liberals. However, the group

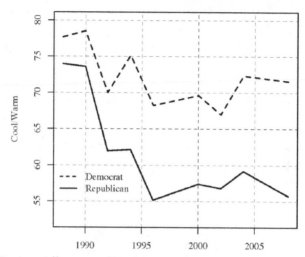

FIGURE 7.6 Partisan Affect toward Environmentalists
Source: American National Election Study Cumulative File, 1948–2012, VCF0229.

of interest is now "environmentalists," or "people seeking to protect the environment" (ANES 2015, VCF0229).

Figure 7.6 plots partisan affect toward environmentalists from 1988 through 2008. Environmentalists were not included in the feeling thermometer question in 2012. In 1988 the divergence between Republicans and Democrats on liking for environmentalists was only 3.7 percent. Among Republicans, 74 percent felt favorably toward those seeking to protect the environment. Among Democrats, 77.7 percent viewed them favorably. Republicans and Democrats jointly felt very warm toward people seeking to protect the environment. However, a pattern of increasing divergence started in the early 1990s. By 2008, only 55.7 percent of Republicans felt favorable toward environmentalists, with 71.6 percent of Democrats favorable. Democratic affect toward environmentalists remained fairly stable between the early 1990s and 2008. However, Republican sentiment toward environmentalists dropped sharply over this period. By 2008, a 15.85 percent divergence had opened between Republican and Democratic attitudes. Thus, the evidence again suggests that the mass public became increasingly divided over societal efforts to protect the environment and that most of the division was driven by changing Republican attitudes.

The Cultural Dimension of Issue Polarization

As discussed in the previous chapter, the Old Guard sought to regain support for the Founders' social contract by connecting their economic issues with cultural matters that had nothing to do with those economic issues. The most prominent cultural issue in this strategy was abortion. However, a variety of

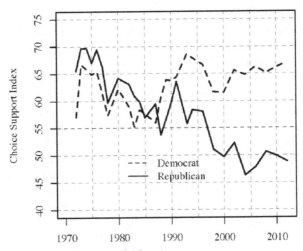

FIGURE 7.7 Partisan Attitudes toward Abortion
Source: General Social Survey Cumulative File, 1972–2012. Support index constructed by averaging GSS responses on ABDEFECT, ABHLTH, ABRAPE, ABNOMORE, ABPOOR, ABSINGLE, ABANY.

other issues were also emphasized, including gays and lesbians, guns, illegal aliens, and social welfare. On its face, it is obvious that Republicans and Democrats currently disagree over these issues. However, the dynamics of how they got there is interesting.

As discussed in the previous chapter, abortion has been a major mobilizing factor among Republicans since the 1980s. Central to debates over abortion has been a woman's right to choose, and how far that choice should extend. In measuring partisan attitudes toward abortion, an index was constructed from seven GSS questions. The specific question wording for each is: "Please tell me whether or not you think it should be possible for a pregnant woman to obtain a legal abortion if . . ." (GSS 2015, ABANY). The questions differ by changing the reason for the abortion: "There is a strong chance of serious defect in the baby" (ABDEFECT). "The woman's own health is seriously endangered by the pregnancy" (ABHEALTH). "She became pregnant as a result of rape" (ABRAPE). "She is married and does not want any more children" (ABNOMORE). "The family has a very low income and cannot afford any more children" (ABPOOR). "She is not married and does not want to marry the man" (ABSINGLE). "The woman wants it for any reason" (ABANY). The responses for each year were aggregated into an index of support for a woman's right to choose ranging from 0 to 100. A score of 0 implies that respondents on average believed that abortion should never be allowed. A score of 100 implies that respondents on average believed that a woman should always be able to obtain an abortion.

Figure 7.7 plots the average partisan score on the choice index for each year from 1972 (the year before *Roe v. Wade*) through 2012. Interestingly, the choice index shows Republicans in 1972 were about 8 points *more* supportive than Democrats of a woman's right to choose, and remained more favorable than Democrats until 1988. This was in spite of Ronald Reagan's highly visible support for a constitutional amendment, as well as his publication of the anti-abortion pamphlet *Abortion and the Conscience of a Nation* (Reagan 1984).

After 1988, Democratic respondents shifted abruptly, becoming more supportive of choice than Republicans by about 7 points. Since 1988, Democrats' average choice support score has remained relatively stable at around 65 points. Republicans became significantly more supportive of choice in 1991. However, after 1991 Republicans' choice support score continually trended lower through time. By 2012, the Republican score was only 48.8 percent, compared with 67.1 percent for Democrats, an 18-point difference. Between 1973 and 2012, Republican support dropped by 20.9 points, while Democratic support barely changed. Thus, the GSS evidence shows that Republicans and Democrats became increasingly divergent over the abortion issue, with much of the divergence after 1991 driven by change in Republican attitudes.

It should be noted, however, that this result could be survey dependent. The GSS bank of questions on abortion is far more refined and extensive than that for the ANES. Nevertheless, the ANES abortion variable, VCF0838, shows that between 1980 and 2012 many Democrats also became more extreme on abortion. Hence, polarization over abortion may well have been symmetrical.

The mass public also increasingly divided over their acceptance of gays and lesbians. This division can readily be observed using the GSS variable HOMO-SEX. Specifically, the question asks whether sexual relations between adults of the same sex is always, almost always, sometimes, or not wrong.

Figure 7.8 plots the percentage of Republicans and Democrats responding that homosexuality is always wrong from 1973 through 2012. Interestingly, opposing partisans were quite close in saying that homosexual relations are always wrong until 1988. Before 1988, an average 78 percent of Republicans and 77 percent of Democrats responded that it was always wrong. However, after 1988 respondents from both parties grew increasingly less likely to respond in this manner. By 2012, about 62 percent of Republicans and about 43 percent of Democrats responded that homosexuality was always wrong, a difference of 19 percent. The increasing acceptance of homosexuality was faster among Democrats than among Republicans. Thus, the parties became increasingly divergent through time over gays and lesbians. The divergence was driven as much by change among Democrats as Republicans or, said differently, an absence of corresponding change among Republicans.

Another cultural issue that has increasingly divided Republicans and Democrats through time is gun control. This issue also divides Americans along urban-rural lines. Rural citizens typically own guns. Hunting and a frontier mentality mean that guns are an integral part of their culture. Among rural citizens, efforts to restrict gun ownership are often met with anger. In urban

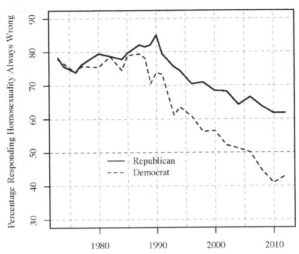

FIGURE 7.8 Partisan Attitudes toward Gays and Lesbians
Source: General Social Survey Cumulative File, 1972–2012, HOMOSEX.

settings, guns are a source of crime and violence. Restrictions on gun ownership are generally viewed more positively and as a means of protecting the public. One can observe mass polarization over the gun issue using the GSS variable GUNLAW. The specific question wording is: "Would you favor or oppose a law which would require a person to obtain a police permit before he or she could buy a gun?" (GSS 2015, GUNLAW).

Figure 7.9 plots the percentage of Republican and Democrat respondents opposing gun licensing from 1972 through 2012. A heavy dashed vertical line marks 1993, the year President Clinton and a Democratic Congress enacted the Brady Handgun Violence Prevention Act. The figure shows that Republicans have always been more opposed to gun control than Democrats. However, the extent of their divergence has changed significantly through time. In 1972, the difference between the Democratic and Republican responses on the GUNLAW question was only 1.7 percent. That difference remained small until 1980 when Republicans suddenly became more opposed to gun control. The difference shot up to 10 percent in 1980 and remained there through 1984. Republicans ran on platforms opposing gun control in 1980, 1984, and afterward (Republican National Committee 1980; see also Republican National Committee 1984). Ronald Reagan was a life-long member of the National Rifle Association (NRA). Thus, the NRA for first time in its 109-year history endorsed a presidential candidate and spent heavily on issue ads in his favor (Ingram 2001).

After the 1984 election, the difference between Republicans and Democrats dropped sharply. By 1991, the divergence between Republicans and Democrats was only 2.2 percent. However, after Clinton's election the 1993 Brady

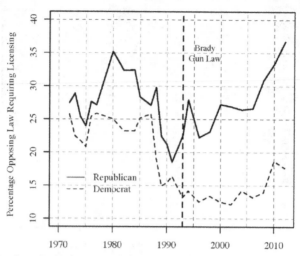

FIGURE 7.9 Partisan Attitudes toward Gun Control
Source: General Social Survey Cumulative File, 1972–2012, GUNLAW.

Handgun Violence Prevention Act was enacted to institute federal background checks on all firearm purchasers in the United States. Figure 7.9 shows that this Democratic legislation sparked a Republican trend that has continued to present. In 1993, the difference between Republicans and Democrats increased to 9 percent and continued increasing through 2012. In 2012 the partisan difference in opposition to gun control was 19.1 percent. Thus, guns are yet another cultural issue dividing the mass public, and the evidence again shows that the division since 1993 was largely driven by ideological change among Republicans.

Partisan attitudes toward illegal aliens have also increasingly divided the mass public through time. To observe this division, the ANES feeling thermometer for illegal aliens (ANES 2015, VCF0233) was used. Again, the specific question wording is given above in the discussion of partisan attitudes toward conservatives and liberals. However, now the group of interest is "illegal aliens."

Figure 7.10 tracks the average Democrat and Republican partisan warmth toward illegal aliens from 1988 through 2012. This question was administered only seven times during this time frame. Nevertheless, clear evidence again emerges of a difference in partisan trends. Republicans felt warm toward illegal aliens in only one year, 1990. All other years show Republican dislike for illegal aliens. Their dislike had grown very intense by 2012, with a score of only 29 on the 100-point scale. Democrats also showed dislike for illegal aliens in 1988, 1994, and 2004. However, all other years show Democrats as either indifferent or warm toward illegal aliens. Republican feelings toward illegal aliens were always more negative than for Democrats. In 1990,

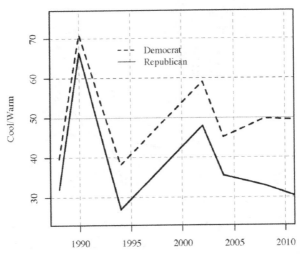

FIGURE 7.10 Partisan Attitudes toward Illegal Aliens
Source: American National Election Study Cumulative File, 1948–2012, VCF0233.

the difference in sentiment between Republicans and Democrats was only 4.60 on the 100-point scale. However, by 2012 the difference had grown to 20 percent. Thus, the partisan divergence over illegal aliens was again driven by Republicans.

Finally, partisans differ fundamentally in their attitudes toward welfare and welfare recipients. Welfare is considered here as a cultural issue because racism and partisan attitudes toward work and dependence are likely associated with partisan welfare attitudes. Welfare recipients are perceived incorrectly by some as predominately African-American and lazy. Such beliefs characterize Republicans more than Democrats. The measure of attitudes toward welfare recipients is again the ANES feeling thermometer for "people on welfare" (ANES 2015, VCF0220).

Figure 7.11 tracks partisan affect toward welfare recipients from 1976 through 2012. The graph shows that Republicans have generally disliked welfare recipients; Democrats have always felt warmer toward this group. The distance has always been great between Democrats and Republicans on the welfare issue. Republicans registered dislike for people on welfare for 11 of the 14 surveys. In contrast, Democrats evaluated people on welfare positively for all surveys. In 1976, the gap between Republicans and Democrats was 9.2 percent. The divergence increased to 13 percent in 1980, as Ronald Reagan was running for the presidency. Reagan's characterization of "welfare queens" during the 1980 campaign apparently had a small effect. A large decline in Republican liking for people on welfare occurred in 1994, as Old Guard Republicans pushed welfare reform in their Contract with America. By 2012 the difference between Republican and Democrat warmth toward

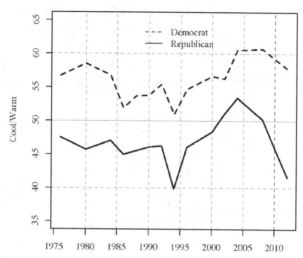

FIGURE 7.11 Partisan Attitudes toward People on Welfare
Source: American National Election Study Cumulative File, 1948–2012, VCF0220.

welfare recipients had grown to its maximum of 16.2 percent, as Republican dislike again approached what it had been in 1994. Thus, partisan division over welfare was again largely due to more negative evaluations by Republicans.

White Evangelicals and the Economic Dimension of Issue Polarization

It requires no analysis to understand that white evangelicals have been a major contributor to divisions over cultural issues such as abortion, gays and lesbians, morality, and family values. However, the argument here is that the Old Guard cunningly and deliberately sought to draw the Christian Right into the Republican Right by connecting these cultural issues with their right-wing economic issues. If the Old Guard was successful in this endeavor, then there should be a systematic relationship between membership in evangelical denominations and attitudes toward economic issues such as size of government, free markets, taxes, support for equal opportunity, and regulating the environment. Was the Old Guard successful in making these connections?

The analyses below use the same economic variables as were discussed above for Figures 7.2 through 7.6. Question wordings are the same. What differs in the analyses below is that instead of evaluating partisan differences on these economic issues, the analyses consider the attitudes of white evangelicals. The evangelical variable was coded as recommended by Leege (1995) in a working paper on the ANES website using the religious denomination variables (ANES 2015, VCF0128a, VCF0152). Nonwhite respondents were excluded from the analysis.

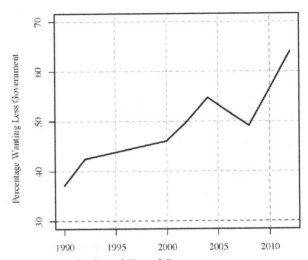

FIGURE 7.12 White Evangelicals and Size of Government
Source: American National Election Study Cumulative File, 1948–2012, VCF9131 and VCF0128a and VCF0152 (whites only).

Figure 7.12 graphs support among white evangelicals for less government from 1990 through 2012. The plot shows definitively that among white evangelicals, support for less government grew sharply and steadily. Also, observe the similar trends between white evangelical support for less government in Figure 7.12 and Republican support for less government in Figure 7.2. In 1990, only 37.1 percent of white evangelicals expressed support for less government. By 2012, white evangelical support for less government had grown to 64 percent. In other words, an economic issue (size of government) that was completely unrelated to religion had been successfully connected with the evangelical community.

Figure 7.13 graphs support among white evangelicals for free markets from 1990 through 2012. A similar pattern emerges, and there is again a close correspondence between white evangelical support for free markets in Figure 7.13 and Republican support for free markets in Figure 7.3. In 1990, only 28.1 percent of white evangelicals believed in free markets. By 2012, white evangelical support for free markets had grown to 50.5 percent. Thus, an economic issue (free markets) that was completely unrelated to religion had again been successfully connected with the evangelical community.

Figure 7.14 plots the relationship between respondents saying their taxes are too high and being a member of a white evangelical denomination. Constructing the GSS religious denomination variable (GSS 2015, DENOM) to represent evangelicals is more difficult than for the ANES analyses above. The GSS did not identify all of the denominational categories that were included in the

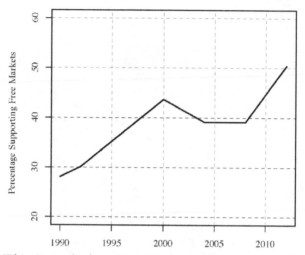

FIGURE 7.13 White Evangelicals and Free Markets
Source: American National Election Study Cumulative File, 1948–2012, VCF9132 and VCF0128a and VCF0152.

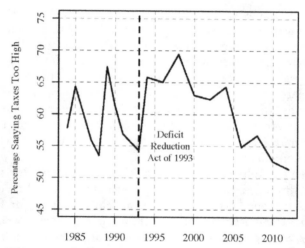

FIGURE 7.14 White Evangelicals and Taxes
Source: General Social Survey Cumulative File, 1972–2012, TAX and recoded DENOM.

ANES coding. A major change was also made to DENOM in 1984 when the number of categories was expanded from 7 to 25 (Davis and Smith 1986). It was impossible to code the evangelical variable before 1984 due to the coarseness of the earlier measure. Further, even after 1984 some evangelical categories were excluded by ANES.

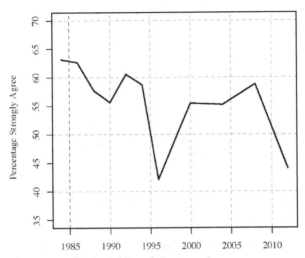

FIGURE 7.15 White Evangelicals and Equal Opportunity
Source: American National Election Study Cumulative File, 1948–2012, VCF9132, VCF0128a, and VCF0152.

Nevertheless, the post-1984 results in Figure 7.14 show a pattern similar to that observed for Republicans in Figure 7.4. Again, in apparent response to the Deficit Reduction Act of 1993, white evangelicals in Figure 7.14 track with Republicans. The increase in the percentage of white evangelicals saying their taxes were too high rose from 54.3 percent in 1993 to 65.8 percent in 1994, an increase of 11.49 percent. The percentage increased to almost 70 percent by 1998 and remained high for about ten years. Thus, the similarity of tax attitudes among white evangelicals and Republicans again suggests that the Old Guard was successful in connecting an economic issue (taxes) that was completely unrelated to religion with evangelical values.

Figure 7.15 plots the relationship between strong support for society promoting equal opportunity and membership in a white evangelical denomination. The trend is not as sharp as that for less government and free markets above, but is present nevertheless. Regressing support for equal opportunity among evangelicals on time produces a significant negative trend coefficient of –0.42. In 1984, the percentage of white evangelicals strongly agreeing that society should ensure equal opportunity was 63.2 percent. By 2012, the percentage was significantly lower at only 44 percent. Comparing Figure 7.15 with Figure 7.5, in 1984 white evangelicals were 13 percent less supportive of equal opportunity than average Democrats, and 6.59 percent more supportive than average Republicans. By 2012, white evangelicals were 21 percent less supportive of equal opportunity than average Democrats, but 10 percent more supportive than average Republicans. Thus, white evangelicals moved away from Democrats and toward Republicans between 1984 and 2012. Again, an economic

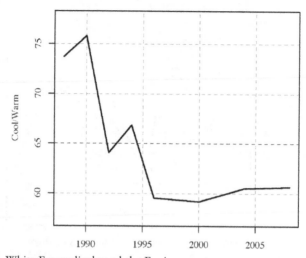

FIGURE 7.16 White Evangelicals and the Environment
Source: American National Election Study Cumulative File, 1948–2012, VCF0229 and VCF0152.

issue completely unrelated to religion (equality of opportunity) was successfully connected with evangelical values.

Finally, the evidence is very persuasive that white evangelicals grew less supportive through time of environmentalism. Figure 7.16 again uses the ANES feeling thermometer for respondent warmth toward people seeking to protect the environment. The graph plots the average warmth toward environmentalists among white evangelicals from 1988 through 2008. Positive feelings toward environmentalists among white evangelicals peaked in 1990, when their average warmth was 75.8. After this, their support dropped sharply to only 59.2 percent by 2000, and remained near this level in 2004 and 2008. Comparing Figure 7.16 and Figure 7.6, the trajectory of white evangelical support for environmentalists again followed a path similar to that for Republicans. In 1988, white evangelicals, Republicans, and Democrats were separated by only about 4 points in their liking for environmentalists. However, by 2012 white evangelicals were only 4.9 points more positive than Republicans, but 10.9 points more negative than Democrats. The negative time trend again strongly suggests that white evangelicals were strongly connected with the anti-environmentalism of Old Guard Republicans. Thus, another issue that was completely unrelated to Christian values, protecting the environment, was again strongly connected through membership in a white evangelical denomination.

White Evangelicals and the New Republican Base

The preceding analyses show that the Old Guard was successful in connecting their economic agenda with a set of highly emotional cultural issues completely unrelated to economics. Through this strategy, they sought to bring a reliable support group, the Christian Right, into the Republican Right. Were they successful in doing so?

The answer to this question has obvious implications for the more theoretical debate over whether increasing mass polarization has been due to ideological change within the political parties (Carsey and Layman 2006; Fiorina and Levendusky 2006; Levendusky 2009b) or due to people switching their party loyalties to align with their ideology (Abramowitz 2010, 69–71; Black and Black 2002; Hetherington and Weiler 2009, 153–59). If white evangelical Christians switched their party loyalties through time, then this change would support the second explanation. In subsequent sections, the switching explanation is evaluated mathematically and empirically. However, significant party switching needs to have occurred for the switching explanation to be plausible.

Time series graphs of two-party identification and the party identification of white evangelicals are jointly important in demonstrating party switching. Figure 7.17A reports the same data as in Figure 6.1, except that Independents are now excluded and the time series is restricted to the same time interval on which white evangelical partisanship can be measured. Figure 7.17B reports the party identification of white evangelicals through time. Heavy dashed vertical lines in Figure 7.17A and B mark the 1980 election. Recall from the previous chapter that the white evangelical vote was crucial to Ronald Reagan's election in both 1980 and 1984.

In 1980, the percentage of the electorate identifying as Republican was only 23 percent, with 45 percent identifying as Democrats. However, Figure 7.17A shows that after the 1980 election a change in party loyalties began occurring. By 1985, 32 percent of the electorate identified as Republican, with only 34 percent identifying as Democrat. The Republican percentage had increased by 9 percent, while the Democratic percentage had dropped by 11 percent. Democratic party identification never returned to the pre-1980 levels. Hence, significant party switching occurred starting in 1980.

What was the basis of this party switching? After the change in party identification started around 1980, a major shift also ensued in the party loyalties of white evangelicals. This shift can be observed by examining the party identification of white evangelicals in the electorate, drawn from the ANES time series on party identification (ANES 2015, VCF9132). Figure 7.17B shows that before 1980 many more white Democrats than white Republicans belonged to evangelical denominations. Pre-1980, around 32 percent of white Democrats and only 22 percent of white Republicans reported belonging to evangelical denominations. After 1980 the relationship moved in the reverse direction. Between 1990 and 2012, the average evangelical membership among white Republicans increased to 32.2 percent. Over this same time span, white Democrat membership in evangelical denominations plummeted. By 2012, only 15.4 percent of white Democrats belonged to evangelical denominations.

A. Party Identification, 1968–2012

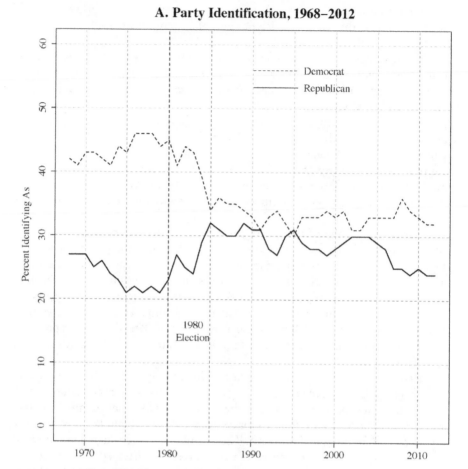

FIGURE 7.17 Party Identification and White Evangelical Party Identification, 1968–2012

Sources: Pew Research Center, Trends in Party Identification from Gallup, 1939–1989, Times Mirror/Pew Research Center, 1990–2012; American National Election Study Cumulative, 1948–2012. Coded from VCF9132, VCF0128a, and VCF0152.

White Democrats either switched parties or were driven out of evangelical denominations.

These time series graphs suggest that party switching occurred after 1980, especially among white evangelicals. The logic of what likely occurred seems compelling. Consider the changing ideology and party switching explanations for the results shown in Figure 7.17B.

Changing ideology: after 1980, nonevangelical Republican partisans suddenly became more evangelical and switched to evangelical religious

B. Party Identification and White Evangelicals

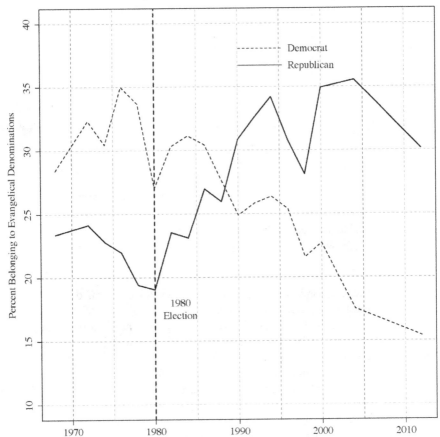

FIGURE 7.17 (*cont.*)

denominations; previously evangelical Democratic partisans became less evangelical and switched to nonevangelical religious denominations? This explanation seems unlikely.

Party switching: religion is a much stronger bond than political partisanship. Therefore, it seems likely that white evangelicals switched their party loyalties to align with their changing ideology. Evangelical white Democrats became evangelical white Republicans, making the Republican Party progressively more evangelical and leaving the Democratic Party progressively less evangelical.

Thus, Figure 7.17 suggests that the Old Guard was successful in bringing the Christian Right into the Republican Right. Did the Old Guard's success translate into a reliable support group for the Republican Party? This question can be answered by observing the through time voting behavior of white evangelicals.

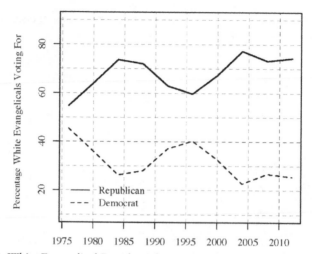

FIGURE 7.18 White Evangelical Presidential Voting
Source: American National Election Study Cumulative, 1948–2012. Coded from VCF0152 and VCF0704a.

The analysis focuses on voting in presidential elections using the question "Who did you vote for in the election for President?" (ANES 2015, VCF0704a).

Figure 7.18 shows the pattern in white evangelical presidential voting from 1976 through 2012. The graph shows that white evangelicals always voted more for Republicans than for Democrats. However, the strength of their support for Republicans varied and grew much stronger through time. In 1976, white evangelical support for Ford was only 54.4 percent, with Carter receiving 45.6 percent. Carter's relatively good showing among white evangelicals was perhaps because he was himself a member of an evangelical denomination, and many evangelicals reside in the South where Carter was a favorite son. In 1980, 64 percent of white evangelicals reported voting for Reagan. In 1984, after catering to the evangelical Christians as discussed in the previous chapter, Reagan's support increased to 73.7 percent. In the 1992 and 1996 elections, white evangelical support for Republican candidates dropped to an average 61.3 percent when another Southern favorite son, Bill Clinton, was elected. Since 2000, an average 73 percent of white evangelicals reported voting for the Republican presidential candidate. That number peaked in 2004, when a whopping 77 percent of white evangelicals voted for George W. Bush. Thus, the Old Guard strategy was successful in capturing a reliable support group.

MEASURING AND EVALUATING MASS POLARIZATION

This section takes a detour from the earlier historical style of analysis by developing more precise measures of polarization than have been used in past quantitative research on polarization. It defines and illustrates three possible scenarios for mass polarization. It then constructs a single, more general measure of mass polarization to be used in the next chapter for evaluating theoretical relations between mass and elite polarization and a potential representation gap.

Defining and Illustrating Three Polarization Types

The word "polarization" derives from the root word "pole," which is a noun deriving from the Greek word "polos" and the Latin word "polus." All three words pertain to an axis through a sphere. An axis through a sphere has two poles at opposite ends. In the physical sciences polarization refers to an alignment with respect to a set of poles, such as with phenomena like north-south magnetic polarization, positively and negatively charged electrical poles, or the alignment of waves relative to their direction of travel (light waves, sound waves, electromagnetic waves, ocean waves, etc.).

However, in the social sciences the word "polarization" has not been used so precisely. Rather, it has taken on several meanings, each implying a different characteristic. Consider the following three dictionary definitions. From http://dictionary.reference.com/browse/polarization, it is "a sharp division ... into opposing factions." From www.thefreedictionary.com/polarization, polarization is "a concentration ... about two conflicting or contrasting positions." From http://en.wikipedia.org, polarization (in politics) is "the process whereby public opinion divides and goes to the extremes." Each of these definitions implies a different concept.

The first definition – a sharp division into opposing factions – is the most commonly used in past literature on party polarization. This phenomenon can be labeled *divergence polarization*. The discussion surrounding Figures 7.2 through 7.12 illustrates divergence polarization for several economic and cultural issues. Relative to electoral polarization, the implication is that the means of two groups increasingly separate. This definition holds no implication that the two groups are actually attracted to opposite ends of a pole (as in the physical world), but simply that they are divergent. This aspect of polarization can be measured using the means (or modes) of opposing groups on some attribute and taking the difference. For example, the difference in the annual mean self-reported liberalism/conservatism of Democrats and Republicans through time is reported below. Using this definition, polarization between Democrats and Republicans is a truism since the two parties have always diverged. Thus, divergence polarization is a matter of degree.

The second definition – concentrating about two conflicting and contrasting positions – focuses on the dispersion of the members of two groups around their respective means. With this definition there is no implication that the means are diverging, just that members are increasingly attracted to their respective group means. This can be labeled *dispersion polarization*. An unpolarized condition would exist when the members of the two groups are very broadly dispersed about their respective means. A polarized condition would exist when the members of two groups are strongly attracted to their respective means. The extreme of polarization would occur with standard deviations of zero, when members of the two parties are so strongly attracted to their respective party means that members do not deviate. This aspect of polarization can be measured by calculating the standard deviation or variance of the distribution of group members about their respective means. For example, the annual standard deviation of the self-reported liberalism/conservatism of Democrats and Republicans through time is reported below. Again, dispersion polarization is relative and may be changing through time.

The third definition – political actors divide and go to the extremes – emphasizes the shape of the distribution of members of the two groups and combines aspects of the first two definitions. This can be labeled *distributional polarization*. Members of the two groups are attracted toward their respective poles (located at the endpoints), which implies changing modes (and means). Further, if all members of the groups move to the poles, then this implies lower dispersion. When all members are at the extremes, then the dispersion of the two distributions again becomes zero.

Under distributional polarization, electoral polarization is higher when most members of the political parties are strongly concentrated at the left and right poles of the two distributions, leaving fewer members near the center. The concepts associated with the third definition can be captured by calculating the relative skewness for the distributions of members of the two groups. Distributional polarization can be asymmetrical. A distribution with increasingly positive skew would be associated with a polarized left party. A distribution with increasingly negative skew would be associated with a polarized right party. Consistent with these ideas, the skewness of the distribution of annual self-reported liberalism/conservatism of Democrats and Republicans through time is reported below. Again, distributional polarization is relative and changing through time, but provides yet another indication of how individuals have aligned themselves with respect to a set of poles.

Figure 7.19 depicts two scenarios each for divergence, dispersion, and distributional polarization. The scale of citizen preferences in this illustration runs from zero to one, with the far left being the liberal pole, and the far right being the conservative pole. Separate distributions are associated with the left and right parties. A line is drawn vertically through the means of the left and right party distributions to mark their respective means (μ_{Left}, μ_{Right}). A line is also drawn vertically through the intersection of the two distributions at I, which is a potential cut point for party loyalty.

The top two graphs in Figure 7.19 illustrate two scenarios for divergence polarization. Consider first scenario A. The two parties' members have means that are separated by 0.10. This closeness depicts a relatively low polarization

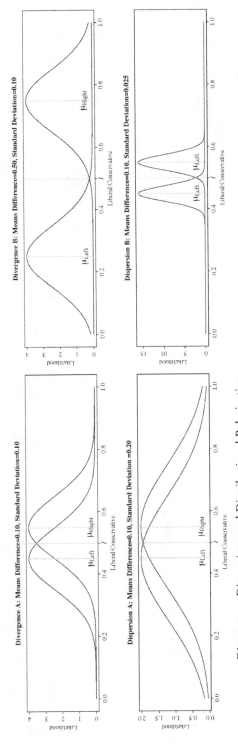

FIGURE 7.19 Divergence, Dispersion, and Distributional Polarization

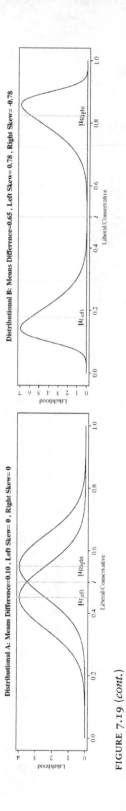

FIGURE 7.19 (*cont.*)

condition in which members are not far apart ideologically. Note that under this condition there is a substantial mass within the two parties at risk of defection. Members of the left party situated to the right of the intersection point *I* of the two distributions are actually closer to the right party mean than to their own party mean. Similarly, members of the right party situated to the left of the intersection point *I* of the two distributions are closer to the left party mean than to their own party mean. Thus, under divergence scenario A there is a high potential for members defecting to the party more closely aligned with their preferences.

Moving to divergence scenario B, the means of the two distributions are now separated by 0.50. The dispersions of the two distributions are the same as in divergence scenario A. The left and right party means have shifted so far to the left and right that there are few members of either party within the overlapping regions of the two curves. Higher polarization clearly exists in scenario B, because the members of the two parties are now much closer to the respective poles at 0 and 1. Under this scenario, few members of the two parties in scenario B are likely to defect, because few are closer to the other party's mean. However, members are also no more tightly attracted to their respective party means than they were in scenario A.

Past polarization studies have considered almost exclusively divergence polarization as defined by the first row of Figure 7.19. That is, they have looked at divergent party means through time, usually at only a few critical points. However, polarization can also occur through changing dispersions and distributions. The middle two graphs in Figure 7.19 illustrate two scenarios for dispersion polarization. The divergence in mean ideologies between left and right is now held constant for scenarios A and B at 0.10. This time it is the dispersions that are changing. Again, consider first dispersion panel A of Figure 7.19. This panel is again intended to show a condition of relatively low polarization. Note that compared to divergence A at the top, members of each party are no more divergent. However, dispersion polarization is even lower because members are less strongly attracted to their respective party means. The overlapping regions to the right and left of the intersection point *I* are much larger. As a result, the potential for defecting is higher, because more members of the two parties are actually closer to the other party's mean than they are to their own party mean.

Moving to dispersion scenario B, divergence polarization is held constant at 0.10. Observe that the potential for defecting to the other party declines with smaller dispersion. With changing party dispersions, the shared region to the right and left of the point of intersection *I* of the two curves drops sharply. In scenario B, the left and right parties have become so strongly attracted to their respective party means that there are few members of either party within the overlapping regions of the two curves. With dispersion polarization, one can think of the party means as attractors that bind members to a fixed ideological position. However, the average members of the two parties are no more divergent in scenario B than they were in scenario A.

Finally, the bottom two graphs in Figure 7.19 illustrate two scenarios for distributional polarization. Again, consider first scenario A, which is intended to depict a low polarization condition. Note that the location of the two distributions is again quite close, as was depicted above in divergence polarization panel A. The left and right preference distributions in scenario A are unskewed. As with the preceding illustrations at scenario A, each party has a substantial proportion of its adherents who are to the right and left of the intersection *I* of the two distributions. Because many adherents are closer to the other party's preferences, this depiction again implies a high potential for defecting to the other party.

Moving to distributional B, the potential for defection declines precipitously with increasing skew. In scenario B there are so few cross-pressured members that defections are highly unlikely. At the extreme of polarization depicted here, the means differences are even greater than was depicted in divergence and dispersion scenarios B above. Of course, the difference between the modes of the two distributions is greater yet. The dispersions of the two distributions are also smaller. Members have divided and moved toward the extreme poles. They are also more concentrated at those poles.

Polarization can take any of these three forms. If it takes the first form, then the means of the two party distributions diverge, with constant dispersion and no skew. If it takes the second form, then the means of the two distributions remain constant, with changing dispersion and no skew. If it takes the third form, then both the means and dispersions of the distributions are changing through time, with skew from the two poles.

Which of the three forms of polarization characterize the American electorate is an empirical question to be answered below. However, before doing so the theoretical mechanisms of polarization will be revisited within the context of these forms.

Formal Analysis of the Theoretical Mechanisms of Mass Polarization

A subsidiary issue within theoretical debates over mass polarization concerns the mechanisms of increasing polarization. If polarization has occurred among the mass public through time, then has that polarization been driven by ideological change or by people switching their party loyalties to align with their ideology?

Advocating the changing ideology explanation, Levendusky states, "When an individual voter transitions . . . I find that voters typically shift their ideology to fit with their party identification; ideology-driven party exit (changing one's party to fit with one's ideology) occurs in only a narrow set of circumstances" (2009b, 3; see also Fiorina and Levendusky 2006; Layman et al. 2006). Yet Levendusky's analysis is hard to reconcile with Black and Black (2002), who state that "Reagan's presidency dramatically transformed [Southern] White partisanship. Between 1968 and 1996 core Republicans expanded from 31 to 53 percent of the Southern White electorate ... Core Democrats have declined to 27 percent of Southern White voters" (2002, 243; see also Abramowitz 2010, 69–71; Hetherington and Weiler 2009, 153–59). Further, the basis of this shift was not purely racial. The South is the most religiously conservative part of the country. As shown earlier, Southern white evangelicals overwhelmingly oppose abortion, homosexuality, and government intrusion into education; they also support free markets, smaller government, and deregulation.

Relative to Figure 7.19, three distinct processes could be responsible for shifts from scenario A to B: shifting ideology, party switching, or partisan demobilization. One potential explanation for increasing mass polarization is shifting ideology *within* the political parties – existing Democrats become more liberal; existing Republicans become more conservative. The evidence reported above in Figures 7.2 through 7.12 suggests significant ideological change occurred through time for both economic and cultural issues, especially among Republicans. Levendusky (2009a) also provides micro-level evidence for this effect occurring between 1992 and 1996. Under this explanation, the percentage of the electorate that is Democrat or Republican does not change. However, those identifying with the political parties change their ideology and may become more attracted to the respective poles. As a result, the Democratic Party becomes more liberal and the Republican Party becomes more conservative, with each party more extreme and cohesive.

Under the shifting ideology theory, the means move further apart, and people can potentially be more strongly attracted to those means. Such effects would be consistent with the divergence and dispersion polarization described in Figure 7.19. People can also change distributionally, rather than symmetrically, moving closer to the respective poles. Such change would also be consistent with the distributional polarization depicted in Figure 7.19. People within the parties become more extreme and cohesive, and there are fewer people near the center of the left and right distributions who might defect. Thus, the implication of the shifting ideology theory is that the means diverge, dispersions decline, and the distributions can become more skewed from the poles.

A second potential explanation in the literature on mass polarization is switching between parties. Figure 7.17 above provided evidence that Democrat to Republican switching occurred among white evangelicals starting after 1980. Such switching may have caused increased mass polarization. In terms of Figure 7.19A, B, and C, those in the overlapping regions of the two curves to the left and right of I are actually closer to the other party's mean than to their own party's mean. As these people learn that their ideology is more compatible with the other party, they defect. As a result, liberal Republicans become Democrats, and conservative Democrats become Republicans. There are more liberals in the Democratic Party and more conservatives in the Republican Party, so both parties become more polarized due to switching.

The distributional implications of switching can be evaluated by considering what happens when those at risk of switching from Figure 7.19A are folded

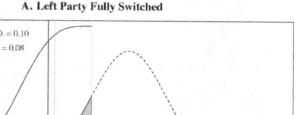

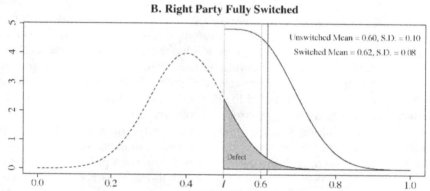

FIGURE 7.20 Distributional Implications of Switching versus Ideological Change

into the other party's distribution. A moderate polarization scenario is used for illustration, with the two party means separated by 0.20 and standard deviations of 0.10. Figure 7.20A and B shows the effects of pure partisan switching. In other words, there are no Independents in the analysis. In panel A, those citizens in the right party distribution (dashed curve) located in the shaded area to the left of *I* are at risk of switching into the left party. In panel B, those citizens in the left party distribution (dashed curve) located in the shaded area to the right of *I* are at risk of switching into the right party.

Now, assume that those switching do not change ideologically. In other words, polarization is purely due to partisan switching and not ideological change. Further, assume that switching is complete and all potential defectors have moved to their more ideologically compatible party. The upper solid-lined plots in Figure 7.20A and B illustrate the probability masses that result from folding these potential defectors into their more compatible distribution. The

C. Left Party, Independents Defect

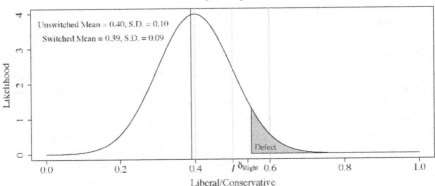

D. Right Party, Independents Defect

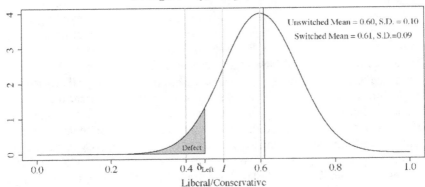

FIGURE 7.20 (*cont.*)

gray vertical lines at 0.40 and 0.60 mark the unswitched party means. The black vertical lines to the left and right mark the switched party means.

Note first that with switching the fairly large regions represented by the two shaded areas in Figure 7.20A and B produce relatively small shifts in the means of the two distributions. The mean of the left party moves to the left (from 0.40 to 0.38), while the mean of the right party moves to the right (from 0.60 to 0.62). Divergence polarization occurs, with the unswitched divergence at 0.20 and the switched divergence at 0.24. This is a change of 20 percent.

Given this percentage, it is highly unlikely that partisan switching can provide a complete explanation for electoral polarization. The empirical section below shows that divergence polarization increased between 1980 and 2012 by almost 300 percent. The implication is that it would be very difficult to achieve this degree of divergence polarization purely through partisan switching. Note further that the standard deviations of the two distributions decline in the top two panels of Figure 7.20A and B (from 0.10 to 0.08). Hence, dispersion polarization also occurs when there is switching.

Finally, note that both distributions become skewed. However, the skew is *not* consistent with the graphs in the bottom row of Figure 7.19. The left party becomes negatively skewed, while the right party becomes positively skewed. With partisan switching, people are *not* increasingly concentrated near the poles of the liberal-conservative continuum. Rather, they are concentrated toward the center of the left-right continuum.

More generally, switching between parties will *always* shift the left party mean to the left and the right party mean to the right. There are fewer conservatives in the left party and fewer liberals in the right party, so the parties become more divergent. Similarly, defections from one party to the other will *always* diminish the within-party dispersions, as fewer people remain who are divergent from the respective party means. However, switching in the absence of ideological change will also *always* result in an increasing concentration of partisans near the center. Hence, partisan switching can potentially explain increased divergence and dispersion polarization, but not distributional polarization as depicted in the bottom row of Figure 7.19. These facts will provide a basis below for evaluating empirically whether polarization in the American electorate has been due to people switching parties or within-party ideological change.

A third and related potential explanation for mass polarization is demobilization. That is, cross-pressured partisans become Independents. Figure 6.1 in the previous chapter showed that the percentage of Independents grew through time. In the commonly espoused version of the sorting theory (e.g., see Fiorina et al. 2011, figure 4.1; Levendusky 2009b, table 1.1), where ideological change drives most polarization, scholars have argued that the percentage of Independents should remain the same with sorting, but not with polarization. However, it is easy to show that shifts from partisans to Independents (a type of switching) will also lead to more extreme parties. Under this scenario, some people in the overlapping part of the two parties' preference distributions in Figure 7.19 no longer wish to identify with their current party. However, they are also disinclined to move to the other party, so they become Independents. These individuals fall outside a range delimited by $\delta_{Left} < I < \delta_{Right}$, where I is the point of intersection of the two distributions on the liberal/conservative scale and $\delta_{Left}, \delta_{Right}$ are arbitrary constants along the bottom axis delimiting the region where people are not inclined to move.

Figure 7.20C and D illustrates the distributional implications of partisans becoming Independents. The shaded areas represent those who become Independents, with the remaining part of each distribution representing those who do not. Note that the remaining distributions become truncated with upper limit for the left party at δ_{Right} and lower limit for the right party at δ_{Left}. Calculating the means and standard deviations of the remaining truncated normal distributions, the means diverge from 0.20 to 0.22 in separation, and the dispersions of both parties decline from 0.10 to 0.09. Movement out of the parties to

Independents leaves fewer moderates in both parties, resulting in distributions that are more extreme and cohesive.

Note, however, the implications of such movements are again inconsistent with the depiction of distributional polarization as shown in the bottom row of Figure 7.19. The left party becomes more negatively skewed, while the right party becomes more positively skewed. Yet distributional polarization requires that the left party be positively skewed and the right party be negatively skewed from their respective poles. Again, this distributional difference provides a basis below for evaluating empirically whether electoral polarization has been due to party switching, demobilization, or within-party ideological change.

Evaluating Mass Polarization Empirically

The preceding section defines polarization in a strictly theoretical sense and evaluates the most likely causes of mass polarization through formal analysis. However, current research lacks the data to measure and map these suggested types of polarization – divergence, dispersion, and distributional – for the electorate in an empirical sense. Accordingly, new general measures of electoral polarization were developed that track the distributions of the partisanship and ideology among the mass public. Details of how these measures were constructed are contained in Appendix A. However, a simplified explanation is given here.

Past research on electoral polarization has relied exclusively on data from the American National Election Studies (ANES) and General Social Surveys (GSS). However, data from these sources are limited in several respects. First, the surveys from these organizations were administered irregularly over time, missing many years. Second, weighting issues are associated with these data, as these organizations occasionally oversampled respondents to study pressing issues of the time. Third, and most important, these data are limited historically. The ANES did not ask the ideology question until 1972. The GSS did not ask ideology and party identification questions until 1974. Therefore, these surveys do not provide the historical coverage that would enable comparing the dynamics of changing electoral polarization over an extended period.

Measuring the concept "electoral polarization" requires a common data source administered regularly over a long time span. Accordingly, a new measure was constructed using the online Roper iPoll database. The database was queried for mass surveys asking respondents about both their ideology and their party identification. Using this query, the individual level data from 115 surveys with 125 ideology questions were obtained over a period extending from 1944 through 2012.

Before 1975, surveys were intermittent and relied on multiple question types for each year. After 1975, surveys were available for each year, but sometimes there were multiple surveys. These potential disparities were addressed through smoothing with the procedure and software WCALC developed by Stimson (1991). The software produced recursively smoothed annual time series running from 1944 through 2012.

The preceding section established a theoretical interest in studying three potential types of polarization: divergence, dispersion, and distributional polarization. Accordingly, the data were divided into Democrat, Independent, and Republican respondents. Then, the mean, standard deviation, and skewness of the partisan distributions were calculated for each survey over time. Independents were excluded from most of the analyses below, as the primary interest is in partisan polarization. Such treatment is also consistent with the analyses reported in Figures 7.2 through 7.12. However, Independents are considered in the next section for empirically evaluating the ideological change versus party switching explanations for party polarization.

Evaluation of Party Switching versus Ideological Change with Empirical Data

The empirical analysis begins by considering how party switching versus ideological change may have affected the dynamics of electoral polarization. Before proceeding, it should be noted that the commonly used approach to evaluating the switching versus ideological change explanations for mass polarization has relied on individual-level data (Carsey and Layman 2006; Erikson and Tedin 1981; Levendusky 2009a; Sundquist 1983). The analysis here provides new insight on this question using aggregate data.

As modeled in Figure 7.20 above, if partisans defect to the other party or become Independents, then the means of the two parties should move by definition toward the party poles. Thus, the question for this first analysis concerns whether such movement occurred during a period when switching was readily apparent. Figure 7.21 provides descriptive evidence about this potential effect.

Figure 7.21A plots the percentages of party identifiers through time for Democrats, Republicans, and Independents from 1944 through 2010. These are the same data as reported in Figure 6.1 of the previous chapter. Figure 7.21B plots the average ideology on the five-point scale of Democrats, Republicans, and Independents for surveys over this same time frame. A horizontal line is drawn in panel B marking the center of the liberal/conservative scale. A vertical line is drawn in both panels at 1980 to mark a potential tipping point for polarization of the American electorate.

Now, consider Figure 7.21A in more detail. The Republican percentage declined steadily from around 1950 through 1979. In 1950, roughly 35 percent of the electorate identified as Republican; by 1979 only 23 percent identified as Republican. Through this same period there were increases in the percentage identifying as Independents. In 1950, roughly 18 percent identified as Independent; by 1979 about 32 percent identified as Independent. From 1950 through 1979 Democrat identifiers remained fairly stable at around 45 percent.

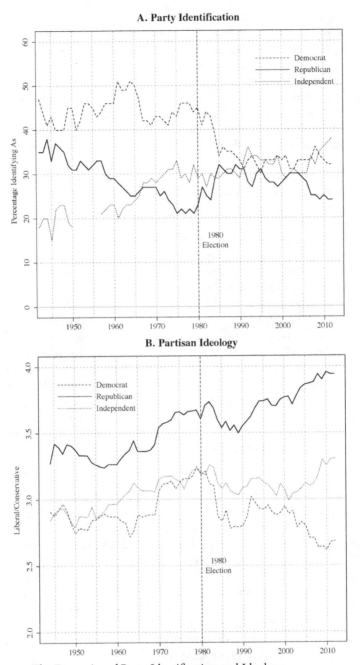

FIGURE 7.21 The Dynamics of Party Identification and Ideology
Sources: Party ID from Pew Research Center, Trends in Party Identification from Gallup, 1939–1989, Times Mirror/Pew Research Center, 1990–2012; Partisan Ideology from Gallup, augmented by surveys from the CBS/*New York Times*, Office of Public Opinion Research, the Roper Organization, and the National Opinion Research Center.

Starting in 1980, Figure 7.21A shows a subsequent drop in Democratic identification. At the same time Republican identification began increasing. The percentage of Democrat identifiers continued to decline throughout the Reagan administration. The percentage of Republican identifiers increased after 1980, dropped during the 1982–83 recession, and then increased again to remain fairly stable thereafter. Between 1979 and 1986 Republican identifiers rose from 23 to 31 percent, a level slightly lower than it had been in 1950. Over this same time frame the percentage of Independent identifiers remained fairly stable, but was considerably higher than in 1950. These movements suggest that some Democrats switched to become Republicans but not Independents during this period. Also, the evidence in Figure 7.17 above suggests that the switching was especially prevalent among white evangelicals.

Turning attention now to Figure 7.21B, if switching by Democratic partisans into Republicans produced divergence polarization, then there should have been divergent movements in partisan means after 1980. The Republican mean should have moved toward the right pole as shown by Figure 7.20B. Movement of right-leaning Democrats to the Republican Party should also have moved Democrats toward the left pole, as the party became more liberal and cohesive.

Figure 7.21B confirms that Democrats became more liberal after 1980 when party switching was occurring. However, Republicans also moved in the liberal direction after 1982. Interestingly, the Reagan administration corresponded with *both* parties moving to the left. This co-movement lasted until about 1992 when the parties began moving in opposite directions. Thus, during the 1980s Reagan's effort to curtail the New Deal social contract apparently sparked a counter-reaction among *both* Democrats and Republicans. Ideological change, rather than partisan switching, seems the more compelling explanation for subsequent polarization.

The Dynamics of Divergence Polarization

Consider now the dynamics of divergence polarization reported in Figure 7.22. Panel A reports the means of the distributions of Republican and Democrat identifiers for each year from 1944 through 2012. The ideology scale runs from 1 to 5. Figure 7.22B reports the divergence between the Republican and Democrat means for each year. Vertical lines are again added to the graphs at 1980.

From 1944 through 1980, panels A and B of Figure 7.22 show that changes in the Republican and Democratic means tracked together through time. Both Republicans and Democrats grew increasingly conservative from the 1960s through 1980. Divergence polarization was at a minimum in 1957 when the mean ideology on the five-point scale for Republicans was 3.13 and that for Democrats was 2.89. Interestingly again, Republicans and Democrats *both* reversed the conservative trend in 1980 to become more liberal throughout the Reagan administration.

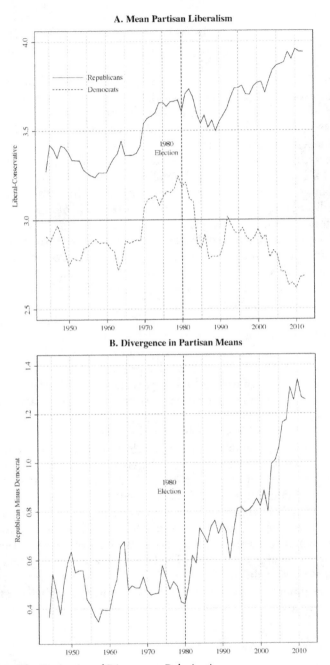

FIGURE 7.22 The Dynamics of Divergence Polarization

This reversal toward increased liberalism after 1980 is consistent with a thermostatic theory of mass behavior (Erikson et al. 2002; Wlezien 1995). Using a thermostatic theory, people from both parties concluded that Reagan's policies were more extreme than those they personally espoused. As a result, they turned more liberal. The reversal in 1980 is also consistent with Stimson's (1999) measure of public mood, which also shows a reversal in the liberal direction after Reagan was elected. The consistency of the measure with the Stimson measure provides construct validity and also gives a theoretical rationale for understanding this change.

However, Figure 7.22B also shows there was increased partisan divergence after 1980. Panel A shows that Republicans and Democrats *both* grew more liberal, but at different rates, thereby producing the divergence. The change in partisan divergence was very sharp between 1981 and 1984. Between 1985 and the Clinton election in 1992, the divergence leveled out. However, note that while divergence occurred, only Democrats moved toward their own pole. Republicans during the 1980s actually moved away from their pole. Thus, considering divergence polarization alone would produce an anomalous prediction relative to what one might ordinarily consider polarization – political actors moving toward the poles.

True polarization with partisans moving toward their polar extremes started only around 1993. In 1993 the Republican mean ideology was 3.68, while the Democrat mean was 2.97. Republicans were well to the right of the center at 3, while Democrats were almost precisely on the center. By 2000, the Republican mean had increased to 3.77, while the Democrat mean was 2.9. Republicans had become even more polarized, while Democrats still remained near the center.

Starting precisely in 2003, polarization started increasing again, and very sharply. This time, Democrats were largely responsible for the increase. In 2003, the Republican mean was 3.78, barely changed from 2000. However, the Democrat mean decreased to 2.78. It is quite likely that the shift in 2003 was a response to George Bush's tax cut for the wealthy or the start of his war on Iraq. Polarization continued to increase very sharply throughout the Bush administration to peak in 2008. In 2008, the Republican mean was 3.9, while the Democrat mean was 2.63. By 2012, Republicans and Democrats in the electorate remained polarized. The Obama presidency and its response to the Great Recession did nothing to increase or diminish divergence polarization. At this point the divergence in party means was roughly three times what it had been in 1980.

The Dynamics of Dispersion Polarization

The divergence between opposing partisans started during the Reagan administration, but movement of both parties toward their respective poles did not start until later. Yet dispersion and distributional polarization may have

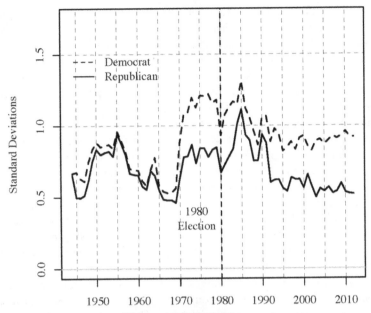

FIGURE 7.23 The Dynamics of Dispersion Polarization

coincided with Reagan. Did Republicans and Democrats both become more cohesive during the 1980s? Figure 7.23 provides evidence for answering this question by reporting the standard deviations of the distributions of Democrats and Republicans from 1944 through 2012.

The time series plots show that the dispersion of partisans around their respective party means initially shifted around 1970–71. Democrats became less ideologically cohesive after most of the Great Society programs were enacted. Between 1944 and 1969, the dispersions of Republicans and Democrats tracked very closely and were almost equal. This similarity, combined with the earlier results on divergence polarization, suggests that both parties were tents for liberals and conservatives.

Between 1970 and 1980, the party dispersions grew sharply different, largely due to Democrats becoming less cohesive. Perhaps Democratic disaffection with the Great Society caused respondents to become less cohesive than earlier. In particular, Southern Democrats may have become increasingly conservative in thermostatic response to what they considered the extreme liberal policies of the Great Society. For whatever reason, Democrats became less cohesive as a party after about 1970–71, and remained so during most of the 1980s. Further, Republicans in the electorate did *not* become more ideologically cohesive during the Reagan administration. Indeed, Figure 7.23 shows that Republicans actually grew less cohesive between 1984 and 1987, relative to their average from 1965 through 1980.

Between 1988 and 1991, Republicans were about equal to their pre-1980 dispersion. However, Republican cohesion increased very sharply starting around 1992. It may have been that the Old Guard had by this time taken greater control of the party, providing a menu that drove liberals and moderates out. For whatever reason, Republicans in the electorate were significantly more cohesive than Democrats after 1992. In contrast, Democrats remained about as dispersed in 2012 as they were in 1992

The substantive implication is that dispersion polarization occurred before and after, but not during the Reagan administration. Republicans actually became more diverse during the Reagan administration. Reagan was clearly a polarizing leader, invoking ideological responses from members of *both* political parties (e.g., see Figures 6.7 and 7.22). However, the dispersional nature of the post–Reagan era reveals a dynamic that has not been well understood until now. Republicans became *less* cohesive during the Reagan administration, but returned to a more cohesive status after Reagan's leadership had ended. Since 1992, the standard deviations of the two party distributions have differed substantially, with Republicans far more attracted to their party means than Democrats. Indeed, Republican cohesion was greater in 2012 than during the Reagan administration. These findings suggest again that Republicans have asymmetrically become more polarized than Democrats.

The Dynamics of Distributional Polarization

Finally, the electoral polarization story is only complete by considering the changing distributions of Republicans and Democrats through time. Accordingly, Figure 7.24 reports the skewness of the Democratic and Republican distributions. In broad overview, the skewness statistics reveal a continuous difference between the average shapes of the Democrat and Republican distributions.

Historically, Democrats in the electorate periodically exhibited positive skew and at other times slightly negative skew. Considering the entire period of analysis, the average skewness for the Democrat distributions was +0.07. Considering the Democratic skew only for the period from 1981 through 2012, the average skewness was −0.003. Both numbers are very close to zero, showing a historically symmetrical distribution for Democrats through time. In other words, Democrats were not distributionally attracted toward the left pole and exhibited far more potential for defection from the overlapping part of their distribution through time.

In contrast, Republicans exhibited negative skew over the entire period from 1944 through 2012. The average skewness for the Republican distributions was −0.51. The average Republican skewness for the period from 1981 through 2012 was −0.40. These differences suggest that Republicans were more consistently attracted toward the right pole. However, they were no more skewed since 1980 than they were before 1980. Considering Figure 7.20B again, these

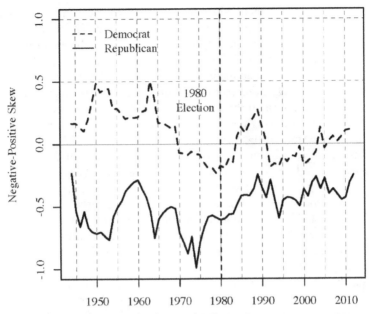

<small>FIGURE 7.24</small> The Dynamics of Distributional Polarization

facts suggest a Republican distribution with less potential for defection from the overlapping part of their distribution.

While these averages are noteworthy, they also hide interesting dynamics that tell us about the changing nature of electoral polarization through time. Figure 7.24 shows that between 1981 and 1989, Democrats became more positively skewed, while after 1980 Republicans became less negatively skewed. This result is again consistent with the results in Figures 7.21 and 7.22. Figure 7.21A shows that both Democrats and Republicans turned increasingly liberal after 1980, regardless of their increasing divergence. Figure 7.22 shows that Republicans grew increasingly diverse after 1980, likely associated with their liberal turn. Consistently, Republicans grew less skewed between 1981 and 1988, as the average Republican became more liberal. From around 1989 through 2012, Republican skew remained relatively constant. Hence, only moderate distributional polarization characterized Republicans since the Reagan administration. Polarization was, therefore, largely of the divergence and dispersion types.

Empirical Distributions of Partisan Polarization through Time

In understanding the changing nature of polarization in the American electorate, it is also useful to holistically consider the distributions for the two parties through time. In keeping with this idea, the mean, standard deviation, and skewness statistics for selected years were used to generate their historical distributions. Based on their substantive interest, the years 1957, 1965, 1979, 1981, 1988, 1995, 2000, 2003, and 2012 were chosen. The year 1957 was the low point of partisan divergence, and the year after the bipartisan Federal Highway Act was passed. The year 1965 marked the height of the Great Society when many legislative enactments occurred on a bipartisan basis. The year 1979 was immediately prior to the presumed start of the Reagan Revolution. The substantive analysis in the previous chapter suggested that significant Old Guard efforts at producing the Reagan Revolution started in this year. The year 1981 marks the start of the Reagan administration. The year 1988 was at the end of the Reagan administration, enabling comparison of polarization with both earlier and later years. The year 1995 marks when Republicans took control of Congress to implement their "Contract with America." The year 2000 was the end of the Clinton administration and denotes the very polarizing George W. Bush/Al Gore election. The year 2003 occurred after the first Bush tax cut for the wealthy and at the start of Bush's war in Iraq. Finally, the year 2012 is the data point closest to the present and reflects a relative peak in divergence polarization.

Using the skew-t distribution (Azzalini and Capitano 2003), the distributions of Republican and Democrat ideological preferences were generated. Results are reported in Figure 7.25. The distributions on the left are the Democrats, and those on the right are the Republicans. Gray vertical lines on each graph mark the respective means of the distributions for the two parties. Black vertical lines mark the respective modes.

Tracking the divergence between the means for each party visually across the nine graphs provides a story similar to that provided in Figure 7.22B. The distances between Democrat and Republican means did not change much until the 1980s. However, the respective means did vary through time. It is just that they tracked together for much of the historical time series as shown in Figure 7.22A. Starting in the 1980s, the means became increasingly divergent through 2012.

In 1957 the Democrat mean was slightly left of center on the scale of liberalism/conservatism. By 1979 Democrats had moved significantly to the right, but moved back again toward the center after 1981. By 2012 Democrats were somewhat more liberal than they were in 1957. In contrast, Republicans had moved considerably to the right through time. In 1957 Republicans were slightly to the right on the scale of liberalism/conservatism. By 1979 the Republican mean had moved farther to the right than at any prior or subsequent point in the historical time series. By 1988, the Republican mean had shifted left. However, by 1995 Republicans had moved again toward the right, and remained increasingly to the right for each year through 2012.

The changing skewness of the progression from 1957 through 2012 is also interesting. Note that skewness of a distribution implies that the mean (gray vertical lines) is different from the mode (black vertical lines). The distance between the means and modes in each graph captures the relative skewness of the distributions. In 1957 the distributions for the two parties were both largely

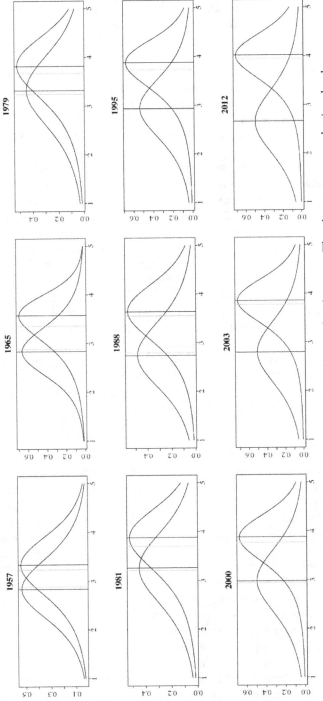

FIGURE 7.25 Historical Empirical Distributions of Partisan Ideology in the Electorate. The plots are generated using the skew-t distribution using the observed means, standard deviations, and skewness statistics for each year. The vertical black lines are modes. The vertical gray lines are means. The left curve represents Democrats, the right curve Republicans.

257

symmetrical, with Democrats exhibiting slightly positive skew and Republicans exhibiting slightly negative skew. By 1965 the Democrat distribution remained fairly symmetrical. However, the Republican distribution had become more skewed and asymmetrical. The modes of the Republican distribution in 1979 and 1981 were well to the right of the mean near around four on the five-point scale. Thus, by 1979 a large mass of Republicans had already grown quite conservative. The mode for Republicans continued increasing from 1979 through 2012, ultimately shifting to above 4.

More generally, the story told by the progression shown in Figure 7.25 is again one of *asymmetric* electoral polarization. Republicans grew increasingly polarized through time, while Democrats became only slightly polarized. Democrats became more liberal since 1957, but fluctuated more and less liberal in interim plots. They became significantly more liberal after 2003, as George W. Bush polarized the American public through tax cuts for the wealthy and the invasion of Iraq. However, the shape of the Democrat distribution remained fairly symmetrical since 1957. The mean of the Democrat distribution was generally located near the mode. Thus, Democrats were not significantly attracted toward the left pole or to the mean.

In contrast, since 1957 and especially after 1979, Republicans moved toward the right pole with declining dispersion. In 2012, the Republican mean was farther to the right than at any other point in modern history, and the Republican mode was even farther to the right. The dispersion of the Republican distribution was also significantly lower, suggesting that Republicans became far more attracted to their respective pole and mean than Democrats. Thus, the electorates of both political parties have contributed to modern polarization, but asymmetrically by Republicans.

A Single Measure of Electoral Polarization

As shown above, polarization involves at least three dimensions: divergence, dispersion, and distribution. The preceding analyses show that no single one of these dimensions can accurately depict modern mass polarization. However, all three dimensions can be used together to do so. As shown in Figure 7.19, each of the three dimensions of polarization can cause the overlap between the partisan distributions to change. For each polarization type, the probability masses in the overlapping parts of the distributions become smaller with increasing polarization. For example, compare the overlap between the empirical partisan distributions in 1957 and 2012 contained in Figure 7.26. The shaded overlap area is much larger between Democrats and Republicans in 1957 than in 2012. Using this concept, a more general measure of mass polarization can be constructed.

When there is total overlap between the two distributions, then the size of the shaded region becomes one. When there is no overlap between the two distributions, then the size of the shaded region becomes zero. Using this fact, a new measure of polarization can be constructed by measuring the empirical

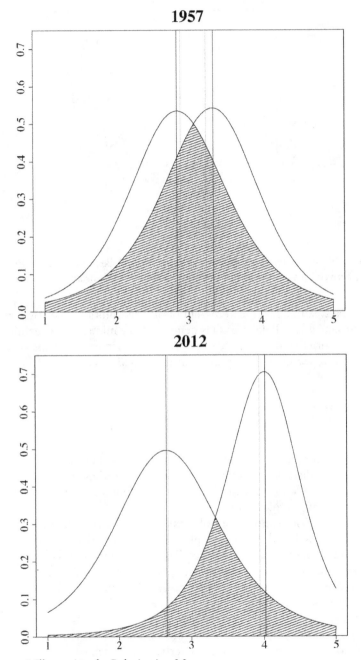

FIGURE 7.26 Illustrating the Polarization Measure.

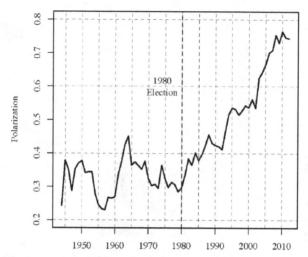

FIGURE 7.27 The Dynamics of Electoral Polarization. Polarization is measured using the overlap between the empirical distributions of Republications and Democrats.

overlap between Democrat and Republican distributions for each year from 1944 through 2012. Polarization is defined as one minus the probability masses associated with the overlap between the two partisan distributions at each point in time. More formally, polarization at time t is defined by

$$Polarization_t = 1 - \left(\int_{I_t}^{1} Left_t \, dx + \int_{0}^{I_t} Right_t \, dx \right),$$

where I_t is the point of intersection of the two distributions at time t, $Left_t$ is the left party distribution at time t, $Right_t$ is the right party distribution at time t, and x is a left-right continuum ranging from 0 to 1. The new measure of polarization ranges from 0 to 1.

The measure of institutional polarization presented in the next chapter will also be calculated in this manner, placing electoral and institutional polarization into the same measurement space. The identical metrics will then be used to compare electoral and institutional polarization, enabling evaluation of whether a representation gap exists between the American electorate and their representatives in Washington. The measures will also be used in an analysis of whether party polarization in American is due more to party elites or changing electorates. Figure 7.27 contains the more general measure of electoral polarization based on these calculations. A vertical dashed line is again drawn on the graph at 1980.

The graph reveals that mass polarization between Republicans and Democrats started in the 1980s. To state the obvious, Ronald Reagan was a highly polarizing figure, even as many Republicans became more liberal during this period. Polarization declined during the George H. W. Bush presidency from 1989 through 1992. This decline probably reflects his less extreme issue positions and appeal to a broader base. After the George H. W. Bush presidency, polarization continued increasing quite sharply. The sharpest change occurred around 1994 (see also Abramowitz and Saunders 1998). As Republicans took control of Congress based on their "Contract with America," between 1995 and 2002, polarization grew more gradually. However, starting in 2003 it increased quite sharply again. Obviously, George W. Bush was also a highly polarizing president with his tax cuts for the wealthy and invasion of Iraq. Polarization increased very sharply through the entire Bush presidency to level off around 2008. Electoral polarization during the Obama presidency continued around this same level. This is not to say that Obama was not polarizing. There was also no decline in polarization during the Obama presidency. Ceiling effects may be associated with electoral polarization, such that it was about as high as it could get by 2008.

CHARACTERIZING ELECTORAL POLARIZATION

The evidence in this chapter should definitively settle any remaining scholarly debate over whether the mass public is polarized in the modern era. It is. Along economic, cultural, and ideological lines, partisans in the electorate have moved toward their respective poles. That movement has involved divergence, dispersion, and distributional changes. However, those movements have been asymmetrical. Republicans have moved much closer to the right pole than Democrats have moved toward the left pole. Republicans in the electorate have become far more concentrated around their party mean than Democrats around their party mean. And Republicans have also shifted more toward the right pole in distribution. Democrats are ideologically only slightly more liberal and cohesive than they were in the 1940s. In contrast, Republicans are much farther to the right and cohesive than at any time in post–New Deal history.

The evidence in this chapter also shows that the primary mechanism of electoral polarization has been ideological change, rather than partisan switching. To be sure, significant party switching occurred during the 1980s among white evangelicals. As planned by the Old Guard, white evangelicals became a reliable support group for Republican candidates. To maintain evangelical support, Republican elites adhered to core evangelical principles on cultural issues. However, party switching alone does not explain the magnitude of changes in Republican ideology through time. The simulation analyses above showed that party switching can account for about a 20 percent divergence by Republicans. However, between 1980 and 2012 divergence polarization increased by almost 300 percent. Further, while partisan switching was occurring in the 1980s, Republicans in the electorate actually moved toward the left pole, rather than to the right pole. Further, virtually all of the issue-specific analyses above showed Republicans in the electorate shifting positions through time on both economic and cultural issues in a manner consistent with changing ideology.

More generally, Republicans in the electorate became increasingly visceral and ideological through time in their dislike for the liberal policies of the New Deal and Great Society. They increasingly favored smaller government, free markets, low taxes on the wealthy, individual responsibility, and weaker regulation. The connection drawn strategically by the Old Guard between these economic issues and highly emotional cultural issues such as abortion, gay rights, guns, illegal aliens, and welfare bolstered Republican support for these economic values. Because of the connection drawn by the Old Guard between the economic and cultural dimensions of party ideology, it became godly once again to believe in unfettered markets, increasing concentrations of wealth, and increasing inequality.

In contrast, the evidence above shows that Democrats in the electorate became less visceral and ideological while consistently supporting New Deal and Great Society programs. The New Deal and Great Society created new economic rents for many groups. In a system designed for inaction, rather than action, those rents were not to be easily taken away. Democrats in the electorate also became more secular and less religious through time, enabling greater polarization along cultural lines. While polarization along cultural lines is significant, the core battle continues over the economic benefits associated with New Deal and Great Society programs.

While the electorate is significantly polarized along both economic and cultural lines, it remains unclear whether the electorate is as polarized as their elected officials in Washington. The next chapter turns toward a systematic analysis of the causes of polarization in Washington and the electorate, and evaluates whether polarization is a top-down or bottom-up phenomenon.

8

Elite Polarization and Democratic Representation

In his farewell address to the nation on September 19, 1796, President George Washington warned about the formation of political parties. He said, "[Parties] serve to organize faction, to give it an artificial and extraordinary force – to put in the place of the delegated will of the Nation, the will of a party . . . [T]hey are likely, in the course of time and things, to become potent engines, by which cunning, ambitious and unprincipled men will be enabled to subvert the power of the people" (Washington 1796). Washington's farewell address suggested that political parties and their representatives would ultimately undermine, rather than follow, public preferences.

Consistently, Old Guard Republicans strategically used an elite-driven strategy in attempting to resurrect the Founders' social contract. No groundswell of public support for Old Guard economic and cultural values occurred in the 1970s or '80s. Yet the Old Guard took over the national Republican Party and subsequently secured smaller government, less regulated markets, and lower taxes on the wealthy. The Old Guard also cunningly connected their economic values with a completely unrelated set of cultural values, thereby recruiting a reliable support group, the Christian Right, into the Republican Right. While the Reagan administration was a start, lasting and significant support for the Founders' social contract required continuing control of the menu of policy choices offered by the Republican Party to the electorate. It also required continuing influence on party representatives in Washington. Did increasing polarization in Washington result from the Old Guard strategy?

Certainly, increased polarization occurred. Past scholarship has documented congressional polarization since the 1980s along liberal-conservative lines using the percentage of party-line votes (Fleischer and Bond 2000a; Stonecash et al. 2003), party unity scores (Fleischer and Bond 2000a; Sinclair 2002; Stonecash et al. 2003), interest group support scores (Stonecash et al. 2003), nominate scores (Fleischer and Bond 2004; Hetherington 2001; Jacobson 2000; McCarty et al. 2008; Theriault 2008), Bayesian common space scores (Clinton et al. 2004), and National Political Awareness Test scores (Ansolabehere et al. 2001a).

While less studied, polarization between presidents and Congress is also evident, as opposing partisans in Congress consistently lined up to challenge most everything a president proposed, and presidents consistently posed an obstacle to opposing partisans in Congress (Binder 2003; Edwards and Barrett 2000; Fleischer and Bond 2000a, 2000b; Pomper 2003; Sinclair 2000, 2002; Wood et al. 2015). There is much anecdotal evidence of these interactions, including Reagan's polarizing effort to rein in New Deal and Great Society programs over Democratic objections in the 1980s, the Clinton–Gingrich standoff over the federal budget and "Contract with America" in the 1990s, Democratic reactions to the Bush tax cuts and invasion of Iraq in the 2000s, and the Boehner/McConnell–Obama battles over stimulating the economy, raising the federal debt ceiling, and the Affordable Care Act after 2009.

American political institutions became hopelessly divided over a wide range of issues, including social programs, regulation, immigration reform, gay marriage, abortion, gun control, stem cell research, global climate change, the size of the military, and so on. (e.g., see Abramowitz 2010; Hetherington and Weiler 2009). While there is a strong consensus that polarization grew higher among Washington elites, it remains important to understand the nature and causes of this phenomenon.

When did elite polarization begin? Was elite polarization a factor that drove mass polarization, as suggested by Washington's farewell address? Was elite polarization merely a reflection of mass polarization? Or might the relationship actually have run both ways, whereby feedback existed from the electorate to representatives, and back from representatives to the electorate? Starting in the late 1980s, Republicans in the electorate grew far more polarized than Democrats and Independents. Was the same asymmetrical pattern present for Washington elites? Was there a representation gap due to polarization, whereby representatives grew more extreme than those who elected them?

PARTY PLATFORMS AND ELITE POLARIZATION

An understudied approach to evaluating elite polarization is observing changes in party platforms through time. Did the Republican Party platforms change systematically through time, suggesting that the menu of policies offered by party elites shifted? Were there also changes in Democratic Party platforms over the same period? If so, then such changes would be consistent with an elite-driven theory of system polarization.

Various scholars have theorized that modern polarization is elite-driven. For example, Fiorina et al. (2011, 29) argue that the electorate appears more polarized because the choices they are given by elites are more polarized. Similarly, Levendusky (2009b, 35) claims that "political change begins with elites and then spreads to the masses." In making this argument he notes that the theoretical foundations for an elite-driven model are well established by past political science research starting with Converse (1964). Converse showed that the larger citizenry was not particularly ideological in the 1960s and tended to be poorly informed. Therefore, the masses could not be the source of ideological polarization.

Similarly, Carmines and Stimson (1980, 1981, 1984, 1986, 1989) posited a theory of issue evolution whereby change was initiated by political elites. They showed that changing issue positions among elites transmits signals to the masses by increasing the clarity of party stances. Citizens' evaluations of these signals and greater clarity can, in turn, result in mass realignment and consequent turnover among political elites.

Along similar lines, Zaller (1992) posited that individuals form opinions on issues as a result of the elite behavior, particularly sensed through the mass media. Mass opinion is largely shaped by elite discourse on the issues (see also Adams 1997; Brody 1991; Hetherington 2001; Layman 2001; Layman and Carsey 2002). According to Zaller, the most politically aware and those attending to elite cues through the media form a consistent belief system. The result is a more polarized electorate. Similarly, Sniderman (2000) argued that citizens' choices have been fixed for them by polarized elites. Citizens use shortcuts promulgated by party elites competing for their allegiance. Consistently, Sniderman and Bullock (2004) focus on menu-dependence, arguing that the citizens' choices are a function of the menu being offered to them by the political parties.

Scholars have also theorized that the political parties engage in conflict extension, rather than conflict displacement, through time. According to Layman and Carsey (2002; see also Carsey and Layman 2006), elites have an incentive to polarize iteratively on new issues while retaining partisan cleavages on past issues. Thus, conflict extension theory would suggest that elites maintained the older partisan cleavage over economic issues, while subsequently adding cultural issues to bolster their base. For each new issue that the parties adopt opposing positions, some new subset of the electorate might be drawn into the party.

Party Platforms and Party Elites

Given the scholarly consensus on growing elite polarization through time, and the known importance of elite messages, the focus here is on the ways in which elite cues, manifest through party platforms, have changed.

Focusing on the party platforms as a reflection of elite polarization differs from past research on this topic. Previous studies of elite polarization have focused almost exclusively on proxy measurement of elite ideology in Congress. For example, McCarty et al. (2008) demonstrate elite polarization through NOMINATE scores, proxy measures of liberal-conservative ideology derived from the universe of roll-call votes in Congress. Groseclose et al. (1999)

developed a model of inflation-adjusted ADA scores, which uses a much smaller subset of congressional roll-call votes to reflect litmus-test liberal/conservative issues. An example of direct measurement of elite ideology is the National Political Awareness Test (NPAT) (Ansolabehere et al. 2001b). NPAT measures are derived from direct surveys of candidates for congressional office. But such measures are rarely, if ever, repeated over time, if not solely because of elite resistance to being surveyed for fear of being audited by members of their constituency. In large part, then, understanding of elite polarization has been built on indirect expressions of preferences through legislative roll-call votes.

In contrast, the party platforms are unique, direct indicators of partisan ideology because they are plainly a construction of party elites. Moreover, and particularly useful for the study of polarization, they are repeated regularly over time. As a result, they offer an instrument for examining the changing nature (and divergence) of elite ideology through a *direct*, repeated measure of elite ideology.

Party platforms spell out the general programs proposed by political parties. They are manifestations of the policy preferences of those most central to the party. These documents are meant to appeal to the party faithful and attract new supporters. Platforms provide members with blueprints for campaigning and for governing after the election (Budge and Hofferbert 1990; Pomper and Lederman 1980, 152–53; Sanbonmatsu 2006, 98, but see King and Laver 1993). They also constitute a communication mechanism for party elites with those who would represent the party. As written documents, platforms are a mechanism for holding party members accountable, thereby facilitating party responsibility. Since the 1970s and the rise of candidate-centered, rather than party-centered elections, they also manifest the preferences of the presidential candidates, as well as all others seeking office under the party banner (Maisel 1993).

Fine (1994) describes in detail how the political party platforms are constructed. Before the presidential nominating conventions, each party's national committee designates a platform writing committee. The platform writing committee conducts hearings. Testimony is typically received from interest groups, trade associations, labor unions, corporations, educational institutions, research institutes, campaign organizations, party committee members, elected officials, and private individuals. While the mechanism for influence by presidents and presidential candidates is unclear, Fine argues that they are "especially important in the platform writing process in the post-reform era" (Fine 1994, 856). After hearing testimony, the platform committee constructs a draft document to be presented to the convention delegates. The convention then deliberates over the draft document, possibly amending it, and then approves the final document.

The platform writing committee is comprised of party leaders from various segments of the political system. For example, the platform writing committee for the Democrats in 2012 consisted of administration officials, governors and former governors, current and former members of Congress, members of think tanks, and representatives of interest groups. The 2012 Republican platform committee was drawn exclusively from members of the Republican National Committee (RNC), which consists of three party leaders from each state and territory.

Scholarly debate surrounds the relevance of party platforms. One controversy concerns whether anyone is paying attention. Some scholars argue that elites use platforms to communicate their policy goals to the public and that the public uses platforms to make voting decisions (Fine 1994; Kidd 2008; Simas and Evans 2011). However, skeptics argue that it is unlikely that a generally uninformed electorate would take the time to process all of the information in lengthy party platforms. Paddock (2010, 713) concedes this point, but argues that, "while most voters do not read party platforms, there is empirical evidence that platform pledges reach voters through indirect means (e.g., news accounts)." A related perspective suggests that the tone of ensuing presidential campaigns serves as an alternative indirect means through which voters can receive information about the party platforms (Simas and Evans 2011, 832).

Others argue that party platforms may not be made for public consumption at all. Instead, party elites use the platforms to ensure the support of "established constituencies" (Monroe 1983). Elites author the platform to lock in the support of some interest groups and sway the support of others. Reinhardt and Victor (2012) argue that interest groups use party platforms as a means to articulate their interests and that parties incorporate group preferences to reward groups that can mobilize voters (evangelicals, labor, environmentalists, etc.). By grouping enough interests together, the platforms are engineered to give the party the best chance of achieving its electoral outcome.

Another debate concerns whether party platforms matter for policy. On one side are the skeptics. Pomper (1988, 144) repeats the classic argument put forth by Ostrogorski (1964, 138–39): "The platform, which is supposed to be the party's profession of faith and its programme of action is only a farce – the biggest farce of all the acts of this great parliament of the party." Similarly, David Truman wrote that "the platform is generally regarded as a document that says little, binds no one, and is forgotten by politicians as quickly as possible after it is adopted" (Truman 1951, 282–83). More recently, Rozell et al. (2006, 34) argue that interest groups "struggle to influence the party platforms – which, in practice, often embody nothing more than the momentary sentiments of a majority of party activists."

On the other side are those reporting evidence that policy makers try to adhere to the goals put forth in their party's platforms. Budge and Hofferbert (1990) claim strong links between election platforms and government outputs, specifically, federal spending priorities. Pomper and Lederman (1980, 164) find that parties attempt to follow through on the pledges made in platforms more than 50 percent of the time.

These debates aside, the party platforms are used here simply to evaluate the changing menu of policies offered by the political parties relating to polarization. Only a few scholars have used party platforms to study polarization. Ginsberg (1972, 1976) analyzed the text of party platforms to study the link between electoral choices and the policy positions taken by major parties. He found that changes in "party cleavages" are linked to electoral realignments associated with "critical conflicts" where one or more parties changes positions in hopes of mobilizing a new segment of the electorate. More recently, polarization scholars have studied party platforms at the state level (Coffey 2011; Paddock 2010). Coffey (2011, 311) credits the renewed interest in party platforms with the advancement of content analysis software that makes it easier to wade through lengthy political texts. Only one study has applied these new techniques to national party platforms. Kidd (2008) used "wordscores" to analyze the content of national party platforms written between 1996 and 2004. Incredibly, he reported that American political parties were not ideologically polarized over this time period – especially on domestic issues. Coffey (2011) argues that this blatantly wrong finding resulted from overreliance on automated text analysis software and a lack of attention to the actual content of the platforms.

The data described below are developed using methods that combine content analytic software techniques with hands-on analysis of the actual content of the platforms. The analyses examine the changing menus of policies offered by partisan elites, manifest through party platforms, for the period 1944–2012. The next section describes in more detail the methods used to analyze the platforms' content, as well as specific analytic procedures.

Text Mining the Platforms

The data come from the thirty-six platforms for the Democratic and Republican parties during presidential election years from 1944 through 2012. The platforms were retrieved as electronic text from the website of *The American Presidency Project* (Peters and Wooley 2012). The platform lengths varied across years from a minimum of 1,375 words in 1944 to a maximum of 38,195 words in 1980 for the Democrats, and from a minimum of 2,755 words in 1948 to a maximum of 35,847 words in 1988 for Republicans. Because the text lengths vary so much, the counts are normalized to platform length to provide comparability. In other words, the focus is on the percentage of the platform devoted to specific issue dimensions. The goal is to extract meaning and quantitative measures from the Democratic and Republican platforms that would reflect the timing and degree of polarization between the parties through time.

Text-mining methodologies were used to extract meaningful quantitative measures from the party platforms. Specific details on how the party platform analysis was performed are contained in Appendix B. Simply put, information is derived by uncovering patterns and trends in the text through a variety of statistical techniques. These techniques include but are not limited to recording frequencies for particular words, finding associations between words, categorizing document text by concept, mapping word importance, and clustering either platforms or terms. Once such techniques are implemented, the analyst turns to interpreting the emerging patterns.

Platforms Cluster Analysis

A hierarchical cluster analysis was first performed. Figure 8.1 reports the dendrogram tree of the platforms cluster analysis. Each platform is labeled by party and year (e.g., R2000 indicates the 2000 Republican Party platform; D2000 indicates the 2000 Democratic Party platform). A gray bracket is superimposed over each of the four major clusters of the tree. The dissimilarity scale on the left measures how similar the clustered platforms are to one another and to the other clusters. Given two political parties of different ideological persuasions, one might expect there to be only two clusters, with each party occupying a distinct cluster. However, the empirically identified clusters suggest different factors driving the clusters. The platform clustering shows both temporal and partisan patterns.

The far left cluster on the tree marked in gray in Figure 8.1 contains five Democratic Party platforms from 1996 through 2012. The second left cluster consists of a mix of twenty Democratic and Republican Party platforms, all before 1980. The first right cluster on the tree contains three Republican and two Democratic platforms between 1980 and 1988. The far right cluster contains six Republican platforms between 1992 and 2012. Note especially from the dissimilarity scale on the left that *after 1980 Republican platforms were very dissimilar* from pre-1980 Republican platforms, pre-1980 Democratic platforms, and from post-1988 Democratic platforms.

The far left cluster, consisting of five Democratic platforms from 1996 through 2012, suggests that the menu offered by Democrats after 1996 was distinct from that provided earlier and from Republicans over this same period. The second left cluster, consisting of eleven Democratic and nine Republican platforms from 1944 through 1976, suggests a period of general similarity between the parties. The first twig on the first branch of the second left cluster shows Democratic and Republican platforms similar in 1944, 1948, and 1952, with these platforms also similar to the Democratic platforms in 1988 and 1992. Observing the dissimilarity scale along the y-axis, these platforms were the most similar of the thirty-six platforms. However, the 1992 Democratic platform was distinct from the others of this branch, suggesting the strong imprint of presidential candidate Bill Clinton. Interestingly, this result is confirmed by case-study evidence that Clinton specifically attempted to eschew traditional liberal priorities in favor of a more centrist platform (Borrelli 2001). Clinton's control over the platform was such that

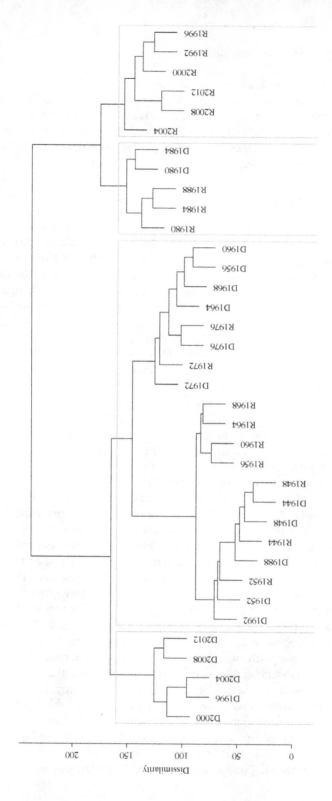

FIGURE 8.1 Cluster Dendrogram of Democratic and Republican Platforms, 1944–2012

the 1992 document was "not just compatible with but thoroughly imbued with the Clinton agenda" (Borrelli 2001, 455).

The second twig of the first branch of the second left cluster shows that Republican platforms from 1956 through 1968 cluster together. These years coincide with the Modern Republicanism of the Eisenhower–Nixon years, again suggesting the presidency's distinct imprint on party platforms. The separate twig for Republican platforms through this era shows they were distinct from both earlier and later eras of the Republican Party, as well as from Democrats. The second branch of the second left cluster shows that Democratic platforms from 1956 through 1976 were similar to one another and to Republican platforms in 1972 and 1976. More generally, Democrats and Republicans appear more similar than dissimilar before 1980. Per the discussion in Chapters 4 and 5, Democrats and Modern Republicans both supported the New Deal social contract before 1980.

After 1980, Old Guard Republicans controlled the party and promoted restoration of the Founders' social contract. The two clusters on the right side of Figure 8.1 contain evidence supporting this argument. The evidence consists of the nine Republican platforms from 1980 through 2012, along with two Democratic platforms in 1980 and 1984. The first right cluster consists of Republican and Democratic platforms during the Reagan era. During this period, Democratic elites incorporated language in their platforms somewhat similar to that of the Republicans. The far right cluster consists solely of Republican platforms starting in 1992.

Focusing on the dissimilarity scale on the y-axis, the results in Figure 8.1 show that Republican platforms after 1980 were very distinct from Republican platforms before 1980. Republican platforms after 1980 were also distinct from Democratic platforms before 1980 and after 1988. Indeed, *post-1980 Republican platforms form a cluster that is more dissimilar than every platform before 1980, Republican or Democratic.* Republicans seemingly became more consistent in the menu offered to their electorate after 1980. Between 1956 and 1968, the earlier Modern Republicans had been distinct from the Democratic Party, but not all that distinct during the 1940s, early 1950s, and 1970s. The similarity of Republican platforms after 1980 suggests that Republican elites offered a menu to their electorate that was much different from earlier. Republicans grew more ideological in promulgating their economic and cultural agenda.

In contrast, post-1996 Democratic platforms are not very dissimilar from earlier Democratic platforms. Observing the dissimilarity scale on the y-axis, Democratic platforms between 1996 and 2012 are similar to Democratic platforms between 1956 and 1972. These results are consistent with the evidence from Chapter 7 suggesting that elite polarization in the modern era is an asymmetrical phenomenon, with Republicans more polarized than Democrats.

These results also show the influence of the Old Guard Republicans and Ronald Reagan. It is well known that, even though convention delegates are

more extreme ideologically than other members of the party (Stone and Abramowitz 1983), they are focused on winning elections, rather than preserving
ideological purity. In 1976, traditional party activists (who backed Ford for the
nomination) outweighed ideological purists (who supported Reagan) (Sullivan
1977). By 1980, Old Guard Republicans and Reagan had gained control of the
party apparatus and convention delegates: 70 percent of Republican convention delegates perceived Reagan as having a better chance against Carter than
Bush (Stone and Abramowitz 1983, 949). For the first time since the New Deal,
the presidential nominee of the Republican Party was viewed as widely elect-
able without sacrificing ideological purity to centrists for electability. As the
nominee, Reagan and the Old Guard exerted influence over the platform
writing process, setting in motion a continuing movement of the Republican
Party to the right.

From Modern Republicanism to Old Guard Conservatism in Republican Platforms

What specifically changed in Republican platforms is observed by comparing
the frequencies of particular stemwords in the 1976 and 1980 platforms. On
examining these two documents, the change from Modern Republicanism
to Old Guard conservatism becomes readily apparent. The 1980 Republican
platform strongly reflected the policies advocated by the Chicago School
intellectuals, wealthy entrepreneurs, evangelical religious activists, right-wing
think tanks, and advocacy groups as discussed in Chapter 6.

Consider some numerical evidence. Along the economic dimension, the
stemwords "tax" and "taxpay" appeared 130 times in the 1980 Republican
platform, primarily in the context of seeking tax cuts for business and individuals, with the largest cuts going to the wealthiest Americans. Comparing this
with the 1976 platform, it reflects an almost three-fold increase in references
to taxes. The stemword "cut" appeared 11.5 times more often in 1980 than
in 1976. Along the regulation dimension, the stemword "regul" was used
47 times, mainly emphasizing the Republican desire to deregulate the economy,
worker health and safety, consumer protection, the environment, equal
employment opportunity, and other areas. This number reflects an about
2.5-fold increase in emphasis on regulation compared with the 1976 platform.
Along the cultural dimension, the stemword "famil" was used 79 times, mainly
emphasizing families and family values essential to rallying the Christian Right.
Again, this number was almost double the emphasis in the 1976 platform.
Along the social dimension, the stemword "social" was used 27 times, mainly
in reference to cutting social programs. This count reflected a more than two-
fold increase over the 1976 platform.

Evaluating specific statements containing these stemwords clarifies how
much the Old Guard Republican philosophy was embedded into the 1980 platform language. Concerning taxes, the platform stated that "the Republican

Party supports across-the-board reductions in personal income tax rates" (Republican National Committee 1980). "Across-the-board" meant giving the same percentage tax cut to all tax groups (a huge benefit to the wealthy). The platform also proposed cutting estate taxes, business taxes, investment taxes, and capital gains taxes; accelerating tax depreciation allowances for businesses; and abolishing the windfall profits tax on the energy industry. Of course, all of these proposals were associated with "trickle-down economics" and aimed at benefiting the commercial class.

Platform language on regulation stated, "Regulatory costs are now running in excess of $100 billion each year, or about $1,800 for every American family ... According to official figures, it takes individuals and business firms over 143 million man-hours to complete 4,400 different federal forms each year ... Regulation also restricts personal choices, tends to undermine America's democratic public institutions, and threatens to destroy the private, competitive free market economy it was originally designed to protect" (Republican National Committee 1980). Among the specific deregulatory recommendations in the platform were clean air, worker health and safety, pesticides, herbicides, antibiotics, food additives and preservatives, auto safety and emissions, consumer protection, equal employment opportunity, energy, and education.

Platform elements concerning equal opportunity and education were tailored to appeal to the Religious Right and bolster the Republican's Southern strategy. The platform stated that "equal opportunity should not be jeopardized by bureaucratic regulations and decisions which rely on quotas, ratios, and numerical requirements to exclude some individuals in favor of others" (i.e., reverse discrimination). The platform called for an end to "harassment of colleges and universities" that were segregationist in their admission policies (such as Bob Jones University; e.g., see Balmer 2007, chapter 1). It also alluded to federal policies toward public and private schools: "Today, parents are losing control of their children's schooling ... The result has been a shocking drop in student performance, lack of basics in the classroom, forced busing, teacher strikes, manipulative and sometimes amoral indoctrination ... We will halt the unconstitutional regulatory vendetta launched by Mr. Carter's IRS Commissioner against independent [private] schools ... We will respect the rights of state and local authorities in the management of their school systems" (Republican National Committee 1980).

Platform statements concerning "family" promoted the Religious Right's conception of family values and were laced with disdain for social welfare. The Republican platform stated, "The Carter Administration and the Democratic Party continue to foster [welfare] dependency ... By fostering dependency and discouraging self-reliance, the Democratic Party has created a welfare constituency dependent on its continual subsidies ... The values and strengths of the family provide a vital element in breaking the bonds of poverty ... Ultimately, the Republican Party supports the orderly, wholesale transfer of all welfare functions to the states" (Republican National Committee 1980).

Concerning abortion, the platform stated, "We will work for the appointment of judges at all levels of the judiciary who respect traditional family values and the sanctity of innocent human life ... [W]e affirm our support of a constitutional amendment to restore protection of the right to life for unborn children. We also support the Congressional efforts to restrict the use of taxpayers' dollars for abortion. We protest the Supreme Court's intrusion into the family structure through its denial of the parent's obligation and right to guide their minor children" (Republican National Committee 1980).

The 1980 Republican platform was not rooted in a groundswell of public support for the policies being endorsed. As discussed in Chapter 6, the Heritage Foundation profoundly shaped the Republican Party platform and subsequent actions of the Reagan administration. Thus, it was a top-down, "no-holds-barred" effort to establish a new agenda for the Republican Party. It was a propaganda document connecting the New Deal social contract's alleged godless government intervention in American society with racial and religious emotions. It was anti-tax, anti-government, anti-regulation, and anti-bureaucracy. It also promised a less active role for the federal government in promoting the general welfare of the nation and ensuring equality of opportunity across groups. In short, it sought a return to the Founders' social contract where government provided rents mostly to the patrician class.

What Made the Platforms Distinct?

Of course, the cluster analysis and preceding discussion are merely descriptive and do not reveal the dynamics of the differences between Democratic and Republican platforms between 1980 and 2012, or what was in them that might have caused increased polarization through time. Accordingly, this section moves to a dimensional analysis of what was actually in the platforms.

Text mining enables producing frequencies of polarizing words, which can be aggregated by dimension and standardized by platform length for the platform year. Text mining of the thirty-six platforms revealed roughly 8,000 unique stemwords for Democratic platforms and 9,000 for Republican platforms. However, not all of these stemwords are relevant to polarization. Accordingly, three different tools were used to help identify stemwords relevant to polarization.

The first tool was a human coding of *all* stemwords as suggesting ideological content from an intuitive perspective. The second was a human coding of only *frequently used stemwords* (at least one standard deviation above the mean number of uses), following the intuition that those words used especially often might drive partisan cleavages. Last, *regression analysis–chosen stemwords* were identified. Knowing that elite polarization increased over time, the counts through time for each of the stemwords, by party, were regressed on a simple time trend and for theoretical reasons (discussed in Chapters 6 and 7), a second time trend that began after 1980. Statistically significant words from these two

Republican Platforms

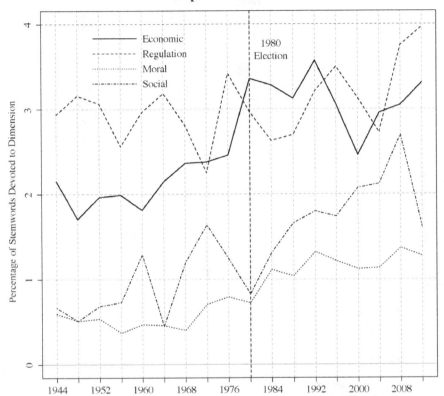

FIGURE 8.2 Dimensional Analysis of Republican and Democratic Platforms, 1944–2012
Sources: Text analysis of political party platforms using the R package *tm*. Platform text obtained from Peters and Wooley (2012)

regressions were deemed atheoretically as polarizing. Thus, polarizing words were defined by their importance for these three indicators. This approach identified 150 polarizing terms for Democrats and 220 polarizing terms for Republicans.

The polarizing terms were then classified into four dimensions: economics (stemwords such as market, entrepreneur, competit), regulation/size of government (stemwords such as environ, size, regul, bureaucrat), morality (stemwords such as abort, faith, gay), and social welfare (stemwords such as voucher, relief, homeless). The full list of polarizing stemwords, by dimension, is contained in the appendix of Jordan et al. (2014).

Time series graphs of the frequencies of polarizing words are reported in Figure 8.2, aggregated by dimension for each party and standardized by platform

Democratic Platforms

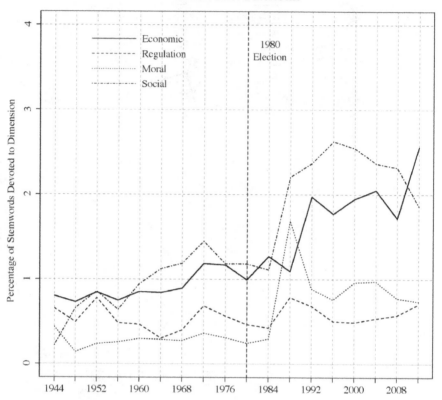

FIGURE 8.2 (*cont.*)

length. A dashed vertical line is drawn at 1980 to mark the point of Republican platform divergence in the cluster analysis. Note especially the economic dimension for the left graph for Republicans. The use of polarizing economic stemwords jumped sharply in 1980, suggesting that the impetus for the divergence observed in the cluster analysis was the Republican focus on free markets, competition, and business. In fact, this is the only dimension that jumped considerably in 1980 for either party, though the use of polarizing words about regulation/size of government had increased earlier in 1976 for Republicans.

Figure 8.2 shows that Republican focus on the economic dimension remained higher after 1980, relative to platforms before 1980. While erratic, the focus on regulation also moved higher after 1980, and became especially important in 2008 and 2012 following the Great Recession. The Republican focus on moral and social issues also increased steadily after 1980 and was higher than before 1980. However, in relative terms economic and regulatory matters consistently occupied a much larger percentage of Republican platforms than moral and social matters. The moral dimension, which includes such matters as abortion and gay rights, occupied the smallest percentage of the Republican platforms even after 1980. Note that economics and regulation/size of government were *always* the most important of the polarizing dimensions for Republicans. This result suggests the primacy of economics in driving Republican elite polarization.

The right side of Figure 8.2 reports the percentage of polarizing words for each dimension in the Democratic platforms. Comparing the Democratic platforms to the Republican platforms, Republicans were always more concerned with economics and regulation than Democrats, but far more so after 1980. The temporal dynamics of the graph also suggest that Democrats subsequently responded to Republican changes, again suggesting that Republicans drove polarization asymmetrically. Polarizing words along each dimension account for a very small percentage of the total words in the Democratic platforms until 1988.

In 1988, the Democratic platform jumped along both the moral and social dimensions. This change likely accounts for why the cluster dendrogram in Figure 8.1 shows that Democratic platforms did not cluster with Republican platforms after 1988. Democratic focus on both moral and social matters increased and remained higher through 2012, with positions opposite from the Republicans. Then, the 1992 Democratic platform jumped in the percentage of stemwords devoted to the economic dimension. Since 1992, Democratic platforms have remained more focused on economic matters than earlier. Thus, a major cleavage separating Democrats from Republicans since 1980 has been economic, with moral and social issues of added importance.

These findings are consistent with the broader literature on polarization and elite cleavages. For example, McCarty et al. (2008) report that elite polarization – as measured through NOMINATE scores – is related to growing economic inequality. Aldrich and Rohde (2000) also report that the first dimension of what they term "conditional party government," a measure of homogeneity of the majority party versus the heterogeneity of the minority party, is almost entirely explained through time by economic issues, relegating social and moral issues to a second dimension of conflict. Additionally, the findings in this section fit with theories of conflict extension, rather than conflict displacement (Layman and Carsey 2002). Only after first polarizing on economic issues did party elites move to secondary social and moral issues. However, they retained their established cleavages on economic issues, rather than polarizing on only a single dimension at a time.

POLARIZATION: AN ELITE-DRIVEN, ELECTORATE-DRIVEN, OR INTERACTIVE PROCESS?

Analysis of changing party platforms through time shows that Republican Party elites shifted the menu of policies offered to the mass public starting in

1980. While this evidence is suggestive, it fails to disentangle whether polarization in the American system was a *purely* top-down, bottom-up, or mutually reinforcing process. Do partisan elites drive polarization by providing a menu or other cues that would cause the electorate to become more polarized (e.g., see Adams 1997; Brody 1991; Carmines and Stimson 1989; Fiorina and Abrams 2009; Fiorina and Levendusky 2006; Fiorina et al. 2011; Hetherington 2001; Layman 2001; Layman and Carsey 2002; Sniderman 2000; Sniderman and Bullock 2004; Zaller 1992)? Is polarization a phenomenon whereby changes in the electorate cause partisan elites to become more polarized (e.g., see Abramowitz 2010; Abramowitz and Saunders 1998, 2008; Bishop 2009; Black and Black 2002; Brewer et al. 2002; Gimpel and Schuknecht 2003; Jacobson 2000; McCarty et al. 2008; Oppenheimer 2005; Stonecash et al. 2003; Theriault 2008)? Or does the relationship run in both directions such that the electorate and party elites affect one another through mutually reinforcing processes (e.g., see Fleischer and Bond 2001, 55–77; Jacobson 2000)?

More specifically, what are the relations between House, Senate, presidential, and electoral polarizations? Do House, Senate, and presidential polarization affect electoral polarization, either singularly or jointly? Does electoral polarization affect House, Senate, and presidential polarization, either singularly or jointly? According to Aldrich and Rohde (2000, 2001), more homogenous Republican and Democratic constituencies should have elected more ideologically pure representatives who also responded to more coherent constituent cues. Or is party polarization an interactive phenomenon? As expressed by Jacobson (2000, 26), the "relationship between mass and elite partisan consistency is inherently interactive."

A related set of questions concerns the potential equilibrium dynamics of the polarization system. Is there a long-term equilibrating relationship between House, Senate, presidential, and electoral polarization? Are there short-term covariations among these variables? How, if at all, does the president fit into this set of relationships? Did presidential polarization exacerbate House and Senate polarization? Did presidential polarization affect polarization of the electorate?

Measuring Congressional Polarization

Past research evaluating polarization in the House or Senate has typically used either Poole and Rosenthal (2000) DW-NOMINATE scores or interest group support scores for individual members of Congress. Both measurement approaches have advantages and disadvantages.

DW-NOMINATE scores are calculated on the universe of all roll call votes. The algorithm used to calculate these scores employs a methodology that makes them directly comparable across Congresses (but not chambers) so that they can be used to track changes in the relative liberalism/conservatism of member voting for a particular chamber across time. A significant limitation is that DW-NOMINATE scores are calculated on the *universe* of all roll call votes, and many of those votes are only marginally relevant to the liberal-conservative dimension. A more important limitation of DW-NOMINATE scores for this study is that they are calculated only for each two-year Congress, and if considering the president (as is done below), they are calculated only over a president's entire term, either four or eight years. As a result, statistical analysis using DW-NOMINATE scores would yield only 33 observations for Congress since 1946, and 12 observations for presidents. This number of observations is generally considered too small for a robust statistical analysis.

In contrast, interest group support scores are calculated for only a subset of roll call votes. During each year, interest groups choose a set of key roll call votes that best reflect their issue positions on matters taken up by Congress. Legislators' votes on these key votes are recorded and compared with the interest group's benchmark positions. The scores are the proportion of members' votes that support the interest group's positions. Support scores for the Americans for Democratic Action (ADA) are available annually from 1947. These scores generally align closely with specific issues discussed earlier as being important to the New Deal social contract.

The number of key votes chosen each year by the ADA for calculating the scores has ranged historically from a low of 7 to a high of 37. The modal number of votes chosen was about 20. A limitation of these scores is that they are intended for comparison of legislators within a single chamber during a single year. The set of votes changes from year to year and across chambers, so that one cannot be sure they are capturing the same liberal/conservative dimension.

However, Groseclose et al. (1999) developed a methodology that enables comparing interest group support scores across both years and chambers. Because the set of votes is not the same across time, the scales that underlie the raw scores can "shift" and "stretch." Thus, Groseclose et al. derive an index, much like an inflation index for consumer prices, that adjusts the scores to be comparable across years and chambers. These inflation-adjusted ADA scores remain limited in that they are calculated using only a subset of legislative votes. This subset of votes is chosen by the ADA for the explicit purpose of separating friends from foes. As a result, the measure may overstate the degree of polarization that exists in each chamber at any point in time. Nevertheless, inflation-adjusted ADA scores by Congress and chamber correlate with Poole and Rosenthal's DW-NOMINATE scores by Congress and chamber at about 0.90. Therefore, one can have some confidence that these scores are a reasonably valid measure.

Because they are annual, yielding 66 time series observations from 1947 through 2012 for both houses of Congress and the president, inflation-adjusted ADA scores are used for the analyses below. Specifically, the procedure developed by Groseclose et al (1999) was used to produce the inflation-adjusted scores from 1947 through 2012 for each member in each year. In updating the measure through 2012, the Anderson and Habel (2009) data were used, and the raw scores for each member from the ADA's website were used to update the measure through 2012. Then, Republicans and Democrats were separated out for each year and chamber.

Finally, the mean, standard deviation, and skewness statistics were calculated for the party scores for each year and chamber. Using these normalized moments, simulated distributions for the two parties were generated, again using the skew-t distribution (Azzalini and Capitano 2003), precisely as was done for the electorate in Chapter 7. Based on these distributions, the probability masses in the overlapping parts of the two distributions were calculated. Again, as with the electorate, the measure of polarization is one minus these probability masses. More intuitively, the measure represents the annual degree of partisan disagreement on the selected issues.

Figures 8.3 and 8.4 present the historical empirical distributions of partisan ideology for the House of Representatives and Senate for the same years as reported for the electorate in Figure 7.25. Note that the x-axis scales are flipped in Figure 8.3 and 8.4 to enable easier comparison of Democrats and Republicans in Congress with the graphs for Democrats and Republicans in the electorate in Figure 7.25. Comparing these graphs with those reported in Figure 7.25, it is apparent that both the House and Senate grew far more polarized than the electorate. Further, as with the electorate, much of the House and Senate polarization was driven by Republicans.

Observing the means (and modes, which are very close) in Figures 8.3 and 8.4 shows that divergence polarization became much more extreme. The parties have always been divergent. For example, the divergences between Democrat and Republican means in the House and Senate in 1957 were only 23.24 and 9.19, respectively, on the 0–100 ADA scale. By 1995, the divergences had grown to 66.27 and 62, respectively. In 2012, the divergences were 71.87 and 69.34, respectively. These changes began in the mid-1980s during the Reagan administration, but accelerated after 1995 and the Republican "Contract with America." It is also noteworthy that both political parties moved much closer to their respective poles through time. However, Republicans moved much closer to the right pole (8.88 points away for House; 6.65 points away for Senate) than Democrats moved to the left pole (19.25 points away for House; 24 points away for Senate). The implication is that *congressional polarization is also an asymmetrical phenomenon, with Republicans significantly more polarized than Democrats.*

Observing dispersion and distributional polarization in the graphs, the distributions for both parties in both chambers exhibit little changing skew but significantly changing dispersions. The distributions for Democrats in the House remained broadly dispersed from the 1950s through 2012. The distributions for Democrats in the Senate narrowed in 1995, broadened somewhat through 2003, and then narrowed again significantly in 2012. The distributions

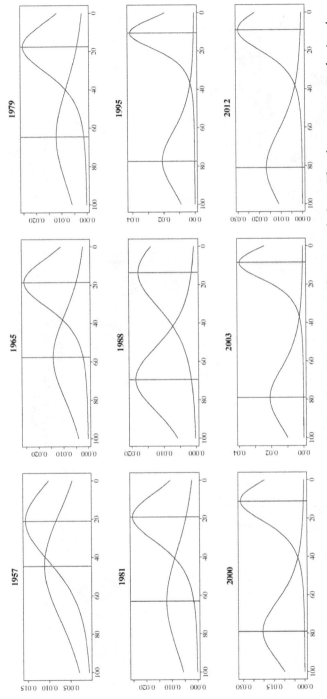

FIGURE 8.3 U.S. House of Representatives Historical Empirical Distributions of Partisan Ideology. The plots are generated using the skew-t distribution using the observed means, standard deviations, and skewness statistics of the House ADA Scores for each year. The vertical black lines are modes. The vertical gray lines are means. The left curve represents Democrats, the right curve Republicans

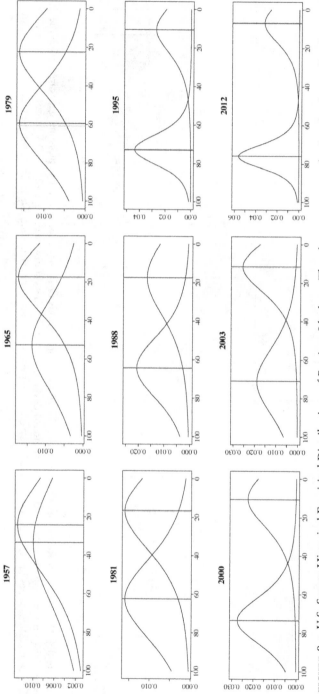

FIGURE 8.4 U.S. Senate Historical Empirical Distributions of Partisan Ideology. The plots are generated using the skew-t distribution using the observed means, standard deviations, and skewness statistics of the Senate ADA Scores for each year. The vertical black lines are modes. The vertical gray lines are means. The left curve represents Democrats, the right curve Republicans

for Republicans in the House narrowed significantly starting in 1995 and remained narrow through 2012. After 1995, the distributions for Republicans in the Senate exhibited less dispersion than earlier. Thus, polarization in Congress involved both changing divergence and dispersion.

Finally, focusing on the overlapping parts of the distributions, the overlap for the House and Senate distributions became much smaller through time than those for the electorate. By 2012, there were very few members of Congress who would vote with the other party. This fact implies that the Fiorina et al. (2011, 204–5) argument, to be discussed below, that elected representatives in Congress became far more polarized than those who elected them might be correct. However, a closer comparison is required to reach this conclusion.

Measuring Presidential Polarization

Past research has also commonly placed presidents into the same space as members of Congress using presidential position-taking on the ADA votes as recorded by *Congressional Quarterly Almanac* (*CQ*) (e.g., see Grafton and Permaloff 2004; Zupan 1992). Each year *CQ* seeks to determine what the president wants in the way of legislative action by examining presidential messages to Congress, press conferences, and other public statements and documents. However, by the time an issue reaches the floor for a vote, it may differ from the form existing at the time the president expressed a position. In such cases, *CQ* analyzes the bill to determine whether the features, on average, reflect the president's current preference. The president is deemed as supporting or not supporting a bill by evaluating his (estimated) position at the time of the vote, which may differ from earlier presidential positions. The presidential ADA score is the proportion of the ADA votes in each year that are recorded as having presidential support by *CQ*.

As with the measures of electoral and congressional polarization, the interest is in the degree of overlap between presidential positions and those of the opposing political party in Congress. As presidents increasingly agree with the other political party, presidential polarization decreases. As presidents increasingly disagree with the other political party, presidential polarization increases. For example, if a president were to agree all the time with the other political party, then there would be no polarization; if a president were never to agree with the other party, then there would be total polarization. Using this construct, the president's *CQ* reported positions on the ADA issues were evaluated during each year to assess his agreement with those of the other political party. The measure of presidential polarization is one minus the proportion of presidential positions for each year that agreed with those of the opposing political party. More intuitively, it gauges how much disagreement presidents had each year with the opposing party in Congress.

Comparing the New Measures

With measures of House, Senate, presidential, and electoral polarization calculated using the same methodology and with a common scale, it now becomes possible to more systematically evaluate the nature of polarization in the American system. Graphing the four measures side by side provides an initial basis for comparison. Accordingly, Figure 8.5 presents three graphs for this purpose. A heavy dashed vertical line again appears in each graph to mark 1980. For easy comparison, Figure 8.5A is the same graph as presented in Figure 7.27. Panels B and C are constructed using the same measurement construct, placing the House, Senate, and president into the same space as the electorate.

Comparing Figure 8.5A and B reveals some similarities. Before 1980, electoral and congressional polarizations were relatively low and absent a significant trend. After 1980, trends developed in both electoral and congressional polarization. As with the electoral polarization time series in panel A, legislative polarization was lowest around 1956 or 1957, increased into the 1960s, and then declined to a stable mean between 1969 and the late 1970s. Starting in the 1980s, congressional polarization began increasing. The upward trend continued until the 1990s and then leveled off near the maxima around 1995 (after the "Contract with America" election when Republicans took control of both the House and Senate). Between 1995 and 2012, House and Senate polarization remained stable and near the maximum. Apparently, legislative polarization experienced a ceiling effect such that it could not increase much further, being about as high as it could go.

Comparing electoral with House/Senate polarization, electoral polarization continued climbing after 1995, while congressional polarization had already leveled off. Electoral polarization grew even more rapidly after 2003, while congressional polarization remained stable near its maximum. Congressional polarization increased at a faster rate between 1981 and 1995 and achieved a higher level than polarization in the electorate. Comparing the ultimate levels for electoral and congressional polarization, the average for Congress between 1995 and 2012 was about 0.95. The maximum for the electorate in 2010 was only about 0.77. Hence, the electorate became increasingly polarized, but was significantly less polarized than Congress. Further, the timing of these changes and rates of change suggest a top-down process. In temporal sequence, elite polarization led electoral polarization.

Finally, Figure 8.5C graphs presidential polarization from 1955 through 2012. The data show that before 1960, presidential disagreement with the opposing party was generally low. Eisenhower was a Modern Republican who continued New Deal programs, expanded Social Security, and launched the largest public works program in American history, the Interstate Highway System. However, the Kennedy–Johnson era from 1961 through 1965 marked a period when presidents often disagreed with the opposing party. Starting in 1966 and continuing until 1980, presidential polarization declined. The

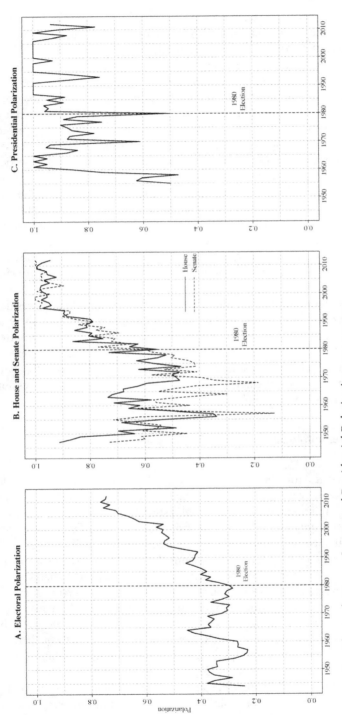

FIGURE 8.5 Electoral, House, Senate, and Presidential Polarization, 1944–2012

Sources: Electoral polarization is from Figure 7.27 for comparison. The House and Senate polarization measures are created using the mean, standard deviation, and skewness of annual ADA scores using the same method as used for the electorate. The House and Senate measures comprise one minus the average proportion of legislators who agree with the other political party on ADA votes. The presidential measure is one minus the average of ADA votes on which the president agrees with the other party

years 1970 and 1980 show sharp drops during the Nixon and Carter administrations. Of course, President Nixon cooperated in 1970 with a Democratic
Congress to pass a plethora of environmental, job safety, and worker health
legislation (Wikipedia 2015b). Similarly, President Carter compromised with
Republicans in 1980 in passing various regulatory reforms and conservation
laws (Wikipedia 2015b). After 1981, presidential disagreement with the opposing party increased again and polarization was saturated at one from 1987
through 1991. From 1992 through 1994, presidential polarization declined,
but increased to saturation again between 1995 and 1998, a likely response by
President Clinton to the Gingrich budget wars and "Contract with America."
Between 2000 and 2006, presidential polarization continued to be saturated at
1. However, starting in 2007 presidential polarization declined. The years
2007 and 2008 mark the start of the Great Recession, when President George
W. Bush became more consensual in addressing the economic emergency.
Presidential polarization increased again starting in 2009, as President Obama
confronted the Republican Party of "No!" (Grunwald 2012b). However,
Obama became somewhat more consensual and willing to compromise from
2010 through 2012.

Visual examination of panel C also shows clearly that Republican presidents
after Reagan were at or near their polar extreme. Hence, after Reagan there was
little room for Republican presidential responsiveness to either the electorate or
Congress. Excluding the Eisenhower years, Democrat presidents were less
polarized than Republican presidents. More generally, the presidential polarization time series does not track closely with the electoral and congressional
polarization time series in panels A and B.

Time Series Methodologies for Evaluating Elite and Electoral Polarization

Competing theories for the causal sequence of polarization, whether elite-
driven, electorate-driven, or interactive, offer no definitive rationale for imposing directional relationships in statistical estimation. That is, polarization
effects could plausibly be top-down, bottom-up, or both. Further, no prior
research has investigated this matter, or whether relations, if they exist, are
only short-term or in long-term equilibrium. Under these circumstances it is
appropriate to let the data speak for themselves using empirical analysis.

Vector autoregression (VAR) (Sims 1980) and vector error correction
(VECM) methods (Engle and Granger 1987; Johansen 1988, 1991, 1994,
1995; Juselius 2006) are the appropriate methods for addressing the preceding
questions. In the analyses below, VAR methods are used first to evaluate the
temporal sequence of relationships and track the dynamics among the four
variables in the polarization system. Each variable in the VAR is treated as
endogenous and regressed on multiple lagged values of itself, as well as multiple
lagged values of the other variables in the system. Impulse responses are

computed to track joint movements among the variables in the system. Computing the impulse responses involves sequentially introducing a shock to each variable and tracking out movements in the other variables using the VAR estimates. It is also typical in VAR analysis to compute tests of Granger causality in which blocks of lags are excluded from the system. Hypothesis tests are then conducted to evaluate the significance of these excluded lags. However, it is well known that such tests are invalid in the presence of cointegration (Freeman et al. 1998; Phillips 1995).

VAR methods are very general, but do not effectively model cointegration and error-correcting relationships. VAR impulse responses are valid even in the presence of cointegration, but the Granger tests are not. Further, VAR methods are incapable of sorting out what part of the responses are due to short- versus long-term relations. If there is cointegration and error correction in the polarization system, then it is appropriate to also estimate relationships using a VECM. The specific techniques applied here are discussed in Juselius (2006) and Lutkepohl (2007, part II). Appendix B contains the relevant technical descriptions.

More simply, a set of variables is called cointegrated if they "track together" through time. For example, Figure 8.5B shows that House and Senate polarization track through time in a bivariate sense. However, it is less obvious that the four variables in Figure 8.5 track together through time in a multivariate sense. If there is a linear combination of these four variables that consistently equilibrates to a stationary error process, then the variables are cointegrated in a multivariate sense.

Appropriate tests were performed to determine whether the four variables were cointegrated. Appendix Table B.1 shows that these variables track together through time in a multivariate sense. The analyses below take this into account and focus on both the VAR and VECM representations of the polarization system. Both representations contain *precisely* the same information, because they are just mathematical transformations of one another. However, focusing on both representations allows emphasizing different aspects of the relationships for interpretation purposes.

The VAR Analysis

Figure 8.6 reports the impulse responses for the VAR(2) polarization system. The approach is to trace the dynamics of a simulated shock through the estimated system using the coefficient matrix. Simulated shocks of one standard error of the regression are introduced for each variable. Upper and lower confidence boundaries around the impulse responses are computed using the method proposed by Sims and Zha (1999). The graphs on the top-down diagonal of Figure 8.6 contain responses in the variable being shocked. Within the rows to the right and left of the corresponding diagonal graphs are the responses of the other variables to the variable being shocked.

288

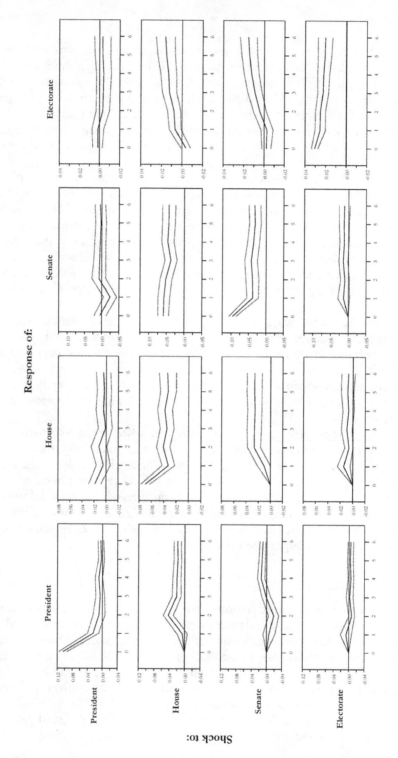

Response of:

FIGURE 8.6 VAR Impulse Responses for Polarization System in Levels

The first row of Figure 8.6 shows the dynamic responses to a simulated one-standard-error shock in presidential polarization. One standard error of the regression for the presidential equation is about 0.10 units on the 0–1 polarization scale. Presidential polarization (row 1, column 1) is not very inertial to its own shocks, having decayed to zero by the second year. House polarization (row 1, column 2) responds immediately to presidential polarization, but becomes unresponsive in subsequent years. Neither the Senate nor the electorate show statistically significant increases after presidents become more polarized. Senate polarization (row 1, column 3) actually declines briefly after presidents become more polarized. The response by the electorate (row 1, column 4) is also negative, but never statistically significant. Thus, the VAR results suggest that presidential polarization temporally leads House polarization, but not Senate and electoral polarization.

The second row of Figure 8.6 shows the dynamic responses to a simulated one-standard-error shock in House polarization. One standard error of the regression for the House equation is about 0.07 units on the 0–1 polarization scale. Observe that House polarization (row 2, column 2) is highly inertial to its own shocks. More important, presidential polarization (row 2, column 1), Senate polarization (row 2, column 3), and electoral polarization (row 2, column 4) all respond strongly to House polarization. About two years after the increase in House polarization, presidential polarization peaks at about 0.04 units on the 0–1 polarization scale and remains significantly responsive through the sixth year. The Senate responds immediately by about 0.06 units, and continues to be responsive to the House shock for the next six years (see also Theriault and Rohde 2011). Increased electoral polarization also becomes significant after about two years, and continues to grow through year six. The House is the most polarizing of the four actors in the system. Of course, this empirical finding conforms to the historical record starting in the mid-1990s when House Speaker Newt Gingrich led a highly cohesive House majority in driving partisan dissensus.

The third row of Figure 8.6 shows the dynamic responses to a simulated one-standard-error shock in Senate polarization. One standard error of the regression for the Senate equation is about 0.11 units on the 0–1 polarization scale. Senate polarization (row 3, column 3) is again highly inertial to its own shocks. More interesting, House polarization (row 3, column 2) is also responsive to Senate polarization, but only about half as responsive as the Senate is to the House. Two years after the Senate shock, House polarization increases by about 0.03 units on the 0–1 polarization scale. Increasing Senate polarization may actually depress presidential polarization (row 2, column 3) by about 0.02 units two years after the shock. Apparently, the Senate is a mildly moderating influence on presidential polarization. The electorate (row 3, column 4) also responds to Senate polarization, following about the same pattern as that for the House.

Finally, the fourth row of Figure 8.6 shows the dynamic responses to a simulated one-standard-error shock in electoral polarization. One standard error of the regression for the electoral equation is a small 0.03 units on the 0–1 polarization scale. Electoral polarization (row 4, column 4) is also inertial to its own shocks. Presidential polarization (row 4, column 1) is unresponsive to electoral polarization. House polarization (row 4, column 2) responds significantly to an increase in electoral polarization, but the increase is only about 0.015 units on the 0–1 polarization scale. Senate polarization (row 4, column 3) does not respond significantly to the electorate, though the result is suggestive. Thus, the VAR results suggest that increased electoral polarization affects House and Senate polarization but is not a huge stimulus to polarized American institutions.

The VECM Analysis

Consider now the results from the VECM(3) representation. Table 8.1 contains estimates for both the short- and long-run effects from the VECM. The numbers in parentheses are t-statistics. Note that t-statistics larger than 1.96 are statistically significant at the 0.05 level. The short-run effects associated with Γ in Equation B.2 in Appendix B are reported in the top part of the table.

Focusing on $\Delta \text{President}_{t-1}$ and $\Delta \text{President}_{t-2}$ in the first two rows of Table 8.1, the response of $\Delta \text{President}$ to itself is negative, suggesting a choppy time path. Consistent with the VAR in levels, ΔHouse responds positively to increasing presidential polarization with a two-year lag. Again corresponding with the VAR analysis above, the response of ΔSenate to increased presidential polarization is negative. Inconsistent with the VAR in levels, the short-term $\Delta \text{Electorate}$ variable responds positively in the short run to increasing presidential polarization with a two-year lag.

Focusing on $\Delta \text{House}_{t-1}$ and $\Delta \text{House}_{t-2}$ in the third and fourth rows, the $\Delta \text{President}$ variable responds significantly to increasing House polarization. Just as with the VAR in levels, presidential and House polarizations are in a mutually reinforcing relationship. ΔHouse and ΔSenate in the second and third numerical columns are negatively responsive to changing House polarization. These results suggest that the House and Senate time paths are not strictly trending upward. Rather, they follow an irregular time pattern as shown in Figure 8.5B. Just as with the levels VAR results, the response of $\Delta \text{Electorate}$ to increasing House polarization is positive and statistically significant in the second year. Of course, two years corresponds with the House electoral cycle.

Focusing on $\Delta \text{Senate}_{t-1}$ and $\Delta \text{Senate}_{t-2}$ in the fifth and sixth rows of Table 8.1, ΔSenate is negatively related to its own lags in the short run, again suggesting the choppy nature of the Senate time series as shown in Figure 8.5B. However, unlike with the levels VAR, previous change in Senate polarization has no short-run effect on $\Delta \text{President}$, ΔHouse, or $\Delta \text{Electorate}$.

Finally, considering $\Delta \text{Electorate}_{t-1}$ and $\Delta \text{Electorate}_{t-2}$ in the seventh and eighth rows of Table 8.1, the only significant relationship is $\Delta \text{House}_{t-1}$. This result is again consistent with the levels VAR. As with the levels VAR, the

TABLE 8.1 *Long- and Short-Run Effects from the VECM Representation*

Variable	ΔHouse	ΔSenate	ΔPresident	ΔElectorate
	Dependent Variable			
Short-Run (Γ)				
ΔHouse$_{t-1}$	−0.47	−0.29	0.11	0.11
	(−4.73)	(−3.80)	(1.79)	(0.47)
ΔHouse$_{t-2}$	−0.09	−0.11	0.18	0.62
	(−0.94)	(−1.64)	(2.84)	(2.87)
ΔSenate$_{t-1}$	−0.10	−0.53	−0.08	−0.09
	(−0.65)	(−4.55)	(−0.84)	(−0.26)
ΔSenate$_{t-2}$	0.17	−0.41	0.15	−0.09
	(1.10)	(−4.10)	(1.57)	(−0.26)
ΔPresident$_{t-1}$	0.02	−0.34	−0.38	0.36
	(0.12)	(−2.56)	(−3.54)	(0.91)
ΔPresident$_{t-2}$	0.50	−0.07	−0.43	1.16
	(2.96)	(−0.59)	(−4.00)	(3.10)
ΔElectorate$_{t-1}$	0.13	−0.07	0.02	−0.05
	(2.13)	(−1.61)	(0.44)	(−0.36)
ΔElectorate$_{t-2}$	0.01	−0.01	−0.03	0.05
	(0.07)	(−0.17)	(−0.83)	(0.38)
Constant	0.27	0.12	0.267	0.05
	(7.14)	(2.09)	(4.124)	(2.16)
Long-Run (α)				
Error Correction$_{t-1}$	0.54	0.20	0.57	0.08
	(7.02)	(1.72)	(4.33)	(1.82)

Note: Estimation of the vector error correction model is by cointegrated maximum likelihood (Johansen and Juselius 1990). The first number in each row for short-run effects is the coefficient on the differenced variable within the Γ matrix in appendix Equation B.2. The first number in the row for long-run effects is the coefficient for the error-correction term in each equation α from $Π = αβ'$ in Equation 8.2. The numbers in parentheses are t-statistics.

House responds to the electorate with a one-year lag. Note, however, that the House response to the electorate is only about one-sixth the size of the elector-ate's response to the House in the third and fourth rows of Table 8.1. Thus, the results again confirm that the electorate is not a major force affecting polariza-tion in Congress or the presidency.

The long-run error corrections shown in Table 8.1 provide additional infor-mation. The error correction estimates (α from the discussion surrounding

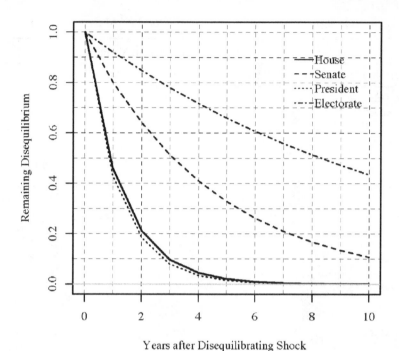

FIGURE 8.7 Error Correction Rates in Polarization VAR. The plots project the
remaining disequilibrium for each actor *t* years after a one-unit disequilibrating shock
to the system.

Equation B.2 in Appendix B) gives the rate of reequilibration after disequil-
brium occurs, say, due to a shock. The error correction that occurs through
the electorate equation is only 0.08 and is statistically significant at only the
0.10 level. This implies that little of the reequilibration after a shock occurs
through the electorate. The House equation provides far more of the reequilibration. On average, about 54 percent of the disequilibrium during each
year is corrected through adjustment by the House. The Senate equation
provides less of the reequilibration. On average, about 20 percent of the
disequilibrum is corrected through the Senate during each year after a shock.
Finally, the president adjusts at about the same rate as the House. About
57 percent of the reequilibration after a shock occurs through adjustment by
the president.

A more intuitive grasp on what these results mean can be obtained by
graphing the rates of error correction from the last row of Table 8.1 after a
simulated one-unit disequilibrating shock in each variable. Figure 8.7 contains these dynamics. The House and President respond very sharply to a
disequilibrating shock. In other words, if the House or President is pushed
away from their equilibrium, the attractor force moving them back to the

common time path is strong. The Senate is less responsive to a disequilibrating shock. However, the attractor force for the electorate is weakest, suggesting that institutions keep the system in a polarized condition, rather than the electorate.

More generally, the statistical analyses show that electoral and elite polarization track together through time (i.e., are cointegrated) and are involved in a long-run equilibrium relationship (i.e., are error correcting). The VAR and VECM results both show a primarily elite-driven process, with the House of Representatives and president playing key roles. As the House and president become more polarized, then so do the Senate and electorate.

However, system polarization is neither a *purely* elite-driven nor a *purely* electorate-driven process. The VAR and VECM results both show that the electorate has a small but statistically significant effect on House polarization. Thus, elites and the electorate are in a mutually reinforcing relationship. Electoral polarization reinforces elite polarization, perhaps through election processes, given the consistent two-year lags in the preceding analyses. And elite polarization subsequently reinforces electoral polarization.

ELITE POLARIZATION AND THE REPRESENTATION GAP

The preceding analyses hold implications for the quality of American democracy. Polarization weakens American democracy if citizen preferences are not aligned with those of their polarized representatives. Extreme elites representing a moderate mass public implies preferences that are not well represented. Extreme elites representing an equally extreme mass public implies appropriate representation.

Scholarly Literature on the Representation Gap

The scholarly literature has recognized the possibility of a representation gap but is divided on whether it exists and on its magnitude. On one side, Fiorina et al. (2011, 204–5) state that "there is a disconnect between the world of contemporary Americans and the political order that purports to represent them. Citizens see a political order that characteristically debates policy proposals more extreme than necessary to address societal issues and community problems, ... and a political order dominated by a political class whose behavior and operating style would be unacceptable outside of politics" (see also Fiorina and Abrams 2009, 21).

Concerning the magnitude of this disconnect, Fiorina and Levendusky (2006, 57) observe that "as elites became more ideologically distinctive over the past quarter-century, ordinary voters recognized this and then changed their positions ... Importantly, however, the pattern among ordinary voters is much weaker than among political elites. While there is almost a total separation between Democratic and Republican members of Congress, ... the mass public is not nearly as ideologically divided as party elites." All of this work is predicated on the belief that most citizens hold moderate views, while their elected representatives are extreme. Hence, there should be a representation gap.

On the other side, scholars argue that polarization in Washington is simply a reflection of polarization in the electorate. Abramowitz (2010, 157) focuses on party activists in the electorate as driving elite polarization. He states, "The evidence ... indicates that members of Congress generally reflect the views of their party's electoral bases: Republicans reflect the views of their party's conservative electoral base, and Democrats reflect the views of their party's liberal electoral base. Polarization in Congress reflects polarization in the American electorate." Similarly, Theriault (2008, 134) argues, "The constituencies of the respective party members have become almost twice as polarized over the last 32 years ... These more polarized constituencies have increasingly cast party-consistent votes in presidential and congressional contests ... Members who cast partisan roll call votes are increasingly casting votes consistent with their constituent preferences." Similarly, Jacobson (2000, 25) states, "Evidence from examination of the electorate, then, is fully consistent with the standard argument that partisan polarization in Congress reflects electoral changes that have left the parties with more homogeneous and more dissimilar electoral coalitions ... [C]hanges in roll call voting reflect changes in electoral coalitions." This work is predicated on the belief that the electorate has become more extreme. Thus, there should be no representation gap or, if it exists, it is small.

The health of American democracy as a result of polarization depends, then, on whether the electorate is also polarized. *If the political parties are polarized, but their electorates are not polarized, then there is a representation gap.* The majority of citizens in the political middle are disenfranchised by the extreme choices they are given and must accept because their political leaders are polarized. Presenting citizens with extreme election choices results in increasingly extreme representatives. The policies resulting from these extreme representatives are also extreme, and are consistent not with most citizen preferences but with the preferences of others with extreme views. Most citizens are forced to choose candidates (in elections) and live with policies (from institutions) that are not consistent with their own preferences.

On the other hand, *if both the political parties and their electorates are polarized, then the representation gap may be diminished or nonexistent.* If most citizens hold preferences near the ends of the liberal-conservative continuum, then the representational system may be healthy. An electorate characterized by ideological extremes produces extreme candidates. Extreme candidates produce polarized election outcomes. Polarized election outcomes result in polarized institutions. Polarized institutions result in extreme policies or no policies at all because of an inability or unwillingness to compromise. In either case, the outcome is reflective of the preferences of polarized citizens.

Evaluating the Representation Gap

Of course, the deficiency of past literature is that no one has attempted to measure the representation gap empirically. Rather, scholars have only argued about its existence/nonexistence. Placing the arguments in the context of the preceding analyses, consider the ideological continuum from the previous chapter running from most liberal to most conservative. Some scholars assume that most citizens reside near the middle of the ideological spectrum. This assumption would seem reasonable, given the median voter theorem that characterizes much social science research (e.g., see Aldrich 1983; Austin-Smith and Banks 1988; Davis et al. 1970; Downs 1957; Enelow and Hinich 1981, 1982, 1984; Riker and Ordeshook 1973; Wittman 1983). Parties, candidates, and elected officials are assumed to cater in a self-interested manner to the middle of the ideological spectrum to maximize their support.

However, the analyses in Figures 8.3 and 8.4 show that congressional Republicans became increasingly concentrated toward the ends of the ideological spectrum after 1980. Congressional Democrats also shifted significantly to the left. Observing Figure 8.5C, presidents also became more polarized. With polarized institutions, representatives may not cater to the middle. Rather, they may cater to the poles for ideological reasons or to satisfy their most politically active constituents. In *The Myth of Presidential Representation*, Wood (2009) documented that modern presidents are not centrists, but better represent their fellow partisans. If members of Congress also reflect the ends of the ideological spectrum rather than the middle, then there may be a representation gap.

Of course, this purported representation gap rests on the assumption that most citizens actually do reside near the middle of the ideological spectrum. The previous chapter showed in Figure 7.25 that Democrats in the electorate moved somewhat to the left after 1980. However, Republicans in the electorate moved far to the right after 1980, becoming increasingly concentrated toward their pole. If elected representatives are polarized to about the same extent as those who elected them, then institutional polarization may merely be reflective of the preferences of polarized citizens.

This debate over the implications of polarization for democratic representation can be resolved empirically. This study has placed polarization for members of Congress and the presidency into the same measurement space as was developed for the electorate in Chapter 7. Intuitively, the polarization measures represent the amount of disagreement between Republicans and Democrats in the House, Senate, presidency, and electorate, using the overlap between their liberal-conservative distributions.

Because the four measures were generated using a common methodology and scale, the empirical representation gaps can now be calculated. They are measured simply by taking the three institutional polarizations minus electoral polarization. Figure 8.8 contains graphs of the measures. Considering panel A, it is clear that House and Senate polarization have almost always been greater

A. House and Senate Representation Gaps

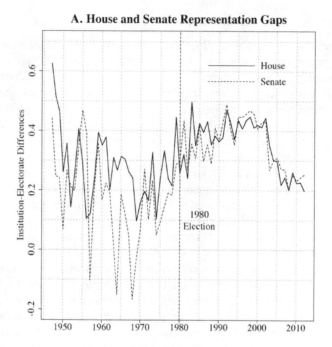

B. Presidential Representation Gap

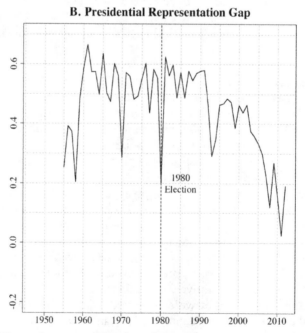

FIGURE 8.8 House, Senate, and Presidential Representation Gaps, 1947–2012. The graphs plot the difference between the institutional polarization in panels B and C and electoral polarization in panel A of Figure 8.5.

than electoral polarization, even since the 1940s. That is, legislative representatives have generally been more extreme than those who elected them. However, there were a few exceptions. The electorate was more polarized than partisans in the Senate in 1957, 1964, and 1968. In all other years, the House and Senate were more polarized than the electorate.

Considering the dynamics of the congressional representation gaps, in 1947, 1948, and 1954, when Republicans had control of the House and Senate, the representation gaps were higher. However, the gap before 1980 averaged only about 0.28 for the House and 0.17 for the Senate on the 0–1 scale. The pre-1980 minima were 0.10 for the House in 1969 and −0.17 for the Senate in 1968.

After 1980, the representation gap widened as members of Congress grew increasingly more extreme than those who elected them. Between 1981 and 2003, the representation gap averaged 0.40 for the House and 0.39 for the Senate. These are large numbers for the range of Figure 8.8. From 2004 through 2012, the representation gap trended downward to about 0.20 for the House and 0.25 for the Senate.

The decline in the representation gap after 2003 was due to increasing electoral polarization (see Figure 8.5), while House and Senate polarization remained stable near their maxima. As the electorate grew increasingly polarized, their elected representatives remained constantly extreme. Hence, assertions by Fiorina and others of a disconnect between citizens and their legislative representatives appears true (Fiorina and Abrams 2009, 21; Fiorina and Levendusky 2006, 57; Fiorina et al. 2011, 204–5). However, contrary to their assertions, the representation gap has grown smaller, not larger, in more recent years.

Considering Figure 8.6B, which contains the presidential representation gap, the plot shows that presidents were far more polarized than the electorate before 2003. This result is consistent with the evidence presented in Wood (2009) showing that presidents are partisans representing their fellow partisans. Before 2003, presidential partisanship diminished at a few points. The Eisenhower years, as well as dips under Nixon in 1970 and Carter in 1980, reflect periods when presidents were more compromising. The presidential representation gap declined again under Clinton in 1993 and 1994, but rose after the 1994 "Contract with America" election. The gap was higher from 1995 through 2003. Then, after 2003 the presidential representation gap trended downward. The minimum occurred in 2011, when the presidential representation gap was only 0.03. The decline in the presidential representation gap was again due to increasing electoral polarization (see Figure 8.5).

CHARACTERIZING POLARIZATION AS AN ELITE-DRIVEN PROCESS

The array of empirical evidence reported in this chapter is consistent with the Old Guard's top-down strategy for restoring the Founders' social contract.

The analysis of party platforms, relationships between elite and electoral polarization, and calculation of the representation gap are all consistent with an elite-driven model.

Concerning the party platforms, the text-mining analysis showed that Republican Party platforms after 1980 clustered together through time and were distinct from Democratic Party platforms before 1980 and after 1988. A distinct breakpoint occurred at 1980 in the menu of policies offered in Republican platforms. The 1980 Republican platform had far greater emphasis than the 1976 platform on taxes, regulation, free markets, social welfare, and moral values. These changed emphases continued and increased through time. The analysis of stemwords in the Republican platforms showed that the economic and regulatory dimensions were consistently much more important for Republicans than the moral and social dimensions. The economic dimension jumped sharply starting in 1980 and continued to grow through the 1990s. The regulatory dimension also increased through 2012. The social welfare and moral dimensions, while much smaller, also increased after 1980.

Concerning the empirical measures of polarization, the graphs in Figure 8.5 of electoral, House, Senate, and presidential polarization show clearly that institutional polarization temporally led electoral polarization. The House and Senate began polarizing about the same time as the electorate in the 1980s. However, the rate at which the House and Senate polarized was much faster than for the electorate. The House and Senate were fully polarized by around 1995, and remained at this high level through the present. At the same time House and Senate polarization was saturated near the maximum, the electorate continued polarizing and did not reach a maximum until near 2012. Using a common measurement metric, House and Senate polarization reached a much higher level than electoral polarization. Again, this difference suggests that elites led electoral polarization temporally.

The statistical analyses of the relationship between institutional and electoral polarizations are also consistent with the elite-driven strategy. In Figure 8.6, House and Senate polarization mutually affected one another, and both temporally led electoral polarization. In the reverse direction, electoral polarization affected House polarization significantly and was nearly significant in affecting Senate polarization. However, the magnitude of the effect of electoral polarization on House and Senate polarization was much smaller. Thus, the analysis suggests a mutually reinforcing relationship, but one that is dominated by party elites.

This mutually reinforcing relationship is confirmed by the error-correction analysis. The short-run effects reported in Table 8.1 show that the House significantly affected the electorate with a two-year lag. In turn, the electorate significantly affected the House with a one-year lag. However, the short-run effect from the House to the electorate was six times larger than that from the electorate to the House. The president also affected polarization of the electorate in the short run, but there was no effect in the opposite direction. The long-run analyses at the bottom of Table 8.1 and graphed in Figure 8.7 show error-correcting relationships dominated by institutions. The House and president are most responsive in returning the polarization system from disequilibrium, while the electorate is least responsive. Hence, institutions led electoral polarization in both the short and long run.

The differential rates at which institutions and the electorate polarized produced an interesting result with regard to the often-hypothesized representation gap. Figure 8.8 shows that there was almost always a representation gap between American elected institutions and the electorate. As Congress polarized after 1981, the gap moved wider through about 2003. However, the increasing polarization among the electorate after 2003 led to a significant decline in the representation gap for both Congress and the president. As a result, the representation gap in 2012 was actually lower than it was in 1980. Interestingly, the reason for this finding is not that institutions became more moderate, and therefore more representative, but that the electorate became more extreme, making polarized institutions appear more representative through time. Citizens moved toward their respective poles, just as their representatives had done earlier.

In conclusion, the Old Guard strategy of restoring significant electoral support for the Founders' social contract was largely accomplished through the activities of party elites. Republican Party platforms from 1980 onward were inculcated with Old Guard economic values advocating small government, low taxes, free markets, and little regulation. The Old Guard cunningly expanded its support among the electorate by adding cultural values to party doctrines. Republican elites in government furthered these efforts by providing a continuous stream of cues consistent with their economic and cultural values. The Republican electorate chose from the menu provided by their party and followed elite cues to become more polarized through time. While the process was primarily elite-driven, it was also self-reinforcing as an increasingly polarized electorate chose even more extreme representatives.

Thus, the Old Guard strategy developed in the late 1970s was largely responsible for increasing polarization of the American system, in both Washington and the electorate.

9

Polarization as the Norm of the American System

Party polarization has been a regular phenomenon throughout American history. As suggested by the title of this book, a war has been waged over *who benefits from government, and at whose expense*. More theoretically, the war has been about *rent-seeking and rent-maintenance by the patrician and plebian classes*. The outcome of this war at any particular time has been predetermined by constraints established by the prevalent interpretation of the American social contract.

The Founders' social contract largely predetermined the outcome of battles from 1789 to 1932. The patrician class received substantial benefits from government during this period, including freedom from significant taxes, high tariffs, cheap money, monetary certainty, and an absence of federal regulation. These benefits were costly to the plebian class, which paid high taxes and prices (due to excises and tariffs), experienced monetary misery (due to economic instability largely caused by the patrician class and the gold standard), and suffered harms flowing from an unfettered market economy (white slavery, child labor, low wages, long working hours, abhorrent working conditions, tainted food and drugs, pollution, monopolistic behaviors, price discrimination, etc.). The war during this period was over whether the Founders' social contract would be maintained to the disadvantage of the plebian class. Due to the original constitutional design, it proved exceedingly difficult to remove rents from the patrician class as their party controlled at least one chamber of Congress or the Court through most of this period.

However, the Great Depression brought the Founders' social contract into wide disrepute. Between 1933 and the late 1970s, it was quite unpopular to be a person of wealth or a Republican. The collapse of the American economy between 1929 and 1932 yielded a new interpretation of the American social contract. From this point forward, the New Deal social contract largely predetermined the outcome of battles over who benefits from government, and at whose expense. The plebian class received substantial benefits of their own through New Deal and Great Society programs and altered constitutional interpretations. These benefits were costly to the patrician class, which paid higher taxes, received no advantage from tariffs, experienced devalued credit instruments, and were constrained by increased regulation. With the political party of the patricians weakened, it was not possible to reverse the rents obtained by the masses before 1980.

After 1980, the party of the patrician class made electoral gains, and polarization over the Founders' and New Deal social contracts reemerged. The party of the patricians continuously attacked programs benefiting the masses and sought to remove costs imposed on them through higher taxes and regulation. The war during this period was over whether the New Deal social contract would be maintained to the disadvantage of the patrician class. Again, it proved exceedingly difficult to remove rents from the plebian class because of the original constitutional design. Those rents had also become an entitlement that if attacked posed significant peril to the party of the patricians.

THE FOUNDERS AND POLARIZATION

Constitution writing for a republic is about establishing the rules of the game of a governmental system that will allocate the scarce political goods and resources of society. Constitution writing is also about effectively resolving conflict that arises over those political allocations. In both respects, the Founders created a system that was skewed toward continuing conflict. *The Founders did not seek to resolve conflict but intended to perpetuate it.*

The Constitution and Polarization

As discussed in Chapter 2, the U.S. Constitution contained specific provisions that benefited the patrician class at significant expense to the plebian class. By taking sides and creating a system favorable to rent-maintenance for the patricians, the Founders perpetuated class conflict.

For example, the Contract Clause in Article 1, Section 10, advantaged creditors by placing limitations on states that ended the popular practice of issuing paper money, thereby diluting debts. It also advantaged creditors by prohibiting states from altering contracts and debt obligations and by making gold and silver the only currency for fulfilling debt contracts. These provisions guaranteed creditors freedom from price inflation that diluted the value of their holdings. However, the debtor class remained a perpetual victim of price deflation that was very prevalent through the nineteenth century up to 1933, making it more difficult to pay off debts. Thus, these provisions of the Constitution established a continuing basis for class conflict from the Founding to the Great Depression.

Further, Article 1, Sections 2 and 9, prohibited direct taxation on any basis other than state population size. Until the Sixteenth Amendment in 1913, people could not be taxed individually based on their wealth or income. Prohibiting direct taxation of individuals gave rents to the propertied class, because the only other means for funding the government was through tariffs and excise taxes. These requirements implied that the patrician class would pay far less than the plebian class in taxes as a proportion of their income or wealth. Rather, the framers placed most of the national tax burden on the plebian class through tariffs and excise taxes. Class dissatisfaction over tariffs and excise taxes was very strong in the nineteenth century through the ratification of the Sixteenth Amendment in 1913. Hence, the Founders established a tax system that was bound to produce class conflict far into the future. That conflict continued even after 1913, as a fundamental basis of polarization in the modern era has been taxes paid by the wealthy.

The provisions of the Constitution and Bill of Rights limiting the power of the federal government also produced persistent class conflict over the abuses of unrestricted and amoral markets. Article 1, Section 8, enumerated the legislative powers of the federal government, while the Tenth Amendment was interpreted to place limits on the federal government exceeding those enumerated powers. Until 1937, the judicial bias was to nullify federal actions not explicitly authorized under Article 1, Section 8, of the Constitution. The basis of this judicial bias was a restrictive interpretation of the Commerce Clause and the Tenth Amendment. By limiting the power of the federal government to those explicitly enumerated in the Constitution, the patrician class benefited greatly, as they were enabled to engage in business practices that injured employees, competitors, segments of the public, and the public at large. Predictably, the plebian class sought relief from these injuries, again producing a more polarized system.

Again, an important function of government is the orderly resolution of conflict. However, the Founders did not intend to create a system that resolved conflict. Rather, their primary purpose was to create a system that would protect the minority from a zealous majority. The representational system created by the Founders was initially skewed toward one particular minority, the propertied class. However, the Founders saw that the system might not always be skewed in this direction. Therefore, they made it difficult to shift from the status quo through a system of separation of powers and competing institutions.

Separation of powers meant that at any point in time it would be difficult to achieve action. If a popular consensus did develop, it would be manifest only in the House of Representatives, the only popularly elected branch of the original government. Such popular consensus could be blocked by the courts or by competing factions through the bicameral legislature or executive. Courts established well in the past could suppress the actions of a contemporaneous majority seeking to impose its will on the minority. Control of the upper legislative branch by a propertied elite could also prevent the people's chamber from taking action that would be injurious to their interests. A president elected by property-holding electors would provide yet another potential check on the threat from a popular consensus.

As discussed in Chapter 2, the Founders feared and detested democracy and crafted a set of institutions intended to prevent popular governance, thereby perpetuating political conflict. The result was an American system where polarization and gridlock became the norm.

The Founders Understood That Polarization Would Be the Norm

Moreover, the Founders' own words show that they believed conflict would be persistent in the American system and that it could not be avoided. As expressed by James Madison in Federalist 10,

From the protection of different and unequal faculties of acquiring property, the possession of different degrees and kinds of property immediately results; and from the influence of these on the sentiments and views of the respective proprietors, ensues a division of the society into different interests and parties ... The latent causes of faction are thus sown in the nature of man; and we see them everywhere brought into different degrees of activity, according to the different circumstances of civil society. A zeal for different opinions concerning religion, concerning government, and many other points, as well of speculation as of practice; an attachment to different leaders ambitiously contending for pre-eminence and power; or to persons of other descriptions whose fortunes have been interesting to the human passions, have, in turn, divided mankind into parties, inflamed them with mutual animosity, and rendered them much more disposed to vex and oppress each other than to co-operate for their common good ... But the most common and durable source of factions has been the various and unequal distribution of property. Those who hold and those who are without property have ever formed distinct interests in society. (Madison 1788b)

The Founders themselves were drawn largely from the propertied class. Observing under the Articles of Confederation what they considered "too democratic" state governments, they feared that a democratic consensus would weaken property rights. Federal and state governments were issuing paper money to the advantage of the numerous debtors who had contributed to the American Revolution. That paper money consistently devalued Revolutionary War bonds held by less numerous creditors. In effect, popularly elected state governments were confiscating property held by unpopular creditors.

The propertied class feared that popularly elected state legislatures would adopt a taxing regime that was to their disadvantage. Thus, the chief end of the new more centralized federal government was not to create a consensual democracy that resolved conflicts. Rather, it was to protect the property of a wealthy minority who, not coincidentally, wrote the Constitution (Beard 1913; McGuire and Ohsfeldt 1984). As expressed by Madison in Federalist 51,

Ambition must be made to counteract ambition ... [A]ll the power surrendered by the people is submitted to the administration of a single government; and the usurpations are guarded against by a division of the government into distinct and separate departments ... Different interests necessarily exist in different classes of citizens. If a majority be united by a common interest, the rights of the minority will be insecure ... Whilst all authority in it will be derived from and dependent on the society, the society itself will be broken into so many parts, interests, and classes of citizens, that the rights of individuals, or of the minority, will be in little danger from interested combinations of the majority. (Madison 1788a)

By pitting faction against faction, a perpetual war of the classes was enabled in which no single faction or party could permanently gain the upper hand.

FORESTS, TREES, AND WHY POLARIZATION IS THE NORM

The Founders' Constitution initiated and enabled the polarization that has existed throughout American history. However, viewed dynamically across American history, party polarization has not been a constant, continuously staying near polar ends. Rather, it has been a time series random walk. A random walk through time will sometimes increase and other times decrease.

Previous analyses of party polarization in America have focused almost exclusively on the period since World War II. However, focusing on recent history risks missing the big picture that emerges by considering polarization through all of American history. The current trend in polarization from the 1980s to present only appears to have reached a critical zenith. Understanding the underlying process that has driven polarization historically requires understanding the dynamic nature of polarization in the American system.

Polarization as an Empirical Regularity

The historical analyses in preceding chapters showed that there were three periods when party polarization increased toward a peak: the Founding Era, the Progressive Era, and the post-1980 period. There were also several periods when polarization was lower: between 1789 and 1792, the Era of Good Feelings from 1815 to 1825, the post–Civil War Reconstruction Era from 1865 to 1879, the 1920s, and the New Deal/Great Society Era from 1933 through 1980.

What was there about these periods that produced increasing/decreasing polarization? Periods of increasing party polarization were all characterized by having two strong political parties battling for class advantage. During the Founding Era, the Federalist Party established advantages for the patrician class, while the anti-Federalist/Democratic-Republican Party sought the removal of patrician advantages and advantages of its own. During the Progressive Era, the "standpatter" Republican Party sought to maintain advantages for the patrician class, while the populist Democrats sought to remove those advantages and extend government benefits more broadly. During the post-1980 period, the Democratic Party sought to maintain New Deal/Great Society advantages for the plebian class, while the Republican Party sought to remove those advantages and distribute government benefits more narrowly.

Another attribute of high polarization periods was substantial activity by party entrepreneurs battling toward partisan ends. During the Founding Era, Madison and Jefferson fought against Hamilton in establishing an anti-Federalist movement. During the Progressive Era, party entrepreneurs such as William Jennings Bryan and Woodrow Wilson fired the passions of Democratic populism. During the post-1980 period, party entrepreneurs such as Paul Weyrich, Ronald Reagan, and Newt Gingrich worked cunningly and deliberately to restore advantage to the patrician class. In each case, party polarization was a strategy for building their respective parties. Increased party polarization was also a consequence of their strategy.

Periods of lower party polarization were all characterized by having a single dominant political party, with a secondary party either in acquiescence or nonexistent. A single political party, the Federalists, emerged immediately after the founding. The Era of Good Feelings followed the death of the Federalist Party after the Hartford Convention and coincided with a period of Democratic-Republican dominance. The post–Civil War reconstruction period followed the North's defeat of the South and coincided with a period of Republican dominance and Democratic impotence. Following World War I, the 1920s was a period of electoral repudiation of the socialist reforms before and during the war, and coincided with a period of Republican dominance and Democratic acquiescence. Finally, the post–New Deal Era followed the Great Depression and World War II and coincided with a period of Democratic dominance and compliant Modern Republicanism.

Each period of one-party dominance occurred following a critical event that upset the competitive balance of a natural two-party system. The Founding Era disparaged the formation of political parties, yet Federalists quickly organized factions sympathetic to the patrician class. The Hartford Convention dealt a deathblow to the Federalists. The Civil War severely wounded the Democrats. Wilson's extreme socialist policies during World War I injured the Democrats. And the Great Depression almost dealt a deathblow to the Republican Party. Yet in each case after a period of one-party dominance, two-party competition returned.

These empirical regularities suggest that when there are two strongly competitive political parties led by zealous party entrepreneurs, then polarization will be high in the American system. A natural question to ask is why *two-party* polarization has been the dominant pattern. Of course, the Founders seemingly had no intention at all of creating a party-based system. Nevertheless, their original representational scheme had that effect due to Article 1, Sections 2 and 3, of the U.S. Constitution. Section 2 provided representation according to the population of each state, with a single representative for each House district.

Section 3 gave each state two senators who were selected by each state. Both electoral schemes implied the disenfranchisement of losers and a strong incentive to not be the loser in a winner-take-all system. The result was competitive two-party polarization.

The plurality voting system in the United States means that voters cast a single vote for a single candidate in each district or state, and the winner of an election is the candidate who receives the most votes. This winner-take-all system means that a one-party system is unstable, as disenfranchised interests always seek reenfranchisement through a second competing party. Further, the winner-take-all system also means that more than two parties is unlikely, because a third party that does not win districts or states will not share the representational benefits. There are also psychological disadvantages for supporting of third parties relative to maintaining support for losers. Thus, two-party polarization has been the norm throughout American history, as divergent class interests have competed for electoral benefits.

The word "polar" implies opposites, implying two. Polarization requires at least two viable parties that gravitate toward the poles. According to this logic, if there is only one political party, then party polarization cannot exist. Further, if there are three or more political parties, then party polarization should be diminished.

Is there an empirical tendency of the American system to have two and only two competitive political parties? From 1789 to 1792, Federalists dominated government. With only one political party, party polarization was low. However, underlying class discontent with Federalist policies was strong. Starting in 1791, Madison and Jefferson began organizing an opposition, resulting in the birth of the Democratic-Republican Party and a subsequent period of high polarization. Similarly, during the Era of Good Feelings only one political party remained after the Hartford Convention, the Democratic-Republicans. Yet, the Democratic-Republican Party soon split into two parties, again representing the patrician and plebian classes. After the Civil War there was only one effective political party, the Republicans. Yet plebian class disadvantage ultimately led to greater party competition culminating in Progressive Era polarization. Finally, after the Great Depression there was again only one effective political party. Yet patrician class disadvantage ultimately led to greater party competition culminating in post-1980 polarization. Hence, periods of one-party dominance have always given way to subsequent periods of two-party competition.

Have third parties ever successfully dissipated two-party polarization by creating a third pole, moderating the natural tendency toward class polarization? A third party has succeeded only once in American history, when Republicans displaced Whigs between 1852 and 1856. After the Republican Party rose, the Whig Party quickly died out, again leaving only two political parties.

Third parties have sometimes split voter loyalty to one of the two major political parties. For example, the Progressive Party in 1912 nominated Theodore

Roosevelt as their presidential candidate, splitting the Republican Party and leading to the election of Woodrow Wilson, who received only 42 percent of the popular vote. The American Independent Party in 1968 nominated George Wallace as their presidential candidate, splitting the Democratic Party and resulting in the election of Richard Nixon with only 43 percent of the popular vote. The Reform Party in 1992 nominated Ross Perot as their presidential candidate, resulting in Bill Clinton being elected president with only 43 percent of the popular vote. Other instances of third parties affecting elections have also occurred, most notably in 2000 when the Green Party vote in Florida made the difference between George W. Bush and Al Gore being elected president. Bush won the electoral vote, but received roughly half a million fewer votes than Gore.

While third parties have occasionally been influential of presidential elections, they have seated few representatives in Congress. In most instances where third parties have arisen, they have died out quickly over the next few elections. However, ideological commitment can increase third-party endurance. For example, the Libertarian Party has existed since 1971, and the Green Party has existed since 1990. Nevertheless, there is a strong empirical tendency of the American system toward two-party polarization.

A Formal Expression of the Two-Party Polarization Norm

These empirical regularities suggest an underlying force causing the system to equilibrate to two highly competitive political parties. This underlying force is similar to physical processes occurring in nature when two species occupying the same ecosystem compete for a common resource. Biologists and population scientists have described the dynamics of two-species competition using a pair of differential equations first proposed by Lotka (1910, 1920) and Volterra (1926).

Applying this model to party competition for a common resource, voter support, in a winner-take-all party system, the dynamics can be expressed as follows:

$$\frac{dx_1}{dt} = r_1 x_1 \left(1 - \left(\frac{x_1 + a_{12} x_2}{K_1} \right) \right) + I_{t50} \tag{9.1}$$

$$\frac{dx_2}{dt} = r_2 x_2 \left(1 - \left(\frac{x_2 + a_{21} x_1}{K_2} \right) \right) - I_{t50} \tag{9.2}$$

where

K_1, K_2 = natural proportions of support for party 1 and 2
x_1, x_2 = actual proportions of support for party 1 and 2
r_1, r_2 = social discontent rate of return parameter for party 1 and 2
a_{12}, a_{21} = efficiency of party entrepreneurs in gaining support
I_{t50} = a critical event at t_{50} affecting proportional changes in support for party 1 and 2

The equilibriums for these differential equations are given:

$$x_1^* = \frac{K_1 - \alpha_{12}K_2}{1 - \alpha_{12}\alpha_{21}}; \; x_2^* = \frac{K_2 - \alpha_{21}K_1}{1 - \alpha_{12}\alpha_{21}}$$

A full set of phase portraits for these equations can be found in Bomze (1983). However, simple graphical dynamics for the two political parties are presented here.

Figure 9.1 illustrates the two-party dynamics for a winner-take-all system such as has always existed in the United States. Figure 9.1A shows movement to system equilibrium when there is only one initial political party, but a second party arises to represent a competing social class. For example, one could think of the Right Party (solid line) in this graph as the Federalists and the Left Party (dashed line) as the Democratic-Republicans starting around 1791. From having no initial support, the Left Party moves to a competitive equilibrium over about twenty-two periods to approach the support for the Right Party.

The rate of movement is a function of the competing party's social discontent parameters, r_1, r_2, and, to a lesser extent the party entrepreneur parameters, α_{12}, α_{21}. The social discontent parameters represent the underlying class dissatisfaction with the status quo of costs and benefits from government. When there is no class dissatisfaction, the party remains in its stable equilibrium state, being held there strongly by an attractor force (r_1 for the Right Party). When there is a lot of social discontent, due to high costs and low benefits, then the attractor force rapidly moves support toward the natural equilibrium (r_2 for the Left Party). If class dissatisfaction is low, then movement to the new equilibrium is slower (dot-dashed line).

The party entrepreneur parameters represent the relative efficiency of party leaders in gaining support. The dotted line in Figure 9.1A shows that effective party entrepreneurs increase the rate at which a second party moves to its new equilibrium, as well as affects the final level of that equilibrium. In this simulation, the Left Party with effective entrepreneurs matches support for the Right Party after only fourteen periods and achieves equilibrium higher than that for the Right Party. For example, Madison and Jefferson were quite efficient in gaining support for Democratic-Republicans after 1791, eventually winning control of all three branches of government by 1801. The overall point is that movement from one to two parties occurs naturally toward the two equilibriums x_1^*, x_2^* due to class dissatisfaction, the efforts of party entrepreneurs, and the winner-take-all nature of the party system.

Figure 9.1B shows the simulated effect of a critical event at t_{50}, which upsets the balance of the competitive two-party system. One could think of a critical event such as the Great Depression, which caused previously dominant Republicans to lose support between 1933 and 1980. With that loss of support came decreasing polarization and acquiescent Modern Republicanism. Note that

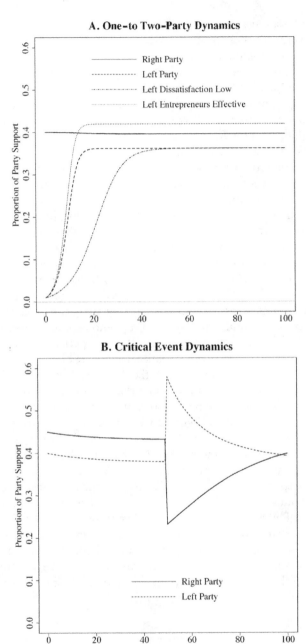

FIGURE 9.1 Simulated Dynamics of a Two-Party System
Source: Dynamic model based on Lotka–Volterra equations.

Right Party losses at t_{50} were Left Party gains. However, the Right Party and Left Party were still sticky to their equilibriums x_1^*, x_2^* due to the social force exerted by the competing classes.

As in Figure 9.1A, the rates at which each party returns its respective equilibrium remain a function of the social discontent parameters, r_1, r_2, and the party entrepreneur parameters, α_{12}, α_{21}. For example, Republican Party entrepreneurs such as Ronald Reagan, Paul Weyrich, and Newt Gingrich accelerated the rate of return to equilibrium for Republicans after 1980. As discussed earlier, polarization was a deliberate and cunning strategy that party entrepreneurs used to attract more support. After the change in entrepreneurship, Right Party gains increased Left Party losses. Ultimately, the system moved back into a competitive two-party balance. At the same time, party polarization increased.

What about polarization in a multiparty system? Intuitively, multiparty systems have more than two poles, so polarization should be diminished. Parties no longer line up in direct opposition to one another. Conflict is dispersed among multiple entities and across multiple policy dimensions. This intuition, while compelling, disregards the class basis of party polarization. In multiparty systems, parties are generally forced to form governing coalitions. Sartori (1966) argued that polarization among the public is a basis for coalitional polarization in multiparty systems, a phenomenon he labeled "polarized pluralism." Hence, even multiparty systems can experience party polarization.

Regardless, multiple competitive political parties are highly unlikely to exist for long in the United States because of the Founders' representational design. Duverger (1951, 1972) argued that more than two political parties is unlikely in a plurality voting system for two reasons. Weak parties are often fused into one of the major parties, such as occurred when the People's Party and Free Silver Party merged into the Democrats in 1896. Additionally, voters generally eliminate third parties by understanding that they have no chance for success, such as has occurred many times in American history. While Duverger's Law is not an absolute (see especially Benoit 2006; Riker 1982), and there are counter-examples of plurality voting systems supporting multiple parties in Great Britain, Canada, India, and the Philippines, the rule has held very strongly in the United States.

The thesis that a third party cannot easily compete in a winner-take-all system can also be described using a differential equation model. Consider a dynamical system in which a third party attempts to enter a stable two-party system. The following equation captures the dynamics of success or failure for the third party:

$$\frac{dx_3}{dt} = \alpha_{3_{12}}(1-\beta)x_3(x_3-B)(K_3-x_3) \tag{9.3}$$

where

x_0 = proportion of support at t_0 for third party
x_3 = proportion of support at t for third party

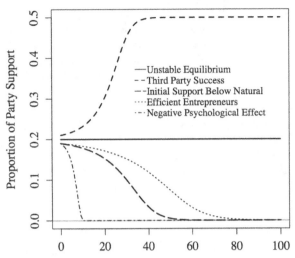

FIGURE 9.2 Dynamic Model of Third Party Entry

K_3 = natural proportion of support for the third party
$\alpha_{3_{12}}$ = efficiency of party entrepreneurs in building support
β = psychological effect on voters of supporting a loser (0...1)
B = fair representation bias point (0.5 in a winner-take-all system)

This equation has only one equilibrium, and that equilibrium is unstable at $x_0 = K_3$ (solid line in Figure 9.2). When the third party's initial support precisely equals it natural level of support, then the system is stable. Any deviation at all from this equality drives support away from the stable point, with the third party almost always failing.

Figure 9.2 depicts some of the other possible dynamics of third party entry into a stable two-party system. If $x_0 > K_3$, then the third party succeeds (dashed line). That is, if its initial support is greater than its natural level of support, then the party succeeds to eventually displace one of the two parties in the system. This outcome has occurred only once in American history. When anti-slavery Whigs merged with anti-slavery Democrats to form the Republican Party between 1852 and 1856, the new party had sufficient initial support to survive. Subsequently, the Whig Party quickly died out and the Republican Party became the second party in the two-party system.

If $x_0 < K_3$, then the third party always fails (long dashed). This has been the most common outcome through American history, as third parties have come and gone. However, Figure 9.2 shows that the rate at which a third party fails is a function of $\alpha_{3.12}$ and β. That is, the third party can survive a while longer when its entrepreneurs are effective (dotted line). The third party fails more rapidly when supporting a loser causes members to be more psychologically distressed (dot-dashed line). For example, Ralph Nader was very effective in establishing and maintaining the Green Party over an extended period, and Green Party members were seemingly unaffected psychologically by perpetually supporting a losing cause. Regardless, most third parties fail quite rapidly due to the negative psychological effect of supporting a losing party. If the party never achieves representation, then there is little incentive for voters to offer their support. Hence, the U.S. representational system is heavily biased against the survival of a competitive third party.

These simple models describe the natural forces that can make two-party polarization the norm for the American system. As suggested by Equations 9.1 and 9.2, the system always gravitates toward two parties. When there has been only one political party in American history, social class discontent and party entrepreneurs have sparked the rise of a second party seeking benefit from government. When one or the other political party loses support, say, due to a critical event, forcing it to acquiesce in the class warfare, then polarization declines. However, the acquiescent party eventually regains support over time to produce new two-party competition. Changing social dissatisfaction and party entrepreneurs can accelerate this process. Further, as suggested by Equation 9.3, more than two parties cannot exist for long in a stable two-party system due to the winner-take-all nature of the system. Hence, there are seldom more than two poles representing the competing social classes.

Of course, these are just mathematical models, but they do correspond with empirical reality in the American system.

FINAL OVERVIEW

It is common for citizens, pundits, politicians, and social scientists alike to lament the extent of polarization and governmental dysfunction in the modern era. Allegedly, polarization runs rampant through the electorate as states and neighborhoods divide along sharply drawn ideological lines. Polarization is deemed even greater in Congress as members are reflective of their polarized districts, and party discipline holds them in line to produce institutional gridlock. Presidents are also seen as polarized, typically behaving as representatives of their fellow partisans, rather than representatives of the nation at large (e.g., see Wood 2009; Wood et al. 2015).

However, focusing on dire present circumstances sidesteps the real reason for studying party polarization. It is an important research concept worthy of scientific investigation in itself. Future research should seek greater understanding of party polarization as a research concept by considering a broader perspective than is possible by focusing purely on the present. It should also consider party polarization as a system-wide process, rather than focusing on single institutions or the electorate.

The lessons of history tell us that modern party polarization will decline at some point, perhaps due to a critical event or mistake by one of the two major political parties. After a period of declining polarization, the process will start again toward another zenith. This pattern has been repeated multiple times through American history, and will likely be the pattern for the future.

Accordingly, scholars should seek to understand factors that alter these patterns. The preceding analyses suggest that the dynamics of polarization should be affected by the magnitude of class dissatisfaction with the status quo. The dynamics should also be strongly affected by party entrepreneurs who translate class dissatisfaction into party support. These two factors are also likely to be simultaneously related to one another. Party entrepreneurs draw support to political parties by fomenting greater class dissatisfaction. In turn, the ability of party entrepreneurs to translate class dissatisfaction into party support depends on the magnitude of class dissatisfaction.

One suggestion for future research is for scholars to evaluate how class dissatisfaction and party entrepreneurs affect party polarization and are related to one another. The statistical analyses in Chapter 8 provide a start toward this end. Party polarization was found to be largely elite-driven, suggesting that party entrepreneurs are important to system-wide polarization. However, party polarization is an interactive process, largely driven from the top, but marginally affected from the bottom.

Historically, party entrepreneurs have been important to escalating class conflict in all eras of American history. Madison and Jefferson were fomenters of class dissatisfaction and also responded to pre-existent class dissatisfaction. Similarly, William Jennings Bryan was important to class dissatisfaction during the Progressive Era. Bryan was an instigator through his fiery speeches, as well as being responsive to pre-existing class dissatisfaction. Finally, multiple party entrepreneurs were responsible for increased party polarization since the 1980s. The Heritage Foundation, under the leadership of Paul Weyrich, strategized bringing the Christian Right into the Republican Right. Ronald Reagan and Newt Gingrich were effective at rallying citizens toward right-wing causes.

One obvious party entrepreneur that has been missing from much past research on party polarization is the American president. Presidents have generally been treated as victims of polarization, rather than causes of polarization. Yet presidents are ideological leaders who often conflict with ideological leaders in Congress. Observing the obvious hostility between presidents and Congress since the 1980s through the present should convince most that presidents are relevant and probably a focal point of Washington polarization. Reagan's attack on New Deal and Great Society programs, Clinton's budget wars with the Gingrich Republicans, George W. Bush's trials against anti-Bush tax cut/ anti-war Democrats, and Obama's tribulations against the Republican Party of "No!" provide convincing anecdotal evidence that presidents are important to this process.

Yet past polarization research has emphasized elite-driven polarization as originating largely from congressional and party leaders. Most of the literature has focused on the House of Representatives (but see Lee 2008; Theriault 2008,

2013; Theriault and Rohde 2011), perhaps because of the more direct connection of the electorate with House members or because of its measurables (i.e., rules in the House with no equivalent concept in the Senate). While not dismissing the role of congressional leaders (they can be entrepreneurs too), it seems clear that presidents should be considered important to polarization of both institutions and the electorate. Indeed, presidents should be central to this process, given their much greater visibility, media attention, and formidable agenda setting, legislative, and executive powers.

Thus, party polarization should be considered holistically as a system-wide and path-dependent phenomenon. Rather than focusing on a single institution or chamber, future research should consider polarization as involving multiple institutions and their interactions. Hostility between presidents and opposing partisans produces escalating hostility and antagonistic behaviors. Hostility between the parties within and across legislative chambers can also produce cascading responses. Allies of the president and across chambers tend to cooperate in joint reaction against opposing partisans. In other words, party polarizations depend on behaviors encompassing the entire system, rather than just between the electorate and partisans in a single chamber of Congress.

Thus, future researchers are encouraged to take a broader view than simply focusing on the present. They should seek to understand the nature of the polarization process viewed in larger historical perspective. Future researchers should also study polarization holistically as a natural and system-wide process involving multiple actors. With such approaches, a deeper understanding can be achieved of party polarization as a research concept worthy of investigation.

Appendix A

This appendix elaborates on the construction of the measures of electoral polarization used in Chapters 7 and 8. The individual-level data from 115 surveys with 125 ideology questions were used in constructing the electoral polarization measures. Before 1975, surveys were intermittent, and following Ellis and Stimson (2009), multiple question types were used for some early years. The data came from seven survey organizations – Gallup, CBS/*New York Times*, ABC, *Los Angeles Times*, the Office of Public Opinion Research, the Roper Organization, and the National Opinion Research Center – although overwhelmingly from Gallup. Such questions took one of four forms with some minor variation in question wording by survey:

- "Identification": "How would you describe your views on most political matters? Generally, do you think of yourself as liberal, moderate, or conservative?"
- "Go left": "Which of these policies would you like to have the Government follow: go more to the left by following more of the views of labor and other liberal groups, go more to the right by following more of the views of business and conservative groups?"
- "Join": "If our political parties were reorganized and there was one for Conservatives and the other for Liberals – which party do you think you would like to join?"
- "Preference": "Other things being equal, would you like to see a liberal or a conservative nominated as the presidential candidate of your party in 1960?"

Obviously, of the four question types, the identification questions are the most content-valid indicators of people's ideology. Accordingly, identification questions were used to generate the measure as much as possible. Identification questions were used for most of the series before 1975 with such questions asked in 1944, 1947, 1948, 1950, 1954, 1955, 1957, 1964, 1965, 1969, 1970, and 1973. However, this coverage is incomplete. Therefore, the pre-1975 data were augmented with surveys asking questions of the other types. Identification questions constitute the entire series after 1975 as survey houses standardized their methodologies and asked the identification question at least annually thereafter.

The selection criteria for the surveys were as follows. If, in any year, there was a Gallup survey that utilized the identification question to query ideology, that survey was used. If there was not a Gallup survey, but there was another survey house that used the identification question, that survey house was used. Before 1975, using the search criteria from Ellis and Stimson (2009), when identification questions were not available, ideology questions were collected and recorded from every survey that included both a partisanship and an ideology question. From 1975 onward, the entire measure was constructed from identification questions. Especially after 1975, there were often multiple surveys for each year asking the identification question. Accordingly, when the data became available more regularly, two surveys were sampled from each year: one in or close to March, and another in or close to September (allowing for deviations to enable collecting the "identification" questions). After 1991, the entire series was constructed from identification questions from Gallup. Overall, the data collection effort was limited by data availability before 1975, but followed a regular pattern after 1975. However, there is no reason to believe that this measure is affected by the unique surveys used. The list of surveys used to construct the measure is available at http://people.tamu.edu/~b-wood.

Typically, the surveys included responses that range from very liberal to very conservative. However, the surveys differed in how these categories were coded. Therefore, the surveys were recoded into a common scheme as follows. In each survey, the very liberal response was coded 1; liberal was coded 2; moderate was coded 3; conservative was coded 4; and very conservative was coded 5. This coding scheme yields a five-point scale, with liberal on the left pole (1) and conservative on the right pole (5). Some early surveys did not have a "very" liberal/conservative option. Thus, data for these surveys were coded into the 2/3/4 categories, as appropriate. For partisanship, Democrat was coded 1; leans Democrat was coded 2; Independent was coded 3; leans Republican was coded 4; and Republican was coded 5.

As described earlier, this study considers three different types of polarization: divergence, dispersion, and distributional polarization. Thus, the data were divided into Democrats, Independents, and Republicans. Then, the mean, standard deviation, and skewness of the partisan distributions were calculated for each survey over time. In every instance, partisans – strong, regular, or weak – were coded with their party, working from the findings that even "weak" partisans are often much more consistent than their self-prescribed label indicates (Keith et al. 1992).

Prior to 1975, surveys were intermittent, relying on multiple question types for some years. After 1975, there were often multiple surveys for each year asking the identification question. These potential disparities were addressed through smoothing with the procedure and software WCALC developed by Stimson (1991). The software produced a recursively smoothed annual time series for each of the three polarization measures running from 1944 through 2012. The final measures are thus smoothed time series of the mean, standard deviation, and skewness for the distributions of ideology during each year for Democrats, Independents, and Republicans.

As a validity check, the measure constructed with the 125 questions was compared with the ideology information from the American National Election Studies (ANES) and General Social Surveys (GSS), two of the most popular sources of data on polarization. For both the GSS and the ANES, an ideology measure was constructed that both ignored independents and coded independents as partisans. Both measures are substantively similar to the measures used here, except that the measures used here extend much further back in time and are not intermittent.

Also, a measure was created that leveraged information from all three sources – the polls, the GSS, and the ANES – into a single measure of ideology. This measure also behaves substantively similarly to the final measure used in this study. The GSS, however, exhibits behavior that is not reflected in either the ANES or the polls' measures of ideology for some of the period under study. Therefore, a measure of ideology relying only on the ANES and the polls' data was created. Again, this measure behaved substantively similarly to the final measure used in this study.

Some might also wonder whether the inclusion of different types of questions prior to 1975 affects the validity of the measure through time. Two comments are relevant to this concern. First, as discussed earlier, identification questions were used whenever possible to construct the measure of ideology. Second, a separate measure of ideology that used only the identification questions – supplemented by the ANES data, for the reasons discussed above – was developed as a validity check. Again, this measure behaves substantively similarly to the final measure used in this study. The measure used here is preferable because it contains more data and extends further back in time.

Finally, some might wonder whether the electoral polarization measure exhibits evidence of polarization only because of the expansion of response categories over time. That is, around 1970, surveys began to ask whether respondents identified as "very" liberal or conservative. To ensure that evidence of polarization was not simply an artifact of increasing the number of response categories, we also constructed a three-point measure of respondent ideology over time, coding "very" liberal/conservative as simply liberal/conservative. Again, this measure behaved substantively similarly to the final measure used in our study.

Each of these measures – the ANES (both with Independents ignored and Independents randomly assigned), the GSS (both with Independents ignored and Independents randomly assigned), the polls alone (both with Independents ignored and Independents randomly assigned and with the ideological response category collapsed to three points), all three combined (both with Independents ignored and Independents randomly assigned), the polls/ANES (both with Independents ignored and Independents randomly assigned), and the polls/ANES measure with only identification questions (both with Independents ignored and Independents randomly assigned) – is available to the scholarly community at http://people.tamu.edu/~b-wood/replication.html.

Appendix B

TEXT-MINING METHODOLOGY

This section discusses the text-mining methods used in the party platform analysis in Chapter 8. Instructive examples demonstrating text mining can be found in Francis and Flynn (2010). A more comprehensive introductory text is Weiss et al. (2010). Basically, text mining is the process of deriving high-quality information from text input.

Text mining requires the analyst first to load and precondition the documents by eliminating extraneous terms and information. The entire set of documents is loaded just as a quantitative dataset is loaded into common statistical packages. However, the documents must be preconditioned to get the associated word counts into a matrix form. The entire body of texts is called a corpus. The corpus is processed to remove numbers, punctuation, and white space. Stop words (such as *the, is, at, which, on,* etc.) are removed using a stop word dictionary. All words are converted to lowercase text. Then, all words are converted to their stems, with endings removed (demonstration/demonstrated becomes demonstrat; national/nationhood becomes nation, etc.). Once the corpus is preconditioned in this manner, an alphabetically sorted document term matrix is created containing counts of all of the remaining words. The document term matrix contains the documents in the rows and counts of unique words in each document in the columns. Finally, sparse terms are removed from the document term matrix according to some arbitrary criterion (e.g., removing terms from the matrix so that no more than 5 percent of any column is null). The resulting document term matrix then becomes the data for analysis.

The R programming language (R Project 2015) was used with the statistical package *tm* (Feinerer 2008; Feinerer et al. 2008) to preprocess the documents in this manner and as an engine for the initial analysis. This package was used to create the document term matrix for use with other R functions and packages. It was also used to develop term frequencies for each stemword within documents and to find word associations. Analyses were conducted separately on the Democratic and Republican platforms, as well as combining them within a single corpus.

Using the corpus, hierarchical cluster analyses wer conducted using the built-in R function *hclust*. Cluster analysis is a set of techniques for partitioning a set of objects (in this case party platforms) into relatively homogeneous subsets based on their inter-object similarities. A cluster is defined by the similarity of its members, where similarity is determined using a geometric measure of vector distance. Once the distance between objects is calculated, an algorithm is applied to cluster the objects into subgroups based on their inter-object similarities. The document term matrix was first scaled using the built-in R function *scale* to standardize the columns for each term. Then, the Euclidian distance between each column was calculated using the built-in R function *dist*. The resultant distances were then clustered hierarchically using *hclust* and a variety of clustering algorithms.

K-means clustering was used to identify a bend in the plot of within-groups sum of squares for extracted clusters from two to ten. This approach is recommended to determine the proper number of clusters to initiate the algorithm (similar to interpreting a scree plot in factor analysis) (Everitt and Hothorn 2009, 251). Based on this plot, a four-cluster dendrogram tree defined by using Ward's (1963) minimum variance method is reported below. At the broadest, the entire set of platforms may be considered a single cluster, while at the finest, each platform can be considered a separate cluster. Ward's method incrementally adds data points that are closest to all members of an existing cluster, thereby producing compact, spherical clusters. Note that the results reported in this chapter do not deviate significantly when the initial number of clusters is set at five or more.

VAR AND VECM METHODOLOGY

This section describes the technical details of the VAR and VECM methodologies used in Chapter 8. To understand the time series analyses, one must understand that every cointegrated VAR has both a levels VAR and a differences VECM representation. Note that the two representations are totally equivalent, because each is just a mathematical transformation of the other (the mathematics are in Lutkepohl 2007, part II). The levels VAR(p) representation is written as follows:

$$y_t = A_1 y_{t-1} + \ldots + A_p y_{t-p} + \varepsilon_t \tag{B.1}$$

In this equation p is the lag order of the VAR, y_t is a vector of k endogenous integrated and potentially cointegrated variables, A_p is a matrix of coefficients associated with each lag of the k variables, and ε_t is a k-dimensional vector of the disturbances from the VAR equations.

The variables in such a VAR process are called cointegrated of order $CI(d,b)$ if all components of y_t are integrated $I(d)$ at the same order and there exists some linear combination $z_t = \beta' y_t$ with $\beta = (\beta_1, \ldots, \beta_k)' \neq 0$ such that z_t is I $(d-b)$. For example, if all components of y_t are $I(1)$, as in the analysis below, and $\beta' y_t$ is stationary $I(0)$, then $y_t {\sim} CI(1,1)$ (Lutkepohl 2007, 245). The vector β is called the cointegrating vector. A system consisting of cointegrated variables is called a cointegrated process.

The preceding levels VAR(p) model can be rewritten in VECM form as follows.

$$\Delta y_t = \Pi y_{t-1} + \Gamma_1 \Delta y_{t-1} + \ldots + \Gamma_{p-1} \Delta y_{t-p+1} + \varepsilon_t \tag{B.2}$$

In this equation, Π is a matrix that captures the long-run dynamics and Γ_p is a matrix that depicts the short-run dynamics. The matrix Π can be further decomposed into two parts such that $\Pi = \alpha\beta'$. The vector α represents the rate of return from disequilibrium for each VAR equation (the error correction components), while β depicts the scaled cointegrating vector. Note that the cointegrating vector β is not unique. Therefore, one element of β is typically normalized to one.

A starting point analysis is estimating a VAR and VECM to determine the appropriate number of lags (p) for the endogenous variables in the four equations. If too many lags are included, then relationships may be attenuated; if too few lags are included, then relationships can be magnified. In order to determine the appropriate lag length, the VAR and VECM were estimated in levels and differences respectively for lag lengths from one to five years. Three information criteria were then used to discern the appropriate lag length. Using Akaike's information criterion (Akaike 1973), Schwarz's Bayesian criterion (Schwarz 1978), and Hannan and Quinn's information criterion (Hannan and Quinn 1979), the appropriate models were found to be VAR(2) and VECM(3). Note that a VECM(3) actually contains only two lags due to the mathematical transformation from Equation B.1 to Equation B.2 above. These models make sense intuitively because of the two-year electoral pattern associated with the House, Senate, and electorate.

Table B.1 contains the statistical evidence for whether the four variables in the polarization system are cointegrated in a multivariate sense. The stationarity tests are estimated using CATS 2.0 (Dennis 2006) with RATS time series software (Doan 2014). The stationarity tests in the top part of the table show that the residuals from the House, Senate, presidential, and electoral polarization VAR equations are all definitively nonstationary, with p-values of 0.00 for the null hypotheses of stationarity. Hence, it is possible for these relations to be cointegrating.

Are they in fact cointegrated? The Johansen trace tests in the bottom part of Table B.1 evaluate the number of cointegrating vectors in the VAR system.

TABLE B.1 *Stationarity and Cointegration Tests for the Polarization System*

Stationarity Tests	Equation			
	House	Senate	President	Electorate
χ^2_3	35.82 (0.00)	37.06 (0.00)	16.88 (0.00)	42.52 (0.00)
Johansen Trace Tests Cointegrating Rank	Eigenvalue	λ_{Trace}		
$r = 0$	0.617	82.61 (0.00)		
$r = 1$	0.342	35.18 (0.24)		
$r = 2$	0.117	15.25 (0.56)		

Note: The stationarity and cointegration tests are those implemented in CATS 2.0 (Cointegration Analysis of Time Series). For the stationarity tests, the null hypothesis is stationarity. The stationarity tests are Lagrange multiplier statistics with three degrees of freedom and 5 percent critical values of 7.815. The cointegrating rank tests are the Johansen trace tests with Bartlett small sample corrections. The Johansen statistic tests the null hypothesis that there are at most r cointegrating vectors versus the alternative that there are $r+1$. The numbers in parentheses for all tests are p-values for rejecting the null hypotheses.

With a four-variable VAR it is possible to have at most three cointegrating vectors. The null hypothesis that $r = 0$ (no cointegrating vectors) is definitively rejected with p-value 0.00. However, the null hypothesis that $r = 1$ (one cointegrating vector) is not rejected with p-value 0.24. Thus, the statistical results in Table B.1 show that there is one cointegrating vector in the polarization system containing House, Senate, presidential, and electoral polarization. More technically, $y_t \tilde{\ } CI(1,1)$.

References

ABC News/*Washington Post.* 1990. "USABCWP.90399.R03." University of Connecticut: The Roper Center for Public Opinion Research.

    1993. "USABCWP.934930.Q013." University of Connecticut: The Roper Center for Public Opinion Research.

    1996. "USABCWP.011096.R10." University of Connecticut: The Roper Center for Public Opinion Research.

    2010. "USABCWP.121310A.R20." University of Connecticut: The Roper Center for Public Opinion Research.

Abramowitz, Alan I. 2010. *The Disappearing Center.* New Haven, CT: Yale University Press.

Abramowitz, Alan I., and Kyle L. Saunders. 1998. "Ideological Realignment in the U.S. Electorate." *Journal of Politics* 60 (3):634–52.

    2008. "Is Polarization a Myth?" *Journal of Politics* 70 (2):542–55.

Adams, Greg. 1997. "Abortion: Evidence of Issue Evolution." *American Journal of Political Science* 41 (3):718–37.

Adams, John. 1790. "Discourses on Davila." *Gazette of the United States.*

Adams, Val. 1963. "TV: Coverage of March." *New York Times,* March 29.

AIDS.gov. 2014. "A Timeline of AIDS" [accessed March 11, 2015]. Available at www.aids.gov/hiv-aids-basics/hiv-aids-101/aids-timeline/.

Akaike, Hirotogu. 1973. "Information Theory and the Extension of the Maximum Likelihood Principle." Paper presented at the 2nd International Symposium on Information Theory, Budapest.

Aldrich, John H. 1983. "A Downsian Spatial Model with Party Activism." *American Political Science Review* 77 (4):974–90.

    1995. *Why Parties?* Chicago, IL: University of Chicago Press.

Aldrich, John H., and David W. Rohde. 2000. "The Consequences of Party Organization in the House: The Role of the Majority and Minority Parties in Conditional Party Government." In *Polarized Politics: Congress and the President in a Partisan Era,* ed. J. R. Bond and R. Fleischer. Washington, DC: Congressional Quarterly Press.

2001. "The Logic of Conditional Party Government: Revisiting the Electoral Connection." In *Congress Reconsidered*, 7th ed., ed. L. C. Dodd and B. I. Oppenheimer. Washington, DC: CQ Press.

Alsop, Stewart. 1964. "Can Goldwater Win?" *Saturday Evening Post*, July 20, 19–24.

Alston, Lee J. 1983. "Farm Foreclosures in the United States during the Interwar Period." *Journal of Economic History* 43 (4):885–903.

Altschuler, Glenn C., and Stuart M. Blumin. 2009. *The GI Bill: A New Deal for Veterans*. New York: Oxford University Press.

Ambrose, Steven E. 1984. *Eisenhower the President*. New York: Simon and Schuster.

1990. *Eisenhower: Soldier and President*. New York: Simon and Schuster.

American Experience. 1990a. *Nixon*. Washington, DC: Public Broadcasting System.

1990b. *Nixon: Domestic Politics*. Washington, DC: Public Broadcasting System.

Americans for Tax Reform. 2015. *About Americans for Tax Reform*. Americans for Tax Reform [accessed February 10, 2015]. Available at www.atr.org/about.

Anderson, Sarah, and Philip Habel. 2009. "Revisiting Adjusted ADA Scores for the U.S. Congress, 1947–2007." *Political Analysis* 17 (1):83–88.

Anderson, Terry. 2004. *The Pursuit of Fairness*. New York: Oxford University Press.

ANES. 2015. *ANES Time Series Cumulative Data File Codebook*. electionstudies.org [accessed February 26, 2015]. Available at www.electionstudies.org/studypages/cdf/cdf.htm.

Ansolabehere, Stephen Jr., James M. Snyder, and Charles Steward III. 2001a. "Candidate Positioning in U.S. House Elections." *American Journal of Political Science* 45 (1):136–59.

2001b. "The Effects of Party and Preferences on Congressional Roll-Call Voting." *Legislative Studies Quarterly* 26 (4):533–72.

Ansolabehere, Stephen, Jonathan Rodden, and James M. Snyder Jr. 2006. "Purple America." *Journal of Economic Perspectives* 20 (2):97–118.

ARL. 1984. *Congress Defeats School Prayer Amendment, "Equal Access."* Americans for Religious Liberty [accessed October 20, 2014]. Available at www.arlinc.org/newsletters/1984-2-12.pdf.

Aronson, Sidney. 1964. *Status and Kinship in the Higher Civil Service*. Cambridge, MA: Harvard University Press.

Ashford, Nicholas Askounes. 1976. *Crisis in the Workplace: Occupational Disease and Injury*. Cambridge, MA: MIT Press.

Austin-Smith, David, and Jeffrey Banks. 1988. "Elections, Coalitions, and Legislative Outcomes." *American Political Science Review* 82 (2):405–22.

Azzalini, A., and A. Capitano. 2003. "Distributions Generated by Perturbation of Symmetry with Emphasis on a Multivariate Skew-t Distribution." *Journal of the Royal Statistical Society B* (65):367–89.

Bagby, Wesley M. 1962. *The Road to Normalcy: The Presidential Campaign and Election of 1920*. Baltimore: Johns Hopkins Press.

Bailey, Michael A. 2012. *Measuring Court Preferences, 1950–2011: Agendas, Polarity, and Heterogeneity*. Washington, DC: Georgetown University.

Baker, Wayne. 2006. *America's Crisis of Values: Reality and Perception*. Princeton, NJ: Princeton University Press.

Ball, Howard. 2006. *Hugo L. Black: Cold Steel Warrior*. New York: Oxford University Press.

Ballotpedia. 2016. *United States House of Representatives, 2016*. The Encyclopedia of American Politics [accessed March 15, 2016]. Available at http://ballotpedia.org/United_States_House_of_Representatives_elections.

Balmer, Randall. 2007. *Thy Kingdom Come: How the Religious Right Distorts Faith and Threatens America*. New York: Basic Books.

Bancroft Library. 2014. *Slaying the Dragon of Debt: Fiscal Politics and Policy from the 1970s to the Present*. University of California, Berkeley [accessed December 16, 2014]. Available at http://bancroft.berkeley.edu/ROHO/projects/debt/government shutdown.html.

Bank, Steven A., Kirk J. Stark, and Joseph J. Thorndike. 2008. *War and Taxes*. Washington, DC: Urban Institute Press.

Barga, Michael. 2014. *The Long Depression (1873–1878)*. The Social Welfare History Project. Available at www.socialwelfarehistory.com/eras/the-long-depression/.

Barlett, Bruce. 2014. "How LBJ Pushed through the Kennedy Tax Cut." *New York Times*, February 14.

Bartels, Larry M. 2006. "What's the Matter with What's the Matter with Kansas?." *Quarterly Journal of Political Science* 1 (1):201–26.

2008. *Unequal Democracy: The Political Economy of the New Gilded Age*. Princeton, NJ: Princeton University Press and Russell Sage Foundation.

Bass, S. Jonathan. 2001. *Blessed Are the Peacemakers: Martin Luther King, Jr., Eight White Religious Leaders and the "Letter from Birmingham Jail."* Baton Rouge: Louisiana State University Press.

Beard, Charles A. 1913. *An Economic Interpretation of the Constitution of the United States*. New York: The Free Press.

Bell, Barbara Currier. 2013. *Looking Back on Environmental Moves in November 1963*. Milford Mirror [accessed June 4, 2014]. Available at www.milfordmirror.com/10422/looking-back-on-environmental-moves-in-november-1963/.

Benoit, Kenneth. 2006. "Duverger's Law and the Study of Electoral Systems." *French Politics* 4 (1):69–83.

Bensen, Lee. 1961. *Turner and Beard: American Historical Writing Reconsidered*. New York: The Free Press.

Bercovitch, Sacvan, ed. 2003. *The Cambridge History of American Literature*, vol. 5: *Poetry and Criticism, 1900–1950*. Cambridge University Press.

Bernanke, Ben S. 2000. "Nonmonetary Effects of the Financial Crisis in the Propagation of the Great Depression." In *Essays on the Great Depression*, ed. B. S. Bernanke. Princeton, NJ: Princeton University Press.

Bernstein, Irving. 1991. *Promises Kept: John F. Kennedy's New Frontier*. New York: Oxford University Press.

2013. "Chapter 5: Americans in Depression and War." In *History at the Department of Labor*. Washington, DC: Department of Labor.

Bernstein, Samuel. 1956. "American Labor in the Long Depression, 1873–1878." *Science & Society* 20 (1):59–83.

Beschloss, Michael. 2007. *Presidential Courage: Brave Leaders and How They Changed America 1789–1989*. New York: Simon and Schuster.

Best, Gary Dean. 1991. *Pride, Prejudice, and Politics: Roosevelt versus Recovery, 1933–1938*. New York: Praeger.

Binder, Sarah A. 2003. *Stalemate: Causes and Consequences of Legislative Gridlock.* Washington, DC: Brookings Institution.

Bishop, Bill. 2009. *The Big Sort.* New York: Mariner Books.

Black, Earl, and Merle Black. 2002. *The Rise of Southern Republicans.* Cambridge, MA: Belknap Press of Harvard University Press.

Blackwell, Christopher W. 2003. *The Development of Athenian Democracy,* ed. A. Mahoney and R. Scaife. The Stoa: A Consortium for Electronic Publication in the Humanities [www.stoa.org]. Available at www.stoa.org/projects/demos/democ racy_development.pdf.

Blais, André, and Stephane Dion, eds. 1991. *The Budget Maximizing Bureaucrat: Appraisals and Evidence.* Pittsburgh, PA: University of Pittsburgh Press.

Bomze, I. 1983. "Lotka–Volterra Equation and Replicator Dynamics: A Two-Dimensional Classification." *Biological Cybernetics* 48:447–53.

Borrelli, Stephen A. 2001. "Finding the Third Way: Bill Clinton, the DLC, and the Democratic Platform of 1992." *The Journal of Policy History* 13 (4):429–62.

Bound, John, and Sarah Turner. 2002. "Going to War and Going to College: Did World War II and the G.I. Bill Increase Educational Attainment for Returning Veterans?" *Journal of Labor Economics* 20 (4):784–815.

Boyd, James. 1970. "Nixon's Southern Strategy 'It's All in the Charts.'" *New York Times,* 25, 105–11.

Bradford, Charles H. 1981. "The Department of Commerce." In *Mandate for Leadership: Policy Management in a Conservative Administration,* ed. C. L. Heatherly. Washington, DC: The Heritage Foundation.

Brady, David W. 2010. "Party Coalitions in the US Congress: Intra- v. Interparty." In *The Oxford Handbook of American Political Parties and Interest Groups,* ed. L. S. Maisel, J. M. Berry, and G. C. Edwards III. New York: Oxford University Press.

Brady, David W., and Hahrie C. Han. 2006. "Polarization Then and Now." In *Red and Blue Nation?,* ed. P. S. Nivola and D. W. Brady. Palo Alto, CA, and Washington, DC: Brookings/Hoover.

Brewer, Mark D., Mark D. Mariani, and Jeffrey M. Stonecash. 2002. "Northern Democrats and Party Polarization in the House." *Legislative Studies Quarterly* 27 (August):423–44.

Brody, Richard A. 1991. *Assessing the President: The Media, Elite Opinion, and Public Support.* Palo Alto, CA: Stanford University Press.

Brokaw, Tom. 2001. *The Greatest Generation.* New York: Random House.

Brown, Richard D. 1976. "The Founding Fathers of 1776 and 1787." *William and Mary Quarterly* 33:465–80.

Brown, Robert E. 1956. *Charles Beard and the Constitution: A Critical Analysis of "An Economic Interpretation of the Constitution."* Princeton, NJ: Princeton University Press.

Bryan, William Jennings. 1896. *A Cross of Gold.* American Rhetoric, Online Speech Bank [accessed February 6, 2016]. Available at www.americanrhetoric.com/ speeches/williamjenningsbryan1896dnc.htm.

Bryce, James. 1888. *The American Commonwealth.* Liberty Fund ed., 3 vols. New York: Macmillan, vol. 2.

Buchanan, James M. 1977. "Democracy in Deficit: The Political Legacy of Lord Keynes." In *Collected Works of James M. Buchanan,* ed. D. R. Henderson. Indianapolis, IN: Library of Economics and Liberty.

2015. "James M. Buchanan (1919–2013)." In *Concise Encyclopedia of Economics,* ed. D. R. Henderson. Indianapolis, IN: Library of Economics and Liberty.

Buchanan, James M., and Gordon Tullock. 1961. *The Calculus of Consent: Logical Foundations of Constitutional Democracy.* Ann Arbor: University of Michigan Press.

Budge, Ian, and Richard Hofferbert. 1990. "Mandates and Policy Outputs: US Party Platforms and Federal Expenditures." *American Political Science Review* 84 (1):111–31.

Burden, Barry C., and David C. Kimball. 2002. *Why Americans Split Their Tickets.* Ann Arbor: University of Michigan Press.

Bureau of Economic Analysis. 2014a. *Gross Domestic Product.* St. Louis: Federal Reserve Bank of St. Louis.

2014b. "Gross Domestic Product (GDPA)." In *Gross Domestic Product.* Washington, DC: U.S. Department of Commerce.

2014c. "Gross Private Domestic Investment (GDPIA)." In *Gross Domestic Product.* Washington, DC: U.S. Department of Commerce.

2014d. "Personal Consumption Expenditures (PCECA)." In *Gross Domestic Product.* Washington, DC: U.S. Department of Commerce.

2014e. "Personal Income Per Capita (A792RC0A052NBEA)." In *Gross Domestic Product.* Washington, DC: U.S. Department of Commerce.

Bureau of Labor Statistics. 2012. "Employment Status of the Civilian Population." In *The 2012 Statistical Abstract: Historical Statistics.* Washington, DC: U.S. Department of Commerce.

2014a. *Consumer Price Index Data from 1913 to 2014.* Bureau of Labor Statistics [accessed July 25, 2014]. Available at www.usinflationcalculator.com/inflation/consumer-price-index-and-annual-percent-changes-from-1913-to-2008/.

2014b. *Labor Force Statistics from the Current Population Survey.* Bureau of Labor Statistics [accessed July 25, 2014]. Available at http://data.bls.gov/timeseries/LNS14000000.

Bureau of the Census. 1940, 1960. *Census of Population and Housing.* U.S. Census Bureau [accessed February 10, 2014]. Available at www.census.gov/newsroom/cspan/1940census/CSPAN_1940slides.pdf.

1970. "Death Rate, for Selected Causes: 1900 to 1970." *In Vital Statistics on Health and Medical Care.* Washington, DC: U.S. Census Bureau.

1976. "Historical Statistics of the United States." Department of Labor. Washington, DC.

2014a. *Current Population Survey.* U.S. Census Bureau [accessed February 10, 2014]. Available at www.census.gov/hhes/socdemo/education/data/cps/historical/index.html.

2014b. *A Look at the 1940 Census.* U.S. Census Bureau [accessed February 10, 2014]. Available at www.census.gov/newsroom/cspan/1940census/CSPAN_1940slides.pdf.

Burnham, Walter Dean. 1970. *Critical Elections and the Mainsprings of American Politics.* New York: W. W. Norton.

Burns, Ric. 1999. *New York: A Documentary Film.* Washington, DC: Public Broadcasting System.

Burt, Martha R. 2010. "Causes of the Growth of Homelessness during the 1980s." *Housing Policy Debate* 2 (3):901–36.

Bush, George H. W. 1988. *Address Accepting the Presidential Nomination at the Republican National Convention in New Orleans, August 18.* The American Presidency Project [accessed December 11, 2014]. Available at www.presidency.ucsb.edu/ws/?pid=25955.

Bush, George W. 2000. *Governor George W. Bush – Acceptance Speech, Philadelphia, PA, August 3, 2000*. 4President.us [accessed February 2, 2015]. Available at www.4president.org/speeches/bushcheney2000convention.htm.

Caldeira, Gregory A. 1987. "Public Opinion and the U.S. Supreme Court: FDR's Court-Packing Plan." *American Political Science Review* 81 (4):1139–53.

Calhoun, Daniel. 1979. "Continual Vision and Cosmopolitan Orthodoxy." *History and Theory* 18 (3):257–86.

Calmes, Jackie. 2008. "In Bailout Vote, a Leadership Breakdown." *New York Times*, September 29.

Cambridge Reports. 1980. "USCAMREP.80OCT.R203." University of Connecticut: The Roper Center for Public Opinion Research.

Campbell, Angus, Philip Converse, Warren Miller, and Donald Stokes. 1960. *The American Voter*. New York: Wiley.

Canes-Wrone, Brandice. 2006. *Who Leads Whom? Presidents, Policy, and the Public*. Chicago, IL: University of Chicago Press.

Canes-Wrone, Brandice, and Kenneth W. Shotts. 2004. "The Conditional Nature of Presidential Responsiveness to Public Opinion." *American Journal of Political Science* 48 (Oct.):690–706.

Canes-Wrone, Brandice, Michael C. Herron, and Kenneth W. Schotts. 2001. "Leadership and Pandering: A Theory of Executive Policymaking." *American Journal of Political Science* 45 (July):532–50.

Cannadine, David. 2006. *Mellon: An American Life*. New York: Knopf.

Caputo, Richard K. 2011. *U.S. Social Welfare Reform*. New York: Springer.

Carmines, Edward G., and James A. Stimson. 1980. "The Racial Reorientation of American Politics." In *The Electorate Reconsidered*, ed. J. C. Pierce and J. L. Sullivan. Beverly Hills, CA: Sage.

   1981. "Issue Evolution, Population Replacement, and Normal Partisan Change." *American Political Science Review* 75 (1):107–18.

   1984. "The Dynamics of Issue Evolution: The United States." In *Electoral Change in Industrial Democracies*, ed. R. J. Dalton, P. A. Beck, and S. C. Flanagan. Princeton, NJ: Princeton University Press.

   1986. "On the Structure and Sequence of Issue Evolution." *American Political Science Review* 80:902–21.

   1989. *Issue Evolution: Race and the Transformation of American Politics*. Princeton, N.J.: Princeton University Press.

Carsey, Thomas, and Geoffrey Layman. 2006. "Changing Sides or Changing Minds? Party Identification and Policy Preference in the American Electorate." *American Journal of Political Science* 50 (1):464–77.

Carson, Clayborne. 1998. *Autobiography of Martin Luther King*. New York: Warner Books.

CBS News. 2008. *Poll: U.S. Concerned but Split on Bailout: CBS News Survey Shows That Americans Fear Effects of Financial Crisis But Are Not Convinced Bailout Plan Is the Answer*. CBS News.

CBS News/*New York Times*. 1980a. "USCBS.102980.R06A." University of Connecticut: The Roper Center for Public Opinion Research.

   1980b. "USCBSNYT.80ELEC.RG." University of Connecticut: The Roper Center for Public Opinion Research.

CDC. 2001. "*MMWR: Morbidity and Mortality Weekly Report.*" Washington, DC: Centers for Disease Control and Prevention.

Center for the Study of the Pacific Northwest. 2013. *Lesson Fifteen: Industrialization, Class, and Race: Chinese and the Anti-Chinese Movement in the Late 19th-Century Northwest.* Center for the Study of the Pacific Northwest [accessed May 31, 2013]. Available at www.washington.edu/uwired/outreach/cspn/Website/Classroom Materials/Pacific Northwest History/Lessons/Lesson 15/15.html.

Chamberlain, Kenneth. 2012. "Resignation, Retirement, and Reelection: How the 112th Congress Compares with the 111th." *National Journal*, December 3, 2012.

Chang, Roberto. 1997. "Is Low Unemployment Inflationary?" Economic Review, *Federal Reserve Bank of Atlanta* 1997 (1):4–13.

Chen, Edwin. 1995. "Gingrich: Today's Medicare Will 'Wither.'" *Los Angeles Times*, October 26.

Chernow, Ron. 2004. *Alexander Hamilton.* New York: Penguin.

Clarfield, Gerard. 1975. "Protecting the Frontiers: Defense Policy and the Tariff Question in the First Washington Administration." *William and Mary Quarterly* 32 (July):443–64.

Clermont, Betty. 2009. *The Neo-Catholics: Implementing Christian Nationalism in America.* Atlanta, GA: Clarity Press.

Cleveland, Grover. 1888. *Annual State of the Union.* The American Presidency Project [accessed November 20, 2012]. Available at www.presidency.ucsb.edu/ws/index .php?pid=29529.

Clinton, Joshua D., Simon Jackman, and Douglas Rivers. 2004. "The Statistical Analysis of Roll Call Data." *American Political Science Review* 98 (2):355–70.

Clinton, William Jefferson. 1992. *Presidential Debate in East Lansing, Michigan, October 19, 1992.* The American Presidency Project [accessed December 11, 2014]. Available at www.presidency.ucsb.edu/ws/index.php?pid=21625.

Clymer, Adam. 1980. "Displeasure with Carter Turned Many to Reagan." *New York Times*, November 9.

CNN Interactive. 2014. "The Budget Battle" [accessed December 16, 2014]. Available at www.cnn.com/US/9512/budget/budget_battle/index.html.

Coffey, Daniel. 2011. "More Than a Dime's Worth: Using State Party Platforms to Assess the Degree of American Party Polarization." *PS: Political Science and Politics* 44 (2):331–37.

Cohen, Adam Seth. 2009. *Nothing to Fear: FDR's Inner Circle and the Hundred Days That Created Modern America.* New York: Penguin.

Cohen, Robert. 2003. *Dear Mrs. Roosevelt: Letters from Children of the Great Depression.* Chapel Hill: University of North Carolina Press.

Cohen, Tom. 2012. "In Polarized Washington, Two Worlds Apart." In *CNN Politics.* Washington, DC: CNN.

Collier, Kenneth. 1994. "Eisenhower and Congress: The Autopilot Presidency." *Presidential Studies Quarterly* 24 (Spring):309–25.

Combs, Jerald A. 1970. *The Jay Treaty: Political Battleground of the Founding Fathers.* Berkeley: University of California Press.

Commager, Henry Steele. 1958. "The Constitution: Was It an Economic Document?" *American Heritage* 10 (Dec.):58–61.

Congressional Budget Office. 2012. *Estimated Impact of the American Recovery and Reinvestment Act on Employment and Economic Output from October 2011 through December 2011*. Washington, DC: Congressional Budget Office.

Connelly, Marjorie. 1994. "Portrait of the Electorate: Who Voted for Whom in the House." *New York Times*, November 13, 1.

Converse, Philip. 1964. "The Nature of Belief Systems in Mass Publics." In *Ideology and Discontent*, ed. D. Apter. New York: Free Press.

Coolidge, Calvin. 1925. "Address to the American Society of Newspaper Editors, January 17, 1925." In *Public Papers of the Presidents*. Washington, DC: U.S. Government Printing Office.

Cooper, Michael L. 2004. *Dust to Eat: Drought and Depression in the 1930s*. New York: Clarion Books.

Council of Economic Advisors. 2014. "Gross Federal Debt." In *Economic Report of the President*. Washington, DC: The White House.

Cowan, Bill. 2016. "*Barack Obama Interview with Bill Cowan*." CBS News.

Cowen, David J., Richard Sylla, and Robert E. Wright. 2006. "The U.S. Panic of 1792: Financial Crisis Management and the Lender of Last Resort." NBER DAE Summer Institute, July 2006, and XIV International Economic History Congress, Session 20, "Capital Market Anomalies in Economic History." Helsinki, Finland.

CQ Almanac Online. 1950a. *Minimum Wages*. CQ Almanac. Available at http://library.cqpress.com/cqalmanac/cqal49-1400347.

1950b. *Minimum Wages Housing Act of 1949 S 1070 – P.L. 171*. CQ Almanac [accessed February 3, 2014]. Available at http://library.cqpress.com/cqalmanac/cqal49-1399761.

1951. *Social Security Act*. CQ Almanac [accessed February 19, 2014]. Available at http://library.cqpress.com/cqalmanac/cqal50-1377221.

1954. *What the 83rd Congress Did*. CQ Almanac [accessed March 3, 2014]. Available at http://library.cqpress.com/cqalmanac/document.php?id=cqal54-1360607.

1961. *Congress 1961*. CQ Almanac [accessed February 9, 2014]. Available at http://library.cqpress.com/cqalmanac/cqal61-1372531.

1962. *Congress 1962 – The Year in Review*. CQ Almanac [accessed March 3, 2014]. Available at http://library.cqpress.com/cqalmanac/cqal62-1325714.

1963. *Congress 1963 – The Year in Review*. CQ Almanac [accessed June 22, 2014]. Available at http://library.cqpress.com/cqalmanac/cqal63-1316541.

1964. *Congress 1964 – The Year in Review*. CQ Almanac [accessed February 23, 2014]. Available at http://library.cqpress.com/cqalmanac/cqal64-1303830.

1965. *Congress 1965 – The Year in Review*. CQ Almanac [accessed July 19, 2014]. Available at http://library.cqpress.com/cqalmanac/cqal65-1258600.

1966. *Congress 1966 – The Year in Review*. CQ Almanac [accessed April 7, 2014]. Available at http://library.cqpress.com/cqalmanac/cqal66-1300992.

1967. *Congress 1967 – The Year in Review*. CQ Almanac [accessed June 29, 2014]. Available at http://library.cqpress.com/cqalmanac/cqal67-1313941.

1968. *Congress 1968 – The Year in Review*. CQ Almanac [accessed June 11, 2014]. Available at http://library.cqpress.com/cqalmanac/cqal68-1283260.

1969. *President Makes Changes in Government Machinery*. CQ Almanac [accessed July 22, 2014]. Available at http://library.cqpress.com/cqalmanac/document.php?id=cqal69-871-26652-1245901.

1970a. *Environmental Quality Council.* CQ Almanac [accessed July 22, 2014]. Available at http://library.cqpress.com/cqalmanac/cqal69-1248484.

1970b. *Welfare Reform: Disappointment for the Administration.* CQ Almanac [accessed July 22, 2014]. Available at http://library.cqpress.com/cqalmanac/cqal70-1292329.

1971. *Major Anti-Pollution Measures Clear 91st Congress.* CQ Almanac [accessed July 22, 2014]. Available at http://library.cqpress.com/cqalmanac/cqal70-1292699.

1973a. *Clean Water: Congress Overrides Presidential Veto.* CQ Almanac [accessed July 22, 2014]. Available at http://library.cqpress.com/cqalmanac/cqal72-1249049.

1973b. *Coastal Zone Management Bill Clears in 1972.* CQ Almanac [accessed July 22, 2014]. Available at http://library.cqpress.com/cqalmanac/cqal72-1249717.

1973c. *Congress Approves Moratorium on Sea Mammal Killing.* CQ Almanac [accessed July 22, 2014]. Available at http://library.cqpress.com/cqalmanac/cqal72-1249699.

1973d. *Congress Clears Nixon's Revenue-Sharing Plan.* CQ Almanac [accessed July 22, 2014]. Available at http://library.cqpress.com/cqalmanac/cqal72-1251510.

1973e. *Ocean Pollution.* CQ Almanac [accessed July 22, 2014]. Available at http://library.cqpress.com/cqalmanac/cqal72-1249016.

1974a. *Compromise Manpower Training and Jobs Bill Cleared.* CQ Almanac [accessed July 22, 2014]. Available at http://library.cqpress.com/cqalmanac/cqal73-1228346.

1974b. *Enactment of the War Powers Law over Nixon's Veto.* CQ Almanac [accessed July 22, 2014]. Available at http://library.cqpress.com/cqalmanac/cqal73-1227822.

1975. *Congress Reforms Budget Procedures.* CQ Almanac [accessed July 22, 2014]. Available at http://library.cqpress.com/cqalmanac/cqal74-1224091.

1981. *Congress Enacts President Reagan's Tax Plan.* CQ Almanac [accessed October 16, 2014]. Available at http://library.cqpress.com/cqalmanac/document.php?id=cqal81-1171841&type=toc&num=6.

1986. *Congress Enacts Sweeping Overhaul of Tax Law.* CQ Almanac [accessed October 16, 2014]. Available at http://library.cqpress.com/cqalmanac/document.php?id=cqal86-1149342.

1993. "Deficit-Reduction Bill Narrowly Passes." *In Congressional Quarterly Almanac.* Washington, DC: Congressional Quarterly.

1995. *GOP Throws Down Budget Gauntlet.* CQ Almanac [accessed December 16, 2014]. Available at http://library.cqpress.com/cqalmanac/document.php?id=cqal95-1099934.

1998a. "Reconciliation Package: Spending Cuts." In *Congressional Quarterly Almanac.* Washington, DC: Congressional Quarterly.

1998b. "Reconciliation Package: Tax Cuts." In *Congressional Quarterly Almanac.* Washington, DC: Congressional Quarterly.

Crain, W. Mark, and Robert D. Tollison. 1979. "The Executive Branch in the Interest Group Theory of Government." *Journal of Legal Studies* 8 (June):555–67.

Currie, David P. 1990. *The Constitution in the Supreme Court: The Second Century, 1888–1986.* Chicago, IL: University of Chicago Press.

Cushman, Barry. 2012. "The Limits of the New Deal Analogy." In *Notre Dame Law School Legal Studies.* South Bend, IN: Notre Dame Law School.

Daily Advertiser 1820. *Journal of Debates and Proceedings in the Convention of Delegates Chosen to Revise the Constitution of Massachusetts.* Boston: Boston Daily Advertiser.

Danziger, Sheldon. 1997. *America Unequal*. Cambridge, MA: Harvard University Press.

Davis, G. Cullom. 1962. "The Transformation of the Federal Trade Commission, 1914–1929." *Mississippi Valley Historical Review* 49 (3):437–55.

Davis, James A., and Tom W. Smith. 1986. *General Social Survey, 1972–1986: Cumulative Codebook*. National Opinion Research Center.

Davis, Mike. 2000. *Prisoners of the American Dream: Politics and the Economy in the History of the U.S. Working Class*. New York: W. W. Norton.

Davis, O.A., and Melvin A. Hinich. 1966. "A Mathematical Model of Policy Formulation in a Democratic Society." In *Mathematical Applications in Political Science II*, ed. J. L. Bernd. Dallas, TX: Southern Methodist University Press.

Davis, O.A., Melvin A. Hinich, and Peter Ordeshook. 1970. "An Expository Development of a Mathematical Model of the Electoral Process." *American Political Science Review* 64 (2):426–48.

de Rugy, Veronique. 2003. "Tax Rates and Tax Revenue: The Mellon Income Tax Cuts of the 1920s." In *Tax and Budget Bulletin*. Washington, DC: Cato Institute.

Dean, John W. 2012. "The Politics of Polarization and Obstructionism." *Verdict: Legal Analysis and Commentary from Justicia*, November 16.

Deaton, Angus. 2013. *The Great Escape: Health, Wealth, and the Origins of Inequality*. Princeton, NJ: Princeton University Press.

——— 2014. "Inequality and Rent-seeking: An Interview with Angus Deaton." In *Demographics*, ed. R. Rolfes. New York: GFG: The GailFosler Group.

Deeben, John P. 2012. "Family Experiences and New Deal Relief." *National Archives Prologue Magazine* 44 (2):1–10.

Democratic National Committee. 1912. *Democratic Party Platform*. Democratic Party. Available at www.presidency.ucsb.edu/ws/index.php?pid=29590.

DeNavas-Walt, Carmen, Bernadette D. Proctor, and Jessica C. Smith. 2013. "Income, Poverty, and Health Insurance Coverage in the United States: 2012." In *Current Population Reports*, P60–245. Washington, DC: U.S. Census Bureau.

Dennis, Jonathan G. 2006. *CATS in RATS: Cointegration Analysis of Time Series Version 2*. Evanston, IL: Estima.

Department of Labor. 2014. *The Job Safety Law of 1970: Its Passage Was Perilous*. U.S. Department of Labor [accessed July 19, 2014]. Available at www.dol.gov/dol/aboutdol/history/osha.htm.

Department of State. 2014. *The Postwar Economy: 1945–1960*. U.S. Department of State [accessed April 3, 2014]. Available at http://countrystudies.us/united-states/history-114.htm.

Diggins, John Patrick. 1981. "Power and Authority in American History: The Case of Charles Beard and His Critics." *American Historical Review* 86 (October): 701–30.

Diggs-Brown, Barbara. 2011. *Strategic Public Relations: Audience Focused Practice*. Boston: Cengage Learning: Wadsworth.

Dike-Wilhelm, Steven. 2006. "Works Progress Administration." In *Encyclopedia of U.S. Labor and Working-Class History*, ed. E. Arneson. New York: Routledge.

DiMaggio, Paul, John Evans, and Bethany Bryson. 1996. "Have American's Social Attitudes Become More Polarized?" *American Journal of Sociology* 102 (3): 690–755.

Doan, Thomas A. 2014. *RATS Version 9*. Evanston, IL: Estima.

Docksai, Ronald F. 1981. "The Department of Education." In *Mandate for Leadership: Policy Management in a Conservative Administration*, ed. C. L. Heatherly. Washington, DC: The Heritage Foundation.

Doherty, Thomas. 2014. *Assassination and Funeral of President John F. Kennedy*. The Museum of Broadcast Communications [accessed May 29, 2014]. Available at www.museum.tv/eotv/kennedyjf.htm.

Dorsen, Norman. 2006. "The Selection of Supreme Court Justices." *International Journal of Constitutional Law* 4 (4):652–63.

Douglas, Susan Jeanne, and Meredith Michaels. 2005. *The Mommy Myth: The Idealization of Motherhood and How It Has Undermined All Women*. New York: Simon and Schuster.

Douglass, John Aubrey. 2000. "Earl Warren's New Deal: Economic Transition, Postwar Planning, and Higher Education in California." *Journal of Policy History* 12 (4): 473–512.

Downs, Anthony. 1957. *An Economic Theory of Democracy*. New York: Harper and Row.

Draper, Robert. 2012. *Do Not Ask What Good We Do: Inside the House of Representatives*. New York: Simon and Schuster.

Dreier, Peter. 2004. *Reagan's Legacy: Homelessness in America*. National Housing Institute [accessed October 17, 2014]. Available at www.nhi.org/online/issues/135/reagan.html.

Dubin, Michael J. 2002. *United States Presidential Elections 1788–1860*. Jefferson, NC: McFarland.

Duverger, Maurice. 1951. *Les partis politique*. Paris: Librairie Armand Collin.

  1972. "Factors in a Two-Party and Multiparty System." In *Party Politics and Pressure Groups*, ed. M. Duverger. New York: Thomas Y. Crowell.

Ebenstein, Alan O. 2007. *Milton Friedman: A Biography*. New York: Macmillan.

Eckert, Allan W. 1995. *That Dark and Bloody River*. New York: Bantam Books.

Econ Journal Watch. 2007. "Economists against Smoot-Hawley." *Econ Journal Watch* 4(3):345–58 [accessed May 23, 2013]. Available at http://econjwatch.org/articles/economists-against-smoot-hawley.

Edwards, George C. III. 1989. *At the Margins: Presidential Leadership of Congress*. New Haven: Yale University Press.

Edwards, George C. III, and Andrew Barrett. 2000. "Presidential Agenda Setting in Congress." In *Polarized Politics: Congress and the President in a Partisan Era*, ed. J. R. Bond and R. Fleisher. Washington, DC: Congressional Quarterly Press.

Edwards, Lee. 1997. *The Power of Ideas*. Ottawa, IL: Jameson Books.

Edwards, Rebecca. 2014. *Silver Party Platform* [accessed March 15, 2014]. Available at http://projects.vassar.edu/1896/silverparty.html.

Eichengreen, Barry J. 1995. *Golden Fetters: The Gold Standard and the Great Depression, 1919–1939*. New York: Oxford University Press.

Eisenhower, Dwight David. 1954. *Annual Message to the Congress on the State of the Union, January 7, 1954*. The American Presidency Project [accessed March 30, 2014]. Available at www.presidency.ucsb.edu/ws/index.php?pid=10096.

  1955. *Annual Message to the Congress on the State of the Union, January 6, 1955*. The American Presidency Project [accessed March 30, 2014]. Available at www.presidency.ucsb.edu/ws/index.php?pid=10416.

1956. *Annual Message to the Congress on the State of the Union, January 5, 1956.* The American Presidency Project [accessed March 30, 2014]. Available at www .presidency.ucsb.edu/ws/index.php?pid=10704.

1963. *Mandate for Change, 1953–1956.* New York: Doubleday.

1996. "To Milton Stover Eisenhower, 9 October 1953." In *The Papers of Dwight David Eisenhower,* ed. L. Galambos. Baltimore, MD: Johns Hopkins University Press.

Eisner, Marc. 2000. *Regulatory Politics in Transition.* Baltimore, MD: Johns Hopkins University Press.

Elkins, Stanley, and Eric McKitrick. 1993. *The Age of Federalism.* New York: Oxford University Press.

Ellis, Christopher, and James A. Stimson. 2009. "Symbolic Ideology in the American Electorate." *Electoral Studies* 28 (3):388–402.

Ellis, Joseph J. 2002. *Founding Brothers: The Revolutionary Generation.* New York: Vintage.

Elwell, Craig K. 2011. *A Brief History of the Gold Standard in the United States.* Washington, DC: Congressional Research Service.

Enelow, James M., and Melvin J. Hinich. 1981. "A New Approach to Voter Uncertainty in the Downsian Spatial Model." *American Journal of Political Science* 25 (3):483–93.

1982. "Ideology, Issues, and the Spatial Theory of Elections." *American Political Science Review* 76 (3):493–501.

1984. *The Spatial Theory of Voting: An Introduction.* New York: Cambridge University Press.

Engemann, Kristie M. 2014. *Banking Panics of 1931–33.* Federal Reserve Bank of St. Louis [accessed March 18, 2014]. Available at www.federalreservehistory.org/ Events/DetailView/21.

Engle, Robert F. III, and Clive W. J. Granger. 1987. "Co-Integration and Error Correction: Representation, Estimation, and Testing." *Econometrica* 55 (Mar.):251–76.

Erikson, Robert S., and Kent L. Tedin. 1981. "The 1928–1936 Partisan Realignment: The Case for the Conversion Hypothesis." *American Political Science Review* 75 (4):951–62.

Erikson, Robert S., Michael B. MacKuen, and James A. Stimson. 2002. *The Macro Polity.* New York: Cambridge University Press.

Ermentrout, Robert Allen. 1982. *Forgotten Men: The Civilian Conservation Corps.* Pompano Beach, FL: Exposition Phoenix Press.

Everitt, Bryan S., and Torsten Hothorn. 2009. *A Handbook of Statistical Analyses Using R,* 2nd ed. Boca Raton, FL: Chapman and Hall.

Fairlie, Henry. 1973. *The Kennedy Promise: The Politics of Expectation.* New York: Doubleday.

Federal Highway Administration. 2014. "Table MV-200." In *Highway Statistics, Summary to 1995.* Washington, DC: U.S. Federal Highway Administration.

Federal Register. 1981. *Executive Order 12291 – Federal Regulation.* Washington, DC: Federal Register.

2014. *Federal Register & CFR Publication Statistics – Aggregated Charts.* Washington, DC: Federal Register.

Feinerer, I. 2008. "An Introduction to Text Mining in R." *R News* 8 (2):19–22.

Feinerer, I., K. Hornik, and D. Meyer. 2008. "Text Mining Infrastructure in R." *Journal of Statistical Software* 25 (5):1–54.

Fels, Rendigs. 1949. "The Long-Wave Depression, 1873–97." *Review of Economics and Statistics* 31 (1):69–73.

Ferling, John. 1992. *John Adams: A Life*. New York: Oxford University Press.

Ferrie, Joseph P. 2013. "Table Ac414–418 – Change in the Farm Population through Births, Deaths, and Migration: 1920–1970." In *Historical Statistics of the United States: Millennial Edition Online*: Cambridge University Press.

Fetter, Daniel K. 2014. "The 20th-Century Increase in US Home Ownership: Facts and Hypotheses." In *Housing and Mortgage Markets in Historical Perspectives*, ed. E. White, K. Snowden, and P. Fishback. Chicago, IL: University of Chicago Press.

Fine, Terri Susan. 1994. "Lobbying from Within: Government Elites and the Framing of the 1988 Democratic and Republican Platforms." *Presidential Studies Quarterly* 24 (4):844–63.

Fiorina, Morris P., and Samuel J. Abrams. 2009. *Disconnect: The Breakdown of Representation in American Politics*. Norman: University of Oklahoma Press.

Fiorina, Morris P., and Mattthew S. Levendusky. 2006. "Disconnected: The Political Class versus the People." In *Red and Blue Nation? Characteristics and Causes of America's Polarized Politics*, ed. P. S. Nivola and D. W. Brady. Washington, DC: Brookings Institution Press.

Fiorina, Morris, Samuel J. Abrams, and Jeremy C. Pope. 2011. *Culture War?: The Myth of a Polarized America*, 3rd ed. New York: Longman.

Fleischer, Richard, and Jon R. Bond. 2000a. "Congress and the President in a Partisan Era." In *Polarized Politics*, ed. J. R. Bond and R. Fleisher. Washington, DC: CQ Press.

2000b. "Partisanship and the President's Quest for Votes on the Floor of Congress." In *Polarized Politics*, ed. J. R. Bond and R. Fleisher. Washington, DC: CQ Press.

2001. "Evidence of Increasing Polarization among Ordinary Citizens." In *American Political Parties: Decline or Resurgence?*, ed. R. F. Jeffrey, E Cohen, and Paul Kantor. Washington, DC: CQ Press.

2004. "The Shrinking Middle in the U.S. Congress." *British Journal of Political Science* 34 (3):419–51.

Foner, Eric. 1995. *Free Soil, Free Labor, Free Men: The Ideology of the Republican Party before the Civil War*. New York: Oxford University Press.

2006. *Give Me Liberty! An American History*. New York: W. W. Norton.

Foner, Philip S. 1986. *May Day: A Short History of the International Workers' Holiday, 1886–1986*. New York: International Publishers.

Ford, Gerald R. 1974a. *Address to a Joint Session of the Congress on the Economy, October 8, 1974*. The American Presidency Project [accessed August 21, 2014]. Available at www.presidency.ucsb.edu/ws/?pid=4434.

1974b. *Proclamation 4311 – Granting Pardon to Richard Nixon, September 8, 1974*. The American Presidency Project [accessed August 20, 2014]. Available at www.presidency.ucsb.edu/ws/?pid=4696.

1975. *Proclamation 4383 – Women's Equality Day, 1975, August 26, 1975*. The American Presidency Project [accessed August 21, 2014]. Available at www.presidency.ucsb.edu/ws/?pid=23839.

Ford, Henry. 1930. "Ford Lays Slump to Era of Laziness: Promises Renewed Prosperity with World-Wide Return to Love of Toil." *New York Times*, October 3.

1931. "Good Times Here, Henry Ford Avers: Nation Is Prosperous but Only a Few Know It." *New York Times*, March 15.

FoxNews.com. 2011. "Nebraska Sen. Ben Nelson Announces Retirement." *Fox News*.

Francis, Louise, and Matt Flynn. 2010. "Text Mining Handbook." In *Casualty Actuarial Society*. Arlington, VA: E-Forum.

Frank, Thomas. 2004. *What's the Matter with Kansas?* New York: Henry Holt.

Freedman, Russell. 2005. *Children of the Great Depression*. New York: Clarion Books.

Freeman, John R., Daniel Hauser, Paul Kellstedt, and John Williams. 1998. "Long-Memoried Processes, Unit Roots, and Causal Inference in Political Science." *American Journal of Political Science* 42 (4):1289–327.

Friedman, Milton. 1960. *A Program for Monetary Stability*. New York: Fordham University Press.

   1990. "The Crime of 1873." *Journal of Political Economy* 98 (Dec.):1159–94.

Friedman, Milton, and Rose Friedman. 1980. *Free to Choose: A Personal Statement*. New York: Harcourt Brace Jovanovich.

Friedman, Milton, and Simon Kuznets. 1945. *Income from Independent Professional Practice*. National Bureau of Economic Research [accessed September 23, 2014]. Available at http://papers.nber.org/books/frie54-1.

Friedman, Milton, and Jacobson Schwartz. 1963. *A Monetary History of the United States, 1867–1960*. Princeton, NJ: Princeton University Press.

Friedman, Milton, and George J. Stigler. 1946. *Roofs or Ceilings? The Current Housing Problem*. Irvington on Hudson, NY: Foundation for Economic Education.

Frum, David. 2000. *How We Got Here: The 70s the Decade That Brought You Modern Life – For Better or Worse*. New York: Basic Books.

Fuelner, Edwin J. Jr. 1981. "Forward." In *Mandate for Leadership: Policy Management in a Conservative Administration*, ed. C. L. Heatherly. Washington, DC: The Heritage Foundation.

Galbraith, John Kenneth. 2009. *The Great Crash, 1929*. New York: Houghton Mifflin Harcourt.

Gales, Joseph. 1834. *Debates and Proceedings in the Congress of the United States, March 3, 1789–March 3, 1791*. Edited by J. Gales. Vol. 2. Washington, DC: Gales and Seaton.

Gallup. 1968a. "Gallup Poll #758." University of Connecticut: The Roper Center for Public Opinion Research.

   1968b. "Gallup Poll #1968–0765: 1968 Presidential Election." University of Connecticut: The Roper Center for Public Opinion Research.

   1968c. "USGALLUP.769.Q17." University of Connecticut: The Roper Center for Public Opinion Research.

   1980a. "USGALLUP.1162.Q09B." University of Connecticut: The Roper Center for Public Opinion Research.

   1980b. "USGALLUP.1163.Q07C." University of Connecticut: The Roper Center for Public Opinion Research.

   2014. *Presidential Job Approval Center: Key Statistics*. Gallup, Inc. Available at www.gallup.com/poll/124922/Presidential-Approval-Center.aspx.

Gayner, Jeffrey. 1995. *The Contract with America: Implementing New Ideas in the U.S.* The Heritage Foundation [accessed December 12, 2014]. Available at www.heritage.org/research/lecture/the-contract-with-america-implementing-new-ideas-in-the-us.

Gergen, David, and Michale Zuckerman. 2012. "What's Wrong with American Politics." *CNN Opinion*. Washington, DC: CNN.

Gimpel, James A., and Jason E. Schuknecht. 2003. *Patchwork Nation: Sectionalism and Political Change in American Politics*. Ann Arbor: University of Michigan Press.

Ginsberg, Benjamin. 1972. "Critical Elections and the Substance of Party Conflict, 1844–1968." *Midwest Journal of Political Science* 16 (4):603–25.

Ginsberg, Benjamin 1976. "Elections and Public Policy." *American Political Science Review* 70 (1):41–49.

Gittinger, Ted, and Allen Fisher. 2004a. "LBJ Champions the Civil Rights Act of 1964." *Prologue Magazine*.

——— 2004b. "LBJ Champions the Civil Rights Act of 1964, Part 2." *Prologue Magazine*.

Glass, Andrew. 2007. "When the GOP Torpedoed Nixon." *Politico*.

Goldberg, R. A. 1997. *Barry Goldwater*: New Haven: Yale University Press.

Goldwater, Barry M. 1960. *Conscience of a Conservative*. New York: Victor Publishing.

Good, Chris. 2012. *Norquist's Tax Pledge: What It Is and How It Started*. ABC News [accessed December 11, 2014]. Available at http://abcnews.go.com/blogs/politics/2012/11/norquists-tax-pledge-what-it-is-and-how-it-started/.

Goodwin, Richard N. 1995. *Remembering America: A Voice from the Sixties*. New York: HarperCollins.

Gordon, David. 2010. "Southern Cross." *The American Conservative*, April 1.

Gore, Albert W. 2000. *Al Gore 2000 on the Issues, ECONOMY*. 4President.us [accessed February 2, 2015]. Available at www.4president.us/issues/gore2000/gore2000economy.htm.

Gould, Lewis L. 1980. *The Presidency of William McKinley*. Lawrence: University of Kansas Press.

——— 2003. *Grand Old Party: A History of the Republicans*. New York: Random House.

Graff, Henry F. 2002. *Grover Cleveland*. New York: Time Books.

Grafton, Carl, and Anne Permaloff. 2004. "Supplementing Zupan's Measurements of the Ideological Preferences of U.S. Presidents." *Public Choice* 118 (January):125–31.

Greenburg, Jan Crawford. 2007. *Supreme Conflict: The Inside Story of the Struggle for Control of the United States Supreme Court*. New York: Penguin Books.

Greene, John Robert. 2000. *The Presidency of George W. Bush*. Lawrence: University Press of Kansas.

Groseclose, Tim, Steven D. Levitt, and James M. Snyder Jr. 1999. "Comparing Interest Group Scores across Time and Chambers: Adjusted ADA Scores for the U.S. Congress." *American Political Science Review* 93 (1):33–50.

Grunwald, Michael. 2012a. *The New New Deal: The Hidden Story of Change in the Obama Era*. New York: Simon and Schuster.

——— 2012b. "The Party of No." *Time*, September 3.

GSS. 2015. *General Social Survey Cumulative File Codebook*. National Opinion Research Center [accessed February 26, 2015]. Available at www3.norc.org/GSS+Website/Browse+GSS+Variables/Mnemonic+Index/.

Hadden, Jeffrey. 1993. "The Rise and Fall of American Televangelism." *Annals of the American Academy of Political and Social Science* 527 (May):113–30.

Haider-Markel, Donald P. 1998. "Political Parties, U. S." In *Encyclopedia of AIDS: A Social, Political, Cultural and Scientific Record of the HIV Epidemic*, ed. R. A. Smith. Chicago, IL: Fitzroy-Dearborn.

Hall, Joe. 1962. "JFK Scored So-So with 87th Congress." *Eugene Register-Guard*, October 14, 37.

Hamilton, Alexander. 1790a. *First Report on Public Credit*. American State Papers, House of Representatives, 1st Congress, 2nd Session [accessed September 13, 2012]. Available at http://memory.loc.gov/cgi-bin/ampage?collId=llsp&fileName= 009/llsp009.db&recNum=19.

1790b. *Second Report on Public Credit*. American State Papers, House of Representatives, 1st Congress, 3rd Session [accessed September 13, 2012]. Available at http:// memory.loc.gov/cgi-bin/ampage?collId=llsp&fileName=009/llsp009.db&recNum=19.

1791a. *Opinion on the Constitutionality of the National Bank*. Yale Law School [accessed September 13, 2012]. Available at http://avalon.law.yale.edu/18th_cen tury/bank-ah.asp.

1791b. *Report on Manufactures* [accessed September 12, 2012]. Available at www .constitution.org/ah/rpt_manufactures.pdf.

1904a. "Hamilton to Jay Cabinet Paper, May 6, 1794." In *The Works of Alexander Hamilton*, ed. H. C. Lodge. New York: G. P. Putnam's Sons.

1904b. "Points to Be Considered in the Instructions to Mr. Jay, Envoy Extraordinary to Great Britain, April 23, 1794." In *The Works of Alexander Hamilton*, ed. H. C. Lodge. New York: G. P. Putnam's Sons.

1904c. *The Works of Alexander Hamilton*, ed. H. C. Lodge. 12 vols. New York: G. P. Putnam's Sons, vol. 2.

Hamilton, Alexander, and Rufus King. 1904. "Camillus." In *The Works of Alexander Hamilton*, ed. H. C. Lodge. New York: G. P. Putnam's Sons.

Hammond, Michael E. 1981. "The Department of Justice." In *Mandate for Leadership: Policy Management in a Conservative Administration*, ed. C. L. Heatherly. Washington, DC: The Heritage Foundation.

Hannan, E. J., and B. G. Quinn. 1979. "The Determination of the Order of an Autoregression." *Journal of the Royal Statistical Society* B41:190–95.

Hansen, Mogens Herman. 1999. *The Athenian Democracy in the Age of Demosthenes: Structure, Principles, and Ideology*. Norman: University of Oklahoma Press.

Harris. 1974a. "Harris Survey, Sep, 1974." University of Connecticut: The Roper Center for Public Opinion Research.

1974b. "iPoll Question Details, Impeach the President." In *iPoll Databank*. University of Connecticut: Roper Center.

Harris, Richard A., and Sidney M. Milkis. 1996. *The Politics of Regulatory Change: A Tale of Two Agencies*. New York: Oxford University Press.

Hartley, William B. 1969. *Estimation of the Incidence of Poverty in the United States, 1870–1914*. Economics, University of Wisconsin, Madison, WI.

Heath, Jim F. 1975. *Decade of Disillusionment: The Kennedy-Johnson Years*. Bloomington: Indiana University Press.

Heatherly, Charles L., ed. 1981. *Mandate for Leadership: Policy Management in a Conservative Administration*. Washington, DC: The Heritage Foundation.

Hechler, Ken, and George M. Elsey. 2006. "The Greatest Upset in American Political History: Harry Truman and the 1948 Election." *White House Studies* 6 (1):83–94.

Heilbroner, Robert, and Aaron Singer. 1999. *The Economic Transformation of America: 1600 to Present*, 4th ed. New York: Harcourt, Brace.

Heilbroner, Robert, and William Milberg. 2012. *The Making of Economic Society*, 13th ed. New York: Pearson.

Helderman, Rosalind S. 2012. "Retiring Rep. Steve LaTourette: You Have to 'hand over your wallet and your voting card' to Extremes." *Washington Post*, July 31.

Henderson, David R., ed. 2008. "Milton Friedman (1912–2006)." In *The Concise Encyclopedia of Economics*. Indianapolis, IN: Liberty Fund.

———. 2016. *Rent Seeking*. Library of Economics and Liberty [accessed January 12, 2016]. Available at www.econlib.org/library/Enc/RentSeeking.html.

Hetherington, Marc J. 2001. "Resurgent Mass Partisanship: The Role of Elite Polarization." *American Political Science Review* 95 (3):619–31.

———. 2009. "Review Article: Putting Polarization in Perspective." *British Journal of Political Science* 39 (2):413–48.

Hetherington, Marc J., and Jonathan D. Weiler. 2009. *Authoritarianism and Polarization in American Politics*. New York: Cambridge University Press.

Hibbs, Douglas A. 1982. "President Reagan's Mandate from the 1980 Elections: A Shift to the Right?" *American Politics Research* 10 (4):387–420.

Higgs, Robert. 2005. *Government and the Economy: The World Wars*. The Independent Institute [accessed November 20, 2012]. Available at www.independent.org/pdf/working_papers/59_government.pdf.

Hill, William. 1893. "Protective Purpose of Tariff Act of 1789." *Journal of Political Economy* 2 (1):54–76.

Himmelstein, Jerome L. 1989. *To the Right: The Transformation of American Conservatism*. Berkeley: University of California Press.

Himmelstein, Jerome L., and James A. McRae Jr. 1984. "Social Conservatism, New Republicans, and the 1980 Election." *The Public Opinion Quarterly* 48 (3):592–605.

Hinish, James E. 1981. "Regulatory Reform: An Overview." In *Mandate for Leadership: Policy Management in a Conservative Administration*, ed. C. L. Heatherly. Washington, DC: The Heritage Foundation.

Hoagland, William. 1984. "Perception and Reality in Nutrition Programs." In *Maintaining the Safety Net*, ed. J. C. Weicher. Washington, DC: American Enterprise Institute.

Hogeland, W. 2006. *The Whiskey Rebellion: George Washington, Alexander Hamilton, and the Frontier Rebels Who Challenged America's Newfound Sovereignty*. New York: Scribner.

Holt, Michael F. 2003. *The Rise and Fall of the American Whig Party: Jacksonian Politics and the Onset of the Civil War*. New York: Oxford University Press.

Hood, J. Larry. 1993. "The Nixon Administration and the Revised Philadelphia Plan for Affirmative Action: A Study in Expanding Presidential Power and Divided Government." *Presidential Studies Quarterly* 23 (1):145–67.

Hoover, Herbert. 1928. *The New Day: Campaign Speeches of Herbert Hoover, 1928*. Palo Alto, CA: Stanford University Press.

Hoover, Herbert. 1930. "Speech to the American Bankers Association, October 3, 1930." In *Public Papers of the Presidents*. Washington, DC: U.S. Government Printing Office.

———. 1931. "Address to the Indiana Republican Editorial Association at Indianapolis, June 15, 1931." In *Public Papers of the Presidents*. Washington, DC: U.S. Government Printing Office.

1932. "Annual Message to the Congress on the State of the Union. December 6." In *Public Papers of the Presidents*. Washington, DC: U.S. Government Printing Office.

Horner, William T. 2010. *Ohio's Kingmaker: Mark Hanna, Man and Myth*. Athens: Ohio University Press.

Hovde, Ellen, and Muffie Myer. 2004. *"Liberty! The American Revolution."* Twin Cities Public Television for the Public Broadcasting System.

2009. *The Crash of 1929*. Documentary. Washington, DC: Public Broadcasting System.

Howe, Daniel Walker. 1984. *The Political Culture of the American Whigs*. Chicago, IL: University of Chicago Press.

Hudson, Deal W. 2008. *Onward, Christian Soldiers: The Growing Political Power of Catholics and Evangelicals in the United States*. New York: Simon and Schuster.

Hughes, Jonathan R. T. 1991. *The Governmental Habit Redux*. Princeton, NJ: Princeton University Press.

Hunter, James Davidson. 1991. *Culture Wars: The Struggle to Define America*. New York: Harper-Collins.

Hunter, James Davidson, and Alan Wolfe. 2006. *Is There a Culture War? A Dialogue*. Washington, DC: Brookings Institution Press.

Hunter, Robert. 1904. *Poverty*. New York: Macmillan.

Hunter, Robert P. 1981. "The Department of Labor." In *Mandate for Leadership: Policy Management in a Conservative Administration*, ed. C. L. Heatherly. Washington, DC: The Heritage Foundation.

Hutson, James H. 1984. "The Creation of the Constitution: Scholarship at a Standstill." *Reviews in American History* 12 (Dec.):463–77.

Ingram, Frederick C. 2001. "National Rifle Association of America." In *International Directory of Company Histories*. New York: Encyclopedia.com.

Internal Revenue Service. 2013. *Corporation Income Tax Brackets and Rates, 1909–2002*. Internal Revenue Service [accessed May 29, 2013]. Available at www.irs.gov/pub/irs-soi/02corate.pdf.

Irwin, Douglas A. 2003. *The Aftermath of Hamilton's "Report on Manufactures."* Cambridge, MA: National Bureau of Economic Research.

Jackson, Robert Houghwout. 1979. *The Struggle for Judicial Supremacy: A Study of Crisis in American Power Politics*. New York: Octagon Books.

Jacobs, Lawrence R., and Robert Y. Shapiro. 2000. *Politicians Don't Pander*. Chicago, IL: University of Chicago Press.

Jacobson, Darien B., Brian G. Raub, and Barry W. Johnson. 2006. *The Estate Tax: Ninety Years and Counting*. Washington, DC: Internal Revenue Service.

Jacobson, Gary C. 2000. "Party Polarization in National Politics: The Electoral Connection." In *Polarized Politics: Congress and the President in a Partisan Era*, ed. J. R. Bond and R. Fleischer. Washington, DC: Congressional Quarterly Press.

Jeffers, H. Paul. 2000. *An Honest President: The Life and Presidencies of Grover Cleveland*. New York: William Morrow.

Jefferson, Thomas. 1791. *Jefferson's Opinion on the Constitutionality of the National Bank* [accessed September 12, 2012]. Available at http://avalon.law.yale.edu/18th_century/bank-tj.asp.

Jensen, Merrill. 1964. *The Making of the U.S. Constitution*. Princeton, NJ: Princeton University Press.

Jenson, Richard. 2001. "Democracy, Republicanism, and Efficiency, 1885–1930." In *Contesting Democracy: Substance and Structure in American Political History, 1775–2000*, ed. B. E. Shafer and A. J. Badger. Lawrence: University of Kansas Press.

Jeong, Gyung-Ho, Gary J. Miller, and Itai Sened. 2009. "Closing the Deal: Negotiating Civil Rights Legislation." *American Political Science Review* 103 (04):588–606.

Johansen, Soren. 1988. "Statistical Analysis of Cointegrating Vectors." *Journal of Economic Dynamics and Control* 12 (1):231–54.

1991. "Estimation and Hypothesis Testing of Cointegrating Vectors in Gaussian Vector Autoregressive Models." *Econometrica* 59:1551–80.

1994. "The Role of the Constant and Linear Terms in Cointegration Analysis of Non-Stationary Variables." *Econometric Reviews* 13 (2):205–29.

1995. *Likelihood-based Inference in Cointegrated Vector Autoregressive Models*. Oxford: Oxford University Press.

Johansen, Soren, and Katarina Juselius. 1990. "Maximum Likelihood Estimation and Inference on Cointegration, with Applications to the Demand for Money." *Oxford Bulletin of Economics and Statistics* 52 (2):169–210.

Johnson, Haynes. 2003. *Sleepwalking through History: America in the Reagan Years*. New York: W. W. Norton.

Johnson, Lyndon Baines. 1964a. *Annual Message to the Congress on the State of the Union, January 8, 1964*. The American Presidency Project [accessed May 28, 2014]. Available at www.presidency.ucsb.edu/ws/index.php?pid=26787.

1964b. *Remarks at the University of Michigan, May 22, 1964*. The American Presidency Project [accessed May 28, 2014]. Available at www.presidency.ucsb.edu/ws/?pid=26262.

1964c. *Remarks upon Signing the Economic Opportunity Act, August 20*. The American Presidency Project [accessed May 28, 2014]. Available at www.presidency.ucsb.edu/ws/?pid=26452.

Jones, Charles O. 1975. *Clean Air*. Pittsburgh, PA: University of Pittsburgh Press.

Jordan, Soren, Clayton Webb, and B. Dan Wood. 2014. "The President, Polarization, and the Party Platforms, 1944–2012." *The Forum* 12 (1):169–89.

Juselius, Katarina. 2006. *The Cointegrated VAR Model*. New York: Oxford University Press.

Kafer, Peter. 2004. *Charles Brockden Brown's Revolution and the Birth of American Gothic*. Philadelphia: University of Pennsylvania Press.

Kanazawa, Mark T., and Roger G. Noll. 1994. "The Origins of State Railroad Regulation: The Illinois Constitution of 1870." In *The Regulated Economy: A Historical Approach to Political Economy*, ed. C. Goldin and G. D. Libecap. Chicago, IL: University of Chicago Press.

Katz, Michael B., and Mark J. Stern. 2001. "Poverty in Twentieth Century America." In *America at the Millennium Project*. Philadelphia: University of Pennsylvania.

Kaufman, Bruce. 2010. "Chicago and the Development of Twentieth-Century Labor Economics." In *The Elgar Companion to the Chicago School of Economics*, ed. R. B. Emmett. Northampton, MA: Edward Elgar.

Keith, Bruce E., David B. Magleby, Candice J. Nelson, Elizabeth Orr, and Mark C. Westlye. 1992. *The Myth of the Independent Voter*. Berkeley: University of California Press.

Kennedy, John F. 1960. *The New Frontier*. American Rhetoric Online Speech Bank [accessed May 20, 2014]. Available at www.americanrhetoric.com/speeches/jfk1960dnc.htm.

——. 1961. *Inaugural Address, January 20, 1961*. The American Presidency Project. Available at www.presidency.ucsb.edu/ws/?pid=8032.

——. 1962. *Special Message to the Congress on Transportation, April 5, 1962*. The American Presidency Project. Available at www.presidency.ucsb.edu/ws/?pid=8587.

——. 1963a. *Radio and Television Report to the American People on Civil Rights, June 11, 1963*. The American Presidency Project. Available at www.presidency.ucsb.edu/ws/?pid=9271.

——. 1963b. *Special Message to the Congress on Improving the Nation's Health, February 7, 1963*. The American Presidency Project. Available at www.presidency.ucsb.edu/ws/?pid=9549.

Kenyon, Cecelia. 1955. "Men of Little Faith: The Anti-Federalists and the Nature of Representative Government." *William and Mary Quarterly* 12 (Jan.):3–43.

Keynes, John Maynard. 1936. *The General Theory of Employment, Interest, and Money*. New York: CreateSpace Independent Publishing Platform.

Keyserling, Leon H. 1960. "The Wagner Act: Its Origin and Current Significance." *George Washington Law Review* 29 (1960):199–233.

Keyssar, Alexander. 2009. *The Right to Vote: The Contested History of Democracy in the United States*. New York: Basic Books.

Kidd, Quentin. 2008. "The Real (Lack of) Difference between Republicans and Democrats: A Computer Word Score Analysis of Party Platforms, 1996–2004." *PS: Political Science and Politics* 41 (3):519–25.

Kimble, James J. 2006. *Mobilizing the Home Front: War Bonds and Domestic Propaganda*. Dallas: Texas A&M University Press.

King, Gary, and Michael Laver. 1993. "On Party Platforms, Mandates, and Government Spending." *American Political Science Review* 87 (3):774–50.

King, Larry. 2001. "The Best of Interviews with Gerald Ford." *CNN Transcripts*. New York: CNN.

Kleppner, Paul. 1973. "The Greenback and Prohibition Parties." In *History of U.S. Political Parties*, vol. 2: *1860–1910, The Gilded Age of Politics*, ed. A. M. J. Schlesinger. New York: Chelsea House/RR Bowker.

Kolko, Gabriel. 1965. *Railroads and Regulation, 1877–1916*. Princeton, NJ: Princeton University Press.

Kriner, Douglas L., and Andrew Reeves. 2015. *The Particularistic President: Executive Branch Politics and Inequality*. New York: Cambridge.

Krueger, Anne. 1974. "The Political Economy of the Rent-Seeking Society." *American Economic Review* 64 (3):291–303.

Krugman, Paul. 2007. "Who Was Milton Friedman?" *New York Review of Books*, 1–10.

Kyle, Richard. 2011. *Evangelicalism: An Americanized Christianity*. New Brunswick, NJ: Transaction.

Laffer, Arthur. 2013. *The Laffer Curve: Past, Present, and Future*. Heritage Foundation [accessed June 11, 2013]. Available at www.heritage.org/research/reports/2004/06/the-laffer-curve-past-present-and-future.

Landes, William M., and Richard A. Posner. 1975. "The Independent Judiciary in an Interest-Group Perspective." *Journal of Law and Economics* 18 (Dec.):875–901.

Layman, Geoffrey. 2001. *The Great Divide*. New York: Columbia University Press.

Layman, Geoffrey, and Thomas M. Carsey. 2002. "Party Polarization and 'Conflict Extension' in the American Electorate." *American Journal of Political Science* 46 (4):2002.

Layman, Geoffrey, Thomas Carsey, and Juliana Menasca Horowitz. 2006. "Party Polarization in American Politics: Characteristics, Causes, and Consequences." *Annual Review of Political Science* 2006 (9):83–110.

Lee, Francis. 2008. "Agreeing to Disagree: Agenda Content and Senate Partisanship, 1981–2004." *Legislative Studies Quarterly* 33 (2):199–222.

Leege, David C. 1995. *Religiosity Measures on the National Election Studies: A Guide to Their Use in Voting Studies*. American National Election Studies [accessed March 7, 2015]. Available at www.electionstudies.org/conferences/1995Values/1995Values_Leege.pdf.

Lernoux, Penny. 1989. "A Reverence for Fundamentalism." *The Nation*, 513–16.

Leuchtenburg, William E. 2006. "New Faces of 1946: An Unpopular President. A War-Weary People. In the Midterm Elections of 60 Years Ago, Voters Took Aim at Incumbents." *Smithsonian*.

Levendusky, Matthew. 2009a. "The Microfoundations of Mass Polarization." *Political Analysis* 17 (2):162–76.

Levendusky, Matthew. 2009b. *The Partisan Sort*. Chicago, IL: University of Chicago Press.

2013. "Party Polarization in American Politics." In *Oxford Bibliographies Online: Political Science*, ed. R. Valelly. New York: Oxford University Press.

Lewis, David E. 2003. *Presidents and the Politics of Agency Design*. Palo Alto, CA: Stanford University Press.

Lewis, Jack. 1985. *The Birth of EPA*. Environmental Protection Agency [accessed July 24, 2014]. Available at http://classic-web.archive.org/web/20060922192621/http://epa.gov/35thanniversary/topics/epa/15c.htm.

Library of Congress. 2013. *Thomas Jefferson: Establishing a Federal Republic*. Library of Congress [accessed December 30, 2013]. Available at www.loc.gov/exhibits/jefferson/jefffed.html.

Lipset, Seymore Martin, and Earl Raab. 1981. "The Election and the Evangelicals." *Commentary* 71 (3):25–31.

Lipset, Seymour Martin, and Earl Raab. 1973. *The Politics of Unreason: Right Wing Extremism in America, 1790–1970*. New York: Harper & Row.

Lockwood, B. 2008. "Pareto Efficiency." In *The New Palgrave Dictionary of Economics*, ed. S. N. Durlauf and L. E. Blume. Basingstoke: Palgrave Macmillan.

Loevy, Robert D. 1985. "The Presidency and Domestic Policy: The Civil Rights Act of 1964." In *The American Presidency*, ed. D. C. Kozak and K. N. Ciboski. Chicago, IL: Nelson Hall.

Longmore, Paul K. 1999. *The Invention of George Washington*. Charlottesville: University Press of Virginia.

Los Angeles Times Exit Poll. 1996. "USLAT.96EXIT.QN." University of Connecticut: The Roper Center for Public Opinion Research.

Lotka, A. J. 1910. "Contribution to the Theory of Periodic Reaction." *Journal of Physical Chemistry* 14 (3):271–74.

1920. "Analytical Note on Certain Rhythmic Relations in Organic Systems." *Proceedings of the National Academy of Science* 6:410–15.

Lutkepohl, Helmut. 2007. *Introduction to Multiple Time Series Analysis*. New York: Springer.

MacDonald, John. 1995. "Gingrich Has Difficulty Escaping Medicare Comments." *Hartford Courant*, November 11.

Macey, Jonathan R. 1987. "Competing Economic Views of the Constitution." *Faculty Scholarship Series*, Yale Law School Legal Scholarship Repository. New Haven, CT.

Macey, Jonathan R. 1988. "Transaction Costs and the Normative Elements of the Public Choice Model: An Application to Constitutional Theory." *Virginia Law Review* 74 (1):471–518.

Maclay, William. 1790. *The Journal of William Maclay: United States Senator from Pennsylvania, 1789–1791*. Maclay's Journal – Chapter XIV. Relations with France and the Excise [accessed September 14, 2012]. Available at http://memory.loc.gov/cgi-bin/ampage?collId=llmj&fileName=001/llmj001.db&recNum=394&itemLink=D?hlaw:1:./temp/~ammem_0A2T::%230010395&linkText=1.

Madison, James. 1787. *Notes on the Debates in the Federal Convention*. The Avalon Project [accessed September 12, 2012]. Available at http://avalon.law.yale.edu/subject_menus/debcont.asp.

Madison, James. 1788a. *The Structure of the Government Must Furnish the Proper Checks and Balances between the Different Departments, Independent Journal*. New Haven: The Avalon Project.

1788b. *The Union as a Safeguard against Domestic Faction and Insurrection (continued), Daily Advertiser*. New Haven: The Avalon Project.

Main, Jackson T. 1960. "Charles A. Beard and the Constitution: A Critical Review of Forrest McDonald's We the People." *William and Mary Quarterly* 17 (1):86–102.

1961. *The Antifederalists: Critics of the Constitution, 1781–1788*. Chapel Hill: University of North Carolina Press.

Maisel, L. Sandy. 1993. "The Platform-Writing Process: Candidate-Centered Platforms in 1992." *Political Science Quarterly* 108 (4):671–98.

Manley, John F. 1973. "The Conservative Coalition in Congress." *American Behavioral Scientist* 17 (2):223–47.

Mann, Robert. 2011. *Daisy Petals and Mushroom Clouds: LBJ, Barry Goldwater, and the Ad That Changed American Politics*. Baton Rouge: Louisiana State University Press.

Mann, Thomas, and Norman J. Ornstein. 2012. "Five Delusions about Our Broken Politics." *The American Interest*.

Markham, Jeremy W. 2002. *A Financial History of the United States*. 3 vols. New York: M. E. Sharpe, vol. 1.

Martin, Andrew D., and Kevin M. Quinn. 2002. "Dynamic Ideal Point Estimation via Markov Chain Monte Carlo for the U.S. Supreme Court, 1953–1999." *Political Analysis* 10 (2):134–53.

Martin, Andrew, Kevin Quinn, and Lee Epstein. 2004. "The Median Justice on the United States Supreme Court." *North Carolina Law Review* 83:1275–320.

Martin Luther King Research and Education Institute. 2014. *Watts Rebellion (Los Angeles, 1965)*. Martin Luther King, Jr. Research and Education Institute [accessed June 12, 2014]. Available at http://mlk-kpp01.stanford.edu/index.php/encyclopedia/encyclopedia/enc_watts_rebellion_los_angeles_1965/.

Mason, Robert. 2014. *The Republican Party and American Politics from Hoover to Reagan*. New York: Cambridge University Press.

Mayer, George H. 1967. *The Republican Party 1854–1966*, 2nd ed. New York: Oxford University Press.

McCarty, Nolan, Keith T. Poole, and Howard Rosenthal. 2008. *Polarized America: The Dance of Ideology and Unequal Riches*. Cambridge, MA: MIT Press.

McConnell, Grant. 1967. *The Modern Presidency*. New York: St. Martins Press.

McConnell, Mitch. 2010. "Mitch McConnell: Top Priority, Make Obama a One Term President" YouTube video, 0:07 [accessed March 3, 2017]. Available at www .youtube.com/watch?v=W-A09a_gHJc.

McCorkle, Pope. 1984. "The Historian as Intellectual: Charles Beard and the Constitution Reconsidered." *American Journal of Legal History* 28 (4):314–63.

McCullough, David. 1992. *Truman*. New York: Simon and Schuster.

2001. *John Adams*. New York: Simon and Schuster.

McDonald, Forest. 1958. *We the People: The Economic Origins of the Constitution*. Chicago, IL: University of Chicago Press.

1965. *E Pluribus Unum: The Formation of the American Republic, 1776–1790*. Boston: Houghton-Mifflin.

McDougall, Walter A. 2008. *Promised Land, Crusader State: The American Encounter with the World since 1776*. New York: Houghton Mifflin.

McElvaine, Robert S. 1993. *The Great Depression: America 1929–1941*. New York: Three Rivers Press.

2009. *Grand Theft Jesus: The Hijacking of Religion in America*. New York: Crown.

McFarland, Gerald W. 1975. *Mugwumps, Morals, and Politics, 1884–1920*. Amherst: University of Massachusetts Press.

McGuire, Robert A. 2003. *To Form a More Perfect Union: A New Economic Interpretation of the Constitution of the United States*. New York: Oxford University Press.

McGuire, Robert A., and Robert L. Ohsfeldt. 1984. "Economic Interests and the American Constitution: A Quantitative Rehabilitation of Charles A. Beard." *Journal of Economic History* 44 (2):509–19.

1986. "An Economic Model of Voting Behavior over Specific Issues at the Constitutional Convention of 1787." *Journal of Economic History* 46 (1):79–111.

1989. "Self-Interest, Agency Theory, and Political Voting Behavior: An Economic Model of Voting Behavior over Specific Issues at the Constitutional Convention of 1787." *American Economic Review* 79 (1):219–34.

McKinley, Albert Edward. 1905. *The Suffrage Franchise in the Thirteen English Colonies in America*. Philadelphia: University of Pennsylvania Press.

McThenia, Andrew W. Jr. 1973. "An Examination of the Federal Water Pollution Control Act of 1972." *Washington and Lee Law Review* 30 (2):195–222.

McWilliams, Wilson C. 1981. "The Meaning of the Election." In *The Election of 1980: Reports and Interpretations*, ed. G. M. Pomper and M. M. Pomper. New York: Chatham House.

Mellon, Andrew. 1924. *Taxation: The People's Business*. New York: Macmillan.

Merrill, Thomas W. 2003. "Childress Lecture: The Making of the Second Rehnquist Court: A Preliminary Analysis." *St. Louis University Law Journal* 47 (Spring): 569–620.

Meyer, Muffie. 2007. *Alexander Hamilton*. The American Experience. PBS.

Midgley, J. 1992. "Introduction: American Social Policy and the Reagan Legacy." *Journal of Sociology and Social Welfare* 19 (1):3–28.

Milkis, Sidney M., and Michael Nelson. 1999. *The American Presidency: Origins and Development*. Washington, DC: Congressional Quarterly Press.

Miller, John C. 1960. *The Federalists: 1789–1801*. New York: Harper and Row.

Miller, Steven P. 2014. "The Evangelical Presidency: The Reagan's Dangerous Love Affair with the Christian Right." *Salon*, May 18.

Miller Center. 2013. "Domestic Affairs." In *American President: Herbert Hoover (1874–1964)*, ed. D. E. Hamilton. Charlottesville, VA: The Miller Center.

———. 2014. *Essays on Harry S. Truman and His Administration*. Miller Center [accessed March 28, 2014]. Available at http://millercenter.org/president/truman/essays/biog raphy/1.

Miroff, Bruce. 1976. *Pragmatic illusions: The Presidential Politics of John F. Kennedy*. New York: McKay.

Moffitt, Robert, and Douglas A. Wolf. 1987. "The Effect of the 1981 Omnibus Budget Reconciliation Act on Welfare Recipients and Work Incentives." *Social Service Review* 61 (2):247–60.

MoJo News Team. 2012. "Full Transcript of the Mitt Romney Secret Video." September 19.

Monroe, Alan D. 1983. "American Party Platforms and Public Opinion." *American Journal of Political Science* 27 (1):27–42.

Moore, Charles, ed. 1927. *George Washington's Rules of Civility and Decent Behavior*. Boston: Houghton Mifflin.

Moore, Geoffrey H., and Victor Zarnowitz. 1986. "Appendix A: The Development and Role of the National Bureau of Economic Research's Business Cycle Chronologies." In *The American Business Cycle: Continuity and Change*, ed. R. J. Gordon. Chicago, IL: University of Chicago Press.

Morris, Charless. 2004. *The Blue Eagle at Work: Reclaiming Democratic Rights in the American Workplace*. Ithaca, NY: Cornell University Press.

Mouw, Ted, and Michael E. Sobel. 2001. "Culture Wars and Opinion Polarization: The Case of Abortion." *American Journal of Sociology* 106 (4):913–43.

Mundell, Robert A. 1971. *The Dollar and the Policy Mix*. Princeton, NJ: Princeton University.

Nathan, Richard P. 1983. *The Administrative Presidency*. New York: Wiley.

———. 2011. *Anniversary of President Nixon's National Television Address on the "New Federalism."* Yorba Linda, CA: Richard M. Nixon Library.

National Democratic Platform – Breckinridge Faction. 1860. *National (Southern) Democratic Platform (John C. Breckenridge)* [accessed March 12, 2015]. Available at www.ushist.com/general-information/1860_national_presidential_election_plat forms.shtml.

National Democratic Platform – Douglas Faction. 1860. *National (Northern) Democratic Platform (Stephen A. Douglas)* [accessed March 12, 2015]. Available at www.ushist.com/general-information/1860_national_presidential_election_platforms .shtml.

National Institute of Mental Health. 2014. *Important Events in NIMH History*. National Institute of Mental Health [accessed October 17, 2014]. Available at www.nih.gov/about/almanac/archive/1999/organization/nimh/history.html.

National Opinion Research Center. 1968. "*NORC Amalgam Study #4050.*" University of Connecticut: The Roper Center for Public Opinion Research.

NBC News/Associated Press. 1980. "USNBCAP.63.R04." University of Connecticut: The Roper Center for Public Opinion Research.

NBC News/*Wall Street Journal.* 1993. "*USNBCWSJ.93SEPT.R08C5.*" University of Connecticut: The Roper Center for Public Opinion Research.

NBER. 1954a. *Personal Saving for the United States, Series Q1074AUSQ163SNBR.* National Bureau of Economic Research [accessed February 6, 2014]. Available at www.nber.org/chapters/c2644.pdf.

———. 1954b. *Personal Saving for the United States, Series Q1091AUSQ027NNBR.* National Bureau of Economic Research [accessed February 6, 2014]. Available at www.nber.org/chapters/c2644.pdf.

———. 1957. *The Measurement and Behavior of Unemployment.* National Bureau of Economic Research [accessed February 6, 2014]. Available at www.nber.org/chapters/c2644.pdf.

———. 2013a. "Net Profits of All Corporations (Series ID: 09048)." *In NBER Macrohistory Database.* Washington, DC: National Bureau of Economic Research.

———. 2013b. "Number of Business Failures for the United States (Series ID: M09028USM474NNBR)." In *NBER Macrohistory Database.* Washington, DC: National Bureau of Economic Research.

———. 2014a. *Business Cycle Expansions and Contractions.* Washington, DC: Department of Commerce.

———. 2014b. "Number of Concerns in Business (A10030USA173NNBR)." In *NBER Macrohistory Database.* Washington, DC: National Bureau of Economic Research.

NCHLA. 2004. *Human Life Amendments: United States Congress (1973–2003).* National Committee for a Human Life Amendment [accessed October 20, 2014]. Available at www.nchla.org/datasource/idocuments/HLAhghlts.pdf.

Nesbitt, Robert C. 1985. "Labor." In *The History of Wisconsin*, vol. 3: *Urbanization and Industrialization, 1873–1993.* Madison: State Historical Society of Wisconsin.

Neuman, W. Lawrence. 1998. "Negotiated Meanings and State Transformation: The Trust Issue in the Progressive Era." *Social Problems* 45 (3):315–35.

Neustadt, Richard E. 1954. "Congress and the Fair Deal: A Legislative Balance Sheet." *Public Policy* 5 (1):349–81.

Nevins, Allan. 1932. *Grover Cleveland: A Study in Courage.* New York: Dodd, Mead.

New York Times. 1886. "Fatal War among Races: Irishmen and Italians Cracking Each Other's Skulls." *New York Times*, September 20.

Nichols, Roy F. 1948. *The Disruption of American Democracy: A History of the Political Crisis That Led Up to the Civil War.* New York: Macmillan.

Niskanen, William A. 1971. *Bureaucracy and Representative Government.* Chicago, IL: Aldine Press.

———. 1975. "Bureaucrats and Politicians." *Journal of Law and Economics* 18 (3):617–44.

Nixon, Richard M. 1969a. *Address to the Nation on Domestic Programs, August 8, 1969.* The American Presidency Project [accessed July 22, 2014]. Available at www.presidency.ucsb.edu/ws/?pid=2191.

———. 1969b. *Special Message to the Congress on Occupational Safety and Health, August 6, 1969.* The American Presidency Project [accessed July 24, 2014]. Available at www.presidency.ucsb.edu/ws/?pid=2181.

1969c. *Special Message to the Congress on Reform of the Federal Tax System, April 21, 1969.* The American Presidency Project [accessed July 22, 2014]. Available at www.presidency.ucsb.edu/ws/?pid=2010.

1969d. *Veto of the Federal Water Pollution Control Act Amendments of 1972, October 17, 1972.* The American Presidency Project [accessed July 22, 2014]. Available at www.presidency.ucsb.edu/ws/index.php?pid=3634&st=veto&st1=.

1970a. *Special Message to the Congress about Reorganization Plans to Establish the Environmental Protection Agency and the National Oceanic and Atmospheric Administration.* The American Presidency Project [accessed July 22, 2014]. Available at www.presidency.ucsb.edu/ws/index.php?pid=2575&st=environmental+protection+agency&st1.

1970b. *Special Message to the Congress on Environmental Quality, February 10, 1970.* The American Presidency Project [accessed July 22, 2014]. Available at www.presidency.ucsb.edu/ws/index.php?pid=2757.

1971a. *Annual Message to the Congress on the State of the Union, January 22, 1971.* The American Presidency Project [accessed July 23, 2014]. Available at www.presidency.ucsb.edu/ws/index.php?pid=3110.

1971b. *Special Message to the Congress on Consumer Protection, February 24, 1971.* The American Presidency Project [accessed July 23, 2014]. Available at www.presidency.ucsb.edu/ws/?pid=3321.

1972a. *Letter to the Senate Minority Leader about the Proposed Constitutional Amendment on Equal Rights for Men and Women, March 18, 1972.* The American Presidency Project [accessed February 16, 2016]. Available at www.presidency.ucsb.edu/ws/?pid=3777.

1972b. *Special Message to the Congress on Health Care, March 2, 1972.* The American Presidency Project [accessed July 26, 2014]. Available at www.presidency.ucsb.edu/ws/?pid=3757.

1972c. *Statement about Signing the Equal Employment Opportunity Act of 1972, March 25, 1972.* The American Presidency Project [accessed July 23, 2014]. Available at www.presidency.ucsb.edu/ws/?pid=3358.

Novak, Michael. 2012. "The Moral Imperative of a Free Economy." In *The 4% Solution: Unleashing the Growth America Needs.* George W. Bush Institute. New York: Crown Business.

Nuxoll, Elizabeth M. 2012. *Biographical Essay, John Jay.* Columbia University [accessed September 27, 2012]. Available at www.columbia.edu/cu/lweb/digital/jay/biography.html.

O'Brien, Denis. 1964. "Goldwater and the Republican Future." *The Tablet*, London: London Publishing, Inc., 5–7.

O'Connor, Alice. 2010. "Bringing the Market Back In: Philanthropic Activism and Conservative Reform." In *Politics and Partnerships: The Role of Voluntary Associations in America's Political Past and Present*, ed. E. S. Clemens and D. Guthrie. Chicago, IL: University of Chicago Press.

Office of the Clerk U.S. House of Representatives. 2012. *Party Divisions of the House of Representatives (1789 to Present).* House of Representatives [accessed September 18, 2012]. Available at http://artandhistory.house.gov/house_history/partyDiv.aspx.

Office of the Historian. 2014. *The Neutrality Acts, 1930s.* U.S. Department of State [accessed February 5, 2014]. Available at http://history.state.gov/milestones/1921-1936/neutrality-acts.

Officer, Lawrence H., and Samuel H. Williamson. 2013. Annual Inflation Rates in the United States, 1775–2013. Measuringworth.com [accessed March 11, 2014]. Available at www.measuringworth.com/inflation/.

Olmstead, Alan L., and Paul W. Rhode. 2013a. "Table Da1–13 – Farms – Number, Population, Land, and Value of Property: 1910–1999 [Annual]." In *Historical Statistics of the United States: Millennial Edition Online*: Cambridge University Press.

2013b. "Table Da578–579 – Farms Operated by Full Owners – Percent Mortgaged, and Mortgage Debt as a Percentage of Value of Land and Buildings: 1890–1961." In *Historical Statistics of the United States: Millennial Edition Online*: Cambridge University Press.

Olsen, Keith. 1973. "The G.I. Bill and Higher Education: Success and Surprise." *American Quarterly* 25 (5):596–610.

Oppenheimer, Bruce I. 2005. "Deep Red and Blue Congressional Districts." In *Congress Reconsidered*, 8th ed., ed. L. C. Dodd and B. I. Oppenheimer. Washington, DC: CQ Press.

Ortiz, Stephen R. 2009. *Beyond the Bonus March and GI Bill: How Veteran Politics Shaped the New Deal Era*. New York: NYU Press.

Ostrogorski, Moisy. 1964. *Democracy and the Organization of Political Parties*, vol. 2: *The United States*. New York: Quadrangle Books.

Paarlberg, Don. 1981. "The Department of Agriculture." In *Mandate for Leadership: Policy Management in a Conservative Administration*, ed. C. L. Heatherly. Washington, DC: The Heritage Foundation.

Packard, Jerrold M. 2003. *American Nightmare: The History of Jim Crow*. New York: St. Martins Griffin.

Paddock, Joel. 2010. "Ideological Polarization in a Decentralized Party System: Explaining Interstate Differences." *Social Science Journal* 47 (2010):710–22.

Page, Benjamin I., and Robert Y. Shapiro. 1985. "Presidential Leadership through Public Opinion." In *The Presidency and Public Policy Making*, ed. G. C. I. Edwards, S. A. Shull, and N. C. Thomas. Pittsburgh, PA: University of Pittsburgh Press.

1992. *The Rational Public: Fifty Years of Trends in American's Policy Preferences*. Chicago, IL: University of Chicago Press.

Parmet, Herbert S. 1983. *JFK: The Presidency of John F. Kennedy*. New York: Doubleday.

Patterson, James T. 1966. "A Conservative Coalition Forms in Congress, 1933–1939." *Journal of American History* 52 (4):757–72.

People's Party. 1892. *The Omaha Platform: Launching the Populist Party*. People's Party [accessed November 8, 2012]. Available at http://historymatters.gmu.edu/d/5361/.

Perlstein, Rick. 2001. *Before the Storm: Barry Goldwater and the Unmaking of the American Consensus*. New York: Nation Books.

Perrett, Geoffrey. 1985. *Days of Sadness, Years of Triumph: The American People, 1939–1945*. Vol. 1. Madison: University of Wisconsin Press.

Peters, Charles, and Timothy Noah. 2009. "Wrong Harry: Four Million Jobs in Two Years? FDR Did It in Two Months." *Slate*.

Peters, Gerhard, and John Wooley. 2012. *Political Party Platforms of Parties Receiving Electoral Votes: 1840–2012*. University of California, Santa Barbara [accessed December 10, 2012]. Available at www.presidency.ucsb.edu/platforms.php.

2013. *Voter Turnout in Presidential Elections*. University of California, Santa Barbara [accessed May 30, 2013]. Available at www.presidency.ucsb.edu/data/turnout.php.

Pew Research Center. 2008. *Economic Bailout: Public Remains Closely Divided Overall, but Partisan Support Shifts*. Pew Research Center for the People and the Press, October 6.

Phillips, A. William. 1958. "The Relation between Unemployment and the Rate of Change in Money Wage Rates in the United Kingdom, 1861–1957." *Economica* 25 (Nov.):283–99.

Phillips, P. C. B. 1995. "Fully Modified Least Squares and Vector Autoregression." *Econometrica* 63 (5):1023–78.

Piketty, Thomas, and Emanuel Saez. 2003. "Income Inequality in the United States, 1913–1998." *Quarterly Journal of Economics* 118 (1):1–39.

Piketty, Thomas, Emmanuel Saez, and Stefanie Stantcheva. 2011. "Optimal Taxation of Top Labor Incomes: A Tale of Three Elasticities." In *National Bureau of Economic Research Working Papers*. Cambridge, MA: National Bureau of Economic Research.

Pomper, Gerald M. 1981. "The Presidential Election." In *The Election of 1980: Reports and Interpretations*, ed. G. M. Pomper and M. M. Pomper. New York: Chatham House.

1988. *Voters, Elections, and Parties: The Practice of Democratic Theory*. New York: Transaction.

2003. "Parliamentary Government in the United States: A New Regime for a New Century." In *The State of the Parties*, ed. J. C. Green and R. Farmer. Lanham, MD: Rowman and Littlefield.

Pomper, Gerald M., and Susan Lederman. 1980. *Elections in America: Control and Influence in Democratic Politics*. New York: Longman.

Poole, Keith. 2014. *Nomination of Potter Stewart to Be Associate Justice of the Supreme Court*. GovTrack.US [accessed March 29, 2014]. Available at www.govtrack.us/congress/votes/86-1959/s58.

Poole, Keith, and Howard Rosenthal. 2012. *Voteview.com*. University of Georgia, Department of Political Science [accessed September 24, 2012]. Available at www.voteview.com.

2000. *Congress: A Political-Economic History of Roll Call Voting*. New York: Oxford University Press.

Popkin, Susan J. 2000. *The Hidden War: Crime and the Tragedy of Public Housing in Chicago*. Rutgers, NJ: Rutgers University Press.

Posner, Gerald. 2000. "The Fallacy of Nixon's Graceful Exit." *Salon*, November 10.

Posner, Richard A. 1974. "Theories of Economic Regulation." *Bell Journal of Economics and Management Science* 5 (2):335–58.

2007. *Economic Analysis of Law*. New York: Aspen.

Public Papers of the Presidents. 1971. *Letter to the Chairman of the Senate Committee on Commerce about Pending Product Safety Legislation, July 19, 1971*. Washington, DC: U.S. Government Printing Office.

1983. "Remarks at the Annual Convention of the National Association of Evangelicals in Orlando, Florida, March 8, 1983." Washington, DC: U.S. Government Printing Office.

1984a. *The President's News Conference, September 17, 1985*. Washington, DC: U.S. Government Printing Office.

1984b. *Remarks at an Ecumenical Prayer Breakfast in Dallas, Texas, August 23, 1984.* Washington, DC: U.S. Government Printing Office.

1984c. *Remarks at the Annual Convention of the National Religious Broadcasters, January 30, 1984.* Washington, DC: U.S. Government Printing Office.

R Project. 2015. *The R Project for Statistical Computing.* R Foundation. Available at www.r-project.org.

Rankin, Robert A. 1995. "President Vetoes GOP Budget Bill Clinton to Reveal His Own Plan Today." *Philadelphia Inquirer,* December 7.

Reagan, Ronald. 1964. *A Time for Choosing* [accessed November 20, 2012]. Available at http://millercenter.org/president/speeches/detail/3405.

1982. *Message to the Congress Transmitting a Proposed Constitutional Amendment on Prayer in School.* The American Presidency Project [accessed October 20, 2014]. Available at www.presidency.ucsb.edu/ws/?pid=42527.

1984. *Abortion and the Conscience of a Nation.* Nashville, TN: Thomas Nelson.

Reinhart, Gina, and Jennifer Victor. 2012. "Competing for the Platform: The Politics of Interest Group Influence on Political Party Platforms in the United States." 108th Annual Meeting of the American Political Science Association. New Orleans, LA.

Reitano, Joanne R. 1994. *The Tariff Question in the Gilded Age: The Great Debate of 1888.* University Park: Penn State University Press.

Republican National Committee. 1856. *Republican Party Platform.* Republican Party [accessed November 20, 2012]. Available at www.presidency.ucsb.edu/ws/index.php?pid=29619.

1860. *Republican Party Platform.* Republican Party [accessed November 20, 2012]. Available at www.presidency.ucsb.edu/ws/index.php?pid=29620.

1976. *Republican Party Platform, August 18, 1976.* The American Presidency Project [accessed July 22, 2014]. Available at www.presidency.ucsb.edu/ws/?pid=25843.

1980. *Republican Party Platform, July 15, 1980.* The American Presidency Project [accessed October 3, 2014]. Available at www.presidency.ucsb.edu/ws/?pid=25844.

1984. *Republican Party Platform, August 20, 1984.* The American Presidency Project [accessed October 3, 2014]. Available at www.presidency.ucsb.edu/ws/?pid=25845.

Revell, Keith D. 2000. "Cooperation, Capture, and Autonomy: The Interstate Commerce Commission and the Port Authority in the 1920s." *Journal of Policy History* 12 (2):177–214.

Ricci, David M. 1994. *The Transformation of American Politics: The New Washington and the Rise of Think Tanks.* New Haven, CT: Yale University Press.

Riker, William H. 1982. "The Two-Party System and Duverger's Law: An Essay on the History of Political Science." *American Political Science Review* 76 (Dec.):753–66.

1984. "The Heresthetics of Constitution-Making: The Presidency in 1787 with Comments on Determinism and Rational Choice." *American Political Science Review* 78 (Jan.):1–16.

Riker, William H., and Peter Ordeshook. 1973. *An Introduction to Positive Political Theory.* Englewood Cliffs, NJ: Prentice-Hall.

Rimmerman, Craig A. 1998. "Presidency, U.S." In *Encyclopedia of AIDS: A Social, Political, Cultural and Scientific Record of the HIV Epidemic,* ed. R. A. Smith. Chicago, IL: Fitzroy-Dearborn.

Robbins, James S. 2008. *Clinton Campaign Reminiscent of 1980 Race*. CBS News/ National Review Online [accessed October 7, 2014]. Available at www.cbsnews .com/news/clinton-campaign-reminiscent-of-1980-race/.

Roberts, Steven V. 1982. "Foes of Abortion Meet with Reagan." *New York Times*, January 23.

Rogers, Will. 1955. *Sanity Is Where You Find It*. Boston: Donald Day.

Rollins, Joe. 1998. "Politicians and Policymakers, U.S." In *Encyclopedia of AIDS: A Social, Political, Cultural and Scientific Record of the HIV Epidemic*, ed. R. A. Smith. Chicago, IL: Fitzroy-Dearborn.

Romer, Christina D. 1992. "What Ended the Great Depression?" *Journal of Economic History* 52 (4):757–84.

Roosevelt, Franklin D. 1933a. *Fireside Chat on Banking, March 12*. The American Presidency Project [accessed November 24, 2013]. Available at www.presidency .ucsb.edu/ws/index.php?pid=14540.

———1933b. *First Inaugural Address, March 4*. The American Presidency Project [accessed November 11, 2013]. Available at www.presidency.ucsb.edu/ws/index.php?pid= 14473.

———1941. *Fireside Chat 19: On the War with Japan (December 9, 1941)*. The American Presidency Project [accessed November 24, 2013]. Available at www.presidency .ucsb.edu/ws/?pid=16056.

Roper. 1974. *Roper Report 74-9, Sep, 1974*. University of Connecticut: The Roper Center for Public Opinion Research.

Rose, Charlie. 2012. "Charlie's Conversation with the President and First Lady." CBS News.

Rose, Jonathan D. 2013. "A Primer on Farm Mortgage Debt Relief Programs during the 1930s." In *Finance and Economics Discussion Series Divisions of Research and Statistics and Monetary Affairs*. Washington, DC: Federal Reserve Board.

Rosenof, Theodore. 1997. *Economics in the Long Run: New Deal Theorists and Their Legacies, 1933–1993*. Chapel Hill: University of North Carolina Press.

Rosensteil, Thomas B. 1992. "Clinton Commercial Rips Bush Tax Pledge." *Los Angeles Times*, October 3.

Rossi, Melissa. 2007. *What Every American Should Know about Who's Running America*. New York: Plume.

Rossiter, Clinton R. 1966. *1787: The Grand Convention*. New York: Macmillan.

Rozell, Mark J., Clyde Wilcox, and David Madland. 2006. *Interest Groups in American Campaigns: The New Face of Electioneering*. Washington, DC: CQ Press.

Rubin, Beth A., James D. Wright, and Joel A. Devine. 1992. "Unhousing the Urban Poor: The Reagan Legacy." *Journal of Sociology and Social Welfare* 19 (1):111–47.

Rude, George. 1964. *Revolutionary Europe: 1783–1815*. New York: Harper and Row.

Rusk, Jerrold G. 2002. *Statistical History of the American Electorate*. Washington, DC: CQ Press.

Rutland, Robert A. 1996. *The Republicans: From Lincoln to Bush*. Columbia: University of Missouri Press.

Saez, Emmanuel, and Gabriel Zuckman. 2016. "Wealth Inequality in the United States since 1913: Evidence from Capitalized Income Tax Data." *Quarterly Journal of Economics* 131(2):519–78.

Safire, William. 2008. *Safire's Political Dictionary*. New York: Oxford University Press.

Sanbonmatsu, Kira. 2006. *Where Women Run: Gender and Party in the United States.* Ann Arbor: University of Michigan Press.

Santoni, G.J. 1986. *The Employment Act of 1946: Some History Notes.* Federal Reserve Bank of St. Louis [accessed March 28, 2014]. Available at http://research.stlouisfed .org/publications/review/86/11/Employment_Nov1986.pdf.

Sartori, Giovanni. 1966. *European Political Parties: The Case of Polarized Pluralism,* ed. J. LaPalombara and M. Weiner. Princeton, NJ: Princeton University Press.

Schaffner, Brian F. 2011. "Party Polarization." In *The Oxford Handbook of the American Congress,* ed. E. Schickler and F. E. Lee. New York: Oxford University Press.

Schlesinger, Arthur M. Jr. 1945. *The Age of Jackson.* New York: Konecky and Konecky.

Schlesinger, Arthur M. 1945b. *The Age of Jackson.* Little, Brown.

1957. *The Crisis of the Old Order: 1919–1933, The Age of Roosevelt,* vol. 1. New York: Houghton-Mifflin.

1958. *The Coming of the New Deal.* Boston: Houghton-Mifflin.

1960. *The Politics of Upheaval.* Boston: Little, Brown.

1965. *A Thousand Days: John F. Kennedy in the White House.* Boston: Houghton Mifflin.

1973. *The Imperial Presidency.* Boston: Houghton Mifflin.

Schneider, William. 1981. "The November 4 Vote for President: What Did It Mean?" In *The American Election of 1980,* ed. A. Ranney. Washington, DC: American Enterprise Institute.

Schuldes, Martin. 2011. *Retrenchment in the American Welfare State: The Reagan and Clinton Administrations in Comparative Perspective.* Zurich: LIT Verlag Münster.

Schulman, Bruce J. 2004. "The Tennessee Valley Authority." In *Poverty in the United States,* ed. A. O'Connor and G. Mink. Santa Barbara: ABC-CLIO.

Schwarz, G. 1978. "Estimating the Dimension of a Model." *Annals of Statistics* 6:461–64.

Senate, U.S. 2014a. *Landmark Legislation: The Civil Rights Act of 1964.* U.S. Senate [accessed June 6, 2014]. Available at www.senate.gov/artandhistory/history/ common/generic/CivilRightsAct1964.htm.

2014b. *"Summary of Bills Vetoed, 1789–Present."* Washington, DC: U.S. Senate.

Shabecoff, Philip. 1981. "Reagan Order on Cost-Benefit Analysis Stirs Economic and Political Debate." *New York Times,* November 6.

Shank, Alan. 1980. *Presidential Policy Leadership: Kennedy and Social Welfare.* New York: University Press of America.

Sharp, James Roger. 1993. *American Politics in the Early Republic.* New Haven, CT: Yale University Press.

Shiller, Robert J. 2013. "Best, Brightest and Least Productive?" *Japan Times,* September 29.

Simas, Elizabeth, and Kevin Evans. 2011. "Linking Party Platforms to Perceptions of Presidential Candidates' Policy Positions." *Political Research Quarterly* 64 (4):831–39.

Simons, Henry C. 1934. "A Positive Program for Laissez-faire: Some Proposals for Liberal Economic Policy." In *Economic Policy for a Free Society,* ed. H. C. Simons. Chicago, IL: University of Chicago Press.

Sims, Christopher A. 1980. "Macroeconomics and Reality." *Econometrica* 48 (Jan.):1–48.

Sims, Christopher A., and T. Zha. 1999. "Error Bands for Impulse Responses." *Econometrica* 67 (5):1113–56.

Sinclair, Barbara. 2000. "Hostile Partners: The President, Congress, and Lawmaking in the Partisan 1990s." In *Polarized Politics*, ed. J. R. Bond and R. Fleisher. Washington, DC: CQ Press.

Sinclair, Barbara. 2002. "The Dream Fulfilled? Party Development in Congress, 1950–2000." In *Responsible Partisanship?: The Evolution of American Political Parties since 1950*, ed. J. C. Green and P. S. Hernson. Lawrence: University of Kansas Press.

Slaughter, Thomas P. 1986. *The Whiskey Rebellion: Frontier Epilogue to the American Revolution.* New York: Oxford University Press.

Smerk, George M. 1965. "The Urban Mass Transportation Act of 1964: New Hope for American Cities." *Transportation Journal* 5 (2):35–40.

Smiley, Gene, and Richard H. Keehn. 1995. "Federal Personal Income Tax in the 1920s." *Journal of Economic History* 55 (2):285–303.

Smith, Gary Scott. 2006. *Faith and the Presidency from George Washington to George W. Bush.* New York: Oxford University Press.

Smith, James Allen. 1991. *The Idea Brokers: Think Tanks and the Rise of the New Policy Elite.* New York: Free Press.

Smith, Jason Scott. 2006. *Building New Deal Liberalism: The Political Economy of Public Works, 1933–1956.* New York: Cambridge University Press.

Smith, Mark C. 2014. "Christian Voice." In *Encyclopedia of American Religion and Politics (Facts on File Library of American History)*, ed. P. A. Djupe and L. R. Olson. New York: Infobase Publishing.

Sniderman, Paul. 2000. "Taking Sides: A Fixed Choice Theory of Political Reasoning." In *Elements of Reason: Cognition, Choice, and the Bounds of Rationality*, ed. M. McCubbins, A. Lupia, and S. Popkin. New York: Cambridge University Press.

Sniderman, Paul, and John Bullock. 2004. "A Consistency Theory of Public Opinion and Political Choice." In *Studies in Public Opinion*, ed. W. E. Saris and P. M. Sniderman. Princeton, NJ: Princeton University Press.

Snowe, Olympia. 2012. "Olympia Snowe: Why I'm Leaving the Senate." *Washington Post*, March 1.

Sorensen, Theodore C. 1965. *Kennedy.* New York: Harper & Row.

Stam, Jerome M., and Bruce L. Dixon. 2014. "Farmer Bankruptcies and Farm Exists in the United States, 1899–2002." In *Agriculture Information Bulletin Number 788.* Washington, DC: U.S. Department of Agriculture.

Steinhauer, Jennifer. 2012. "Weighing the Effect of an Exit of Centrists." *New York Times*, October 8.

Stern, Mark J. 1991. "Poverty and the Life-Cycle, 1940–1960." *Journal of Social History* 24 (3):521–40.

Stern, Seth. 2010. *Justice Brennan: Liberal Champion.* New York: Houghton Mifflin.

Stigler, George J. 1972. "The Theory of Economic Regulation." *Bell Journal of Economics and Management Science* 11 (1):3–21.

Stiglitz, Joseph. 2012. *The Price of Inequality: How Today's Divided Society Endangers Our Future.* New York: W. W. Norton.

Stimson, James A. 1991. *Public Opinion in America: Moods, Cycles, and Swings.* Boulder, CO: Westview Press.

1999. *Public Opinion in America: Moods, Cycles, and Swings*, 2nd ed. Boulder, CO: Westview Press.

Stimson, James A., Michael B. MacKuen, and Robert S. Erikson. 1995. "Dynamic Representation." *American Political Science Review* 89 (Sept.):543–65.

Stone, Walter J., and Alan I. Abramowitz. 1983. "Winning May Not Be Everything. But It's More Than We Thought: Presidential Party Activists in 1980." *American Political Science Review* 77 (3):945–57.

Stonecash, Jeffrey M., Mark D. Brewer, and Mark D. Mariani. 2003. *Diverging Parties: Social Change, Realignment, and Party Polarization.* Boulder, CO: Westview Press.

Sullivan, Denis G. 1977. "Party Unity: Appearance and Reality." *Political Science Quarterly* 92 (4):635-45.

Sundquist, James L. 1968. *Politics and Policy: The Eisenhower, Kennedy, and Johnson Years.* Washington, DC: Brookings Institution Press.

1983. *Dynamics of the Party System: Alignment and Realignment of Political Parties in the United States.* Washington, DC: Brookings Institution.

Swain, Frank. 1981. "The Department of Transportation." In *Mandate for Leadership: Policy Management in a Conservative Administration*, ed. C. L. Heatherly. Washington, DC: The Heritage Foundation.

Taussig, F.W. 1892. *The Tariff History of the United States*, 8th ed. New York: G. P. Putnam's Sons.

Tax Foundation. 2013. *U.S. Federal Individual Income Tax Rates History, 1862–2013.* Tax Foundation [accessed May 29, 2013]. Available at http://tax foundation.org/article/us-federal-individual-income-tax-rates-history-1913-2013-nominal-and-inflation-adjusted-brackets.

Tax Policy Center. 2014. *Tax Expenditures: What Are They and How Are They Structured?* Urban Institute and Brookings Institution [accessed August 20, 2014]. Available at www.taxpolicycenter.org/briefing-book/background/shelters/expenditures.cfm.

Tempalski, Jerry. 2006. "Revenue Effects of Major Tax Bills." Office of Tax Analysis. Assistant Secretary for Tax Policy. Washington, DC: U.S. Department of Treasury.

Thayer, George. 1974. *Who Shakes the Money Tree?: American Campaign Practices from 1789 to the Present.* New York: Simon and Schuster.

Thayer, William Roscoe. 2000. *Theodore Roosevelt: An Intimate Biography.* New York: Bartleby.com.

Theriault, Sean M. 2008. *Party Polarization in Congress.* New York: Cambridge University Press.

2013. *The Gingrich Senators: The Roots of Partisan Warfare in Congress* New York: Oxford University Press.

Theriault, Sean M., and David W. Rohde. 2011. "The Gingrich Senators and Party Polarization in the U.S. Senate." *Journal of Politics* 73 (4):1011–24.

Thorp, Willard Long. 1926. The Annals of the United States of America. In *Business Annals.* Washington, DC: National Bureau of Economic Research.

Time. 1975. "The Vice Presidency: Rocky's Turn to the Right." *Time*, May 12.

1979. "The New Right Takes Aim and Democratic Targets Fear the Bombardment." *Time*, 20–33.

Time/Yankelovich, Skelly, and White. 1974. "Time/Yankelovich, Skelly & White Poll, Sep, 1974." University of Connecticut: The Roper Center for Public Opinion Research.

Times Mirror/Pew Research Center. 2012. *Trend in Party Identification, 1939–2012.* Pew Research Center for the People and the Press [accessed July 21, 2014]. Available at www.people-press.org/2012/06/01/trend-in-party-identification-1939-2012/.

Tollison, Robert D. 1988. "Public Choice and Legislation." *Virginia Law Review* 74 (2):339–71.

Truman, David B. 1951. *The Governmental Process*. New York: Alfred A. Knopf.

Truman, Harry S. 1945. *Special Message to the Congress Presenting a 21-Point Program for the Reconversion Period*. The American Presidency Project [accessed March 24, 2014]. Available at www.presidency.ucsb.edu/ws/?pid=12359.

——— 1947a. *Veto of Bill to Reduce Income Taxes, June 16, 1947*. The American Presidency Project [accessed March 24, 2014]. Available at www.presidency.ucsb.edu/ws/?pid=12670.

——— 1947b. *Veto of the Taft-Hartley Labor Bill, June 20, 1947*. The American Presidency Project [accessed March 24, 2014]. Available at www.presidency.ucsb.edu/ws/index.php?pid=12675.

——— 1947c. *Veto of the Wool Act, June 26, 1947*. The American Presidency Project [accessed March 24, 2014]. Available at www.presidency.ucsb.edu/ws/?pid=12683.

——— 1948. *Veto of the Income Tax Reduction Bill, April 1, 1948*. The American Presidency Project [accessed March 24, 2014]. Available at www.presidency.ucsb.edu/ws/index.php?pid=13142&st=tax+reduction&st1=.

——— 1949. *Annual Message to the Congress on the State of the Union, January 5, 1949*. The American Presidency Project [accessed March 24, 2014]. Available at www.presidency.ucsb.edu/ws/?pid=13293.

Tullock, Gordon. 1967. "The Welfare Costs of Tariffs, Monopolies, and Theft." *Western Economic Journal* 5 (June):224–32.

——— 1993. *Rent Seeking*. Brookfield, VT: Edward Algar.

Ture, Norman B. 1981. "The Department of Treasury." In *Mandate for Leadership: Policy Management in a Conservative Administration*, ed. C. L. Heatherly. Washington, DC: The Heritage Foundation.

TVhistory.TV. 2014. *Television History: The First 75 Years*. TVhistory.TV [accessed April 3, 2014]. Available at www.tvhistory.tv/Annual_TV_Households_50-78.JPG.

United States Senate Office of the Clerk 2012. *Party Division in the Senate (1789 to Present)*. U.S. Senate [accessed September 18, 2012. Available at www.senate.gov/pagelayout/history/one_item_and_teasers/partydiv.htm.

University of Chicago Centennial Catalogues. 2014. *Frank H. Knight*. University of Chicago [accessed September 18, 2014]. Available at www.lib.uchicago.edu/projects/centcat/centcats/fac/facch23_01.html.

Vaisse, Justin. 2010. *Neoconservatism: The Biography of a Movement*. Cambridge, MA: Harvard University Press.

Vanderlip, Frank A. 1932. "What about the Banks?" *Saturday Evening Post*, 205 (19): 3–66.

Voigt, Stefan. 1997. "Positive Constitutional Economics: A Survey." *Public Choice* 90 (1):11–53.

Volterra, V. 1926. "Fluctuations in the Abundance of Species considered Mathematically." *Nature* 118(2972): 558–60.

VRS Election Day Exit Poll. 1992. "Voter Research & Surveys: VOTE_FOR_PRESIDENT TAXING." BC News, CBS News, CNN, NBC News. University of Connecticut: The Roper Center for Public Opinion Research.

Wall, M. Danny. 1981. "The Department of Housing and Urban Development." In *Mandate for Leadership: Policy Management in a Conservative Administration*, ed. C. L. Heatherly. Washington, DC: The Heritage Foundation.

Wanniski, Jude. 1978. *The Way the World Works: How Economies Fail – and Succeed.* New York: Basic Books.

Ward, Joe H. 1963. "Hierarchical Grouping to Optimize an Objective Function." *Journal of the American Statistical Association* 58 (1):236–44.

Warshaw, Shirley Anne. 1991. "The Implementation of Cabinet Government during the Nixon Administration." In *Richard M. Nixon: Politician, President, Administrator*, ed. L. Friedman and W. F. Levantrosser. New York: Praeger.

Washington, George. 1796. *Farewell Address, September 19, 1796.* The American Presidency Project [accessed February 27, 2016]. Available at www.presidency.ucsb.edu/ws/?pid=65539.

Washington Post. 2010. "Charles 'Mac' Mathias Jr.: Principled Moderate Who Aided His State and Country." *Washington Post*, January 26.

——— 2012a. "The Watergate Story, The Government Acts: Part II." *Washington Post*, June 14.

——— 2012b. "The Watergate Story, the Post Investigates: Part I." *Washington Post*, June 14.

——— 2013. "Shutdown Damages Republicans, with Plenty of Pain to Go Around." *Washington Post*, June 14.

Waterman, Richard W. 1989. *Presidential Influence and the Administrative State.* Knoxville: University of Tennessee Press.

Weekly Compilation of Presidential Documents. 2008. Washington, DC: Government Printing Office.

Weiner, Tim. 1997. "Transcripts of Nixon Tapes Show the Path to Watergate." *New York Times*, October 31.

Weingroff, Richard F. 1996. *Federal-Aid Highway Act of 1956, Creating the Interstate System* [accessed February 21, 2016]. Available at www.fhwa.dot.gov/publications/publicroads/96summer/p96su10.cfm.

Weisberger, Bernard A. 2000. *America Afire: Jefferson, Adams, and the First Contested Election.* New York: Harper-Collins.

Weiss, Sholom M., Nitin Indurkhya, and Tong Zhang. 2010. *Fundamentals of Predictive Text Mining.* London: Springer.

Whalen, Charles, and Barbara Whalen. 1985. *The Longest Debate.* Washington, DC: Seven Locks Press.

Whaples, Robert. 1995. "Where Is There Consensus among American Economic Historians? The Results of a Survey on Forty Propositions." *Journal of Economic History* 55 (1):139–54.

Wheelock, David C. 2008. "The Federal Response to Home Mortgage Distress: Lessons from the Great Depression." *Federal Reserve Bank of St. Louis Review* 90 (May/June):133–48.

White House. 2013. *The Budget for Fiscal Year 2013*, Table 6.1. The White House, February 6 [accessed February 7, 2014]. Available at www.whitehouse.gov/sites/default/files/omb/budget/fy2013/assets/hist.pdf.

Whittaker, William G. 2005. *Child Labor in America: History, Policy, and Legislative Issues.* Ithaca, NY: Cornell University Industrial and Labor Relations School.

Wikipedia. 2012. "Laissez-faire" [accessed November 8, 2012]. Available at http://en.wikipedia.org/wiki/Laissez-faire.

2014a. "African-American Civil Rights Movement (1954–1968)." Wikimedia Foundation [accessed April 3, 2014]. Available at http://en.wikipedia.org/wiki/African-American_Civil_Rights_Movement_(1954–68).

2014b. "Constitution of the United States of America." Wikipedia [accessed February 21, 2014]. Available at http://en.wikipedia.org/wiki/United_States_Constitution.

2014c. "George Wallace's 1963 Inaugural Address." Wikimedia Foundation [accessed July 21, 2014]. Available at http://en.wikipedia.org/wiki/George_Wallace's_1963_Inaugural_Address.

2014d. "Ideological Leanings of the Supreme Court Justices." Wikimedia Foundation [accessed March 29, 2014]. Available at http://en.wikipedia.org/wiki/Ideological_leanings_of_U.S._Supreme_Court_justices - cite_note-Bailey2012–16.

2014e. "King Assassination Riots." Wikimedia Foundation [accessed June 12, 2014]. Available at http://en.wikipedia.org/wiki/King_assassination_riots.

2014f. "List of Incidents of Civil Unrest in the United States." Wikimedia Foundation [accessed April 3, 2014]. Available at http://en.wikipedia.org/wiki/List_of_incidents_of_civil_unrest_in_the_United_States.

2014g. "Long Depression." Wikimedia Foundation [accessed April 3, 2014]. Available at https://en.wikipedia.org/wiki/Long_Depression.

2014h. "Mass Racial Violence in the United States." Wikimedia Foundation [accessed June 12, 2014]. Available at http://en.wikipedia.org/wiki/Mass_racial_violence_in_the_United_States.

2014i. "Protests against the Vietnam War." Wikimedia Foundation [accessed June 12, 2014]. Available at http://en.wikipedia.org/wiki/Protests_against_the_Vietnam_War.

2015a. "Contract with America." Wikimedia Foundation [accessed February 3, 2015]. Available at http://en.wikipedia.org/wiki/Contract_with_America.

2015b. "List of United States Federal Legislation, 1901–2001." Wikimedia Foundation [accessed June 9, 2014]. Available at http://en.wikipedia.org/wiki/List_of_United_States_federal_legislation,_1901-2001.

2015c. "United States Senate Elections, 1980." Wikimedia Foundation [accessed February 10, 2015]. Available at http://en.wikipedia.org/wiki/United_States_Senate_elections,_1980.

2016a. "1860 Democratic National Conventions." Wikimedia Foundation [accessed April 5, 2016]. Available at https://en.wikipedia.org/wiki/1860_Democratic_National_Conventions.

2016b. "Legal Tender Cases." Wikimedia Foundation [accessed February 5, 2016]. Available at http://en.wikipedia.org/wiki/88th_United_States_Congress.

Wilentz, Sean. 2005. *The Rise of American Democracy: Jefferson to Lincoln.* New York: W. W. Norton.

Williamson, Samuel H. 2014. What Was the U.S. GDP Then? Measuringworth.com. [accessed March 11, 2014]. Available at www.measuringworth.com/usgdp/.

Wilson, Woodrow. 1914. *Message on Neutrality.* The American Presidency Project [accessed February 3, 2016]. Available at www.presidency.ucsb.edu/ws/index.php?pid=65382.

Winston, David A. 1981. "The Department of Health and Human Services." In *Mandate for Leadership: Policy Management in a Conservative Administration,* ed. C. L. Heatherly. Washington, DC: The Heritage Foundation.

Wittman, Donald. 1983. "Candidate Motivation: A Synthesis of Alternatives." *American Political Science Review* 77:142–57.

Wlezien, Christopher. 1995. "The Public as a Thermostat: Dynamics of Preferences for Spending." *American Journal of Political Science* 39 (4):981–1000.

Wlezien, Christopher. 1996. "Dynamics of Representation: The Case of U.S. Spending on Defense." *British Journal of Political Science* 26 (1):81–103.

Women in Military Service Memorial Foundation. 2014. *Highlights in the History of Military Women*. Women in Military Service for America Memorial Foundation, Inc. [accessed February 6, 2014]. Available at www.womensmemorial.org/Educa tion/timeline.html.

Wood, B. Dan. 1988. "Principals, Bureaucrats, and Responsiveness in Clean Air Enforcements." *American Political Science Review* 82 (1):215–34.

1990. "Does Politics Make a Difference at the EEOC?" *American Journal of Political Science* 34 (2):503–30.

2009. *The Myth of Presidential Representation*. New York: Cambridge University Press.

2010. "Agency Theory and the Bureaucracy." In *Oxford Handbook of American Bureaucracy*, ed. R. F. Durant. New York: Oxford University Press.

Wood, B. Dan, and James E. Anderson. 1993. "The Politics of U.S. Antitrust Regulation." *American Journal of Political Science* 37 (1):1–39.

Wood, B. Dan, and Richard W. Waterman. 1993. "The Dynamics of Political-Bureaucratic Adaptation." *American Journal of Political Science* 37 (2):497–528.

1994. *Bureaucratic Dynamics: The Role of Bureaucracy in a Democracy*. Boulder, CO: Westview Press.

Wood, B. Dan, and Stephen Huss. 2008. "Explaining Attention to Civil Rights Issues." Southern Political Science Association Convention, New Orleans.

Wood, B. Dan, Kelly Arndt, and Soren Jordan. 2015. "Presidents and the Politics of Polarization." American Political Science Association, San Francisco, CA.

Woodward, Bob. 1999. *Five Presidents and the Legacy of Watergate*. New York: Simon and Schuster.

2001. *Greenspan's Fed and the American Boom*. New York: Simon and Schuster.

2005. *The Choice: How Bill Clinton Won*. New York: Simon and Schuster.

Woodward, Bob, and Carl Bernstein. 2005. *All the President's Men*. New York: Bloomsbury.

World War II Museum. 2014a. *African Americans in World War II: Fighting for a Double Victory*. National World War II Museum [accessed February 7, 2014]. Available at www.nationalww2museum.org/assets/pdfs/african-ameri cans-in-world.pdf.

2014b. *WWII Timeline*. National World War II Museum [accessed March 18, 2014]. Available at www.nationalww2museum.org/see-hear/world-war-ii-history/timeline .html.

Yates, Robert. 1787. *Notes of the Secret Debates of the Federal Convention of 1787, Taken by the Late Hon Robert Yates, Chief Justice of the State of New York, and One of the Delegates from That State to the Said Convention*. The Avalon Project [accessed August 26, 2014]. Available at http://avalon.law.yale.edu/18th_century/ yates.asp.

Zaller, John R. 1992. *The Nature and Origins of Mass Opinion*. New York: Cambridge University Press.

Zarnowitz, Victor. 1996. *Business Cycles: Theory, History, Indicators, and Forecasting*. Chicago, IL: University of Chicago Press.

Zupan, Mark A. 1992. "Measuring the Ideological Preferences of U.S. Presidents: A Proposed (Extremely Simple) Method." *Public Choice* 73 (2):351–61.

Index